PROGRAMMING PRINCIPLES WITH COBOL I

Don B. Medley
Professor, Chairman
Computer Information Systems
California State Polytechnic University
Pomona, California

Ronald W. Eaves
Professor
Computer Information Systems
California State Polytechnic University
Pomona, California

Published by

J42   **SOUTH-WESTERN PUBLISHING CO.**

CINCINNATI   WEST CHICAGO, ILL.   DALLAS   PELHAM MANOR, N.Y.   PALO ALTO, CALIF.

ACKNOWLEDGMENT

The following extract from Government Printing Office Form Number 1965-0795689 is presented for the information and guidance of the user:

Any organization interested in reproducing the COBOL report and specifications in whole or in part, using ideas taken from this report as the basis for an instruction manual or for any other purpose is free to do so. However, all such organizations are requested to reproduce this section as part of the introduction to the document. Those using a short passage, as in a book review, are requested to mention "COBOL" in acknowledgement of the source, but need not quote this entire section.

COBOL is an industry language and is not the property of any company or group of companies, or of any organization or group of organizations.

No warranty, expressed or implied, is made by any contributor or by the COBOL Committee as to the accuracy and functioning of the programming system and language. Moreover, no responsibility is assumed by any contributor, or by the committee, in connection therewith.

Procedures have been established for the maintenance of COBOL. Inquiries concerning the procedures for proposing changes should be directed to the Executive Committee of the Conference of Data Systems Languages.

The authors and copyright holders of the copyrighted material used herein

FLOW-MATIC (Trademark of Sperry Rand Corporation), Programming for the UNIVAC® I and II, Data Automation Systems copyrighted 1958, 1959, by Sperry Rand Corporation; IBM Commercial Translator, Form No. F28–8013, copyrighted 1959 by IBM; FACT, DSI 27A5260–2760, copyrighted 1960 by Minneapolis-Honeywell

have specifically authorized the use of this material in whole or in part, in the COBOL specifications. Such authorization extends to the reproduction and use of COBOL specifications in programming manuals or similar publications.

CONTENTS

Preface   **vii**

1. Computer Programs: Recipes for Processing Information   1

Objectives   1
Purpose of a Program   1
Characteristics of an Algorithm   6
Developing the Program Algorithm   7
Algorithm Development: An Example   10
Practice Assignments   19

2. Application Program Development   23

Objectives   23
Problem Definition: The Starting Point   23
Program Development Process   30
Step 1: Analyze the Problem   31
Step 2: Design Program Structure   36
Step 3: Design Program Processing   37
Practice Assignments   50

3. The Process of Programming   57

Objectives   57
Program Development Process: Step 4: Code the Program   57
The COBOL Language   58
COBOL Coding Case Study   67
Program Development Process: Step 5: Testing and
     Debugging   69
Practice Assignments   78

4. Defining Data 89

Objectives 89
Data Relationships 89
Data Hierarchies 90
Data Definition 91
Data Definition Examples 96
Using Working-Storage 96
Defining Initial Data Values 97
Identifying Data Types 98
Editing Data for Printed Output 100
Practice Assignments 105
Programming Assignments 109

5. Converting Data to Information 121

Objectives 121
Processing Data 121
Input/Output Commands 122
Data Movement Commands 125
Calculation Commands 128
Practice Assignments 139
Programming Assignments 142

6. Decision Making, Control, and Repetition 165

Objectives 165
Decision Relationships 165
Repetitions in Programs 188
Counters and Accumulators 193
Flags and Switches 195
Programming Assignments 200

7. COBOL for Files 221

Objectives 221
Building Files in COBOL 221
Environment Division 222
Configuration Section 222
Input-Output Section 223
File Section 224
Procedure Division Instructions 228
Programming Assignments 244

8. Printed Reports   **265**

Objectives 265
Types of Reports 265
Detail Reports 265
Summary Reports 266
Exception Reports 268
Control Reports 272
Report Structures 273
Report Design Practices 280
Report Format Definitions 282
Programming Assignment 285

9. File Principles and Management   **305**

Objectives 305
Makeup of Files 305
File Organization Methods 306
File Types 308
File Storage Media 311
File Processing 313
Creating Serial Files 313
File Sorting and Merging 318
Sequential File Maintenance 322
Practice Assignment 326

10. Using Secondary Storage   **337**

Objectives 337
Secondary Storage Devices 337
Magnetic Tape Recording 338
Magnetic Disk Recording 342

11. Control Break Reports   **355**

Objectives 355
Characteristics of Control Break Reports 355
Preparation of Control Break Reports 357
Case Study 358
Options for Control Break Reports 375
Practice Assignment 380

12. Tables 391

Objectives 391
Tables: What They Are and Why They Are Used 391
Defining Tables 393
Static Tables 395
Accessing Table Data 396
Dynamic Tables 399
References To Tables 401
Table Lookup Techniques 401
Multiple-Level Tables 407
Programming Assignments 411

Appendices 431

A: Collating Sequences 431
B: Reserved Words 434
C: COBOL Language Summary—Abridged 435

Glossary 441

Index 459

PREFACE

PERSPECTIVE

This book, in part, represents an implementation of the *Model Curriculum for Undergraduate Computer Information Systems Education* of the Data Processing Management Association-Education Foundation (DPMA-EF). Specifically, the information presented in this book meets or exceeds the content called for in the suggested outline for course *CIS-2—Applications Program Development I.* Correspondence between this book and the course specifications is assured by the fact that the text was developed under the oversight of the DPMA-EF, with content appropriateness and technical accuracy validated through independent review.

The DPMA-EF curriculum specifies structured program development using COBOL as the vehicle. This decision was made in recognition of COBOL's status as the predominant language for business applications. The curriculum, in turn, is aimed at graduating students qualified as entry-level programmer-analysts in business-oriented computer facilities.

CONTENT LEVEL

This text is designed to support an undergraduate course. It is assumed that students using this text will have completed—or will be enrolled concurrently in—an introductory course in computer information systems (CIS). During the introductory-level course, the student should acquire a general knowledge of the procedures for systems development and program development.

The approach taken to systems and program development in this book is compatible with that of the companion introductory text, *Computer Information Systems: An Introduction,* by Adams, Wagner, and Boyer.

This book is aimed at providing the instructional content for a first semester in a two-semester program for the building of understanding and competence in structured application programming using COBOL. A companion work, *Programming Principles With COBOL II,* provides a basis for the work of the second semester. At the conclusion of the first semester, students should be able to design and develop COBOL programs using sequential files and data structures that encompass one-level tables.

CONTENT HIGHLIGHTS

Although no issue is made about structured or unstructured COBOL, this book, throughout its entire content, routinely presents and reinforces the principles and techniques of structured programming. Further, emphasis is placed on the development of application programs as a means of solving business problems—rather than upon COBOL as a programming language. To that end, this text introduces a minimum subset of the COBOL language. Early chapters are designed to build an understanding of what programs do and where they fit within their business and computer information systems (CIS) organizations. To help establish an understanding of and appreciation for the approach of this book in building the student's learning experience, a brief summary of chapter content follows:

1. Computer Programs: Recipes for Processing Information

Computer programs are described as procedures for solving algorithms. Therefore, it is explained, programs can be no better than the problem definitions on which they are based. The chapter stresses the need to design programs before any writing of instructions takes place. Students are given practice assignments in stating solutions to simple problems.

2. Application Program Development

A systems development life cycle and a process for specifying, designing, and developing programs are reviewed. It is emphasized that the front ends of both systems development and program development projects should concentrate on problem definition and determination of user needs. Thoroughly understood solutions to identified problems are then defined before actual program development takes place. It is stressed that, the more thorough the understanding of problems and definitions of solutions, the easier and more effective will be the actual work of writing programs.

3. The Process of Programming

Tools for structured design and development of programs—including structure charts, flowcharts, and pseudocode—are reviewed. These tools and principles are then related to the divisional structure of COBOL programs. Students are ready, at the conclusion of this chapter, to begin dealing with actual, simple COBOL programs.

4. Defining Data

Students learn the entries and the syntax for defining and describing data in COBOL. They are introduced to the reserve word list as a checkpoint against misuse of terms and have an opportunity to assign names to data elements. Students learn the rules of syntax and style for data definition entries and also master basic rules about the formatting of entries on coding sheets. Descriptions are illustrated profusely with appropriate, handwritten entries on segments of actual COBOL coding sheets.

5. Converting Data to Information

Students are introduced to simple input and output using only ACCEPT and DISPLAY commands. Data manipulation is described using COBOL arithmetic and MOVE instructions. This chapter exposes students to the fundamental data processing capabilities of COBOL.

6. Decision Making, Control, and Repetition

Students learn about the basic types of decision making that form one of the important control constructs in programs. They also learn the roles of sequencing, repetition (iteration), and selection in the continuous processing of data.

7. COBOL for Files

Files are introduced at a level that makes it possible for students to prepare the instructions necessary to read or write batches of records for typical data processing activities. The content of this chapter stops short of explanations about the functions and uses of file devices or of the details of header and trailer records. However, students learn enough so that they can manipulate files and records in memory and prepare complete programs that can be compiled and executed.

8. Printed Reports

Principles and techniques for formatting and producing printed reports are introduced. This chapter takes students through discussion of many common report types. They are introduced to concepts of report headings, footings, detail lines, and to carriage control functions.

9. File Principles and Management

Students build upon the fundamental knowledge of files acquired in Chapter 7. The idea of Chapter 7 is to build enough knowledge to enable students to produce simple, detail reports. In this chapter, they learn more about the organization of files and the more important processes using them. The discussion includes files, records, fields, sorting, collating, and master file updating.

10. Tape and Disk Files

Students expand their knowledge of data structures and file management to encompass the principles of how secondary storage devices operate and how files are written to and read from secondary storage.

In keeping with the CIS curriculum, this book carries file management skills to the level of sequential files on secondary storage devices, leaving more advanced techniques for the second semester and for the companion, advanced programming book in this series.

11. Control Break Reports

This chapter builds knowledge and provides experience in the development of COBOL programs for summary reports. Although the principles of multilevel control break reports are explained, actual examples involve two-level control break reports only. More advanced reports and reporting from direct-access files are left for coverage in the second semester and in the sequel text.

12. Tables

Students learn about defining and using table data in COBOL. Table organization and search techniques are covered and practice assignments are completed at this level. The value of tables in the preparation of output reports is explained thoroughly. Methods described include both tables with content incorporated in programs (static tables) and structures into which data can be read as part of the program execution procedures (dynamic tables). Students are expected to develop competency in using one-level tables only. Multilevel tables are discussed in more depth in subsequent courses.

ACKNOWLEDGMENTS

To assure accuracy and appropriateness for the content of this text, a highly experienced, objective group of persons was asked to review the manuscript during development. The careful readings and thoughtful comments of this group represented, cumulatively, an important contribution to the soundness of this text. Their contributions are acknowledged with sincere thanks.

> Terrence J. Boyer, Mercantile Trust Co., N.A., St. Louis, MO
> Dr. N. D. Brammer, Colorado State University, Ft. Collins, CO
> Ardyn E. Dubnow. Northrop Corporation, Norwood, MA
> Prof. Herbert Rebhun, University of Houston, Houston, TX

A special note of thanks is extended for the manuscript-review services of Dr. Coleman Furr, president of Coleman College, San Diego, who reviewed the text independently, reporting directly to the DPMA-EF regents.

Thanks are also extended to Thomas S. Duck, whose assistance with the program examples is appreciated greatly.

COMPUTER PROGRAMS: RECIPES FOR PROCESSING INFORMATION 1

OBJECTIVES

On completing reading and other learning assignments for this chapter, you should be able to:

1. Define and discuss the terms program, operating system, compiler, application program, COBOL, hardware, software, input, processing, output, and storage.
2. Explain the purpose and function of an algorithm, as well as the need to decompose problems as a means of developing solutions through application programs.
3. Identify and be prepared to apply the three basic steps in the development of a program algorithm.

PURPOSE OF A PROGRAM

A *program* is a set of instructions that causes a computer to perform a series of steps in processing data.

A computer is a collection of wires and electronic components. It either follows instructions or it doesn't. A computer does not have the same intelligence as a human. So, a computer cannot ask what you mean. The responsibility for the completeness and accuracy of instructions resides with the programmer.

For example, look at the definitions above. They define computers and programs in general terms. But what, exactly, is a computer? Also, what, exactly, is meant by processing? In learning to develop computer programs, a good starting point is to learn to use data processing terms with precision.

Consider, for example, the definition that a program consists of instructions that cause a computer to perform processing steps. This is true, but it is so general that it doesn't tell you much. For further understanding, you should know that there are different types of programs. There are programs that manage and control computer equipment and make it work. These are known, broadly, as *operating systems*. There are also programs that enable people to communicate with and use computers. In effect, these programs establish languages that permit people to solve problems through use of terms they can understand. Then, these same language-oriented programs translate instructions written by people into commands that the computer can follow. This type of translation program is called a *compiler*.

One of the most commonly used programming languages in solving business problems is *COBOL (COmmon Business Oriented Language)*. COBOL is one of a large family of programming languages used to define jobs for computer processing. Programs written in the COBOL language are known as *application programs*. An application, simply, is a job to be performed with the aid of a computer—but not entirely by a computer. Applications, or computer information processing systems, involve people, computers, programs, and files of data and information. They also involve the resources (including money) needed to make the whole thing go. Within this context, computers are service devices. Modern computer centers are likened to public utilities. A public utility may deliver electricity to its users. A *computer* is a machine that accepts raw data and delivers information to its users.

These definitions enhance the description of what a program is and what it does. Programs guide the operation of computers. But you may not have a clear idea of just what a computer is. This is not surprising, since the word computer has been overused, to a point at which its meaning has become vague and inexact. If you are to build skills in programming, the term *computer* must have some specific meanings for you.

Computers, Programs, and Data

A computer consists of a series of electronic circuits and devices that are interconnected to function in close coordination. Computer equipment is described as *hardware*. Equipment units are designed to enter (input) data for processing, to do the actual processing, to deliver results (output) to users, and also to store files of data and information for continuing use.

The heart of a computer system, where the actual computing is done, is the *processor*, diagrammed in Figure 1-1. The devices that make up the processor control all functions performed by the computer, including:

- *Input* is the entry and acceptance of data for processing from external devices that feed in new data or from storage units that are part of the computer configuration.

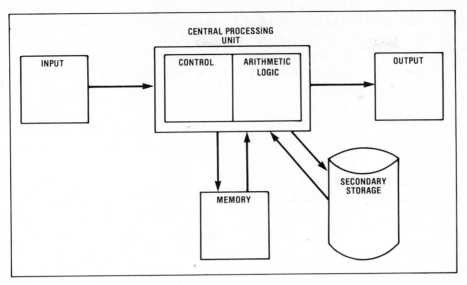

Figure 1-1. Computer processing diagram.

- *Processing* is the actual changing, or transformation, of data into desired information. A computer applies two kinds of processing: logic and control.

- *Output* is the delivery of data or information for further use. This is accomplished by causing data to be printed or displayed on a video screen for use by people or stored for further, later processing.

- *Storage* is the recording of data on devices from which they can be retrieved by the processor under program control. The devices themselves are referred to as *secondary storage*.

To perform these functions, the processor has two main components:

- Memory
- Central processing unit (CPU).

Memory. Computer *memory*, also called *main memory* or *primary storage,* is a high-speed device that records and retains data temporarily in support of processing operations. When a program is entered from external input or retrieved from storage, it remains in memory until processing is completed. Instructions to be executed are withdrawn from memory as needed. The same applies to data to be processed. They are entered from an input device or recalled from storage for holding in memory until needed for processing. No actual processing takes place in memory. But efficient processing would be impossible without support of a high-speed memory.

Central processing unit (CPU). The *central processing unit*, or *CPU*, contains the electronic circuits that carry out the actual processing. The CPU performs its functions in two separate components, the *control unit* and the *arithmetic logic unit (ALU)*.

The control unit, as its name implies, controls all operations of all of the equipment that makes up a computer system. This includes directing the input of data from external devices, the retrieving of programs or data from storage, and the directing of output functions.

The ALU performs the actual processing. Computers execute only two, highly basic, kinds of processing: arithmetic and logic. In most computers, arithmetic functions are limited to taking one numeric value and either adding or subtracting another number from it. Usually, multiplication and division are accomplished through repetitions of addition or subtraction, although some sophisticated processors can perform these jobs directly. Computer logic involves comparison of two values, sensing a condition, and directing further processing on the basis of this condition. The ALU completes one arithmetic or logical function at a time, under direction of the control unit.

Programs.   Collectively, the programs—and the operating procedures for their use—are known as *software*. The elements of hardware and software, combined, form *computer systems*.

Computer systems process *data* and produce *information*. These are two more loosely used terms. What are data? What is information?

Data are raw facts. Items of data include all of the letters of the alphabet, numbers, and any symbols (+ $ − * /) that have been assigned meaning for purposes of computer processing. Spaces between collections of letters, numbers, and symbols also represent data because they play a valid role in transmitting meaning. Data items are also formed from groups of these basic characters, numbers, symbols, and spaces. Examples of typical data item groups include your height, your weight, the color of your eyes, your telephone number, your address, and so on. In summary, data are basic raw materials for data processing or computer information systems.

Information is processed data. That is, information consists of data items that have been modified or combined, producing added value. Consider, for example, the following data items: blue, brown, car, eyes, shirt, dress. Each of these presents a single, raw fact. Combined, they take on new, added meaning and become information: blue eyes, brown dress, brown car, and so on.

In processing data on computers to develop information, bear in mind that a computer is simply a device designed to assist you in your work. It should not be intimidating. True, there may be advanced circuits and highly sophisticated electronic components within a computer; but, as a programmer, you don't have to know about these things. After all, you don't have to be a mechanic to drive a car. Therefore, as far as you are concerned, you can treat a computer as a *black box*. This is a term sometimes used to describe any processing device. You don't have to know about the insides of the black box or what they do.

You do, however, have to understand what happens when you apply instructions or controls to the black box. In other words, you have to know what a computer will do without becoming involved in how it works electronically. Many people use equipment routinely without understanding how it works, just as there are millions of drivers who really don't know the intricate principles of internal combustion or of the moving parts within an automotive engine. All they need to know is how to start the car and make it go. And, in order to be good drivers, they must also know the rules for use of vehicles.

The same applies to computers. You must know a computer's capabilities and what you can expect as a result of actions you take. Just as cars must be operated according to certain rules, so also must certain basic steps be followed in computer processing.

Processing Data

All computer applications and programs follow a standard series of steps, which can be likened to the traffic patterns that govern the use of cars. The processing pattern followed by computer systems is diagrammed in Figure 1-2. This is a straightforward representation of what happens as data are input into a computer, processed, and output as information. The basic cycle involves input, processing, and output, with direct support from data storage units that provide the media for holding input data and the results of processing.

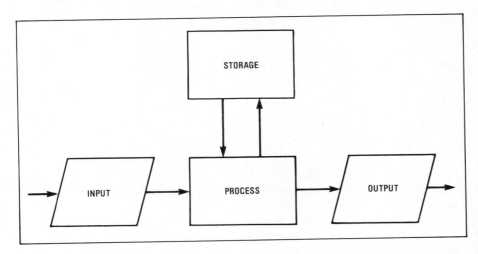

Figure 1-2. The data processing cycle.

Think of it this way: input, processing, and output, supported by secondary storage for a repeated, continuous cycle of computer operation. The idea of continuity of use is an important part of computer processing. This is really what data processing and computer information systems are all about. Writing programs and setting up computers to run them can be time-consuming jobs. It isn't cost-effective to go through the whole business of setting up a computer, for example, if you have to write one paycheck or produce a single invoice. It is highly efficient, however, to prepare programs and set up equipment if you have to write 10,000 paychecks or 6,000 invoices.

Thus, one of the essentials for effective software, including application programs, lies in the repetitious processing of large volumes of data. You must be able to put in data with the same characteristics over and over again and produce the same results, reliably, time after time. Computer information systems are mass volume data processing tools. (This statement applies to any type of business application program. There are scientific situations in which, even though the volume of data is small, the amount of computation involved is so massive that computers represent the only practical tools for solution. However, such scientific applications are beyond the scope of this book.)

In a sense, the requirement of repetition in computer programs has counterparts in many other activities with which you may have been involved. A repeatable program follows a set, routine series of steps. You yourself perform a set, routine series of steps when you follow recipes in preparing certain dishes, when you start your car in the morning, when you type a letter, and so on.

Think back about where the procedures you follow routinely come from. You either learned them from somebody or figured them out for yourself, then followed the pattern in the future. In other words, people establish patterns for doing jobs by looking at overall goals or problems. Then these overall jobs are broken down, *partitioned* or *decomposed*, into a series of steps, or *tasks*, that are followed time after time.

Problem decomposition is an important skill that you will become acquainted with very shortly. Also, repeatability is a basic characteristic necessary for computer programs. As with everyday tasks, computer programming starts by defining the job to be done or problem to be solved, then breaking it down into a series of steps. For program development, the recipe, or series of steps to be followed, is known as an *algorithm*.

Algorithms describe solutions to identified problems. In effect, an algorithm describes the procedures for solving a problem. An algorithm is developed by understanding the goal, or end product required, then decomposing that problem into a series of individual, small, and manageable tasks that, when followed routinely, will lead to producing the desired results.

CHARACTERISTICS OF AN ALGORITHM

To use (and program) computers, you must start by understanding their limitations. First, computers have no judgment that is not predefined, nor do they have any ability to act on their own. They will do only what they are told, following instructions imbedded in programs with exacting detail. Second, you must realize that any instructions that are not included in a program will not be performed by the computer.

This may seem obvious. But it is important to recognize the difference between dealing with people and programming computers. You cannot assume that the computer will know or understand what you want it to do. Recognize also that computers will do what they are told even if the person writing the instructions didn't mean what he or she said. Computers follow instructions explicitly, every time.

To establish the sequence of instructions that a program is to follow, an algorithm is developed. A program algorithm is basically the recipe to be followed by a computer. For computer processing, a program algorithm needs certain characteristics. These traits or characteristics of an algorithm are designed to meet the requirements of computers for processing instructions. These include:

- *Effectiveness.* The algorithm must address the specific problem to be solved and must define the processing that will present a practical solution to that problem.

- *Precision.* Instructions within the algorithm must be precise, and stated in step-by-step descriptions. Nothing can be assumed or overlooked or there will be either an interruption in processing that makes the algorithm impossible to execute or incorrect results produced.

- *Completeness.* Each program must represent a full set of processing steps. Nothing can be left to the judgment or interpretation of a computer. The computer has to be told when to start processing data, what processing to perform, and when to finish. Each program must represent a completed unit of work.

- *Termination.* Each program must have a defined method for stopping when the work is done. Without a specific termination procedure, the computer could simply cycle endlessly without accomplishing anything.

DEVELOPING THE PROGRAM ALGORITHM

A program, remember, is a design for processing. As previously stated, processing is done in a repetitious cycle: input, processing, and output, with storage support.

In carrying out, or *executing*, programs, the computer must operate in the same start-to-finish cycle each time. Processing starts at the beginning and goes through to the end. In program design, however, your first concern is with results. Unless you know where you want to finish, it is impossible to determine exactly where you should begin. Thus, in designing programs, you start by defining your results, or outputs. In other words, you define exactly what information you expect a computer application to deliver.

Once outputs have been defined as the starting point, you can then begin to figure out how to get where you want to go. The next step, then, is to analyze the outputs to determine what inputs are needed to produce them. Thus, input design follows output design.

After input and output are established, you fill in the gaps. That is, you determine the processing that must take place. Processing describes the detailed procedures to be used to convert the input into the desired results.

Algorithm Development Steps

The end result of this design effort is a proper algorithm of the steps that have to be followed in carrying out a solution to a problem.

Development of an algorithm for a computer application follows three basic steps:

1. A statement of the problem to be solved or results to be achieved. This statement must be clear enough so that all parties involved in developing or using a computer application understand fully what results they can expect. This is the description of the output.

2. The resources or ingredients needed to implement the program or realize its goals must be defined. In the case of an application program, the resources to be defined are the data that will be processed. This is the specification for the input.

3. The processing steps to be followed must be laid out, in sequence. Also to be considered are the points at which decisions must be made and all alternatives selected, as well as determinations of how and when to stop the processing. The processing steps must be complete and precise, leaving nothing to chance.

Following the method described above leads to the step-by-step decomposition and orderly solution of problems or development of defined results. Decomposition means that a large job or problem is broken down into a series of manageable parts. The algorithm is generic to job performance and problem solving, no matter what orderly set of activities may be involved. This is why algorithms are sometimes compared to recipes. Developing a computer program can, then, be compared in a general way to baking a cake.

Though these separate activities—developing computer programs and baking cakes—may sound far apart, they actually have many features in common. To illustrate, look at the recipe in Figure 1-3. Consider this as an algorithm. The first step in developing an algorithm is to define end results (outputs). This is done in the heading line above the recipe. The end result is an angel food cake.

The second step in developing an algorithm is to define inputs, ingredients, and resources. In the recipe, the ingredients are listed right at the outset, directly under the description of the end results.

ANGEL-FOOD CAKE

1¼ cups egg whites (10 to 12 eggs)   1¼ teasp. cream of tartar
1 cup plus 2 tablesp. sifted cake flour   1 teasp. vanilla extract
½ cup sifted granulated sugar   ¼ teasp. almond extract
¼ teasp. salt   1 cup sifted granulated sugar

1. About 1 hr. ahead, set out egg whites.

2. When ready to make cake, start heating oven to 375° F. Sift flour with ½ cup sugar 4 times.

3. In large electric-mixer bowl, combine egg whites, salt, cream of tartar, extracts. With electric mixer at high speed (or with egg beater or flat wire whip), beat whites until stiff enough to hold soft, moist peaks.

4. With mixer at same speed, beat in 1 cup sugar, sprinkling ¼ cup at a time over egg whites. Beat until sugar is just blended. (To beat by hand, beat 25 strokes, or turns, after each addition.)

5. Stop mixer. Sift in flour mixture by fourths, folding in each addition with 15 complete fold-over strokes of spoon, rubber spatula, or wire whip and turning bowl often. After all flour has been folded in, give batter 10 to 20 extra strokes.

6. Gently push batter into *ungreased* 4''-deep 10'' tube pan. With spatula, cut through batter once without lifting spatula out of batter.

7. Bake 30 to 35 min., or until cake tester inserted in center comes out clean.

8. Cool by reversing pan, but do not let cake rest on a tabletop. If the tube is not high enough, place it over an inverted funnel. Let the cake hang for about 1½ hours until it is set. Then remove from pan.

9. Do not cut cake with a knife. Use cake divider or 2 forks inserted back to back to pry the cake apart gently.

Figure 1-3. Example of an algorithm—a recipe for angel food cake.

Resources are spelled out as part of the recipe. They include a heated oven and a series of utensils.

The next step in algorithm creation is to describe the processing that will take place. This involves the mixing of ingredients. In carrying out a recipe, you must have the exact ingredients, precisely measured, and mixed in the specified sequence. The same applies in executing a computer program. In the case of an angel food cake, for example, you must sift the flour before you measure it. If you don't, you will have the wrong amount of a key ingredient. Also, you must separate the eggs and then mix them back together again. You might reason that it would do just as well to beat the entire egg and then mix it in. But it wouldn't work that way. You just wouldn't get a light, fluffy angel food cake. You must follow the recipe, exactly.

All of these rules and requirements apply with programs just as they do with recipes. A significant difference, however, lies in the fact that, in developing a program, you can't count on human judgment. You must be much more exact. For example, in a recipe, you might tell a person to "cool the cake to room temperature, then slice and serve." With a computer program, you would have to specify where to put the cake to cool it, what temperature would constitute cooling, what instrument to use for slicing, and how big to make the slices. A computer cannot apply any undefined judgment at all. It needs explicit instructions for every decision and processing step to be carried out.

To demonstrate that the same basic algorithm-development practices apply to computer programs as to angel food cakes, consider a typical business application to be programmed for computer processing.

ALGORITHM DEVELOPMENT: AN EXAMPLE

You are employed by the South Bay Property Management Company. Your employer is in the business of managing large apartment buildings. South Bay Property Managment employs 50 persons. Recently, the company has installed a microcomputer. The main jobs to be handled on the microcomputer are the billing of tenants, the collecting and crediting of rent, and accounting for maintenance costs on all of the buildings. In addition, it has been decided to develop a program to process payroll information on employees and to produce paychecks on a weekly basis.

Management has requested a control listing before actual payroll processing takes place. The list is to include the names of all employees and, for each, data on total hours worked, pay rate, and total pay earned for this pay period. Input for this application will come from weekly time sheets that include employee name, hours worked, and pay rate. Obviously, the computer must calculate the earnings data. To do this, the computer must perform logic operations to determine which employees are entitled to overtime pay. Then, regular pay and overtime pay must be computed separately and consolidated into a single, gross-earnings figure.

This is the problem. The steps followed in producing an algorithm that will serve as a basis for this program are described below.

Algorithm-Development Steps

1. *Define outputs.* In algorithm development, outputs are often defined by preparing a design layout for the report or screen display to be produced. Figure 1-4 shows an output report for this application.

```
            SOUTH BAY PROPERTY MANAGEMENT

     EMPLOYEE          HOURS       PAY        TOTAL
       NAME                        RATE        PAY

     DAVIS     THOMAS  S   40.0     5.15      206.00
     FREDICKS  ROBERT  T   55.8     6.35      404.49
     HENRY     JOHN    D   45.9    10.00      488.50
     JOHNSON   BETTY   B   15.0     5.35       80.25
     JONES     DONALD  S   42.9     7.15      317.10
     KRAMER    MARY    T   35.7     5.24      187.06
     KWAN      ALICE   D   21.5     6.10      131.15
     MORALES   GARY    V   55.0     9.50      593.75
     PEREZ     FRED    J   39.7     4.95      196.51
     STALLONE  MARIA   E   40.0     6.15      246.00
```

2. *Identify needed inputs.* On the basis of identified output, the next step is to figure out what input records must look like if a computer is to produce the defined outputs. In this instance, the needed input data must be present on the weekly time sheet. An example of the time sheet to be used is shown in Figure 1-5.

Figure 1-4. Output report—starting point in algorithm development.

Figure 1-5. Time sheet—an input example.

TIME SHEET DATE: WEEK:

| NAME | HOURS WORKED | | | | | | | | |
	MON	TUE	WED	THUR	FRI	SAT	SUN	TOTAL	INIT
DAVIS, THOMAS S.	8.0	8.0	8.0	8.0	8.0			40.0	
FREDRICKS, ROBERT T.	8.0	8.0	8.0	8.0	16.0	7.8		55.8	
HENRY, JOHN D.	8.0			8.0	8.0	13.0	8.9	45.9	
JOHNSON, BETTY B.						8.0	7.0	15.0	
JONES, DONALD S.	8.0	8.0	10.0	8.9	8.0			42.9	
KRAMER, MARY T.			3.0	8.0	8.0	8.0	8.7	35.7	
KWAN, ALICE D.	8.0	8.0	5.5					21.5	
MORALES, GARY V.	10.0	10.0	10.0	10.0	10.0	5.0		55.0	
PEREZ, FRED J.	8.0	7.7	8.0	8.0	8.0			39.7	
STALLONE, MARIA E.	8.0	8.0	8.0	8.0	8.0			40.0	

3. *Define processing requirements.* The programmer builds an understanding of the processing that must be applied to the input to produce the defined output. This can be done using one or more of the many program design tools that are available. Figure 1-6 shows data records flowing into a computer, indicates the processing that takes place, and shows the format of the output records as they relate to the final report. Based on the understanding of the processing that will take place, the steps required to produce the output can then be described in sequence.

Figure 1-6. Data flow analysis can benefit from a visual diagram showing input, processing, and output of data.

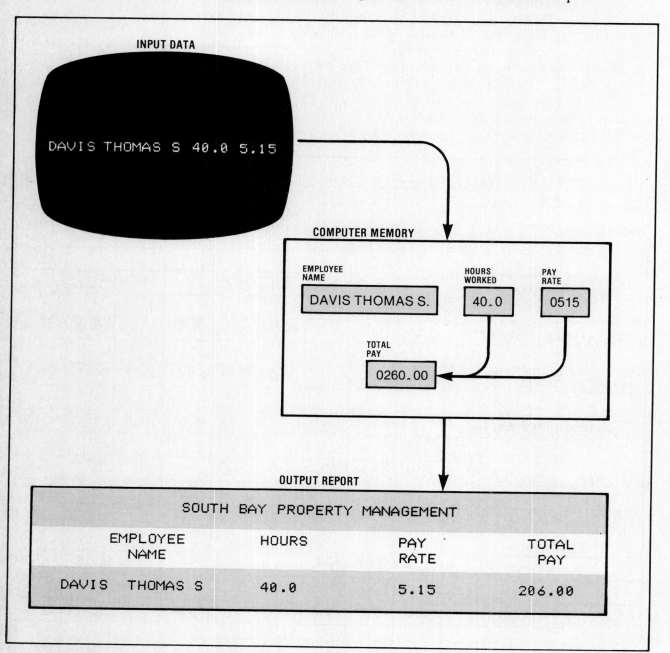

INPUT DATA

DAVIS THOMAS S 40.0 5.15

COMPUTER MEMORY

EMPLOYEE NAME		HOURS WORKED	PAY RATE
DAVIS THOMAS S.		40.0	0515

TOTAL PAY

0260.00

OUTPUT REPORT

SOUTH BAY PROPERTY MANAGEMENT			
EMPLOYEE NAME	HOURS	PAY RATE	TOTAL PAY
DAVIS THOMAS S	40.0	5.15	206.00

One of the design tools that is used to describe the processing logic of programs is *pseudocode*. Pseudocode uses English statements to describe program logic in an easy-to-read, straightforward manner. The writing of pseudocode imposes few syntactical rules on the programmer. Statements need not be complete sentences. Punctuation is limited and indentation patterns are up to the programmer. The only ''requirement'' is that each statement must describe, precisely and unambiguously, what processing will be done to which data. Other requirements may be incorporated in standards developed by individual organizations. In the example in Figure 1-7, pseudocode statements are built around action verbs such as do, perform, move, accept, etc. The emphasis is upon describing what must be done and how each function is to be executed.

The pseudocode statements in Figure 1-7 serve, next, as the basis for the writing of program coding. *Coding,* in turn, is the process of writing instructions that the computer will follow in processing the application. Pseudocode statements form a bridge between describing the processing steps and the writing of a program. Pseudocoding, in effect, is a description of the algorithm for a computer program.

Figure 1-7. Pseudocode statements serve as a basis for program writing.

```
                  (изображение удалено)

Pseudocode:  PAYROLL

PAYROLL-MAINLINE
     Perform Initialization.
     Perform Calculate-payroll UNTIL input employee name equals
         "END OF DATA".
     Perform Termination.
     STOP.

INITIALIZATION
     Display Report Headings.
     Accept an Input Record.

CALCULATE-PAYROLL
     Move card fields to the print area.
     If hours worked is greater than 40
         Compute gross pay including time and one half for over 40 hours.
     Else
         Compute gross pay equal to hours worked times hourly rate.
     Display the Employee Record.
     Accept an Input Record.

TERMINATION
     Display "End of Report" message.
```

Problem Solution: A COBOL Program

Figure 1-8 is the coding for a COBOL program that will implement the payroll algorithm. At this point, you are not ready to write a program of this type. However, do examine the program. Pay particular attention to the portion of the program labeled PROCEDURE DIVISION. This division is the part of a COBOL program that contains the exact instructions that tell the computer what to do. Note the similarities between the COBOL procedures, the actual program statements, and the pseudocode in Figure 1-8. This review will make it clear that program writing, or coding, stems directly from a pseudocoded description of a business problem or need.

Figure 1-8. These COBOL coding sheets contain the statements necessary for development of the sample payroll program. (Illustration continues.)

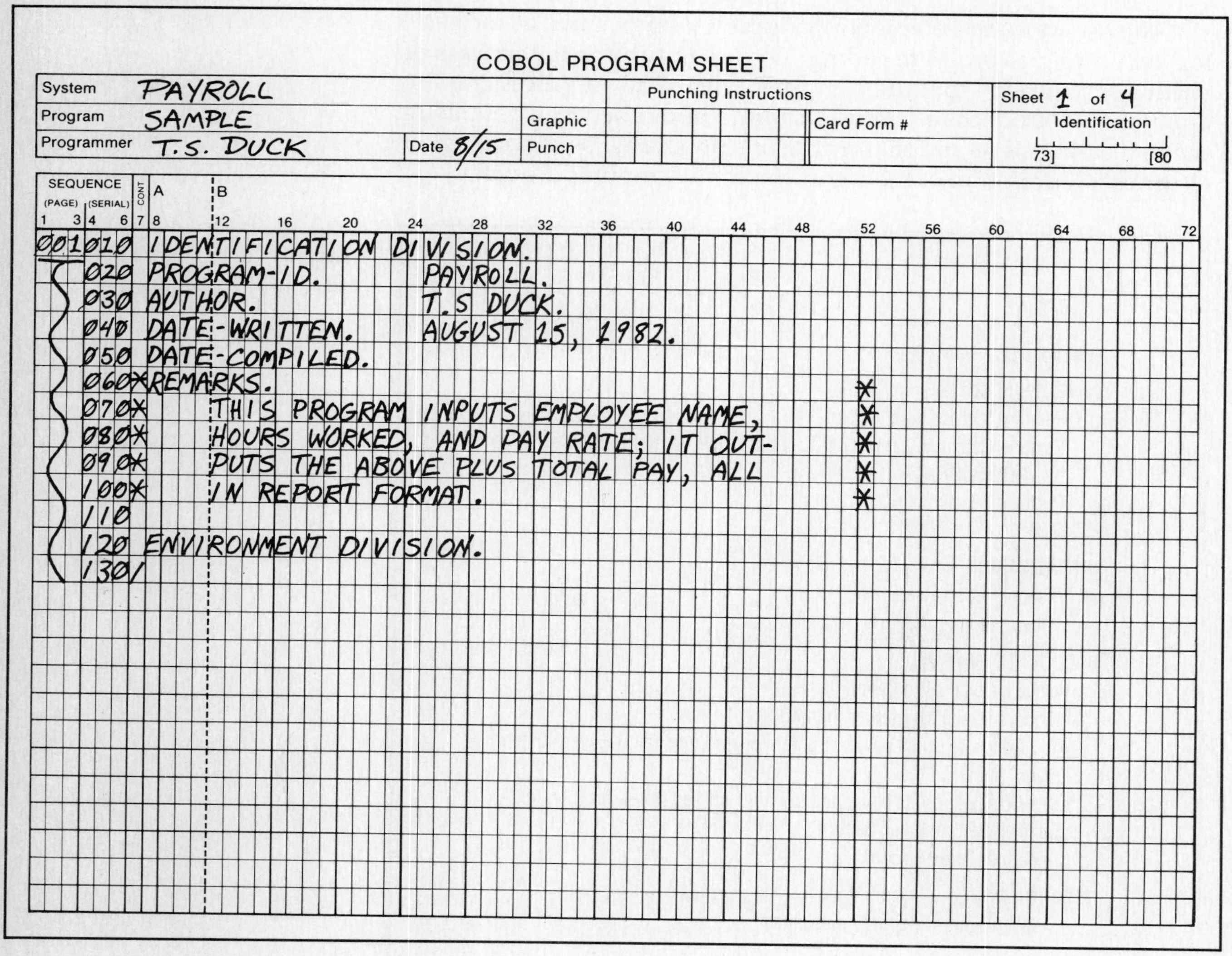

COBOL PROGRAM SHEET

System: PAYROLL
Program: SAMPLE
Programmer: T.S. DUCK   Date 8/15
Sheet 1 of 4

```
001010 IDENTIFICATION DIVISION.
   020 PROGRAM-ID.      PAYROLL.
   030 AUTHOR.          T.S DUCK.
   040 DATE-WRITTEN.    AUGUST 25, 1982.
   050 DATE-COMPILED.
   060*REMARKS.                                         *
   070*     THIS PROGRAM INPUTS EMPLOYEE NAME,          *
   080*     HOURS WORKED, AND PAY RATE; IT OUT-         *
   090*     PUTS THE ABOVE PLUS TOTAL PAY, ALL          *
   100*     IN REPORT FORMAT.                           *
   110
   120 ENVIRONMENT DIVISION.
   130/
```

COBOL PROGRAM SHEET

System: PAYROLL
Program: SAMPLE
Programmer: T. S. DUCK
Date: 8/15
Punching Instructions — Graphic / Punch / Card Form #
Sheet 2 of 4
Identification 73] [80

```
002140 DATA DIVISION.
   150
   160 WORKING-STORAGE SECTION.
   170
   180 01  INPUT-DATA.
   190     05  IN-EMPLOYEE-NAME          PIC X(20).
   200     05  IN-EMPLOYEE-HRS           PIC 9(02)V9.
   210     05  IN-PAY-RATE               PIC 9(02)V99.
   220
   230 01  OUTPUT-LINE.
   240     05  FILLER                    PIC X(03).
   250     05  OUT-EMPLOYEE-NAME         PIC X(20).
   260     05  FILLER                    PIC X(03).
   270     05  OUT-EMPLOYEE-HRS          PIC 9(02)V9.
   280     05  FILLER                    PIC X(04).
   290     05  OUT-PAY-RATE              PIC 9(02)V99.
   300     05  FILLER                    PIC X(02).
   310     05  OUT-TOTAL-PAY             PIC 9(04)V99.
   320
```

COBOL PROGRAM SHEET

System: PAYROLL
Program: SAMPLE
Programmer: T. S. DUCK
Date: 8/15
Punching Instructions — Graphic / Punch / Card Form #
Sheet 3 of 4
Identification 73] [80

```
003330 PROCEDURE DIVISION.
   340
   350 PAYROLL-MAINLINE.
   360     PERFORM INITIALIZATION.
   370     PERFORM CALCULATE-PAYROLL
   380         UNTIL IN-EMPLOYEE-NAME EQUALS "END OF DATA".
   390     PERFORM TERMINATION.
   400     STOP RUN.
   410
   420 INITIALIZATION.
   430     MOVE SPACES TO OUTPUT-LINE.
   440     DISPLAY "               SOUTH BAY PROPERTY MANAGEMENT".
   450     DISPLAY " ".
   460     DISPLAY "     EMPLOYEE           HOURS       PAY        TOTAL".
   470     DISPLAY "       NAME                         RATE        PAY".
   480     DISPLAY " "
   490     ACCEPT INPUT-DATA.
   500
```

COBOL PROGRAM SHEET

System	PAYROLL			Punching Instructions		Sheet 4 of 4
Program	SAMPLE		Graphic		Card Form #	Identification
Programmer	T. S. DUCK	Date 8/15	Punch			73] [80

SEQUENCE (PAGE) (SERIAL)	CONT	A	B

```
004520 CALCULATE-PAYROLL.
   530     MOVE IN-EMPLOYEE-NAME          TO OUT-EMPLOYEE-NAME.
   540     MOVE IN-EMPLOYEE-HRS           TO OUT-EMPLOYEE-HRS.
   550     MOVE IN-PAY-RATE               TO OUT-PAY-RATE.
   560     IF IN-EMPLOYEE-HRS GREATER THAN 40
   570     THEN
   580         COMPUTE OUT-TOTAL-PAY =
   590             IN-EMPLOYEE-HRS * IN-PAY-RATE +
   600             (IN-EMPLOYEE-HRS - 40) * IN-PAY-RATE / Z
   610     ELSE
   620         COMPUTE OUT-TOTAL-PAY =
   630             IN-EMPLOYEE-HRS * IN-PAY-RATE.
   640     DISPLAY OUTPUT-LINE.
   650     ACCEPT INPUT-DATA.
   660
   670 TERMINATION.
   680         DISPLAY " ".
   690         DISPLAY "                    END OF PROCESSING".
```

COBOL Terms

1. PROCEDURE DIVISION.

Summary

A program is a set of instructions that causes a computer to perform a series of steps in processing data. There are different types of programs. Some programs control the functioning of computer equipment. These, broadly, are operating systems. Programs that translate instructions written in human-readable terms to computer language are called compilers. COBOL (COmmon Business Oriented Language) is a programming language that uses such a compiler. Programs written in COBOL to solve specific problems are known as application programs. [*Objective No. 1.*]

A computer is a collection of electronic devices that function together to transform data into information and to communicate results of processing. Computer equipment is called hardware. A computer includes several basic equipment units. One of these is a processor. This is where actual computing is done. The processor includes a memory and a central processing unit (CPU). The memory supports processing by accepting and holding temporarily the programs and data to be processed. The CPU has two components, a control unit and an arithmetic logic unit (ALU). The control unit directs the operation of all devices that make up the computer hardware. The ALU performs arithmetic functions and logical comparisons. These represent the only data processing capabilities of a computer. [*Objective No. 1.*]

The function of the CPU is processing. Other equipment units handle input and output. In addition, computers are supported by secondary storage devices that retain data for processing. Data, in this context, are raw facts, while information consists of processed data that has acquired meaning or value through processing. [*Objective No. 1.*]

Collectively, all programs used to direct computer processing are called software. Together, software and hardware make up computer systems. [*Objective No. 1.*]

Computers are useful tools in situations involving the processing of large amounts of data. For example, it would not pay to set up a computer to produce a single paycheck. But, if a company had thousands of employees, it would be almost essential, today, to process their payroll on a computer. Thus, computers are tools for handling volume jobs. Volumes of work, in turn, require that the processing that takes place be repeatable and reliable. The directions for processing for repeatable, reliable results require precisely written programs. [*Objective No. 2.*]

To design a program for the processing of applications, an algorithm is developed. An algorithm, in effect, states a problem in a form and format suitable for computer solution. Algorithms are developed through a series of orderly steps. The first step is to state the problem. This is done by defining the outputs to be produced by a computer under control of the application program. The second step is to identify the resources needed to solve the problem. This step is completed by defining the data and information inputs needed to generate the identified outputs. The third, final step is to define the processing that must be applied to the input to deliver the specified output. [*Objective No. 2.*]

The algorithm is then described in a series of simple English statements that define what processing is to be applied to which data, in what sequence. These statements, in turn, describe the program to be written. The statements are known as pseudocode. The process of converting pseudocode statements into the instructions that make up a program is known as coding. [*Objective No. 3.*]

Key Terms

1. program
2. operating system
3. compiler
4. COBOL (COmmon Business Oriented Language)
5. application program
6. computer
7. hardware
8. processor
9. input
10. processing
11. output
12. storage
13. secondary storage
14. memory
15. central processing unit (CPU)
16. main memory
17. primary storage
18. control unit
19. arithmetic logic unit (ALU)
20. software
21. computer system
22. data
23. information
24. black box
25. partition
26. task
27. algorithm
28. execute
29. pseudocode
30. coding

Review/Discussion Questions

1. What are operating system programs and what do they do?

2. What is a compiler and what does it do?

3. What are application programs and what is their purpose?

4. What are the elements of computer hardware and how are they interrelated functionally?

5. Why is a computer system used in volume processing situations only and why would it be impractical to use a computer to create a single business document?

6. What is an algorithm and what is its purpose?

7. What are the characteristics of a proper algorithm?

8. What is the importance of decomposition of a problem to computer programming?

9. How is a program algorithm developed?

10. In algorithm development, what is the significance of beginning with definitions of outputs?

11. What is pseudocoding and from what sources is it derived?

Practice Assignments

On the Assignment Sheet that follows, use pseudocode to describe the algorithms for the following activities:

1. Sharpening a pencil with a manually operated pencil sharpener.

2. Printing a list of periodicals in the college library.

Worksheet—Algorithm for Sharpening a Pencil

Program Name: _____

Prepared By: _____

Worksheet—Algorithm for Periodical List

Prepared By: _____

Vocabulary Building Practice—Exercise 1

Write definitions and/or explanations of the terms listed below.

1. program _____
   _____

2. operating system _____
   _____

3. compiler _____
   _____

4. application program _____
   _____

5. computer _____
   _____

6. processor _____
   _____

7. input _____
   _____

8. processing _____
   _____

9. output _____
   _____

10. storage _____
    _____

(over, please)

11. **secondary storage** _____

_____

12. **memory** _____

_____

13. **central processing unit** _____

_____

14. **main memory** _____

_____

15. **control unit** _____

_____

16. **arithmethic logic unit** _____

_____

17. **data** _____

_____

18. **information** _____

_____

19. **black box** _____

_____

20. **partition** _____

_____

APPLICATION PROGRAM DEVELOPMENT 2

OBJECTIVES

On completing reading and other learning assignments for this chapter, you should be able to:

1. Identify the phases of a systems development life cycle and explain the purposes and interrelationships of these phases.

2. Identify the phases of the program development process presented in this chapter and explain the activities and achievements of each phase.

3. Describe the purposes and uses of data flow diagrams and IPO charts.

4. Describe input and output layout forms and explain their values and uses.

5. Describe structure charts and explain the value of the top-down approach to program design that these charts help to implement.

6. Describe the purposes of structured flowcharts, decision tables, and decision trees.

7. Explain the purpose of and describe the development of pseudocode.

8. Describe the functions of sequence, selection, and repetition and explain their importance in program development.

9. Explain walkthroughs and structured walkthroughs, including the differences between these methods and the values derived from each.

PROBLEM DEFINITION, THE STARTING POINT

The problems that lead to the development of computer information systems (CIS) tend to be both extensive and complex. Defining these problems, in itself, can be a major piece of work. In large part, this is because many people, and often multiple business entities, are involved. The basic problems or needs that lead to development of application programs are of a business or organizational nature. Businesses have certain functions that must be completed. As businesses grow, computers increasingly hold the key to meeting these needs.

Typical needs to be met or problems that are solved through use of computers include the issuing of payrolls, the writing of bills to customers, the collecting of payments from customers, the writing of checks to suppliers, the setting up and keeping of books of account and many others. At the management level, data are digested and reported for special meaning in management information systems. For planning purposes, the same data can be used to support decisions on the future directions of an organization.

The point is that many people—and many dollars—are involved in identifying and defining business problems to be solved through the development of computer information systems. To deal with the magnitude and complexity of computer systems development, an activity called a *systems development project* is usually organized. Systems development projects of this type precede the development of computer programs. They deal with the identification of business needs and with the design of methods to meet these needs. A generalized systems development project is a step toward the development of computer programs.

Programs are computer implementations of algorithms. Algorithms, in turn, consist of a series of problem-solving steps. Thus, before an algorithm can be developed, the problem itself has to be identified. This is done with a formal statement, or definition, describing the problem and its requirements.

To put the effort of systems development into perspective, systems development projects frequently wind up costing more than $100,000 and occupying four or five staff years of working time. To make sure that the problem to be solved is really understood and that the project can be completed successfully, projects are organized into a series of phases. This phasing of a project makes it possible to structure the checks and balances necessary to control progress and to protect the investments involved. Organizations use many different types of systems development project structures. A five-phase systems development project structure is provided below as an example of what happens in the process of creating computer information systems.

This project structure is known as a *systems development life cycle.*

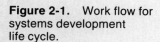

Figure 2-1. Work flow for systems development life cycle.

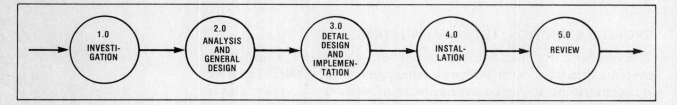

Systems Development Life Cycle

The five phases of a systems development life cycle are:

1. Investigation
2. Analysis and general design
3. Detailed design and implementation
4. Installation
5. Review.

In addition to the five phases, there is an ongoing need for system maintenance—updating the procedures to meet changing requirements or revising them as opportunities for improvement are identified. The work flow of the systems development life cycle is shown in the diagram in Figure 2-1. Content of the five basic phases is summarized below.

Phase 1: Investigation.   This phase consists of a short, organizational set of activities. The phase begins when a manager or executive brings a problem or need to the manager responsible for CIS development. The manager with the need—known as the *user*—works closely with a professional *systems analyst,* a specialist in analysis, design, and development of computer information systems. Results of the investigation phase include:

- Identify the *real* problem. Determine the size and scope of the need or problem and any interrelationships between the procedures studied and those for the rest of the organization.
- Define opportunities and objectives for development of a new computer information system.
- Develop tentative estimates of the *costs and benefits* of the new system. Even though these are tentative, they meet an important principle of computer information systems: there must be enough apparent benefits delivered to justify investment in the cost of development.
- Establish a tentative *schedule and budget* for development of the CIS. The schedule and budget include programming which, in many instances, represents 40 to 50 percent of the cost of systems development.
- Secure management approval to proceed with Phase 2.

Phase 2: Analysis and General Design.   Purposes and activities for the analysis and general design phase include:

- Document the current system. The project study team consisting of users and systems analysts (programmers are not usually on the scene yet) identify and document the business procedures and practices currently in use. They collect copies of forms and operating instructions for any equipment being used. They also document these steps in processing through use of such tools as *systems flowcharts* (Figure 2-2). As appropriate, members of the study team may document existing procedures through use of a *data flow diagram* like the one shown in Figure 2-3. Preparation and use of data flow diagrams are described later in this chapter.

Figure 2-2. Example of system flowchart.

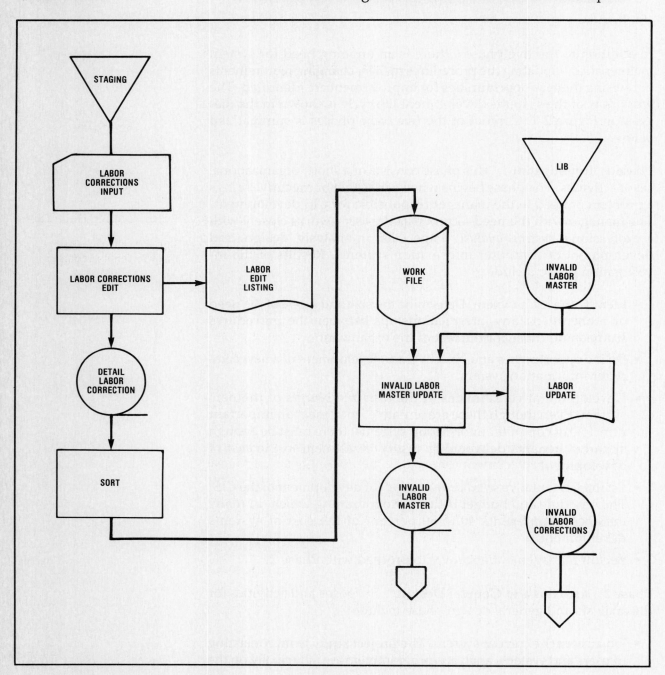

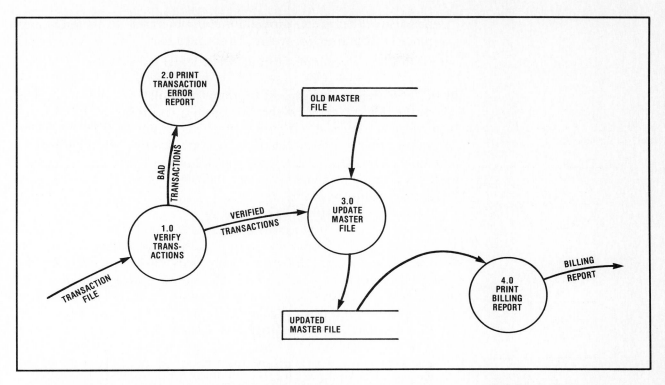

Figure 2-3. Data flow diagram for file updating.

- Identify potential opportunities for improvements in present methods.

- Identify alternative systems or methods that can improve upon current methods. In connection with these tentative solutions to the problem, human-machine *interfaces*, points at which people and equipment interact, should be identified for each alternative approach. In addition, prospective costs and benefits of each alternative should be defined generally.

- Schedules and budgets for the development of a new system to replace existing methods should be refined. Estimates should be closer than they were initially.

- Performance criteria should be established for any system considered as a replacement for existing methods. These are formal statements of expectations for the new or revised procedures should be in quantifiable terms. Decisions about whether to make the changes will be based on these projected improvements and the probabilities that they can be realized.

- The number of alternatives to be considered for systems development is narrowed down. If possible, a final choice on the approach to be used is made during this phase. At the very least, the possibilities to be examined further are narrowed down to two or three alternative approaches.

- Equipment and system software to be used are specified. In particular, if a new set of programs will require additional hardware or software support, provisions must be made to have these in place by the time the system is put into use.

- Secure management approval to proceed with Phase 3.

Phase 3: Detailed Design and Implementation. This is the phase in which the design for computer processing, including programming, is completed. Note that a project is often 50 percent or more completed before programming is initiated. Considerable effort, then, is needed to define the problem and develop the algorithms that serve as the basis for programming. Activities completed during this phase of the systems development life cycle include:

- Design the structure for the programs that will solve the problem. This is done by preparing either flowcharts or data flow diagrams for the new system. In effect, each processing box on the flowchart or each processing step, sometimes called a *bubble,* in a data flow diagram becomes a processing unit within the program. These program units, or parts, are called program *modules.* A module is a set of instructions that accomplishes a limited function or purpose. Every module has only a single point of entry and a single exit. For each program, the relationships among modules are represented in a *structure chart* like the one shown in Figure 2-4. The structure charts identify and relate the processing functions that must be performed to solve the problem through a computer program. The diagram in Figure 2-4 is generic. It illustrates the fundamental structure of most programs. Development of structure charts is discussed extensively in later sections and chapters of this book.

- *Data formats* are designed and specified. Data formats are the organizational structures in which data are represented on forms or in computer files.

- *Processing controls* for the system are established and specified. These controls include a series of steps governing the handling of data. Included are *authorization* of transactions, *validation* of input

Figure 2-4. General structure chart for application programs.

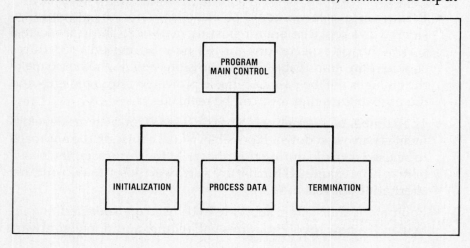

data, *editing* or inspection of results, and *balancing* to be sure that data are complete, accurate, and reliable.

- The internal processing logic for each program module is specified. These logic specifications become the basis for the writing of actual program instructions, or *coding*.

- Develop *test data*. The validity of programs is established by running test data that represent the processing to be done by the finished program. An important aspect of test data is that all conceivable, logical conditions that can be anticipated for the finished system should be included in the test data and processed to be sure that the new programs can deal with such factors.

- Programs are tested and debugged. The actual writing of programs, as indicated above, is known as coding. *Testing* involves the analysis of output produced through use of a program in comparison with expected results. Testing and *debugging* lead to detection of *logical errors*, or improper processing, within programs. Debugging identifies errors in the use of a programming language. These are called errors in *syntax*, or *syntactical errors*.

Phase 4: Installation. During this phase, the system comes into regular, ongoing use. Once a system is tested and has proven to produce correct results, a transition follows into use of the new system for regular, ongoing production. One common approach is to start using the new system in *parallel* with existing methods. Gradually, as the new system proves itself, the old one is phased out.

Phase 5: Review. At the conclusion of each development project, the work is reviewed. The main purpose of these reviews is to verify that the system meets the objectives established at the beginning of development. In addition, the work performed is reviewed as a means of improving systems development methods for future projects.

Maintenance. Almost as soon as it is put into use, a new system develops requirements for *maintenance*, or enhancement and updating. Some of these changes are mandated by business practices, competition, or government requirements. For example, when cost-of-living pay increases become effective, payroll programs must be adjusted. This is a typical maintenance requirement. Also, as new laws come into effect—such as a requirement that banks withhold 10 percent of interest payments on some accounts—programs must be adjusted so that computer systems will conform to regulations.

In summary, the first two phases of a systems development project produce the definition of the problem needed to bring programming into the picture. Programming takes place during the third, detailed design and implementation, phase. Since programming itself is a major activity involving many people and a number of skills, a process approach is also used in the development of application programs. This is described below. And, finally, Phases 4 and 5 involve the placing of the system into production and an ongoing review of the whole process.

PROGRAM DEVELOPMENT PROCESS

The relationship between the overall systems development life cycle and the supporting program development process is shown in Figure 2-5. This diagram highlights the project-type nature of program development. In particular, the life cycle establishes a systematic project approach to the development of programs. This structure, in turn, leads to a system perspective and assigns a rightful place to the work of program coding. Traditionally, one of the major problems in programming, particularly for large systems, has been a natural urge on the part of the programmers to begin writing code. This urge should be resisted until requirements have been adequately defined and the necessary algorithms established. The process approach establishes this perspective by positioning the writing of coding as the fourth among five steps.

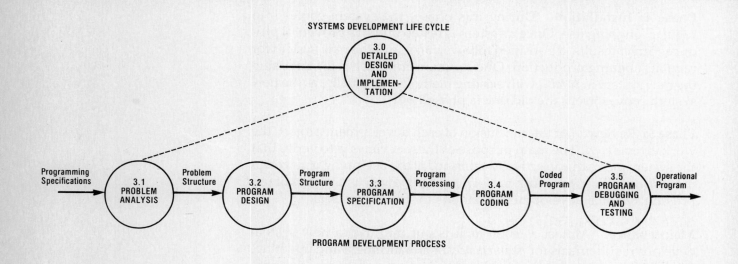

Figure 2-5. Relationship of program development process to systems development life cycle.

The five steps in the overall program development process are identified and described briefly in the discussion that follows. After this description, the first three planning-oriented phases in the process are discussed in further depth. The remainder of the process is covered in Chapter 3. The program development process steps are:

1. *Analyze the problem.* Program specifications provided by the systems development activity are reviewed. The analysis covers requirements for output, input, processing, and any data storage that may be required. The end result of this phase is an understanding of the

nature of the problem and its *structure.* That is, the problem to be solved is broken into a series of identified parts, or components.

2. *Design the program structure.* During this step, the programmer creates a plan of attack to be followed in solving the problem. In doing this, the overall programming requirement is broken down into a series of smaller programming modules. A module, in this context, is a named program building block that includes any defined sequence of contiguous instructions.

3. *Design program processing.* For each identified module, the actual computer processing steps needed are specified. The end result is a documented solution of the problem to be solved—usually stated in pseudocode or represented graphically in structured flowcharts. A structured flowchart is a graphic representation, using standard symbols to picture a computer processing sequence.

4. *Write the program.* The programmer writes the instructions specified in the design. Program instructions consist of a set of statements, or commands, that direct computer processing.

5. *Debug and test the program. Bugs* are errors in a program. Testing has a special meaning in program development. Test procedures determine whether the logical operations—the actual processing—are valid. In other words, the final step in program development validates both the design of the program and the workability of the instructions.

The process of program development proceeds step by step. The structure imposed by the program development process serves, most importantly, to make program development manageable. Without a series of steps, it becomes impossible for the programmer to know exactly where he or she is at any point. With a series of steps, however, it becomes possible to control and direct the programming process.

STEP 1: ANALYZE THE PROBLEM

Analysis begins with a thorough study of program specifications developed as part of a systems development life cycle. Objectives of this step in program development include:

- Understand the problem to be solved.
- Document that understanding.

Documentation of the understanding of program specifications should follow some standard, formal format. Use of a standard method assures that the documentation has meaning for everyone involved. Further, since many people will use this documentation, the format selected is often pictorial, or graphic. Graphic presentation saves time and promotes understanding. In this work, certainly, graphic documentation is more clearly understood than verbal description.

A number of graphic documentation techniques are available for problem analysis. Four commonly used methods are introduced below:

- Data flow diagrams
- Layout forms (input and output)
- IPO charts
- Structure charts.

Data Flow Diagrams

A data flow diagram shows the movement of data through a system of programs or a single program. All processing steps in which the structure or content of data is altered are identified within the data flow diagram. To illustrate, Figure 2-6 is a data flow diagram for the payroll application described at the end of Chapter 1. In Figure 2-6, the circles represent processing steps in which data are transformed in some specified way. The named arrows are the data flows that indicate the movement of data between processes. In effect, the data flow

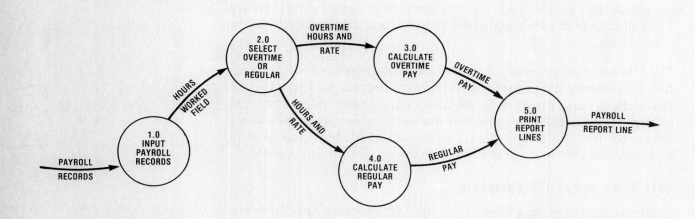

Figure 2-6. Data flow diagram for payroll report program.

diagram is another method of representing the algorithm that describes the program under development.

Layout Forms

Layout forms are standard worksheets used in systems development and programming. These are used to represent the configuration of data to be input to or output from a system. An example of an output layout for a printed document (a report to be generated by the payroll program) is shown in Figure 2-7. The symbols X and 9 are used, respectively, to represent nonnumeric and numeric content for data fields,

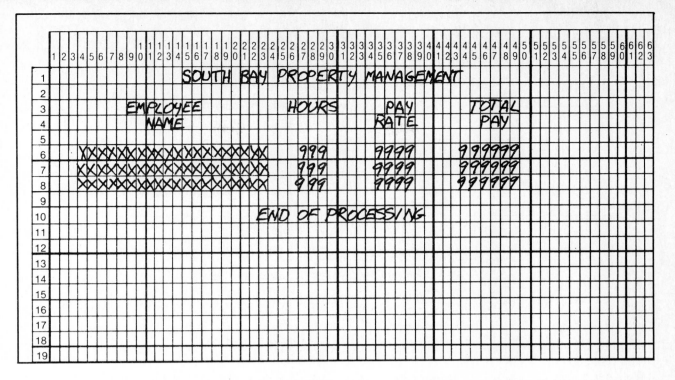

and also to show the sizes of data fields and their corresponding records. The presence of the characters dollar sign ($), comma (,) and period (.) has a special meaning, covered in Chapter 4. Input layouts are usually designed to correspond with the formats of the data media on which they will be recorded—cards, tapes, disks, or display terminals. An input record layout for the payroll program is shown in Figure 2-8.

Figure 2-7. Print layout chart for payrol report.

IPO Charts

IPO charts (Input/Processing/Output charts) document the major processing tasks required to convert the specified input into the desired output. In preparing IPO charts, input and output layout forms are

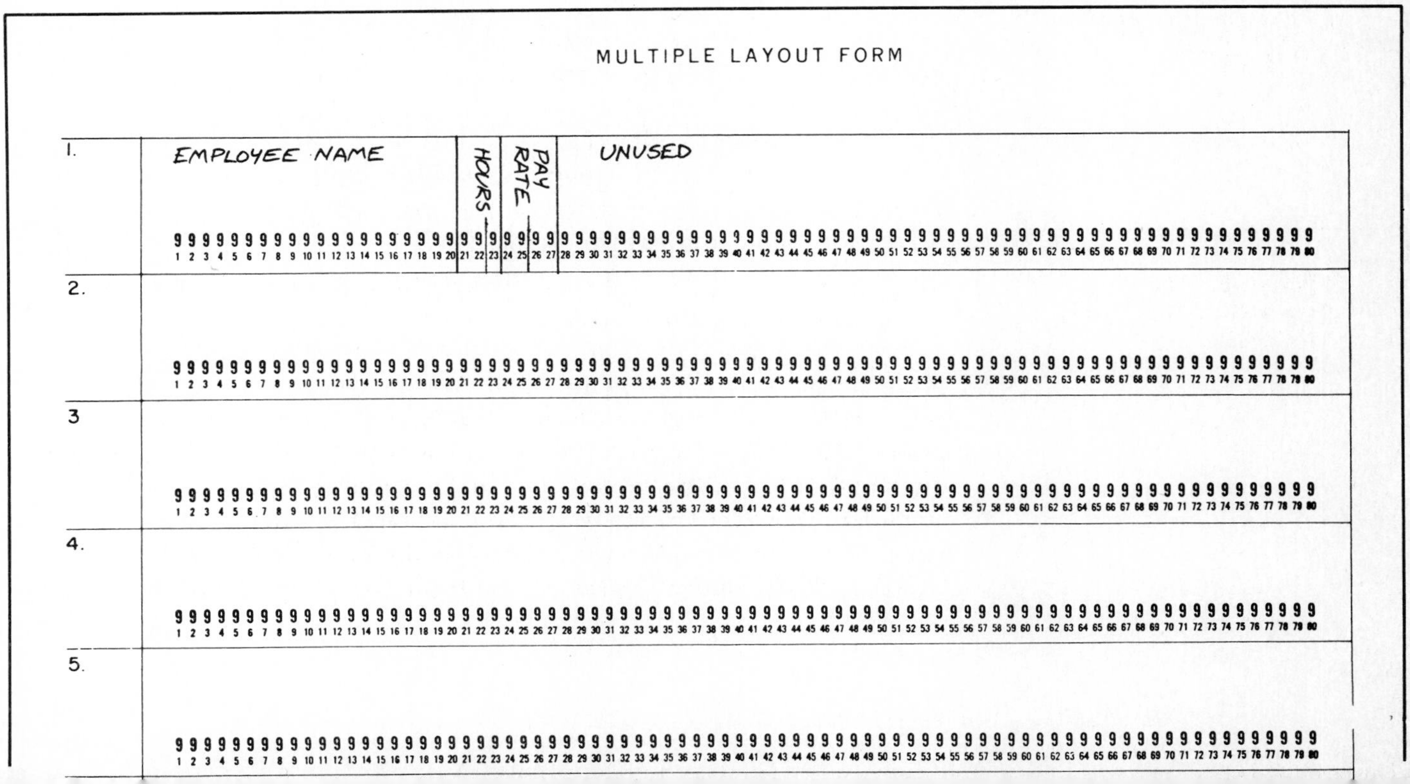

Figure 2-8. Input record layout chart for time card.

IPO CHART				
PROGRAM: PAYROLL REPORT		**PROGRAMMER:** MEDLEY AND EAVES		
MODULE NAME:				
INPUT	PROCESSING		REF:	OUTPUT
TIME CARDS	1. PRINT HEADINGS			PAYROLL REPORT
	2. INPUT DATA			
	3. SET UP PRINT LINE			
	4. CALCULATE TOTAL PAY			
	5. PRINT REPORT LINE			
	6. INPUT DATA			

Figure 2-9. Example of an IPO chart.

analyzed in detail. The processing requirements are then reviewed through reference to program specifications. The program designer can then complete the list of input, processing, and output tasks on the IPO chart.

Figure 2-9 shows an IPO chart for the South Bay Property Management payroll. In reviewing this diagram notice that it deals with *what* steps are performed to convert the payroll input data into the desired report. This chart does not specify *when, how,* or *how often* these processing steps should occur. Since these factors must ultimately be incorporated into an effective program, other techniques such as pseudocode must be used to supplement IPO charts to establish complete program control documentation.

Structure Charts

A fourth commonly used method for documenting and designing program requirements is the structure chart. These are also known as hierarchy charts. Such charts provide a graphic method for breaking programs down into related parts or functions. This process is known as *partitioning* or *decomposition.* Partitioning and decomposition are proven methods for dealing with the complexity of problems to be solved through computer programs. These are techniques which make it possible to break a job down into a series of manageable functions.

A structure chart for the South Bay Property Management payroll is shown in Figure 2-10. As indicated above, a structure chart partitions, or decomposes, a problem into logical parts. Development of a structure chart recognizes that all programs have at least three main components. The diagram in Figure 2-10 shows the standard breakdown. On the top line of the structure chart, known as the top *level,* is the *identifier*—the name of the program itself. At the next level are three parts, represented by boxes. These are the basic components of any CIS program. They are *initiation, main processing,* and *termination.*

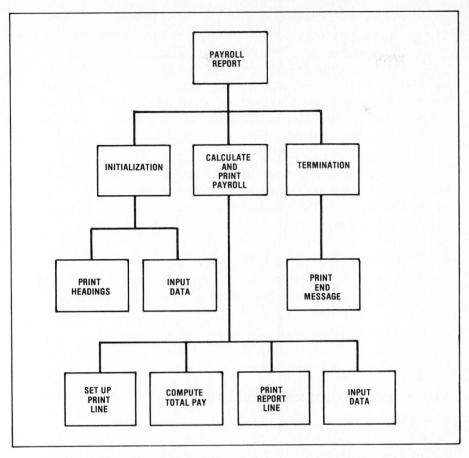

Figure 2-10. Structure chart for payroll program.

As a unit, the diagram in Figure 2-10 can be identified as a *model*, or skeleton, for the program to be developed. The three partitions on the second level of the model serve to decompose the problem into standard parts. It is recognized through this fundamental structure that every program must have steps that initialize, or prepare, the program to receive and process data. There must also be a main processing sequence that actually solves the problem. Then, after all the data are processed, there must be a sequence of steps that close out processing and, in effect, permit the computer to do other work.

The parts, or boxes, of a structure chart are always represented in the same relationship to one another. That is, there are always succeeding levels of boxes that start from the top and work down. Within individual levels, the processing functions represented by the boxes are read from left to right.

This organizational structure is known as a *hierarchy,* or a *hierarchical design*. These charts are also said to follow the *top-down design* method, since the top-level module represents an overview expanded by modules at succeeding levels.

In effect, then, a structure chart presents a two-dimensional diagram of the processing functions to be carried out by the program. One dimension is vertical. This is called the vertical *leg* of the diagram.

The vertical leg shows the superior/subordinate relationship or hierarchy within the program. This vertical dimension indicates which program part, or module, controls or *invokes* what other modules. Note that each box in a structure chart is usually identified as a program module. However, in some early examples, some structure chart boxes may represent only single program statements. To invoke a module simply means that one module causes another module or modules to be executed.

Each level within a structure chart, then, is presented as a single box or series of boxes. These partitions within each lower level are sequenced from left to right in the order in which the modules will be invoked as the program executes. There may be as many levels as needed to complete processing of a given program. In each case, subsequent levels are read from left to right.

Each level, in turn, describes a complete solution to the problem, with each level describing the processing in increasing detail.

Thus, a full structure chart describes a complete solution to a problem—in sufficient detail so that the programmer can use this description as a basis for developing flowcharts or pseudocode descriptions that serve as a basis for actual program writing.

STEP 2: DESIGN PROGRAM STRUCTURE

Step 1 builds a thorough understanding of the nature of the problem to be solved and its overall structure. This understanding is also documented as a basis for further program development activities.

In the second step of the program development process, this understanding of the overall structure of the program should be refined further. The program partitions defined in Step 1 may require further decomposition or may have to be broken apart to produce a more detailed understanding of program requirements.

Data flow diagrams, IPO charts, and structure charts—introduced above as program design tools—are also highly useful in specifying program structures. Often, sets of data flow diagrams, IPO charts, or structure charts are developed to expand, in further detail, individual segments of overall program structures. The programmer then proceeds through several levels of diagrams, or charts, each containing modules that are more precisely defined and more narrowly limited in function than its predecessors. The effect, then, is to specify a series of modules that break a complex program specification down into a set of manageable functions that can be understood clearly and handled individually.

The end products of the second step of the program development process—Design Program Structure—would result in a complete structured specification for the program functions. This structured specification, in turn, forms the basis for the design of program processing, the next step in the program development process.

STEP 3: DESIGN PROGRAM PROCESSING

During this step, the programmer, in effect, forms a bridge between the design of a program structure and the actual writing of program instructions. The work builds upon the program structure design created in Step 2. At this point, the programmer has specifications for a set of modules that can be used to solve the stated problem. Next, the programmer has to develop a design that establishes the sequence in which the modules will be executed and the control logic that will be applied in invoking or skipping modules for their proper order of execution. This processing design forms a basis for the instructions that will be written in the fourth step, discussed in Chapter 3. Four commonly used techniques for documenting the design of program processing are introduced below:

- Pseudocode
- Structured flowcharts
- Decision tables
- Decision trees.

Pseudocode

As described in Chapter 1, pseudocoding is a listed set of descriptions of processing. Descriptions are written in English statements that can be complete sentences or that resemble sentences. This method is flexible in that pseudocoding can be written readily from a structure chart. An advantage, and an additional flexibility for pseudocoding, is that it is not dependent upon any given programming language. Thus, pseudocoding can be used as a basis for design even if the programmer does not know which programming language will ultimately be used.

Figure 2-11 presents the pseudocode for the South Bay Property Management Company payroll program. Compare these English statements with the structure chart in Figure 2-10. The pseudocode statements describe specific processing steps and also indicate the selection control needed to calculate either overtime pay or regular pay. The complete program could now be coded from this pseudocode.

Structured Flowcharts

Structured flowcharts can be used as a basis for program writing. Flowcharts are traditional, general-purpose systems and program design tools. Over the years, a number of purposes have been served and a number of techniques developed for use of flowcharts. In some instances, flowcharts are used to represent, in detail, all of the processing that takes place within an entire system. Whole families of programs are also depicted on some types of flowcharts. Within this text, structured flowcharts are used. A structured flowchart describes the *sequence* of processing and the *controls* applied in implementing a single module

```
Program Name:   PAYROLL-REPORT

PAYROLL-MAINLINE Module.
    Perform Initialization.
    Perform Calculate and Print Payroll
        Until no more data.
    Perform Termination.
    STOP.

INITIALIZATION Module.
    Move spaces to output areas.
    Display Report Headings.
    Accept Input Record.

CALCULATE-AND-PRINT-PAYROLL Module.
    Move Input fields to Output areas.
    If Hours-Worked greater than 40
        Calculate Total-Pay with Overtime
    Else
        Calculate Straight Time Pay.
    Display Output-Record.
    Accept Input-Record.

TERMINATION Module.
    Display "End of Processing" message.
```

Figure 2-11. Pseudocode for payroll program.

within a structure chart. Thus, as programs are designed within this book, structure charts are designed first, then supported by structured flowcharts.

In structured flowcharting, a selected, specific set of symbols is used. This consists of seven forms, or shapes, as illustrated in Figure 2-12. In addition, lines and arrows are used to show direction of flow.

The seven symbols shown in Figure 2-12 are standards selected by the American National Standards Institute (ANSI). Additional symbols are used, widely and regularly. But for structured flowcharting, these seven serve their specific purposes well.

The first symbol in Figure 2-12 is a parallelogram. This identifies any input or output function.

Symbol two, a diamond, identifies a decision point within a module.

The third symbol is a rectangle with double lines at the sides. This identifies a separately defined module (or program subroutine) that is linked into the program that is flowcharted. Typically, these separately identified modules are covered by additional flowcharts.

The fourth symbol is a simple rectangle. This indicates a processing step—any processing step within the module.

Symbol five indicates a termination point for a module—a start or stop function.

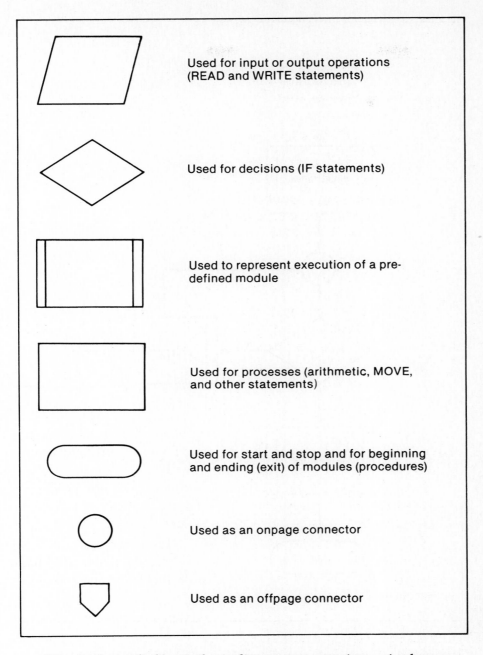

Used for input or output operations
(READ and WRITE statements)

Used for decisions (IF statements)

Used to represent execution of a predefined module

Used for processes (arithmetic, MOVE,
and other statements)

Used for start and stop and for beginning
and ending (exit) of modules (procedures)

Used as an onpage connector

Used as an offpage connector

Figure 2-12. Flowchart symbols of American National Standards Institute (ANSI).

The sixth symbol, a circle, indicates a connecting point between parts of a flowchart.

The final, seventh symbol is an offpage connector. This indicates that the flowchart is continued on another page.

Note that the title of the flowchart in Figure 2-13 is Payroll Mainline. This corresponds with the name of the box at the top level of the structure chart. Then, the names of the subroutines in the rectangles with the double-rule sides correspond with the names of the modules on the second level of the structure chart. Each of these subroutines, in turn,

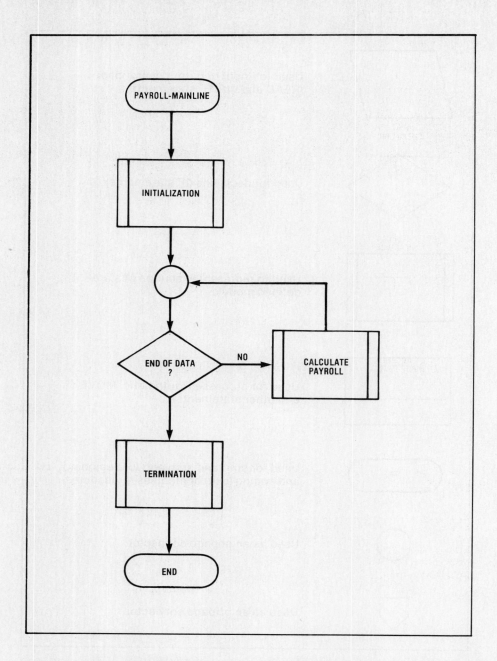

Figure 2-13. Structured flowchart for payroll main control module.

is covered by a separate flowchart. Figure 2-14 shows the initialization flowchart. The Calculate Payroll flowchart is shown in Figure 2-15. The termination subroutine is then flowcharted in Figure 2-16.

From these illustrations, note that a properly prepared structured flowchart has some important, basic characteristics. These include:

• There must be only a single entry into and exit from each structured flowchart. This also applies to each module, or processing step, within every flowchart. Just as the flowchart itself has a single

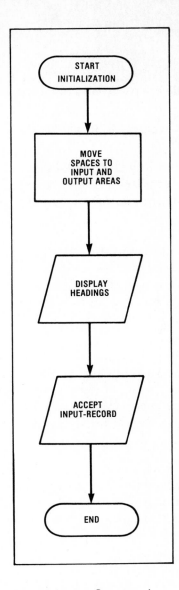

Figure 2-14. Structured flowchart for payroll initialization module.

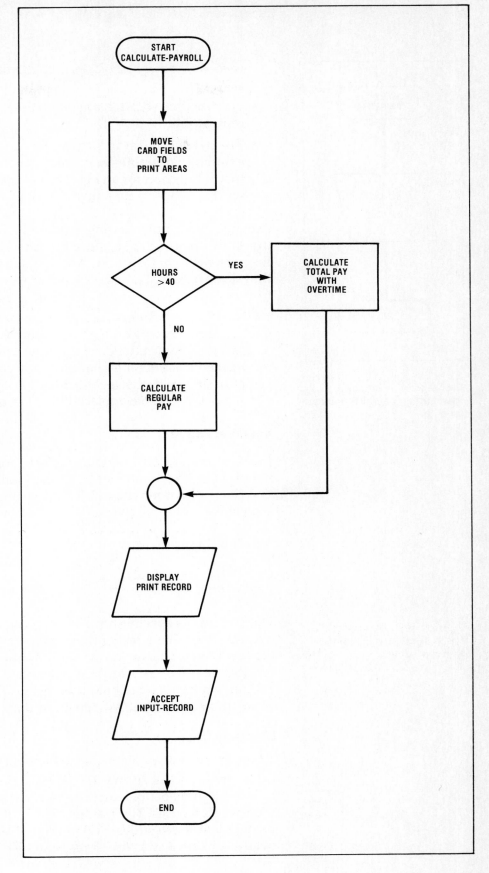

Figure 2-15. Structured flowchart for calculate-payroll module.

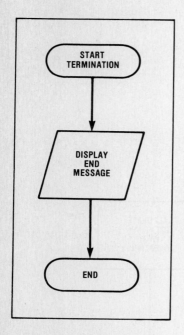

Figure 2-16. Structured flowchart for payroll termination module.

entry and exit, so also does each module have one way in and one way out.

- Each module within a structured flowchart represents a single task or function.

- The overall, physical size of a structured flowchart will be small enough to promote easy, ready understanding. Usually, a structured flowchart for any individual program module, or function, will be complete on a single page.

Advantages of flowcharting include the standardization implicit in the ANSI symbols. Also, since flowcharts are graphic presentations, they are easily understood. Another advantage of flowcharts is that they do an excellent job of showing process flows and controls applied to data.

Many programmers feel that flowcharts are not convenient program design tools. Flowcharts are procedural in nature and, because of this basic characteristic, concentrate upon step-by-step processing requirements. Another limitation of flowcharts is that they may be difficult to redraw when changes in logic must be made. In many organizations, pseudocode has replaced flowcharts as a program design tool.

Decision Tables

Decision tables are long-standing tools for documenting the understanding of policy-type statements. In the example in Figure 2-17, payroll overtime policy for hourly personnel is documented. A decision table is composed of three parts:

- Conditions
- Rules
- Actions.

The conditions specify the selection criteria for the policy regarding overtime pay. The rules represent all possible yes/no combinations of the conditions. The action portion of the decision table is simply the results that can occur from applying the rules. For example, in Figure 2-17, an employee who is not in an hourly pay class would not be paid an overtime premium. All time is paid at the normal hourly rate.

Decision Trees

A *decision tree* is a graphic representation of a decision table. A decision tree conveys no more and no less information than a decision table. However, some people can understand the decision tree more clearly than decision tables. Thus, either or both methods can be used to document processing logic design. The tree in Figure 2-18 illustrates the same overtime pay policy as the corresponding decision table in Figure 2-17.

		RULES			
	CONDITIONS	**1**	**2**	**3**	**4**
1.	HOURLY PAY CLASS	Y	Y	N	N
2.	HOURS WORKED ≤ 50	Y	N	Y	N
	ACTIONS				
1.	PAY 1.5 TIMES RATE FOR OVERTIME	Y	N	N	N
2.	PAY 2.0 TIMES RATE FOR OVERTIME	N	Y	N	N
3.	PAY 1.0 TIMES RATE FOR ALL HOURS	N	N	Y	Y

Figure 2-17. Example of decision table.

Decision tables, decision trees, structured flowcharts, and pseudo-code are all useful methods for documenting the design of program processing. Each method has its advocates and detractors. In this text, structured flowcharts and pseudocode are used.

Elements of a Well-Structured Program

To organize a program for coding, a series of steps is followed. The problem is analyzed. The overall program is partitioned, or decomposed, into modules. These modules are related to each other in hierarchical formats called structure charts. Flowcharts are used to indicate

Figure 2-18. Example of decision tree.

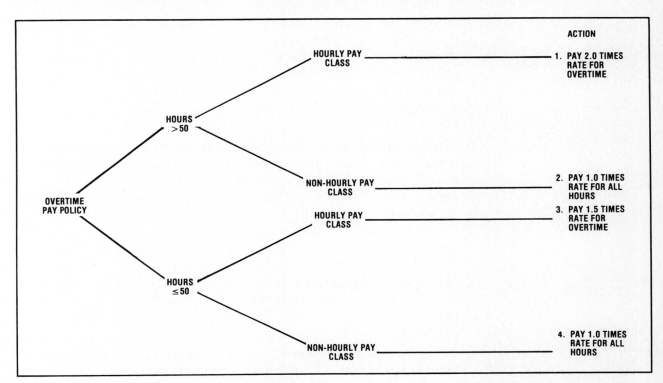

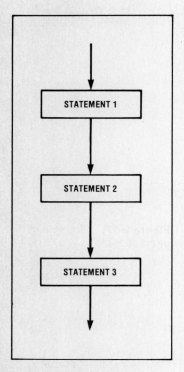

Figure 2-20. Selection construct flowchart.

the sequence in which modules are executed and the controls that are applied.

Extensive studies have been made to identify the types of controls present within operational business programs. These indicate that only three types of controls exist within program structures. These are:

- Sequence
- Selection
- Repetition.

Sequence. *Sequence* is not really a control over a program. Rather, sequence is the normal mode of execution for all instructions. See Figure 2-19. Any program executes instructions or statements in order, as they are written and presented to the computer—*unless* this pattern is altered through a specific control technique. Selection and repetition are the techniques for altering execution sequences.

Selection (case). A *selection* control is built into the Calculate Payroll flowchart, illustrated in Figure 2-15. When this program reaches a logical decision point, a test is performed to indicate whether a condition is true or false. In effect, the program asks a question that can be answered by a *yes* or *no*. In this example, the question is whether an employee worked more than 40 hours. If the answer is no, the record is processed at the standard pay rate. If the answer is yes, overtime pay is calculated. Two alternative sets of instructions are, therefore, available for execution, depending upon the data values present. Thus, the selection construct acts to change the sequential execution of instructions by directing the computer to alternative paths in the program. In a selection construct, the program logic chooses one of two alternate paths of execution on the basis of data values present when the program is running. A simplified selection construct is shown in Figure 2-20.

If programming requirements dictate that more than two alternate paths of logic should be available for selective execution, the situation is known as a *case construct,* or case structure. The case construct is a variation of a selection mechanism. A flowchart of a case structure is shown in Figure 2-21.

Repetition. Program *repetition* is also called *iteration*. This is a mathematical term which indicates that the same processing, or functional handling, takes place repeatedly. It is common in business application programs to repeat processing on all of the records in a file, *until* some predefined condition is met. Typically, this condition will be an end-of-data indicator.

A repetition function is shown in the flowchart for the Payroll Mainline in Figure 2-22. In this case, payroll calculations are made for

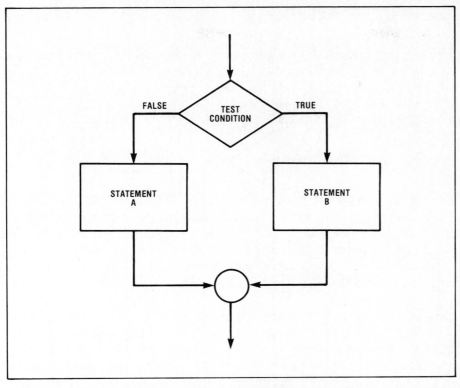

Figure 2-19. Sequence construct diagram.

each employee record *until* an end-of-data marker is sensed. At this point, the program stops calculating and moves into its termination phase.

The program design portion of the program development process serves to produce documents that, in turn, provide a basis for program writing. These documents can include pseudocoding lists or structured flowcharts. With either type of documentation, a proper program can result.

Quality Assurance With Walkthroughs

Before any coding actually begins, a programmer should perform a *walkthrough* of the program logic. Another term for this process is *desk checking*. This means simply that a programmer checks and validates the logic of his or her own program rather than sitting back and waiting for the computer to produce erroneous results.

Structured walkthroughs.   Frequently, a walkthrough becomes a team effort. The programmer who prepared the pseudocode and/or other program design documentation is joined by one or more colleagues. Together, two or three persons step through the processing logic. Such a team activity is called a *structured walkthrough.*

During a structured walkthrough, the programmer, together with participating peers, tracks through all of the processing that will take

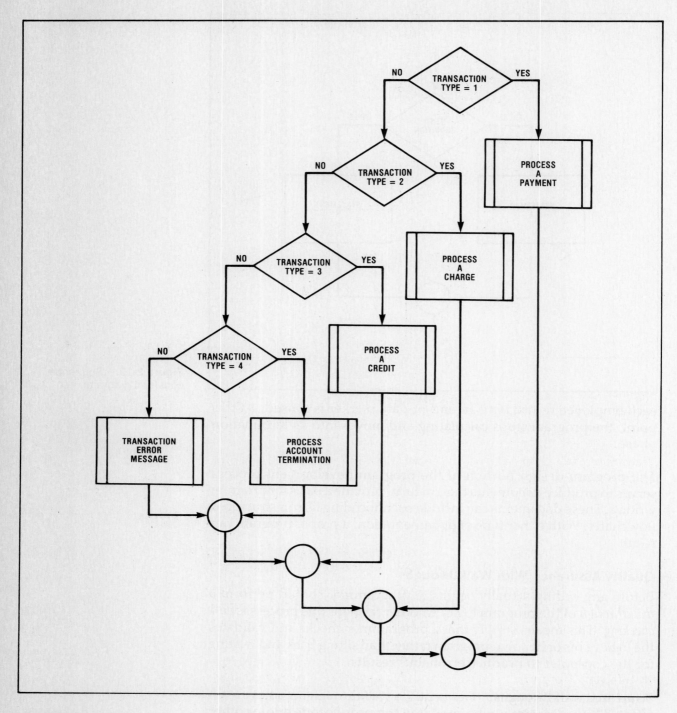

Figure 2-21. Case construct flowchart.

place in a program. The logical conditions called for in the design specifications of the program are manipulated and/or calculated to validate the design. This can be done mentally, with a pencil and paper, or with a desk calculator. Whatever method is used, the results should be the same: The walkthrough team should be satisfied, before any coding begins, that the processing design will produce the specified

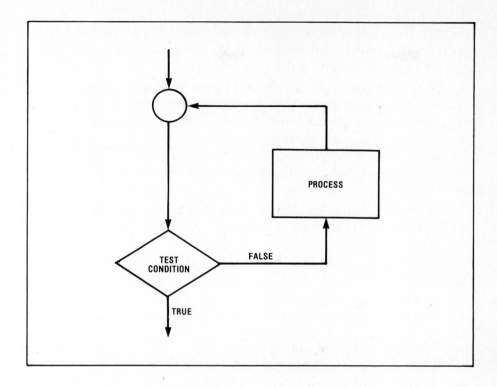

Figure 2-22. Repetition construct flowchart.

results. This is done by actually manipulating the test data and comparing the results derived manually with the predetermined outputs that will test the operational program itself.

In assuring the validity of program logic, it is a sound practice for a programmer to conduct a solo walkthrough first, before checking the program logic in further detail with peers.

Summary

Programs are computer implementations of algorithms that state problems and define a series of steps for the solution of problems.

Systems development follows a series of steps, or phases. Together, these phases form a systems development life cycle. The systems development process is illustrated in this chapter with a five-phase life cycle.

The first phase of the systems development life cycle is called Investigation. The purpose is to react to a request for service that may originate with a user, an operating executive, or even from within the CIS function. In a brief study, the Investigation phase seeks to determine whether the request is feasible and whether it has merit for the organization. If so, approval is given to move into the next phase.

The second phase is Analysis and General Design. This encompasses an in-depth study of existing methods and procedures and a design, from the user's standpoint, of the features to be incorporated into a new computer information system. Feasibility and cost estimates are refined during this phase to support a decision on whether to proceed with development of the new system.

The third phase of the life cycle is Detailed Design and Implementation. A technical solution is devised to implement the general design. Programs are developed to meet the users specifications produced during the previous phase. In addition, all needed equipment is installed. Manuals are prepared to guide and train users in the operation of the new system. At the close of this phase, the new system is ready for actual use.

During the fourth phase, Installation, the new system is brought into operation. At the close of this phase, the new system is running and is in everyday use.

The final phase, Review, calls for two separate evaluations of the results of the systems development project. The first review takes place shortly after the conclusion of the project. While the project team is still together, a learning critique is held to look for improvements both in the newly developed system and also in the project management methodology. About six months after installation, the new system is evaluated again to see if it is delivering the savings and other benefits that were forecast at the outset. [*Objective No. 1.*]

Within the systems development life cycle structure, programs are developed by following a five-step project structure. This structure is designed to assure that adequate planning and design take place before program writing begins. [*Objective No. 2.*]

The first phase of the program development life cycle is Analyze the Problem. Program specifications written with the help of the user are reviewed. An understanding of the problem to be solved and the program to solve that problem are developed. This understanding is documented with data flow diagrams, IPO charts, structure diagrams, and input/output layout forms. [*Objectives Nos. 3 and 4.*]

The second phase is Design the Program Structure. A model is developed for the program that will be produced. The structure of the program involves the relationships between the processing modules needed for implementation. Documentation is through data flow diagrams, IPO charts, and structure charts. [*Objectives Nos. 5 and 6.*]

The third process step is Design Program Processing. Structured flowcharts, pseudocode, decision tables, or decision trees are developed to show the sequence of processing for all steps in the program. [*Objective No. 7.*]

The fourth step is Code the Program. It is significant that the writing of instructions is not undertaken until a quality design has been prepared and a thorough understanding reached about the purpose of the program and the processing to be done.

Key Terms

1. systems development project
2. systems development life cycle
3. systems analyst
4. systems flowchart
5. data flow diagram
6. interface
7. bubble (data flow diagram)
8. module (program)
9. structure chart
10. data format
11. processing control
12. authorization
13. validation
14. editing
15. balancing
16. coding
17. test data
18. testing (program)
19. logical error
20. debugging
21. syntax
22. syntactical error
23. parallel installation
24. maintenance (system)
25. structure (problem)

Step five is Debug and Test the Program. This step finds and eliminates any errors in either code or logic.

This chapter reviews the first three steps of the process in depth. The final two steps are covered in the chapter that follows.

The basic processing functions to be incorporated in business application programs are described. These are sequence, selection, and repetition. [*Objective No. 8.*]

To validate the logic of program design, the programmer conducts a detailed review of the pseudocoding or other design documentation. This activity is known as a walkthrough. The programmer can do this alone or with peers who bring objectivity to the process. When the task is performed by a team, it is known as a structured walkthrough. [*Objective No. 9.*]

Review/Discussion Questions

1. What are the relationships between algorithms and programs?
2. What is the purpose of structuring a systems development project into a series of phases?
3. What are the relationships between the activities in the second and third phases of the systems development life cycle?
4. Why does the systems development life cycle stress a nontechnical design for a new system before technical design and programming take place?
5. What is the significance of the separation of implementation and installation activities into different phases of the systems development life cycle?
6. What are the relationships between the systems development life cycle and the programming process?
7. What is a structure chart and how is it used?
8. What is meant by top-down design of a program?
9. What is a data flow diagram and how are data flow diagrams used?
10. What is the principal use of structured flowcharts?
11. What is the role of record layout forms in program development?

---

26. bug
27. layout form
28. partitioning
29. decomposition
30. IPO chart
31. level (structure chart)
32. identifier
33. initiation
34. main processing
35. termination
36. model (program)
37. hierarchy
38. hierarchical design
39. top-down design
40. leg (structure chart)
41. invoke
42. structured flowchart
43. sequence (processing)
44. control (processing)
45. American National Standards Institute (ANSI)
46. decision table
47. decision tree
48. sequence (program control)
49. selection (program control)
50. repetition (program control)
51. case construct
52. iteration
53. walkthrough
54. desk checking
55. structured walkthrough

Practice Assignments

For each of the assignments described below, use the accompanying work sheets to provide 1) a structure chart, 2) pseudocode, and 3) structured flowcharts to document a program algorithm.

1. Design an algorithm that will input a student record and compute a student's grade point average (GPA).

To compute a grade point average, the grade for each class the student has completed is converted to a numeric equivalent: A = 4, B = 3, C = 2, D = 1, and F = 0. For this problem, all other grades are disregarded and all classes are three-unit courses.

The grade value for each class is multiplied by the number of units for that class. The products of the multiplications for all classes for each student are added and the total is divided by the total number of units completed.

2. Develop an algorithm to balance a personal checkbook.

To balance a personal checkbook account, the returned checks are noted in the check register. The amounts of all checks not returned from the bank are totaled.

All deposits indicated on the bank statement are noted. All deposits entered in the check register but not included in the bank statement are totaled.

Beginning with the ending balance shown on the bank statement, add the total of the deposits not yet credited and subtract the total of the open or uncleared checks. The result should equal your checkbook balance.

Worksheet
Grade Point Average / Structure Chart and Pseudocode

Prepared By: _____

Worksheet
Grade Point Average / Structured Flowchart

Prepared By: _____

Worksheet
Checkbook Balance / Structure Chart and Pseudocode

Prepared By: _____

Worksheet
Checkbook Balance / Structured Flowchart

Prepared By: _____

Vocabulary Building Practice—Exercise 2

Write definitions and/or explanations of the terms listed below.

1. **systems development project** _____

_____

2. **systems development life cycle** _____

_____

3. **systems analyst** _____

_____

4. **systems flowchart** _____

_____

5. **module** _____

_____

6. **structure chart** _____

_____

7. **data format** _____

_____

8. **processing control** _____

_____

9. **logical error** _____

_____

10. **debugging** _____

_____

(over, please)

11. syntax _____

_____

12. system maintenance _____

_____

13. partitioning _____

_____

14. decomposition _____

_____

15. identifier _____

_____

16. initiation _____

_____

17. main processing _____

_____

18. termination _____

_____

19. hierarchical design _____

_____

20. structured flowchart _____

_____

THE PROCESS OF PROGRAMMING 3

OBJECTIVES

On completing reading and other learning assignments for this chapter, you should be able to:

1. Describe and discuss the procedures involved in the writing of instructions for a program.
2. Identify the four divisions of a COBOL program and describe their major functions and purposes.
3. Identify the valid characters that can be used in writing COBOL programs.
4. Describe the use of reserved words in the COBOL language.
5. Enter statements, following examples or instructions, onto COBOL coding sheets.
6. Describe the process of COBOL program compilation.
7. Describe the procedures for testing and debugging programs.
8. Describe the procedures for development of test data for a COBOL program.

PROGRAM DEVELOPMENT PROCESS: STEP 4: CODE THE PROGRAM

After a problem has been analyzed, structured, and a solution designed, the programmer is ready to begin writing the actual instructions that will cause the computer to process the application. It is worth stressing again that program writing is the fourth of five steps in an orderly process for program development.

Many programs are developed under pressures and tensions. Under these circumstances, it can seem attractive to skip some of the preliminaries and get on with the business of writing instructions. Invariably, when this shortcut is taken, it winds up becoming a long way around. Without adequate planning, it is not really possible to be sure that the program identifies and solves the business problem at hand. Further, if the logic is not worked out thoroughly through pseudocoding or through flowcharts drawn in sufficient detail, the program itself will be flawed. Without effective design, it is literally possible to spend more time debugging and testing a program than it takes to write the original instructions.

On the other hand, it can be highly satisfactory, even exhilarating, to write a program and have it run successfully the first time. Chances for this level of success are enhanced immeasurably when the programmer does a thorough job of working out the processing logic before writing instructions. Programming based on sound, logical design will contain fewer errors, or bugs.

As indicated in Chapter 2, logical design through pseudocoding or flowcharting is carried out independently of any specific programming language. In this sense, a programming language is a tool for implementing a design. Hundreds of programming languages, or implementation tools, are available. A sound, logical design will work in a number of appropriate languages. The actual choice of language, then, depends upon policies and operating procedures within individual CIS organizations.

In working your way through this book, you will program in a language that has been chosen for you—COBOL. This is presently the most widely used programming language for business and commercial applications. As a basis for your work in COBOL, the section that follows presents some general background and a brief description of this language.

THE COBOL LANGUAGE

COBOL is an acronym, or abbreviation, that stands for COmmon Business Oriented Language. This concept of a common programming language for business was highly significant at the time COBOL was developed in the late 1950s and early 1960s.

The computer industry was still in its relative infancy during the 1950s. Computers had already proven their potential value. The problem faced by business, industry, and government was in the development of programs to implement computer applications. Up to that time, programs for business applications had been written entirely in what are now called *low-level programming languages*.

There are two general types of languages identified as low-level. One is *machine language*. This means that programmers have to write their instructions in the exact language of the computer. Therefore, machine language programs are written in *binary* notation—entirely with 0 and 1 entries.

A first step toward simplifying the job of communicating with computers was the development of *assembly* or *assembler* languages. These substituted English-language notations along with decimal numbers for the binary coding. However, with assemblers, it was still necessary for programmers to write a separate instruction for each operating function to be executed by a computer. Thus, programmers had to have detailed knowledge of the inner workings of every computer utilized. Programmers were specialized people in short supply. Program writing was difficult—and extremely slow.

It became obvious, during the 1950s, that tools were needed that would make it easier for programmers to communicate with computers. The breakthrough came with introduction of what are known as *high-level languages*. In a high-level language, a single instruction written by a programmer causes a special program within the computer, called a *compiler*, to produce a number of processing instructions. In some instances, complete programming routines can be produced through single instructions entered by programmers.

One of the early high-level languages was *FORTRAN*, an abbreviation for FORmula TRANslator. FORTRAN was designed primarily to solve mathematical or scientific problems. The language made it relatively easy, by comparison with previous methods, for scientists and engineers to communicate with computers in terms of mathematical formulas. A scientist or engineer could write an equation and, with the use of FORTRAN, specify a computer-produced solution for that equation. In those days, it is significant to point out, manufacturers were still making different models of computers for solving scientific problems and for business data processing. Thus, once FORTRAN proved itself for scientific uses, pressure began to mount to provide a similar tool for use with business-oriented computers.

The characteristics that separated scientific and business computing centered around calculation and data-handling requirements. Scientific systems, basically, were designed to do large amounts of numeric processing (early systems could not process alphabetic data at all). Scientific computing rapidly acquired a nickname: *number crunching*. By contrast, business data processing involved the accumulation and manipulation of masses of data. Business computers stressed the ability to store data and to generate comparatively large volumes of output documents.

In the development of a business computing language, the lead was taken by an organization with perhaps the greatest amount of data to process and documents to generate—the United States Department of Defense (DOD). In the late 1950s, the DOD invited a number of representatives from business, industry, government, and universities to participate in a conference charged with development of a business data processing language. The meeting was known as the Conference On DAta SYstems Languages or *CODASYL*. The conference established a number of working committees. By 1960, the first COBOL compiler was released. Subsequently, individual organizations expanded and enlarged upon the original COBOL specifications. During the mid-1960s, the American National Standards Institute (ANSI) entered the picture to produce a universally accepted ANSI-standard COBOL. ANSI working groups continually review and revise COBOL standards. The standard currently in force, which provides the basis for this book, is known as ANSI X3.23—1974 COBOL. Currently, COBOL is undergoing further revision and a new standard specification for the language is expected to be released soon.

Writing COBOL

COBOL is a high-level business-oriented programming language. The term *programming language* has a specific meaning and some special implications. In particular, a distinction should be made between the terms *language* and *compiler*. A language is a set of terms used under specific rules to convey given meanings. Languages have rules *(syntax)* under which writing must be done for clarity. A compiler is a program for translating instructions written in a programming language into the language of computers.

As a language, COBOL has a vocabulary and rules for use of that vocabulary. A subset of the COBOL vocabulary is introduced later in this chapter. The rules for organizing COBOL programs form a logical starting point for understanding the language. To write COBOL programs, you must learn and abide by these rules. Any failure to conform to the rules for structuring a COBOL program will lead you only to futility—an improperly formatted program simply will not be compiled correctly.

Each COBOL program must have its coding organized into four distinct parts, or *divisions*. These four program divisions are:

- **IDENTIFICATION DIVISION.**
- **ENVIRONMENT DIVISION.**
- **DATA DIVISION.**
- **PROCEDURE DIVISION.**

One frequently used tool for the writing of COBOL instructions is a formal, formatted *COBOL Program Sheet*. These are also known as *coding sheets*. The actual coding instructions are organized on these coding sheets within the four divisions identified above. To illustrate, Figure 3-1 shows the coding sheets for the Payroll Mainline program that has been introduced and developed through illustrations in earlier chapters. Refer to these coding sheets to follow the description of the contents for the four divisions that follows.

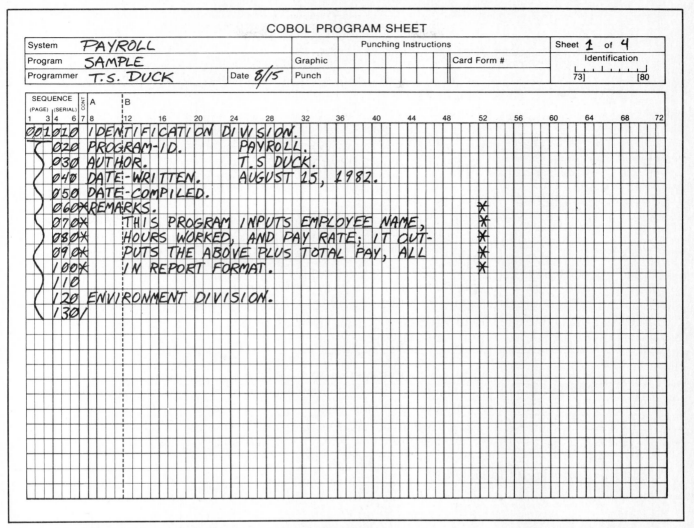

COBOL PROGRAM SHEET

System PAYROLL
Program SAMPLE
Programmer T.S. DUCK   Date 8/15

Punching Instructions
Graphic
Punch
Card Form #

Sheet 1 of 4
Identification
73] [80

```
001010 IDENTIFICATION DIVISION.
   020 PROGRAM-ID.      PAYROLL.
   030 AUTHOR.          T.S DUCK.
   040 DATE-WRITTEN.    AUGUST 15, 1982.
   050 DATE-COMPILED.
   060*REMARKS.                                    *
   070*    THIS PROGRAM INPUTS EMPLOYEE NAME,       *
   080*    HOURS WORKED, AND PAY RATE; IT OUT-      *
   090*    PUTS THE ABOVE PLUS TOTAL PAY, ALL       *
   100*    IN REPORT FORMAT.                        *
   110
   120 ENVIRONMENT DIVISION.
   130/
```

IDENTIFICATION DIVISION. This division has two prerequisite content items. The first is the name of the division itself. The second is the name of the program being presented, identified with the standard term **PROGRAM-ID.** Pay particular attention to the period and the hyphen in this term. Both are required. The identification is incorrect unless entries are complete. Additional documentation may be included through further entries under this division. These serve as comments or descriptions and are used as guides for persons working with the program. Several entries of this type are included in the payroll program.

ENVIRONMENT DIVISION. Entries under this division describe the computer equipment that will be used to compile and run the program. In this sample program, there are no specific, required entries other than the division name. Coding for this division of COBOL programs is discussed in later chapters.

Figure 3-1. These COBOL coding sheets, repeated here for ease of reference, contain the statements necessary for development of the sample payroll program. (Illustration continues.)

COBOL PROGRAM SHEET

```
SEQUENCE
(PAGE)(SERIAL)  A  B
002140 DATA DIVISION.
   150
   160 WORKING-STORAGE SECTION.
   170
   180 01   INPUT-DATA.
   190      05   IN-EMPLOYEE-NAME          PIC X(20).
   200      05   IN-EMPLOYEE-HRS           PIC 9(02)V9.
   210      05   IN-PAY-RATE               PIC 9(02)V99.
   220
   230 01   OUTPUT-LINE.
   240      05   FILLER                    PIC X(03).
   250      05   OUT-EMPLOYEE-NAME         PIC X(20).
   260      05   FILLER                    PIC X(03).
   270      05   OUT-EMPLOYEE-HRS          PIC 9(02)V9.
   280      05   FILLER                    PIC X(04).
   290      05   OUT-PAY-RATE              PIC 9(02)V99.
   300      05   FILLER                    PIC X(02).
   310      05   OUT-TOTAL-PAY             PIC 9(04)V99.
   320
```

COBOL PROGRAM SHEET

```
SEQUENCE
(PAGE)(SERIAL)  A  B
003330 PROCEDURE DIVISION.
   340
   350 PAYROLL-MAINLINE.
   360      PERFORM INITIALIZATION.
   370      PERFORM CALCULATE-PAYROLL
   380          UNTIL IN-EMPLOYEE-NAME EQUALS "END OF DATA".
   390      PERFORM TERMINATION.
   400      STOP RUN.
   410
   420 INITIALIZATION.
   430      MOVE SPACES TO OUTPUT-LINE.
   440      DISPLAY "              SOUTH BAY PROPERTY MANAGEMENT".
   450      DISPLAY " ".
   460      DISPLAY "     EMPLOYEE          HOURS      PAY        TOTAL".
   470      DISPLAY "       NAME                      RATE        PAY".
   480      DISPLAY "
   490      ACCEPT INPUT-DATA.
   500
```

COBOL PROGRAM SHEET

System	PAYROLL			Punching Instructions						Sheet 4 of 4
Program	SAMPLE		Graphic					Card Form #		Identification
Programmer	T.S. DUCK	Date 8/15	Punch							73] [80

```
004520 CALCULATE-PAYROLL.
   530     MOVE IN-EMPLOYEE-NAME            TO OUT-EMPLOYEE-NAME.
   540     MOVE IN-EMPLOYEE-HRS             TO OUT-EMPLOYEE-HRS.
   550     MOVE IN-PAY-RATE                 TO OUT-PAY-RATE.
   560     IF IN-EMPLOYEE-HRS GREATER THAN 40
   570     THEN
   580         COMPUTE OUT-TOTAL-PAY =
   590             IN-EMPLOYEE-HRS * IN-PAY-RATE +
   600             (IN-EMPLOYEE-HRS - 40) * IN-PAY-RATE / 2
   610     ELSE
   620         COMPUTE OUT-TOTAL-PAY =
   630             IN-EMPLOYEE-HRS * IN-PAY-RATE.
   640     DISPLAY OUTPUT-LINE.
   650     ACCEPT INPUT-DATA.
   660
   670 TERMINATION.
   680         DISPLAY " ".
   690         DISPLAY "                              END OF PROCESSING".
```

DATA DIVISION. This division identifies and defines the characteristics of the data to be used in executing the program. In the coding for the payroll program, note that all input and output data elements have been identified.

PROCEDURE DIVISION. This division contains the actual processing instructions that execute the program. The names and descriptions entered through the other divisions can be called up and used within the instructions for this division. Note that the **PROCEDURE DIVISION.** coding for the payroll program is organized according to the modules established in the structure chart. Also note these specific terms:

PERFORM	DISPLAY
STOP	ACCEPT
RUN	IF. . .THEN. . .ELSE
MOVE	

These terms are used in the instructions for this division. These are standard terms, part of the COBOL vocabulary you will be building.

Figure 3-1. Continued.

Each COBOL program will have each of the four divisions described above. In the presentation of program statements to the COBOL compiler, the role of the division corresponds to a chapter in a book. A chapter is a relatively major division of information. For clarity of meaning, further subdivisions are necessary. Within COBOL programs, divisions are subdivided into *sections,* sections into *paragraphs,* paragraphs into *sentences,* and sentences into *clauses.* The structure and content of these subdivisions are covered throughout the rest of this book.

COBOL Character Set

COBOL is a language—a language used to write programs. As a language, COBOL has basic parts and rules that cover its use. In learning COBOL, you follow the same pattern that you do in reading and writing a language. Think back. In learning to read and write your own language, you learned the alphabet, certain punctuation marks, a vocabulary of words, and then rules for writing sentences and paragraphs. The same requirements apply in learning COBOL.

The basic building blocks for the COBOL language are known as a *character set.* Figure 3-2 lists a complete character set for the COBOL language. Basically, this character set consists of all the letters of the alphabet, the digits 0 through 9, and a series of special characters, including $. , ( ) < > and ''. (In some versions of COBOL, a ' is used instead of the ''.)

Some of the characters in this set, clearly, are used for punctuation. For example, every COBOL statement ends with a period (.). The comma (,) is not required in COBOL statements. However, the comma is usable at the programmer's discretion to assure readability or clarity of meaning in program statements.

Other punctuation marks, such as parentheses—( )—and quotation marks—''—have special uses. These are explained in context as the appropriate topics are introduced.

CHARACTER	VALUE	CHARACTER	VALUE
A–Z	LETTER	/	SLASH (VIRGULE, STROKE)
0–9	DIGIT		
	SPACE (BLANK)	(	LEFT PARENTHESIS
.	PERIOD (DECIMAL POINT)	)	RIGHT PARENTHESIS
		+	PLUS SIGN
,	COMMA	−	MINUS SIGN
;	SEMICOLON	=	EQUAL SIGN
"	QUOTATION MARK	>	GREATER THAN SYMBOL
$	DOLLAR SIGN		
*	ASTERISK	<	LESS THAN SYMBOL

Figure 3-2. COBOL character set.

COBOL Naming Rules

The COBOL character set can be used to form two kinds of words. These are *reserved words* and *supplied words* invented by the programmer. Reserved words have special, predefined meanings within the COBOL language. They can be used only for specific purposes or to convey specific meanings. To illustrate, the names of the four divisions of a COBOL program are all reserved words. So are the words describing processing functions within the PROCEDURE DIVISION of the payroll program: PERFORM, STOP, MOVE, DISPLAY, and the others identified earlier. A complete list of COBOL reserved words is given in Appendix B. Make it a practice to refer to this reserved word list regularly.

The content or spelling of programmer-supplied words is limited only by the imagination of the individual. In general, the terms invented by the programmer should describe their functions within the program. Only four simple rules need be followed in developing programmer-supplied words:

1. Supplied words may be any length from 1 to 30 characters.
2. Supplied words may consist of combinations of letters, digits, and the hyphen symbol (-).
3. A hyphen (-) may not be used either to start or to end a word.
4. Programmer-supplied words cannot be identical to reserved words, although reserved words may be used within programmer-supplied words.

To illustrate, the following are examples of valid and invalid programmer-supplied words:

- **SOC-SEC-NO**   Valid term because it follows all of the rules given above.

- **TOTAL%**   Invalid because it uses the symbol %. % is a special character that may not be used in programmer-supplied words.

- **STUDENT-NAME**   Valid.

- **NAME**   Valid.

- **NUMBER**   Invalid because it is a reserved word.

- **STUDENT-NUMBER**   Valid because the reserved word is not by itself.

- **TOTAL COST**   Invalid because of the imbedded blank character.

- **-QUANTITY**   Invalid because of leading hyphen.

COBOL Coding Sheet

Figure 3-3 is the first page of the coding sheet for the payroll program, with annotations added to indicate the conventions for the writing of COBOL instructions.

Note that the coding sheet is a data input form. It is ruled into a series of 80-column lines. A single character is entered in each ruled box. Entries in certain positions on the coding sheet have special meaning to the COBOL compiler. Thus, you should learn to think of coding entries in terms of their program significance. Bear in mind that the coding sheet is an input form that will be used to capture your program through a keypunch machine, terminal, or other data input device. The special, significant positions on the coding sheet include the following:

Figure 3-3. Annotated COBOL coding form.

- Columns 1 through 6 are reserved for indicating line numbers for program entries. Generally, line numbers are assigned in units of

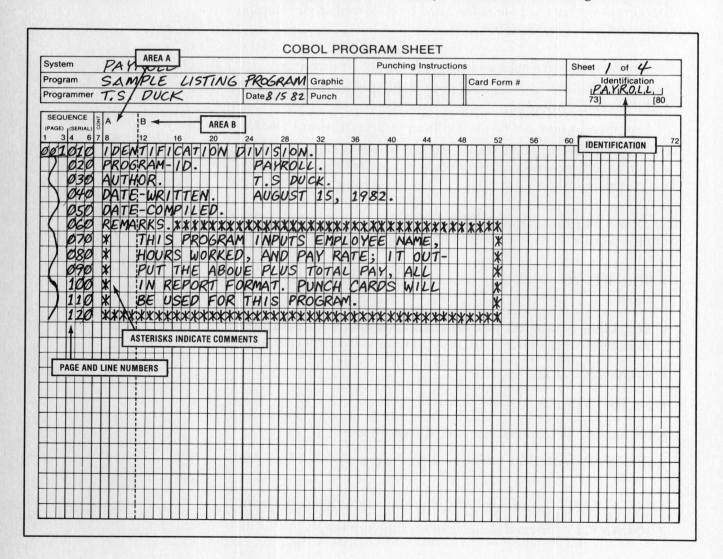

tens. This makes it possible to insert additional coding instructions without renumbering the entire program.

- Column 7 may be blank or may contain one of two special characters. These are the asterisk—(*)—or the slash—(/). The asterisk identifies a comment line in the program. A comment line is a description or other information entry designed for people, not for compiling. Therefore, an * in column 7 tells the compiler not to translate that line. A / in column 7 indicates a *page eject* function on the compilation listing. When the compiler sees this symbol, it will produce coding that will cause the printer on which the program listing is produced to end entries on the page that is in use and start a new page.

- Column 8 begins the A margin or area. The A area is used as the starting point for entries of the names of all divisions, sections, and paragraphs. All such entries *must* begin in the A area.

- Column 12 begins the B margin or area. Notations for any instructions to be executed must begin at the B margin or at some point to the right of this margin. No instructions should be listed beginning to the left of the B margin.

- Column 72 is the end of a valid COBOL entry line. Any notations to the right of column 72 will be ignored by the compiler.

- Columns 73–80 are reserved for the programmer's use in identifying the program or for other labeling purposes.

COBOL CODING CASE STUDY

The coding on the sheets reproduced in Figure 3-1 represents a complete COBOL program for the Payroll Mainline application. Reviewing these coding entries, note that:

- The IDENTIFICATION DIVISION entries name the program and provide a series of optional entries, including the name of the programmer, the date the program was written, and the compilation date. There is also a remarks section that describes the program and its use.

- The entries under the ENVIRONMENT DIVISION are not yet required at this stage of program development.

- Under the DATA DIVISION, names have been assigned to the data fields identified in program specifications as described in Chapter 1.

- The coding within the PROCEDURE DIVISION is significant because this describes the actual processing that will take place.

A point has been made of the fact that writing instructions becomes relatively simple if design documentation has been executed properly.

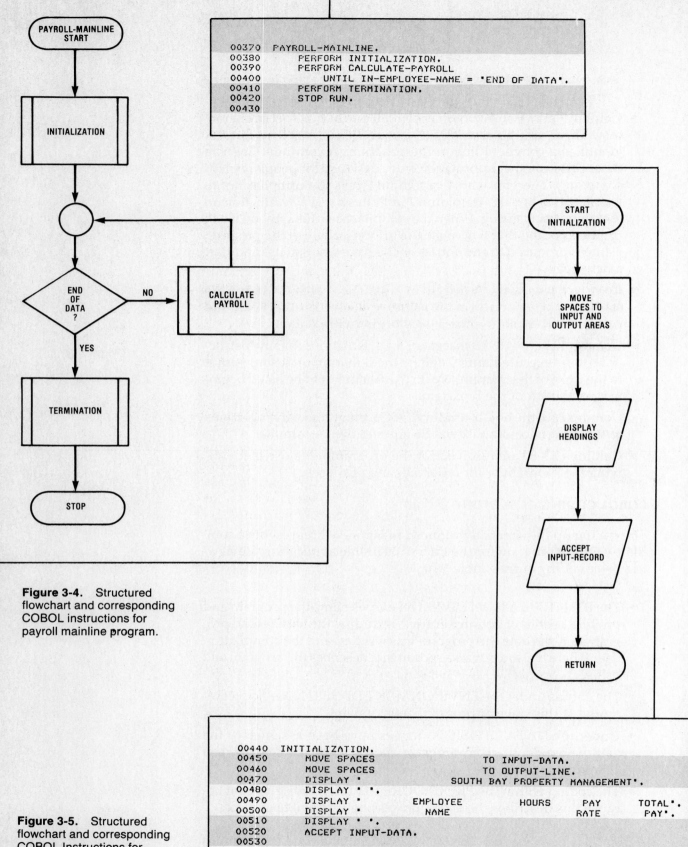

```
00370    PAYROLL-MAINLINE.
00380        PERFORM INITIALIZATION.
00390        PERFORM CALCULATE-PAYROLL
00400            UNTIL IN-EMPLOYEE-NAME = "END OF DATA".
00410        PERFORM TERMINATION.
00420        STOP RUN.
00430
```

Figure 3-4. Structured flowchart and corresponding COBOL instructions for payroll mainline program.

```
00440    INITIALIZATION.
00450        MOVE SPACES                    TO INPUT-DATA.
00460        MOVE SPACES                    TO OUTPUT-LINE.
00470        DISPLAY "                    SOUTH BAY PROPERTY MANAGEMENT".
00480        DISPLAY " ".
00490        DISPLAY "        EMPLOYEE        HOURS      PAY       TOTAL".
00500        DISPLAY "          NAME                    RATE        PAY".
00510        DISPLAY " ".
00520        ACCEPT INPUT-DATA.
00530
```

Figure 3-5. Structured flowchart and corresponding COBOL Instructions for payroll initialization program.

To illustrate this point, consider sections within the PROCEDURE DIVISION as they relate to the corresponding structured flowcharts.

The Payroll Mainline flowchart and its corresponding coding for lines 00370 through 00420 are shown in Figure 3-4. The lines within the program state the actions that the symbols in the flowchart represent. The three lines of functional symbols are represented by three PERFORM commands. Line 00400 describes the repetition structure within this program module. Note how the repetition of the CALCULATE module is controlled by a data name assigned in the DATA DIVISION.

Figure 3-5 includes both the instructions and the flowchart for the Initialization function. The reserved terms used as commands include MOVE, DISPLAY, and ACCEPT. Note that, following the DISPLAY commands, the data entries have been aligned in the positions they will occupy in the report. To indicate printing of a blank line, two quotation mark entries have been made around a blank space (lines 0480 and 0510). This tells the computer output device to leave a blank line.

At this point, note also that each statement in this program module is written on a separate line, by itself, and that each statement, on every line, ends with a period.

The instructions and flowchart for the Calculate Payroll module of the program are shown in Figure 3-6. Pay particular attention to the coding for the selection mechanism (IF. . .THEN. . .ELSE) instructions in this module. Some sentences in this module occupy more than one coding sheet line. In such cases, the period should appear only at the end of the complete sentence. Specific COMPUTE commands are applied to the processing of data identified under definitions included in the DATA DIVISION of the program. Again, observe that the program commands correspond directly with the symbols in the flowchart.

Figure 3-7 contains both the coding and the flowchart for the Termination module of the Payroll Mainline program. As indicated, these commands instruct the computer to generate a blank line (line 0700) following the completion of the output report. This is followed by a line identifying the END OF PROCESSING.

In summary, the coding within the PROCEDURE DIVISION describes the logical steps in the program that have already been established through the use of structured flowcharts. A direct, simple translation process leads to acceptable, quality COBOL coding.

PROGRAM DEVELOPMENT PROCESS: STEP 5: TESTING AND DEBUGGING

Once a program has been coded fully, it is ready for the next, final step in the programming process. This involves testing and debugging to eliminate any errors or unforeseen problems. Included in the testing and debugging phase is a necessary first step which must be completed before anything else can happen. This is *compilation* of the program. The

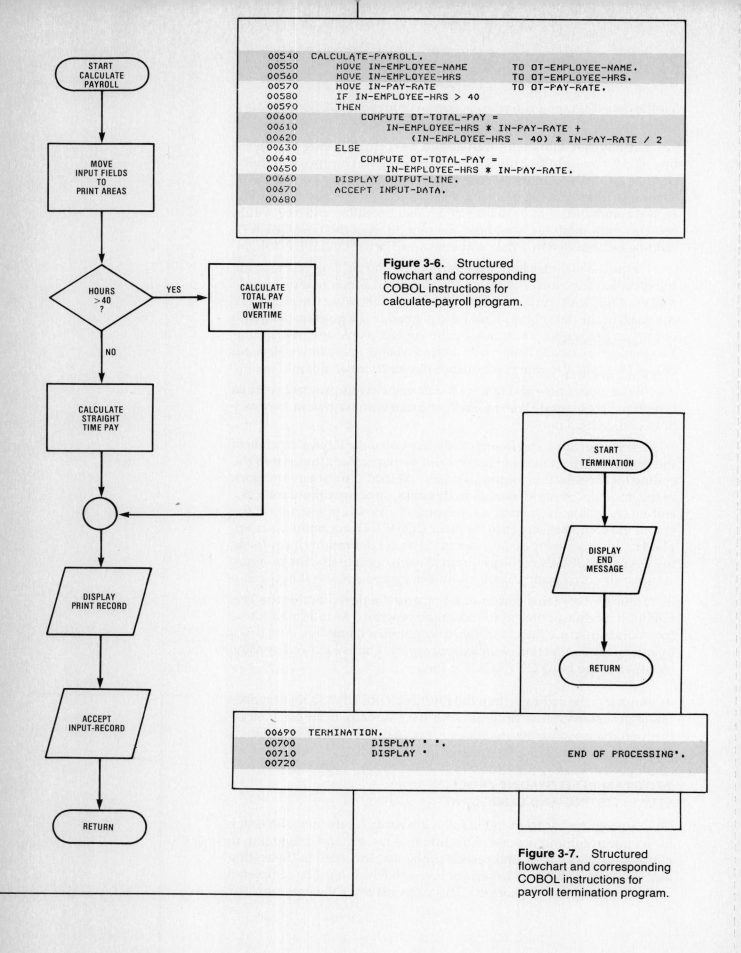

```
00540    CALCULATE-PAYROLL.
00550        MOVE IN-EMPLOYEE-NAME          TO OT-EMPLOYEE-NAME.
00560        MOVE IN-EMPLOYEE-HRS           TO OT-EMPLOYEE-HRS.
00570        MOVE IN-PAY-RATE               TO OT-PAY-RATE.
00580        IF IN-EMPLOYEE-HRS > 40
00590        THEN
00600            COMPUTE OT-TOTAL-PAY =
00610                IN-EMPLOYEE-HRS * IN-PAY-RATE +
00620                    (IN-EMPLOYEE-HRS - 40) * IN-PAY-RATE / 2
00630        ELSE
00640            COMPUTE OT-TOTAL-PAY =
00650                IN-EMPLOYEE-HRS * IN-PAY-RATE.
00660        DISPLAY OUTPUT-LINE.
00670        ACCEPT INPUT-DATA.
00680
```

Figure 3-6. Structured flowchart and corresponding COBOL instructions for calculate-payroll program.

```
00690    TERMINATION.
00700        DISPLAY ' '.
00710        DISPLAY '                        END OF PROCESSING'.
00720
```

Figure 3-7. Structured flowchart and corresponding COBOL instructions for payroll termination program.

source program, consisting of the program statements prepared by the programmer, must be submitted to the compiler. The COBOL compiler, in turn, generates a machine-language program, known as the *object program.* This compilation must take place before the program can be executed. Errors in the use of the COBOL language—called *syntactical errors*—are identified, isolated, and corrected by the programmer during the compilation process. After that, the object program can be used to execute a set of test data. This post-compilation testing identifies any processing errors, or *logical errors,* in the basic design of the program. If logical errors are to be corrected, changes must be made in the source program which, in turn, must be recompiled and retested.

COBOL Compilation

Compilation of COBOL programs is carried out in a five-step process, as described below.

Compilation Step 1. Figure 3-8 diagrams the processing during this step. This shows the main memory of the processor of a computer in relation to secondary storage used, as well as with input accepted.

This diagram notes that, as is necessary in virtually any system, the main memory of the processing unit has an operating system in place. This is the main, or primary, systems software program that makes the computer function. Other software that can be brought into memory as needed from the secondary storage file include the COBOL compiler and other systems support software.

In this first compilation step, the initial input data are identified as *JCL.* The initials JCL stand for *Job Control Language.* This is a language that is used to identify programs being submitted and also software and equipment support requirements for their processing. Any input submitted for processing under an operating system will need initializing JCL statements.

The actual JCL coding used to compile COBOL programs will vary with equipment configurations and operating conventions in individual computer installations. Therefore, before you compile your own

Figure 3-8. COBOL compiling sequence (1): JCL causes COBOL compiler to be loaded into memory.

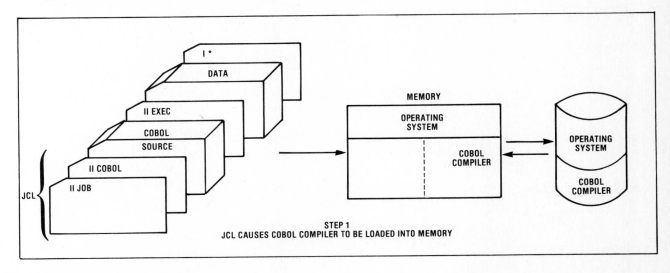

STEP 1
JCL CAUSES COBOL COMPILER TO BE LOADED INTO MEMORY

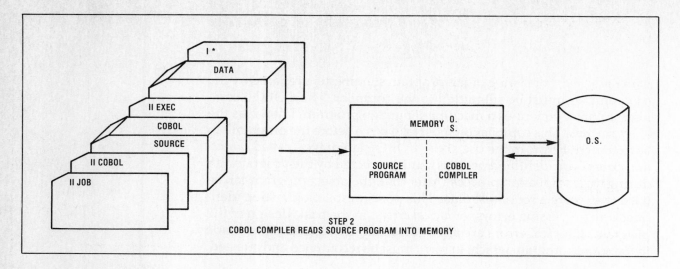

STEP 2
COBOL COMPILER READS SOURCE PROGRAM INTO MEMORY

Figure 3-9. COBOL compiling sequence (2): COBOL compiler reads source program into memory.

COBOL programs, get specific instructions either from your instructor or from the data center you use.

To complete the first compilation step, the JCL entry instructs the operating system to find and read into memory the COBOL compiler.

Compilation Step 2. During the second compilation step, diagrammed in Figure 3-9, the COBOL compiler takes over and causes the COBOL source program to be read into memory. At the close of Step 2, both the COBOL compiler and the source program may be in memory.

Compilation Step 3. Once the source program is in memory, the actual translation process begins. Each COBOL source statement is processed under control of the compiler. For each statement, the compiler checks the syntax initially. If the syntax is correct, object program coding is generated and written to secondary storage. At the same time, a compilation post-list is created for later output to a printer or terminal. If improper syntax has been used, an error message is generated as part of the program listing. However, no object coding for this instruction can be generated. Thus, no corresponding entry is made on the secondary storage file.

At the end of Step 3, as shown in Figure 3-10, one of two conditions will exist. Either your program was compiled completely with no syntax errors, or error messages were generated as part of the printout. If the program compiled completely, you are ready to go on to Step 4. If compilation could not be completed, you have to correct the errors in the source coding, then go back to Step 1 to begin compilation all over. Before you can go on to the next step, you must have a compiled program. In other words, execution of the final two steps in the compilation process is conditional—an object program free of syntax errors is needed.

Compilation Step 4. Once you have a successful compilation of your source program, it is necessary to enter a second set of JCL statements. This instructs the operating system supervisor to bring the newly compiled object program into memory. The COBOL compiler is no longer needed and may, therefore, be displaced by the object program. Once

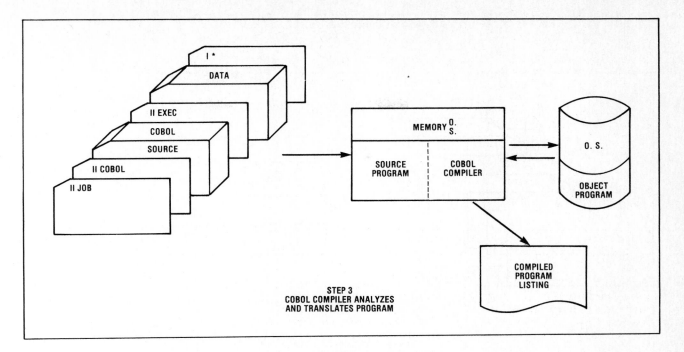

STEP 3
COBOL COMPILER ANALYZES
AND TRANSLATES PROGRAM

the object program is in place, the supervisor turns over control of processing to this application program. These procedures are flowcharted in Figure 3-11.

Compilation Step 5. As the final step in the process, the test data are read into the processing unit memory and processed, item by item, as shown in Figure 3-12. The needed output report is generated. Data produced may also be stored.

Testing and Debugging Activities

As described above, syntactical errors are corrected during the compilation process. As part of Step 3 in compilation, it is necessary to deal with any coding errors identified by the computer. Although COBOL compilers are somewhat different from each other, it is universal that any

Figure 3-10. COBOL compiling sequence (3): compiler analyzes and translates program.

Figure 3-11. COBOL compiling sequence (4): newly compiled object program brought into memory; displaces compiler.

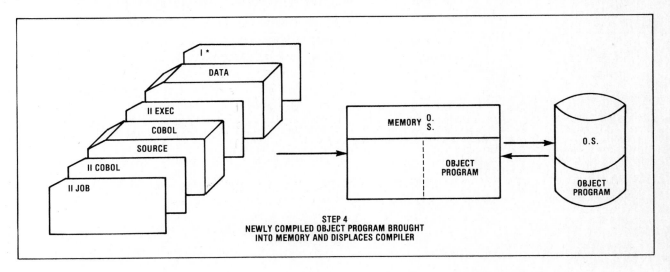

STEP 4
NEWLY COMPILED OBJECT PROGRAM BROUGHT
INTO MEMORY AND DISPLACES COMPILER

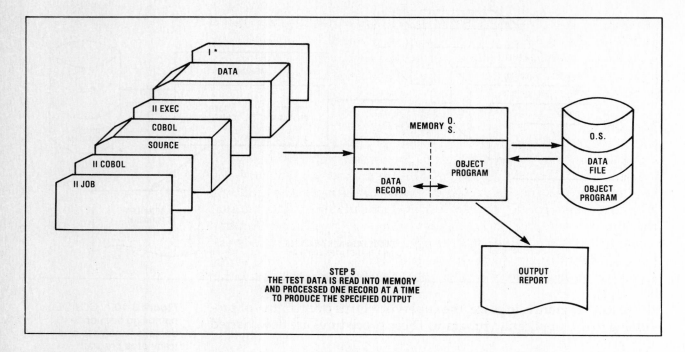

STEP 5
THE TEST DATA IS READ INTO MEMORY
AND PROCESSED ONE RECORD AT A TIME
TO PRODUCE THE SPECIFIED OUTPUT

Figure 3-12. COBOL compiling sequence (5): test data are read into memory and processed one card at a time to produce the specified output.

Figure 3-13. Sample COBOL error messages (IBM).

instruction that cannot be compiled will trigger an error message. The error message, at minimum, will identify the specific line of the program at which the compiler detected the erroneous entry. Also, there will be a description indicating the type of error that has occurred. Some compilers will also generate messages suggesting corrective entries that will eliminate the problem. Examples of compiler-produced error messages are given in Figure 3-13. At any rate, by the time a program is ready for production use, it no longer has any syntactical errors.

Logical, or processing, errors represent a separate phase of testing and debugging. A logical or processing error, in brief, occurs any time a program delivers unexpected or erroneous results in output. If a programmer has worked effectively and correctly through the design phase

20	TEST	10. 23. 59	NOV 12, 1982

CARD	ERROR MESSAGE	
52	IKF1043I-W	END OF SENTENCE SHOULD PRECEDE 10 ASSUMED PRESENT.
81	IKF1001I-E	NUMERIC LITERAL NOT RECOGNIZED AS LEVEL NUMBER BECAUSE STATUS ILLEGAL AS USED. SKIPPING TO NEXT LEVEL, SECTION OR DIVISION.
151	IKF1043I-W	END OF SENTENCE SHOULD PRECEDE 10 ASSUMED PRESENT.
189	IKF4042I-E	SYNTAX REQUIRES FILE-NAME IN CLOSE STATEMENT. FOUND INPUT DELETING TILL LEGAL ELEMENT FOUND.
206	IKF3001I-E	299-FORMAT-RECORDS NOT DEFINED. STATEMENT DISCARDED.
243	IKF4044I-C	SPACE (AL) SHOULD NOT BE MOVED TO NUMERIC FIELD. SUBSTITUTING ZERO
244	IKF4004I-E	STATUS IS ILLEGALLY USED IN MOVE STATEMENT. DISCARDED.
261	IKF3002I-E	TITLE-1 NOT UNIQUE. DISCARDED.
262	IKF3001I-E	TITLE-2 NOT DEFINED. DISCARDED.

of the development process, there should be no logical errors. Such problems should have been eliminated as a result of the structured walkthrough. However, it is always necessary to verify that a program produces accurate and complete results. One of the common methods of program testing is called *top-down testing*.

Top-down testing. Program testing follows the same top-down pattern as program design. That is, during a walkthrough or a logical tracing of the processing steps, the programmer starts at the top level of the structure chart, making sure that all of the logical requirements have been met and that the initial module invokes the succeeding modules correctly. The same procedure is followed for each leg of the program, checking modules from left to right, making sure that each module is properly invoked and that processing control is passed on to the next module, right through to program termination. Validation proceeds across each level, in succession, before the walkthrough goes on to the next level.

For the structure chart presented in the previous chapter, Figure 2-4, testing would proceed as follows:

1. The module called PROGRAM-MAIN-CONTROL would be tested. This should verify that the module invokes the three modules at the next lower level—in the correct order.

2. Proceeding from left to right, the INITIALIZATION module is reviewed. The contents of the module are examined for completeness, accuracy, proper structure, and assurance that this module interfaces correctly with the main control module.

3. The PROCESS-DATA module is tested in the same manner as the INITIALIZATION module.

4. The TERMINATION module is also tested in the same manner.

5. Testing continues at succeeding, lower levels of modules, progressing from top to bottom and left to right until all modules are validated.

This top-down approach to testing should be followed routinely for any situation in which program logic is being validated. The same procedure would be applied if the program, at execution, produced erroneous results. The problem is somewhere in the logical design of the program. Therefore, top-down testing of program logic is the way to find such errors.

Constructing test data. To make sure that each program is valid, test data should meet certain criteria:

- All test data should be constructed *before* the program is coded. In this way, the standards are in place before the coding begins. The programmer can then use the test data for walkthroughs of logical design.

- Results to be produced by the program should be predefined. That is, based on the test data provided, the outputs should be established in advance so that they can be used in walkthroughs and in actual testing at execution time.

- Test data must be comprehensive. The data must cause every logical processing condition within the program to be executed. This scope should also encompass anticipated error conditions. The test data must also represent every type of erroneous input that can be anticipated in actual application of the system.

- Test data must invoke and require execution of every module in the program.

COBOL Terms

1. IDENTIFICATION DIVISION.
2. ENVIRONMENT DIVISION.
3. DATA DIVISION.
4. PROCEDURE DIVISION.
5. PROGRAM-ID.
6. PERFORM
7. STOP
8. RUN
9. MOVE
10. DISPLAY
11. ACCEPT
12. IF. . .THEN. . . ELSE
13. END OF PROCESSING

Summary

The fourth step in the program development process is to code, or write, the program. This is done by creating step-by-step instructions in a programming language. The programming language to be used throughout this book is COBOL, an acronym for COmmon Business Oriented Language. COBOL was developed with the encouragement of the United States Department of Defense to meet a need for preparing business-oriented programs with extensive capabilities for the building and handling of files. [*Objective No. 1.*]

Each COBOL program has four required divisions:

The IDENTIFICATION DIVISION is used to name the program. Optionally, this division can contain entries that identify the programmer, the user, or other relevant information about the program. A brief abstract describing what the program does is often included in this division through use of comment entries.

The ENVIRONMENT DIVISION describes the computer equipment on which the program will be executed.

The DATA DIVISION identifies and defines all data elements to be processed by the program.

The PROCEDURE DIVISION contains the actual processing instructions that execute the program. [*Objective No. 2.*]

COBOL programs may be written with characters that include all letters of the alphabet, numbers from 0 through 9, and such special characters as $. , ( ) < > and '' or '. [*Objective No. 3.*]

Two types of words are used in writing COBOL programs. Reserved words are those that have specific meanings to the compiler. They may not be used for any other purpose. Examples include PERFORM, STOP, MOVE, and DISPLAY. Supplied words are invented by the programmer to identify the program and the data elements. Supplied words may not be identical with reserved words. They may contain from one to 30 characters, and may not begin or end with a hyphen. Blank spaces may not be used within COBOL programmer-supplied names; hyphens should be used to fill spaces that might otherwise be blank. Example: SOC-SEC-NO. [*Objective No. 4.*]

COBOL instructions, or code, may be written on program sheets that are ruled for entry of one character per box. (Programs can also be written at on-line terminals.) A set of conventions is given for entries onto coding sheets. These should be followed for all programs. [*Objective No. 5.*]

Program compilation is achieved in five steps. The first step involves JCL (Job Control Language) entries that identify the hardware and software support requirements for the program. The second step is to input the source coding for the program for processing by the compiler. The third step is actual compilation, including correction of any syntactical errors. This step is repeated until all syntax errors have been removed. In the fourth step, additional JCL instructions are entered, causing the object program to be brought into memory and executed. In the fifth step, actual test data are introduced and processed. The results of this processing are used to validate the logic and completeness of the program. [*Objective No. 6.*]

The final step in the program development process is testing and debugging. Bugs are errors in syntax and logic. The compiler generates error messages that identify the incorrect entry and the line in the program at which syntax errors occur. Some compiler messages suggest corrections for syntax errors.

It is also necessary to check programs for logical errors. These cause incorrect processing and produce incorrect results when the program is used to process test data. [*Objective No. 7.*]

Identification of logical errors can be the most difficult and costly part of programming. To minimize problems, techniques are reviewed for checking logic and also for construction of sets of test data. These methods include testing on a top-down basis and construction of test data so as to utilize and validate all processing functions within the program. [*Objective No. 8.*]

Key Terms

1. low-level language
2. machine language
3. binary
4. assembly language
5. high-level language
6. compiler
7. FORTRAN (FORmula TRANslator)
8. number crunching
9. programming language
10. syntax
11. division
12. COBOL program sheet
13. coding sheet
14. data element
15. field
16. section
17. paragraph
18. sentence
19. clause
20. character set
21. reserved word
22. supplied word
23. comment line
24. page eject
25. compilation
26. source program
27. object program
28. syntactical error
29. logical error
30. JCL (Job Control Language)
31. top-down testing

Review/Discussion Questions

1. What is the role of the IDENTIFICATION DIVISION?
2. What is the purpose of the ENVIRONMENT DIVISION?
3. How are entries in the DATA DIVISION and the PROCEDURE DIVISION related in the execution of a COBOL program?
4. Why is it invalid to use a reserved word for a data name?
5. What are the rules for writing programmer-supplied words?
6. In what columns of the coding sheet are program lines numbered?
7. What is the significance of an asterisk (*) in column 7 of a COBOL coding sheet?
8. Where are the A and B margins on COBOL coding sheets?
9. How are syntactical errors identified and corrected?
10. How are logical errors detected and corrected?
11. What are the attributes of a good set of program test data?

Practice Assignments

Project 1

WORK SITUATION

You are a programmer at North Shore Computer Supplies, Inc. The company sells a line of products known as supplies and auxiliary equipment for the data processing field. Included are printer ribbons, stock paper for computer printouts, standard business forms, punched cards, magnetic tape, magnetic storage disk packs, diskettes, cabinets, desks, data entry work stations, chairs, and other furniture items.

PROGRAMMING ASSIGNMENT

The marketing manager of North Shore has been asked by the company president to review and recommend a plan for promotion and compensation of the company's sales personnel. To do this, the marketing manager has come to you and asked for a computer-produced report that will identify, list, and provide compensation information on the company's senior sales personnel. The personnel files already exist within your company's computer systems. This is a simple application development assignment involving producing a report.

INPUT

A record layout for the input data to be processed is shown in Figure 3-14. In addition, a set of input test data is also provided in Figure 3-15.

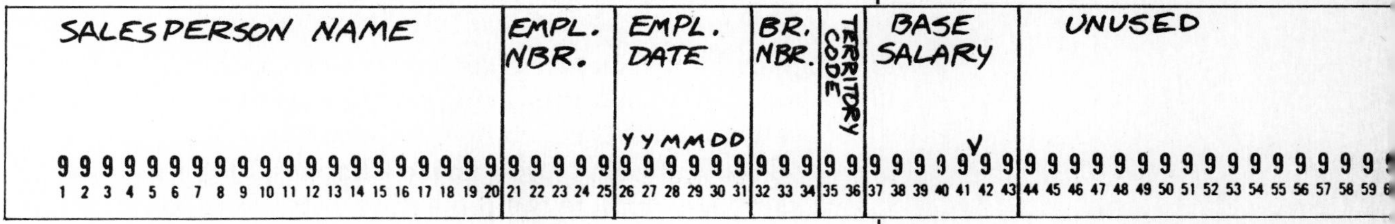

Figure 3-14. Input record layout for sales report program.

OUTPUT

A sample of the output report you are to produce is provided in Figure 3-16.

Figure 3-15. Input data for sales report program.

Figure 3-16. Output report for sales report program.

PROCESSING REQUIREMENTS

As appropriate, further assignments in this text describe any special processing requirements associated with the program you are to develop.

On this assignment, your only special requirement is the selection date to be applied in processing salesperson records. You are to select records with employment dates of a value earlier than 12/31/80.

TASK 1

Space for a structure chart for this program has been provided on an accompanying work sheet. The program has been named in the rectangle at the top level. Using the general program structure chart in Chapter 2 (Figure 2-4) as an example, complete the remaining entries on this structure chart.

TASK 2

On the accompanying work sheet, a structured flowchart has been provided for the first module in the program, entitled Sales-Mainline. Using a flowcharting template, prepare flowcharts for the three other modules: Initialization, Print Salesperson, and Termination.

TASK 3

Hand calculate and format the expected results. Perform a walkthrough of your structured flowcharts, using the test data provided. Be sure that the test data provided are processed in manually executed steps that replicate the processing in the program—and that the processing of the data produces the desired results.

Project 2

ASSIGNMENT

In Chapter 1, a program is introduced that produces a payroll report for South Bay Property Management Company. In this assignment, you are to enter the COBOL program from Figure 1-8 into your computer. Using the test data in Figure 3-17, compile, test, and debug the program until your result is the same as the sample in Figure 3-18.

Figure 3-17. Payroll input file.

```
DAVIS        THOMAS    S4000515
FREDICKS     ROBERT    T5580635
HENRY        JOHN      D4591000
JOHNSON      BETTY     B1500535
JONES        DONALD    S4290715
KRAMER       MARY      T3570524
KWAN         ALICE     D2150610
MORALES      GARY      V5500950
PEREZ        FRED      J3970495
STALLONE     MARIA     E4000615
END OF DATA
```

Figure 3-18. Payroll output report.

```
              SOUTH BAY PROPERTY MANAGEMENT

        EMPLOYEE            HOURS       PAY       TOTAL
          NAME                          RATE       PAY

     DAVIS       THOMAS   S    40.0     5.15     206.00
     FREDICKS    ROBERT   T    55.8     6.35     404.49
     HENRY       JOHN     D    45.9    10.00     488.50
     JOHNSON     BETTY    B    15.0     5.35      80.25
     JONES       DONALD   S    42.9     7.15     317.10
     KRAMER      MARY     T    35.7     5.24     187.06
     KWAN        ALICE    D    21.5     6.10     131.15
     MORALES     GARY     V    55.0     9.50     593.75
     PEREZ       FRED     J    39.7     4.95     196.51
     STALLONE    MARIA    E    40.0     6.15     246.00
```

Worksheet—Payroll Structure Chart

Program Name: _____

Prepared By: _____

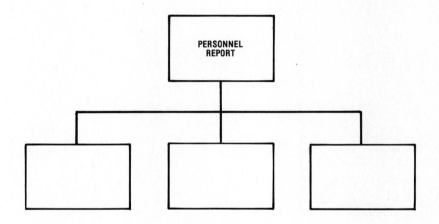

Worksheet—Payroll Structured Flowchart

Program Name: _____

Prepared By: _____

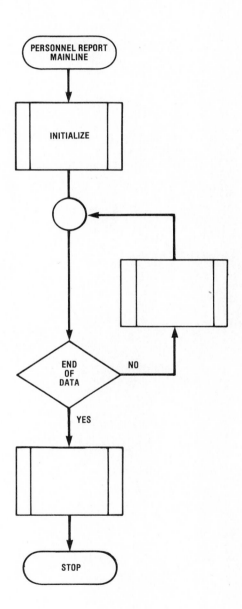

INITIALIZE

PRODUCE
REPORT

TERMINATION

Vocabulary Building Practice—Exercise 3

Write definitions and/or explanations of the terms listed below.

1. **low-level language** _____
_____

2. **machine language** _____
_____

3. **assembly language** _____
_____

4. **high-level language** _____
_____

5. **compiler** _____
_____

6. **COBOL division** _____
_____

7. **data element** _____
_____

8. **field** _____
_____

9. **section** _____
_____

10. **paragraph** _____
_____

(over, please)

11. sentence _____

_____

12. clause _____

_____

13. character set _____

_____

14. reserved word _____

_____

15. supplied word _____

_____

16. comment line _____

_____

17. source program _____

_____

18. object program _____

_____

19. top-down texting _____

_____

20. PROCEDURE DIVISION. _____

DEFINING DATA 4

OBJECTIVES

On completing reading and other learning assignments for this chapter, you should be able to:

1. Define and describe data files, records, fields, and characters.
2. Define and use correctly the term hierarchy as it applies to data and program module relationships.
3. Apply acceptable COBOL names to program modules, records, and data fields.
4. Assign level numbers to DATA DIVISION items.
5. Prepare DATA DIVISION entries for the WORKING-STORAGE section.
6. Prepare entries that define initial data values.
7. Prepare entries that identify types of data, including named constants, figurative constants, and literals.
8. Prepare entries that edit data for printed output.

DATA RELATIONSHIPS

COBOL is a business data processing language. As described in Chapter 3, COBOL was developed specifically because of the needs of business applications for the accumulation and manipulation of large volumes of data.

Because COBOL was designed to provide efficient and flexible data-handling capabilities, the COBOL language has some special, stringent requirements for defining and describing data to be input, processed, output, and stored. In working through this chapter, you will build the basic knowledge and skills necessary to define data for processing by your COBOL programs.

DATA HIERARCHIES

COBOL programs, as described in the previous chapter, are hierarchically structured. The basic data hierarchy that applies for the majority of COBOL applications is diagrammed in Figure 4-1. The diagram illustrates that a *file* is composed of a set of related *records*. Records, in turn, consist of one or more related *fields*. A field is composed of one or more *characters*. The key terms used in this diagram identify relationships among data items, as discussed below.

Figure 4-1. Hierarchical data relationships—payroll program.

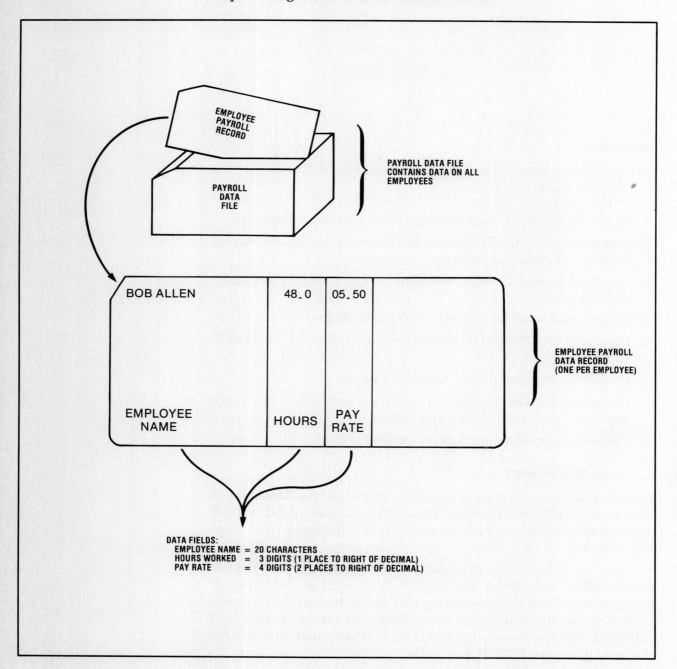

PAYROLL DATA FILE CONTAINS DATA ON ALL EMPLOYEES

EMPLOYEE PAYROLL DATA RECORD (ONE PER EMPLOYEE)

DATA FIELDS:
EMPLOYEE NAME   = 20 CHARACTERS
HOURS WORKED   = 3 DIGITS (1 PLACE TO RIGHT OF DECIMAL)
PAY RATE   = 4 DIGITS (2 PLACES TO RIGHT OF DECIMAL)

File

A *file* is a collection of data items, called records, related to one another according to their content.

A COBOL-processed data file can be compared to a physical filing cabinet in an office. Think of the salesperson reporting application program on which you worked at the end of Chapter 3. A file of salesperson information might occupy a drawer in a cabinet, or perhaps an entire cabinet, depending on the size of the company.

Files can vary widely in size and scope. Within the salesperson file, data relating to the employment and performance of individual employees would be accumulated. A file, by definition, then, is an accumulation of data records with related content.

Record

A *record* is part of a file. The chief characteristic of a record is that it contains a collection of data items, or fields, that relate to a single entity. For instance, a student record could contain the student's name, class standing, and the courses in which the student is currently enrolled. All these data refer to a single entity; that is, an individual student. An accumulation of student records, then, would consitute a student master file.

Field

A *data field* is part of a record. Putting it another way, records are made up of fields of data related to a single entity. A field is the basic, processing-oriented unit of data used within programs.

Individual fields may consist of single or multiple characters. In the salesperson reporting program, the fields you encountered included name, employee number, date of employment, and so on.

Character

A *character* is the smallest unit of data that can be presented to a COBOL program. The character set acceptable to COBOL programs is identified in Chapter 3. Data fields are formed from one or more characters. In turn, fields form records, which build files.

You may also hear the term *byte* used to identify data characters. A byte, basically, is a hardware-oriented description of the basic unit of data while character is a logically oriented term. This text is concerned with the use of data, rather than in how data are physically stored. Therefore, the more general term, character, is used.

DATA DEFINITION

Within COBOL programs, definitions must be given for all units of data to be processed. Note that, in using records in COBOL programs, all positions within the record must be accounted for with proper data definitions.

The components of COBOL *data definitions* include:

- Hierarchical level number
- A unique data name
- A description of the data type
- Size or length of the data.

Assigning Level Numbers

Level numbers are assigned to establish hierarchical relationships among data items. Remember, a given record may include a number of separate fields. Fields, in turn, may have subfields, or parts. For example, in Figure 4-2, the date field has been subdivided into month, day, and year.

In establishing level numbers, certain rules must be followed and numeric entries used in specific ways. For example, the designation 01 identifies the named collection of data as a record. This numeric entry must be in the A margin on the coding sheet.

Fields within records may be identified, and entered in any column to the right of the B margin. Level number assignments may range from 2 to 49 for fields and subfields. The programmer can use any of these numbers. However, in structured programming, it is common practice to establish a structured pattern for level numbers. This book uses a pattern based on a repetition of the value 5. That is, successive field levels within a record are assigned numbers of 5, 10, 15, 20, and so on. Other practices might use 03, 05, 07, or other numbers in an odd sequence, or 02, 04, 06, 08, or other even sequences.

One practice permitted by the COBOL language, for example, is to identify independent data items—those not defined as parts of records—with the level number 77. The revision to the COBOL language currently under consideration will delete this level number. Therefore, this practice is not used in this book and is to be discouraged.

Figure 4-2. Example of COBOL record definition.

Another level number, 88, has a special meaning within the COBOL language. This is covered in a later chapter.

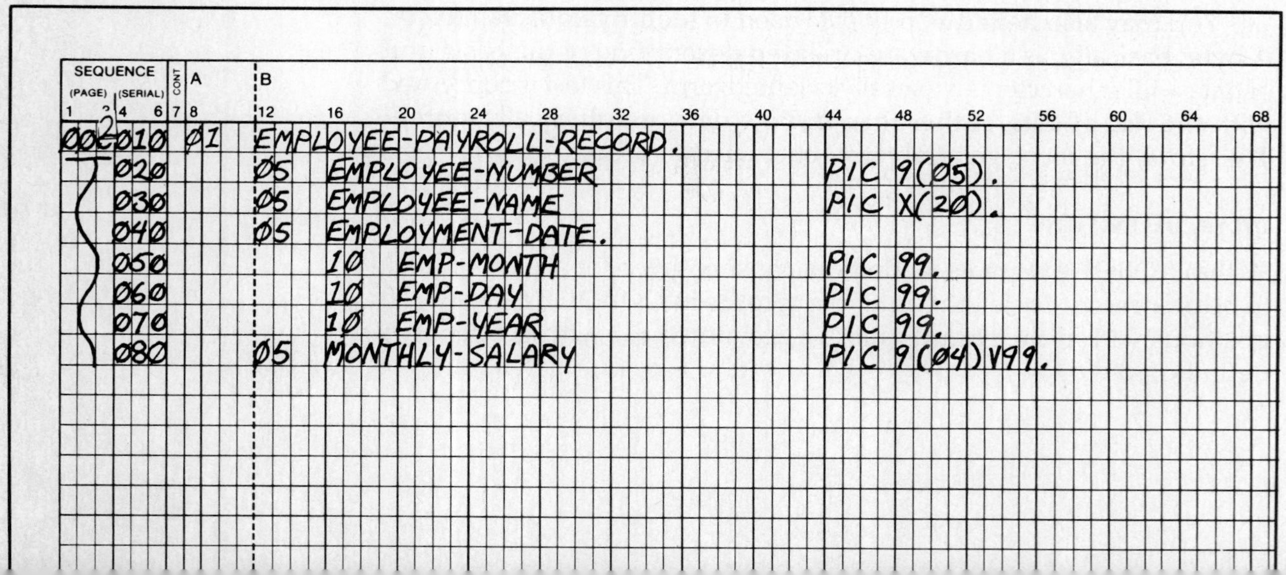

```
SEQUENCE          CONT  A    B
(PAGE) (SERIAL)
1    3 4    6 7 8  12   16   20   24   28   32   36   40   44   48   52   56   60   64   68
00G010  01   EMPLOYEE-PAYROLL-RECORD.
   020   05      EMPLOYEE-NUMBER                    PIC 9(05).
   030   05      EMPLOYEE-NAME                      PIC X(20).
   040   05      EMPLOYMENT-DATE.
   050      10      EMP-MONTH                       PIC 99.
   060      10      EMP-DAY                         PIC 99.
   070      10      EMP-YEAR                        PIC 99.
   080   05      MONTHLY-SALARY                     PIC 9(04)V99.
```

Naming Data

The programmer is responsible for assigning names to all separately identifiable items of data to be presented to each program. The rules for assigning these names are:

- Each name must be between one and 30 characters long.
- Names must consist of letters, digits, or the hyphen symbol (-). No blanks or other special symbols are allowed.
- Each name must contain at least one alphabetic character.
- A name may not start or end with a hyphen (-).
- Reserved words (listed in Appendix B) may not be used.

Some examples of valid data names: INPUT-RECORD, EMPLOYEE-NAME, COST, and AMOUNT. Invalid data-name examples include: INPUT, -TOTAL%, LAST NAME and FIRST.

In complying with these rules, certain conventions, or practices, may be helpful. For example, all data names should be unique. No two data names within an application system or a given program should be the same. The COBOL language does not actually require this uniqueness of identification. However, considerable extra effort is needed to use nonunique names. Therefore, it is much more practical to assign each piece of data its own, unique name.

As another sound practice, you will make your COBOL documentation more readable and useful if the data names you assign describe the content of the items. This facilitates the ongoing maintenance of the program.

In writing names, it is a good practice to be as complete as possible, abbreviating only when necessary. Remember, you have up to 30 characters to use. You don't gain anything by conserving characters in the name if clarity of meaning is lost. For example, in the salesperson report program, it would be a better practice to assign a name such as EMPLOYEE-NAME. The hyphen joins the two words, making the name more readable than if it were run together. (Remember: the space character is not usable in data names.) By contrast, a data name such as E-NA would give you something you have to remember indefinitely, without providing any offsetting benefits. That's why it is a good practice to make your names as complete as possible.

It is also a good practice, as has been done in the examples you have seen so far, to assign a prefix to each data name. This is not necessary and there are no rules that say you *must* use prefixes. However, when it comes to organizing data, as you will see in subsequent discussions, prefixes can help you to remember where data are used within your program. Thus, in the examples within this book, there will be brief (two-character) prefixes used on all data names. These indicate the function of the data item. For example, IN designates an input data item. Out is abbreviated OT or OU. WORKING-STORAGE is abbreviated WS. This type of identifier, again, becomes invaluable in establishing sources and uses of data items.

As stated previously, a programmer must define all fields of a record. In some cases, however, there will be positions of records that are unused or blank. These unused areas of records must still be identified. The COBOL reserved word FILLER is assigned as the name for any unused or blank parts of records.

Describing Data

The name is just one component in a data definition. Other components, as identified in Figure 4-2, are the PICTURE clause and the LEVEL NUMBER.

The PICTURE clause, basically, is a description, in computer processing terms, of the data item.

In writing the PICTURE clause, you must begin with one of two terms. You may use the full word PICTURE. Or you may use an abbreviation: PIC.

After this initial identifier, you must enter a code that tells the program what kind of data are contained in the item. Three symbols are used for this purpose. A 9 symbol indicates that the field contains the *numeric* digits 0–9 only. An A symbol identifies *alphabetic* data—the letters A–Z and blank spaces only. An X symbol identifies the presence of *alphanumeric* data. An alphanumeric field within a COBOL program may contain any valid COBOL characters.

For data that are going to be used in calculations within a program, the 9 symbol must be used in the PICTURE clause. All arithmetic operations must use data defined as numeric. The PICTURE X description offers maximum flexibility in defining data for all purposes other than calculation. Therefore, as a matter of programming convention, only the symbols 9 and X will be used in this text.

In addition to identifying content as numeric or alphanumeric, the PICTURE clause must also indicate the length, or size, of the field. This can be done in either of two ways. Either the basic symbol can be repeated to represent the number of positions in the field, or the number of positions can be entered with a number in parentheses following the PICTURE symbol. For example, a five-digit numeric field could be indicated in either of these ways: 99999 or 9(5). An alphanumeric field of four characters could be identified in either of these ways: XXXX or X(4).

If a numeric field contains a decimal point, the symbol V is used to indicate the position of the decimal point. The V symbol is symbolic only. That is, neither the V nor a decimal point is actually stored with the data. Rather, the symbol marks the position where the decimal should be. This is called an *implied decimal point*. When a numeric field is output, the decimal point will not be printed automatically. Rather,

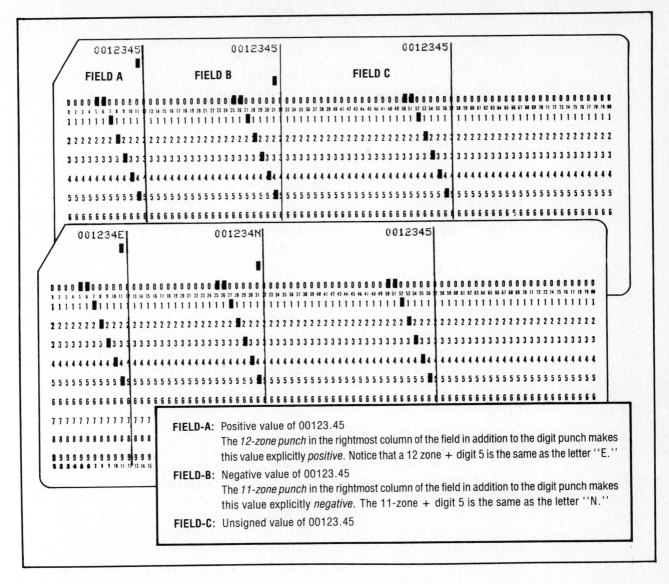

FIELD-A: Positive value of 00123.45

The *12-zone punch* in the rightmost column of the field in addition to the digit punch makes this value explicitly *positive*. Notice that a 12 zone + digit 5 is the same as the letter "E."

FIELD-B: Negative value of 00123.45

The *11-zone punch* in the rightmost column of the field in addition to the digit punch makes this value explicitly *negative*. The 11-zone + digit 5 is the same as the letter "N."

FIELD-C: Unsigned value of 00123.45

if a decimal point is desired, it is specified as part of a function called editing, covered later in this chapter.

A typical decimal notation for data definition purposes might be 99V99. As an alternative, this could also be written as 9(2)V9(2). Still another option would be the notation 9(2)V99. Numeric fields may be no longer than 18 digits regardless of the placement of the implied decimal point.

Signed data. If a numeric field contains an algebraic sign (+ or −) this condition must be indicated in the PICTURE clause. This is done by placing an S symbol before entering any 9 symbols, with no space between the S and the first 9. Thus, a three-digit signed field would be encoded: S999 or S9(3).

The sign in the actual input data item is usually stored as part of the digits in the field, and not as a separate character. This is referred to as an *imbedded overpunched* sign. Figure 4-3 illustrates the use of this

Figure 4-3. Sample punched cards showing locations of imbedded algebraic signs.

imbedded sign in a punched card field. Actual sign representation is dependent upon the vendor and model of computer used. This test assumes an imbedded overpunched sign is used.

DATA DEFINITION EXAMPLES

The content of a data definition will depend on the use to which the data items will be put. If a single data field has subfields that can be used separately, it is known as a *group item*. A data definition for a group item may not have a PICTURE clause. However, data name and level number clauses are needed as shown in the EMPLOYMENT-DATE field in Figure 4-4. Conversely, then, the absence of a PICTURE clause automatically identifies a group item.

If all of the data in a defined item are to be used as a single field, this is called an *elementary item*. For elementary data items, PICTURE clauses are necessary. To illustrate, consider an assignment to describe a payroll record for a COBOL program. Data fields incorporated in this record include employee number, employee name, month of employment, date of employment, year of employment, and monthly salary. A sample data definition for this record, with corresponding input entries on a punched card, are shown in Figure 4-4.

Record Descriptions

In the record description example in Figure 4-4, there is a close relationship between the way fields are physically arranged in the data record and the sequence of field definitions required by COBOL. A record description in COBOL begins with the first position at the left end of the record and proceeds rightward. Each field to be used in the program must be defined completely. As shown in Figure 4-4, each field is defined under the 01 record name in exactly the same sequence as for the established physical order within the record. This practice must always be followed.

The 01 record name entry and its defined parts (fields) constitutes a *logical record*. It is called a logical record because it defines a complete unit of data that is to be acted upon as an entity by the program. Depending on the types of storage media used, records may be stored individually, one record at a time, or in a *physical record* group called a *block*. The relationship between logical records and their physical record storage representations is described in Chapter 10.

USING WORKING-STORAGE

The DATA DIVISION of a COBOL program has two major parts. These are the FILE SECTION and the WORKING-STORAGE SECTION. Files, as defined earlier, are collections of related records. Files also form a set of records used in processing applications. Examples presented so far have not required the use of the FILE SECTION. Procedures for building and handling files are covered in a later chapter.

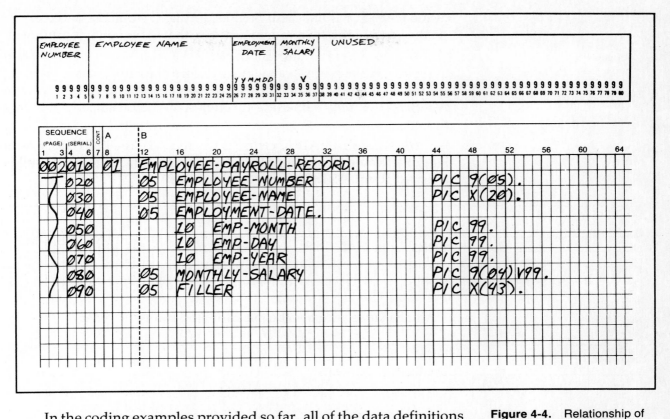

Figure 4-4. Relationship of input record layout to COBOL record definition—payroll program.

In the coding examples provided so far, all of the data definitions included have been within the WORKING-STORAGE SECTION. In general practice, the WORKING-STORAGE SECTION is used for temporary, or *transient*, data that will be applied within a specific program. WORKING-STORAGE can, therefore, be thought of as "scratch pad" memory in which you write figures and messages temporarily to help you solve a problem. Examples of data units defined in WORKING-STORAGE include:

- Independent data used one time only
- Calculation constants such as tax rates, discount percentages, and so on
- Heading lines for printed reports
- Accumulators
- Counters
- Logic switches used as a basis for program control over module selection or repetition functions.

DEFINING INITIAL DATA VALUES

To fulfill the purpose of many programs, it is necessary to define known initial, or starting, values for data fields. For example, suppose one of the requirements of a payroll processing program was to count the number of records handled. Before starting, it would be necessary to set the value of this field to zero to assure that a true count is produced.

In some programming languages, a separate instruction is needed to set accumulator areas of memory to zero before processing begins. Within COBOL programs, the most convenient and reliable way of handling this requirement is through a VALUE clause in the data definition.

When used, a VALUE clause is written after the PICTURE clause length attributes. For example, a data definition for a field that builds a record count might be entered as follows:

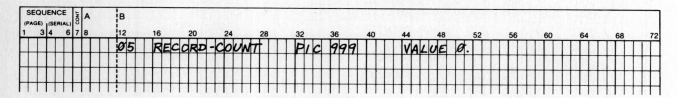

VALUE clauses can also be used for alphanumeric data:

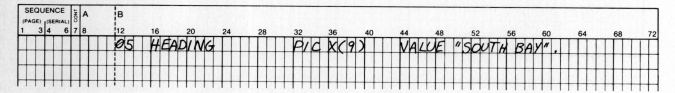

Uses for VALUE clauses include:

- Set initial starting contents for WORKING-STORAGE data. Examples include setting accumulator fields to zero, page numbering, or invoice numbering. Note that the initial content can be set at any value. Zero values are commonly used. However, other values can be entered as appropriate to an application.

- Content of report titles, headings, or footings (titles for totals at the bottom of reports) can be established.

- The VALUE clause may not be used in the FILE SECTION, except as part of 88 level number entries.

IDENTIFYING DATA TYPES

Two types of data records may be defined within COBOL programs:

- *Variables* are named data items that may change from record to record with the execution of the program. An example is the field SALESPERSON-NAME. A new salesperson name will be presented with each data record in the sales analysis system.

- *Constants* are fixed data that do not change in the course of processing. Three types of constants may be defined within COBOL programs, as described below.

Named constant. A *named constant* is one that has an identified function within the program. Examples: TAX-RATE, DISCOUNT. Sample entries:

SEQUENCE		C O N T	A	B															
(PAGE)	(SERIAL)																		
1	3 4	6 7	8	12 16 20 24 28 32 36 40 44 48 52 56 60 64 68 72															
				05 TAX-RATE PIC V999 VALUE .065.															
				05 DISCOUNT PIC V99 VALUE .04.															

(NOTE: When a V is used to show an implied decimal point, the VALUE must show the actual decimal point.)

Figurative constant. *Figurative constants* are reserved COBOL words for which the compiler assigns specific values. The more commonly used figurative constants are:

- SPACE or SPACES are alternative terms that indicate that a blank character will be placed in every position in a defined field.
- ZERO, ZEROS, or ZEROES means that a decimal 0 will be placed in every position in a defined field.

Examples of this use:

SEQUENCE		C O N T	A	B															
(PAGE)	(SERIAL)																		
1	3 4	6 7	8	12 16 20 24 28 32 36 40 44 48 52 56 60 64 68 72															
				05 RECORD-COUNT PIC 999 VALUE ZERO.															
				05 FILLER PIC X(5) VALUE SPACE.															

Literals. *Literals* are numeric and alphanumeric values used in the exact place and within the context described.

Numeric literals may be either signed or unsigned and may consist of whole numbers, decimals, or mixed decimals. In the examples below, the literals are the digits following the word VALUE.

SEQUENCE		C O N T	A	B															
(PAGE)	(SERIAL)																		
1	3 4	6 7	8	12 16 20 24 28 32 36 40 44 48 52 56 60 64 68 72															
				05 LINE-LIMIT PIC 99 VALUE 55.															
				05 FACTOR PIC 9V9 VALUE 1.5.															

Alphanumeric literals are enclosed in quotation marks, using the single or double quotation marks required by specific COBOL compilers. An example of an alphanumeric literal:

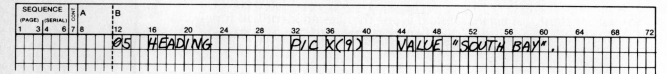

When this entry is used in an output instruction, it will cause the word SOUTH BAY to be printed. Alphanumeric literals may consist of any string of valid COBOL characters positioned within quotation marks. Consult the reference manual for your own computer system to determine whether quotation marks ('') or a single quote (apostrophe ') is used for alphanumeric literals.

Literals may appear in PROCEDURE DIVISION commands and also in DATA DIVISION entries as part of the VALUE clause. For example:

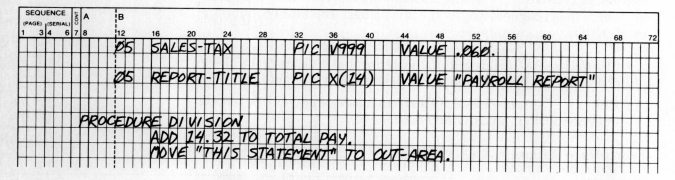

EDITING DATA FOR PRINTED OUTPUT

As indicated earlier, data definitions identify the positions of decimal points, but decimal points are not stored within data fields. In addition, numeric data fields usually do not include such other punctuation marks as the dollar sign ($) or the comma (,).

There are many situations, however, in which full punctuation is needed for numeric outputs. For example, in writing checks, it is sometimes necessary to include decimal points and dollar signs. In management reports, use of punctuation is often necessary to convey the desired meaning.

In addition, adjustment of the content of numeric fields may also clarify the meaning of output reports. For example, within computer storage, there may be a number of leading (left) zeros in numeric fields. It helps to make reports understandable if these unneeded zeros are removed, or suppressed.

To prepare numeric fields for properly punctuated and formatted outputs, a process called *editing* is used. This involves moving numeric data to a special editing picture clause to suppress leading zeros, insert punctuation, or replace certain characters within a field.

Insertion characters may be used to punctuate numeric data. This involves introduction of characters that are not included in stored records. Insertion characters in COBOL include: $, . / + − B 0 CR DB. The meanings of these insertion characters are as follows:

- The $ is appended to the left of a field with a dollar-amount value.
- The , is inserted into numeric fields to improve readability by identifying thousand positions in large numbers.
- The . identifies the decimal point in numeric fields, as appropriate.
- The / (slash mark or stroke) is used commonly to separate the digits in a numeric field representing a calendar date.
- The + appends the appropriate algebraic plus or minus symbol to signed numeric fields.
- The − appends either a minus sign or a blank to signed numeric fields.
- The symbols B and 0 indicate, respectively, a blank space and a zero to be inserted into an alphanumeric field.
- The symbol CR identifies a credit balance in a report or on a business document, identifying a field with a negative numeric value.
- The symbol DB indicates a debit balance, also identifying a negative numeric value.

Examples of printed output fields using insertion characters are shown in Figures 4-5 through 4-8.

DATA IN STORAGE	EDIT PICTURE CLAUSE	EDITED OUTPUT
120182	PIC 99/99/99	12/01/82
040583	PIC 99/99/99	04/05/83
011283	PIC 9/99/99	01/12/83
558469803	PIC 999B99B9999	558 46 9803
123456	PIC 99B99B99	12 34 56
612	PIC 999000	612000
7591	PIC 999900	759100

Figure 4-5. Examples of editing with blank, zero, and slash.

DATA IN STORAGE	EDIT PICTURE CLAUSE	EDITED OUTPUT
65.00	PIC 99.99	65.00
3346.50	PIC $ 9,999.99	$ 3,346.50
1234.56	PIC 9,999.99	1,234.56
4895	PIC 9,999.99	4,895.00
0057.10	PIC $ 9,999.99	$ 0,057.10

Note: ‸ indicates implied decimal point.

Figure 4-6. Examples of editing with dollar sign, comma, and period.

DATA IN STORAGE	EDIT PICTURE CLAUSE	EDITED OUTPUT
− 8640	PIC 9999 −	8640 −
+ 8640	PIC 9999 −	8640
− 9135	PIC − 9999	− 9135
+ 9135	PIC − 9999	9135
− 2526	PIC + 9999	− 2526
+ 2526	PIC + 9999	+ 2526
− 4500	PIC 9999 +	4500 −
+ 4500	PIC 9999 +	4500 +

Figure 4-7. Examples of editing with fixed plus and minus symbols.

DATA IN STORAGE	EDIT PICTURE CLAUSE	EDITED OUTPUT
− 125	PIC 999CR	125CR
− 36.08	PIC 99.99CR	36.08CR
+ 44.30	PIC 99.99CR	44.30
− 44.30	PIC 99.99DB	44.30DB
− 125	PIC 999DB	125DB
+ 6805	PIC 9999DB	6805

Figure 4-8. Examples of editing with CR and DB symbols.

Replacement characters actually substitute for characters stored in data records. These substitutions may be made in numeric fields only and only for leading, nonsignificant zeros. Replacement characters available in COBOL include Z * $ + −.

- The Z replaces nonsignificant leading zeros with blank spaces.
- The * can be used to fill out a printed field in replacement of nonsignificant zeros. The asterisk sign is often called a check-protection character and is used in writing checks.
- The use of multiple $ symbols suppresses leading zeros and causes the dollar sign to "float" in the position to the left of the leftmost significant digit in the numeric field.
- Multiple + and − signs can also be floated to suppress leading zeros and to imprint the appropriate algebraic sign.

Examples of output fields using replacement characters are shown in Figures 4-9 and 4-10.

DATA IN STORAGE	EDIT PICTURE CLAUSE	EDITED OUTPUT
00608	PIC ZZZZZ	608
0123.45	PIC ZZZZ.99	123.45
0000	PIC ZZZZ	
0000	PIC ZZZ9	0
0005.64	PIC Z,ZZ9.99	5.64
0005.64	PIC *,***.99	****5.64
0008.00	PIC $*,***.99	$****8.00
9715.00	PIC *,***.99	9,715.00
0375.55	PIC **,***.99	***375.55

Figure 4-9. Examples of zero suppression using blank and asterisk replacement.

Note: ˎ indicates implied decimal point.

DATA IN STORAGE	EDIT PICTURE CLAUSE	EDITED OUTPUT
− 00350	PIC − − − −9	− 350
− 0008.93	PIC −,− − − −.99	− 8.93
+ 0008.93	PIC −,− − − −.99	8.93
+ 0465.00	PIC +,+ + +.99	+ 465.00
− 0004.65	PIC +,+ + +.99	− 4.65
0237.50	PIC $$,$$$.99	$237.50
0019.87	PIC $$,$$$.99	$19.87
0000.61	PIC $$,$$$.99	$.61

Figure 4-10. Examples of zero suppression with floating plus, minus, and dollar signs.

Generally, numeric data are the only kinds of outputs that require editing. However, on occasion, it may be necessary to insert blanks or slashes in alphanumeric fields. Figure 4-11 shows examples of alphanumeric editing.

DATA IN STORAGE	EDIT PICTURE CLAUSE	EDITED OUTPUT
122582	PIC XX/XX/XX	12/25/82
040182	PIC XX/XX/XX	04/01/82
122582	PIC XXBXXBXX	12/25/82
AB650	PIC XXBXXX	AB 650
A153C	PIC XBXXXBX	A 153 C

Figure 4-11. Examples of alphanumeric editing.

Summary

One of the main purposes behind the development of the COBOL language was to enhance file handling capabilities. Therefore, an understanding of the structures and relationships of data files and their components is essential to effective COBOL programming.

A file is a collection of records related to each other according to their content. A record is a part of a file that contains a collection of data items that relate to a single entity. A field is part of a record; a subfield is part of a field. A field or subfield is the most basic of data items with meaning for processing purposes. Fields or subfields, in turn, consist of characters—individual letters, numbers, or symbols. [*Objective No. 1.*]

In writing COBOL programs, all separately identifiable items of data must be described within the DATA DIVISION. Defined data are identified by a hierarchical level number, a unique data name, and a descriptive PICTURE that includes an indication of size. [*Objective No. 2.*]

Each type of record to be used within a program must be assigned a name that is entered onto a coding sheet according to a set hierarchical structure. The name is preceded by a 01 level number entered into the A margin of a coding sheet. Alphanumeric descriptors can then be entered from the B margin rightward. Fields may be named in any column to the right of margin B. Level numbers assigned to fields may be between 2 and 49. [*Objective No. 3.*]

COBOL Terms

1. PICTURE
2. PIC
3. FILE SECTION.
4. FILLER
5. WORKING-
   STORAGE
   SECTION.
6. VALUE
7. SPACE(S)
8. ZERO(S)(ES)
9. CR
10. DB

Key Terms

1. file
2. record
3. field
4. character
5. byte
6. data definition
7. numeric field
8. alphabetic field
9. alphanumeric field
10. implied decimal point
11. imbedded over-punched sign
12. group item
13. elementary item
14. logical record
15. physical record
16. block
17. transient data
18. variable
19. constant
20. named constant
21. figurative constant
22. literal
23. editing
24. insertion character
25. replacement character

Specific rules must be followed in assigning data names. Each name must be between one and 30 characters long. Names may be composed of any combination of letters, digits, or the hyphen symbol. No other symbols are acceptable. A name may not start or end with a hyphen (-). Reserved words may not be used as data names. [*Objectives Nos. 4 and 5.*]

The WORKING-STORAGE SECTION is used chiefly for temporary, or transient, data to be referenced by the program. In defining data for use in WORKING-STORAGE, VALUE clauses can be used. In addition, data are identified by types—variables or constants. [*Objectives Nos. 6 and 7.*]

Data in numeric fields are stored without any punctuation marks. For clarity of meaning, symbols such as $ * . , + – are often added to printed reports. This is done by following the editing procedures described and illustrated. [*Objective No. 8.*]

Review/Discussion Questions

1. What is a data file?
2. What is a data record?
3. What is a data field?
4. What are the relationships of files, records, fields, and characters of data?
5. How are hierarchical levels of data items established within COBOL programs?
6. What are the rules for naming data items within COBOL programs?
7. What information is provided within a PICTURE clause used in the DATA DIVISION?
8. What options are available for designating the sizes of data fields within COBOL PICTURE clauses?
9. What are data variables?
10. What are data constants?
11. What is a literal?
12. How can numeric data fields be modified through editing?

Practice Assignments

A.   On the line at the right of each data name given below, enter an I if the term is invalid or a V if it is valid. For invalid terms, state the reason for your entry.

SALES-AMOUNT _____

QUANTITY _____

DATE _____

CODE124 _____

STUDENT-MAME _____

12-RECORDS _____

UNIT PRICE _____

12A

ORDER-POINT- _____

$DOLLARS _____

493 _____

B.   Write complete data definition statements in the blank spaces beneath each of the following fields:

1. An accumulator to hold a total of quantities ordered (six-digit integer).

    _____

2. A nine-digit Social Security number.

    _____

3. A 25-character faculty name that includes last name (12 characters), first name (12 characters), and a middle initial (one character).

    _____

4. A grade point average of three digits (two places to the right of the decimal point).

    _____

5. A signed accumulator that has been initialized to zero and will provide for totals on credit card balances of up to $10,000.00.

    _____

6. A numeric field containing the constant 3.1416 (pi).

_____

7. A 30-character field to be used to underline parts of a report that contains a string of dashes (hyphens).

_____

C. Write a COBOL description for the student record in Figure 4-12 and for the inventory record in Figure 4-13.

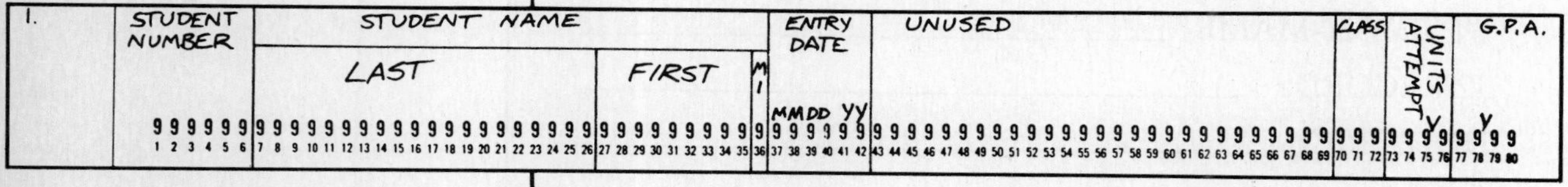

I.	STUDENT NUMBER	STUDENT NAME		M I	ENTRY DATE	UNUSED	CLASS	UNITS ATTEMPT	G.P.A.
		LAST	FIRST		MMDD YY				
	999999	99999999999999999999	99999999	9	999999	99999999999999999999999999	999	99999	999
	1 2 3 4 5 6	7 8 9 10 11 12 13 14 15 16 17 18 19 20 21 22 23 24 25 26	27 28 29 30 31 32 33 34 35	36	37 38 39 40 41 42	43 44 45 46 47 48 49 50 51 52 53 54 55 56 57 58 59 60 61 62 63 64 65 66 67 68 69	70 71 72	73 74 75 76	77 78 79 80

Figure 4-12. Student record layout for use in practice assignment.

Student record. _____

_____

_____

_____

_____

_____

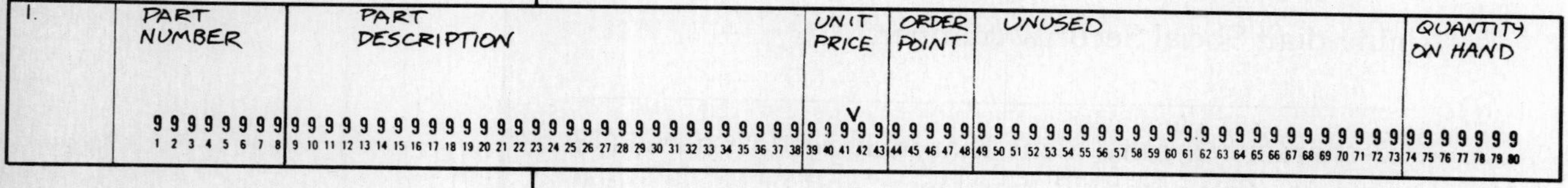

I.	PART NUMBER	PART DESCRIPTION	UNIT PRICE	ORDER POINT	UNUSED	QUANTITY ON HAND
	99999999	999999999999999999999999999999	99999	99999	9999999999999999999999999999	9999999
	1 2 3 4 5 6 7 8	9 10 11 12 13 14 15 16 17 18 19 20 21 22 23 24 25 26 27 28 29 30 31 32 33 34 35 36 37 38	39 40 41 42 43	44 45 46 47 48	49 50 51 52 53 54 55 56 57 58 59 60 61 62 63 64 65 66 67 68 69 70 71 72 73	74 75 76 77 78 79 80

Figure 4-13. Inventory record layout for use in practice assignment.

Inventory record. _____

_____

_____

_____

_____

_____

D.   Write a COBOL record description for the following output definitions. Provide for the indicated edit functions.

1. Output print record.

Field	Print Positions	
Department number	4–6	
Employee number	10–15	
Social Security number	19–29	XXX-XX-XXXX
Name	33–58	
Current month sales	62–71	XX,XXX.XX-
Month last year sales	75–84	XX,XXX.XX-
Year-to-date sales	88–99	$XXX,XXX.XX-

2. Output print record.

Field	Print Positions	
Loan number	5–10	
Principal amount	15–24	XXX,XXX.XX
Monthly payment	30–38	XX,XXX.XX
Impounds amount	45–52	X,XXX.XX
Principal portion of payment	60–68	XX,XXX.XX
Interest portion of payment	75–83	XX,XXX.XX
New balance amount	90–99	XXX,XXX.XX

E.   Show the value of edited results for each of the listed fields. A V in a field indicates an implied decimal point.

	Sending Picture	Contents	Receiving Picture	Edited Results
1.	9(5)	54321	9(6)	_____
2.	9(5)	54321	9(4)	_____
3.	9(5)V99	54321^12	9(5).99	_____
4.	9(5)V99	54321^12	9(5)	_____
5.	9(5)V99	54321^12	ZZZZ9.99	_____
6.	9(5)V99	00321^00	ZZ,ZZZ.ZZ	_____
7.	9(5)V99	00321^00	$Z,ZZZ.99	_____
8.	S9(5)V99	–00321^00	----9.99	_____
9.	S9(5)V99	+00321^12	----9.99	_____
10.	9(5)V99	00321^12	$$$,$$$.99	_____
11.	9(5)V99	00321^12	***,***.99	_____
12.	9(5)V99	00021^12	ZZ,ZZZ.99CR	_____

F. Fill in the missing entries for the blank fields in the MOVE statements below. A ^ in the code indicates an implied decimal point. A b indicates a blank character.

Sending Picture	Contents	Receiving Picture	Edited Results
1. X(5)	APPLE	X(7)	_____
2. X(6)	_____	X(7)	ORANGEb
3. X(6)	_____	XX/XX/XX/	12/31/82
4. 9(6)	030383	_____	b3/03/83
5. 9(4)V99	0013V65	_____	bb$13.65
6. S9(5)	−00541V22	_____	bb541.22__
7. _____	01236V00	$$$,$$$.99	b$1,236.00
8. _____	+0654V32	Z,ZZZ.99	bb654.32+

Programming Assignments

For the programming assignment given below, make sure all of the following tasks are completed:

1. Review the structure or module hierarchy chart for this assignment.

2. Prepare or complete documentation of processing logic with structured flowcharts *and* pseudocode.

3. Define sample data to be used to test your program logic and prepare expected results for that data.

4. Conduct a walkthrough of your program structure and logical design. Do this by yourself, under guidance of your instructor, or in cooperation with a fellow student.

5. Write, compile, test, and debug the program you have designed.

Purpose: Produce a listing of student grade point averages.

Input: A set of records in the following format:

Position	Field
1–6	Student number (numeric)
7–26	Student name (alphanumeric)
27–27	Class level code (one digit)
28–30	Grade point average (two decimal places)
31–34	Units completed (one decimal place)

Figure 4-14 is an input record layout for student grade point records. Figure 4-15 is a structure chart for this application.

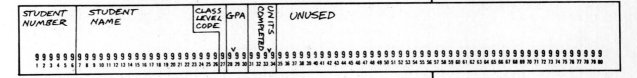

Output: A listing of the contents of each input record, in the following format:

Figure 4-14. Student grade point layout for use in practice assignment.

Print Position	Field
33–38	Student number
5–24	Student name
55–58	Grade point average (9.99)
44–48	Units completed (ZZZ.9)

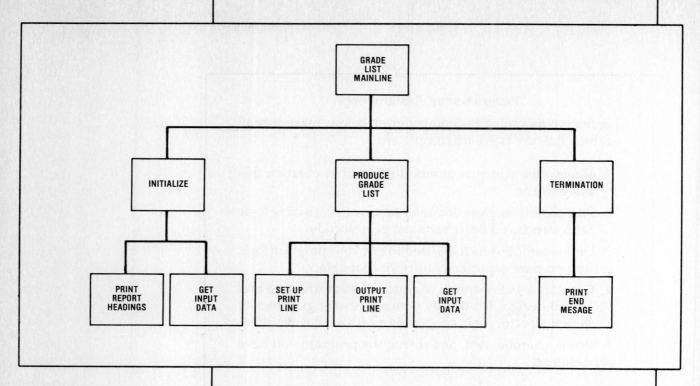

Figure 4-15. Structure chart for grade point list program. For use in practice assignment.

Figure 4-16 is a print record layout for this output report.

Processing Requirements: 1) One line printed per input record. 2) Create a set of eight to 12 sample input records.

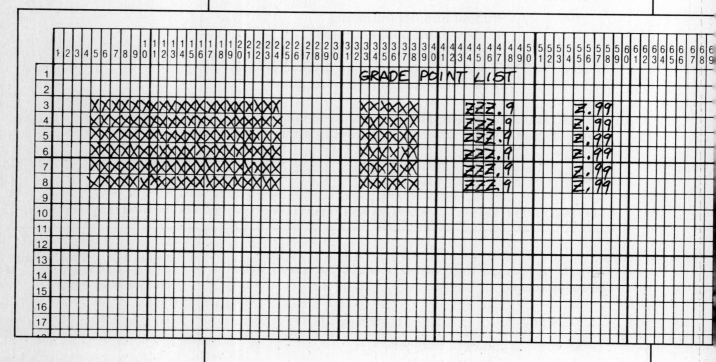

Figure 4-16. Print record layout for grade point list. For use in practice assignment.

Worksheet for Structured Flowchart

Program Name: _____

Prepared By: _____

Worksheet for Pseudocode Specifications

Program Name: _____

Prepared By: _____

COBOL PROGRAM SHEET

System		Punching Instructions		Sheet	of
Program		Graphic		Identification	
Programmer	Date	Punch	Card Form #	[73]	[80]

SEQUENCE
(PAGE) (SERIAL)
1 3 4 6 7 8 CONT A B 12 16 20 24 28 32 36 40 44 48 52 56 60 64 68 72

COBOL PROGRAM SHEET

System				Sheet	of

Program		Punching Instructions			Identification
		Graphic		Card Form #	
Programmer	Date	Punch			[73] [80]

SEQUENCE				A	B														
(PAGE)	(SERIAL)	CONT																	
1 3	4 6	7	8	12	16	20	24	28	32	36	40	44	48	52	56	60	64	68	72

COBOL PROGRAM SHEET

System			
Program			
Programmer			

Punching Instructions

	Graphic			Card Form #
Date	Punch			

Sheet	of
Identification	
	73] [80

SEQUENCE																										
(PAGE)	(SERIAL)	CONT	A	B	16	20	24	28	32	36	40	44	48	52	56	60	64	68	72
1	3 4	6 7 8		12															

COBOL PROGRAM SHEET

System

Program

Programmer

Punching Instructions

Graphic

Punch

Date

Card Form #

Sheet   of

Identification

[73]   [80]

SEQUENCE

(PAGE) (SERIAL)

1 3 4   6 7

CONT

8

A   B

12 16 20 24 28 32 36 40 44 48 52 56 60 64 68 72

COBOL PROGRAM SHEET

System	
Program	
Programmer	

	Punching Instructions		Sheet of
	Graphic	Card Form #	Identification
Date	Punch		

SEQUENCE
(PAGE) (SERIAL)

1	3 4	6	7 8	CONT

A   B

1 3 4 6 7 8 | 12 16 20 24 28 32 36 40 44 48 52 56 60 64 68 72

73 [80]

COBOL PROGRAM SHEET

System				Sheet	of

Program			Punching Instructions			Card Form #		Identification

| Programmer | | Date | | Graphic | | | | |
| | | | | Punch | | | | [73] [80] |

SEQUENCE			CONT	A	B																
(PAGE) (SERIAL)																					
1 3	4	6	7 8		12	16	20	24	28	32	36	40	44	48	52	56	60	64	68	72	

Vocabulary Building Practice—Exercise 4

Write definitions and/or explanations of the terms listed below.

1. file _____

   _____

2. record _____

   _____

3. field _____

   _____

4. character _____

   _____

5. byte _____

   _____

6. data definition _____

   _____

7. numeric field _____

   _____

8. alphabetic field _____

   _____

9. alphanumeric field _____

   _____

10. implied decimal point _____

    _____

(over, please)

11. **group item** _____

_____

12. **elementary item** _____

_____

13. **logical record** _____

_____

14. **physical record** _____

_____

15. **block** _____

_____

16. **transient data** _____

_____

17. **variable** _____

_____

18. **constant** _____

_____

19. **literal** _____

_____

20. **editing** _____

_____

CONVERTING DATA TO INFORMATION 5

OBJECTIVES

On completing reading and other learning assignments for this chapter, you should be able to:

1. Describe and apply the COBOL commands for input and output functions, including ACCEPT and DISPLAY.

2. Describe and apply the COBOL commands for data movement, including the MOVE statements for both numeric and alphanumeric data.

3. Describe and apply the COBOL commands for calculation including ADD, SUBTRACT, MULTIPLY, DIVIDE, and COMPUTE statements, as well as associated options for rounding and adjusting output field sizes to reflect the results of computations.

PROCESSING DATA

The purpose of a computer business application is to process data to produce information. Data become information when they are combined with other data items or transformed for new or added meaning through computation within a computer system. COBOL provides a number of instructions that control processing and, through processing, control the conversion of data into information.

This chapter introduces several basic processing commands of the COBOL language. For introductory purposes, complexities are kept to a minimum. Therefore, although you learn how to perform and control processing within a COBOL program, this text avoids forcing you into the more advanced techniques associated with setting up and manipulating data files until you have a broader base of experience.

The processing commands, or *verbs,* covered in this chapter are broken down into three groups:

- Input/output commands
- Data movement commands
- Calculation commands.

INPUT/OUTPUT COMMANDS

Two of the commands used to control input and output within COBOL programs are ACCEPT and DISPLAY. Input operations use the AC-CEPT command. The DISPLAY command is used for output.

ACCEPT Command

In general, the ACCEPT command is used to bring in limited amounts of data without defining files. (There are other input commands, but these require the use of files and are covered in later chapters.)

This command causes the computer to read and input for processing the value of one *identifier*—the data named and defined under a single data name in the WORKING-STORAGE SECTION of the DATA DIVISION of a program. When the ACCEPT command is executed, a single identified unit of data is input. This can be a single field, a group of fields, or a complete record. The limit for processing under the AC-CEPT command is a single record of data for each command executed.

(NOTE: COBOL compilers for some makes or models of equipment or operating rules in some data centers may restrict the use of the ACCEPT verb, particularly for student programs. You may find yourself in a situation in which you are not permitted to use the ACCEPT verb. If this occurs, follow an alternate procedure: Turn to Chapter 9 of this book, entitled *COBOL for Files.* Read and study the sections on the READ command. Substitute the READ procedures for the ACCEPT instructions presented here.)

Several options are available for use with the ACCEPT instruction, as seen in Figure 5-1.

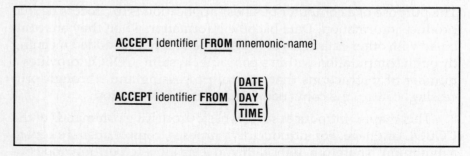

Figure 5-1. The ACCEPT command.

- ACCEPT identifier. This is the simplest format for use of the command. On execution, this instruction will cause occurrence of one value for the identifier to be input to working storage. The input device used is the *default* unit specified by the COBOL compiler. Each COBOL compiler will automatically select an input device if none is specified by the programmer. To find out what the default input device is for the system you are using, consult the COBOL reference manual for your specific machine, or ask your instructor. In many instances, the default input device will be a card reader or the operating console for the system.

- An optional command format for the ACCEPT instruction includes identification of the input device to be used. As indicated, the verb ACCEPT is followed by an identifier. Then the optional entry [FROM] is given. Following this, the programmer specifies one of the optional input devices that may be specified with this command. These optional devices are described below.

Note that the COBOL term [FROM] is within brackets and is underscored. Within the COBOL language, an entry in brackets is optional. Underscored items indicate required entries. As explained above, you don't have to identify an input device to use an ACCEPT command. If you don't use the optional format, the compiler will default to an input device it selects. However, if you want to specify the device to be used at your option, then you must add a [FROM mnemonic-name] clause to your command and identify the *mnemonic-name* in the SPECIAL-NAMES paragraph. Within the COBOL language, mnemonic-names are used by programmers to assign names to specific hardware devices.

The following example would cause the computer to accept a card record from a card reader.

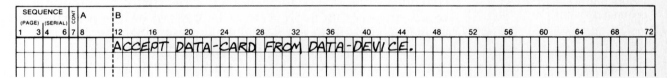

In the above example, the card reader has been assigned the mnemonic-name DATA-DEVICE by the programmer. This is done with an entry in the SPECIAL-NAMES paragraph of the ENVIRONMENT DIVISION of a COBOL program. The notation:

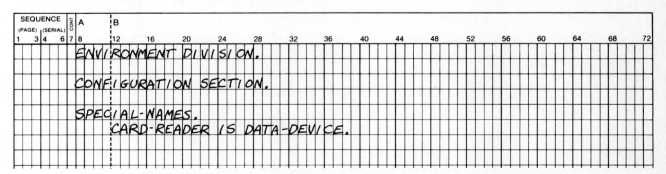

The notation below illustrates use of an ACCEPT command for input of a single field from the operator's console of a computer.

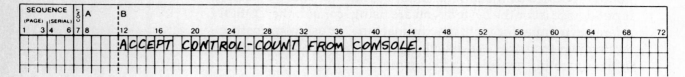

DISPLAY Command

The DISPLAY command causes a COBOL program to execute a limited output function. The command covers a field, group of fields, or any data units up to one complete record.

The output can go to any appropriate device within a computer system. If no specific output device is specified, a default instruction from the compiler will be executed. This usually causes the output data to be printed on the device designated as the *system printer*. However, some compilers output to operator consoles. The option term used for output device selections is [UPON mnemonic-name]. Figure 5-2 shows the formal format used for entry of DISPLAY commands in the COBOL language.

$$\underline{\text{DISPLAY}} \quad \begin{Bmatrix} literal\text{-}1 \\ identifier\text{-}1 \end{Bmatrix} \quad \begin{bmatrix} literal\text{-}2 \\ identifier\text{-}2 \end{bmatrix} \quad [\underline{\text{UPON}}\ mnemonic\text{-}name] \quad \begin{Bmatrix} \text{SYSOUT CONSOLE} \\ mnemonic\ name \end{Bmatrix}$$

Figure 5-2. The DISPLAY command.

To illustrate use of this command, the instruction that follows would cause a COBOL program to display a record count on the computer console.

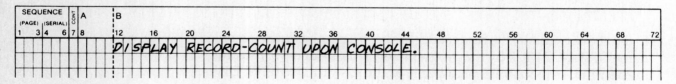

To cause the system to display the record count on a terminal, the command would be written as follows:

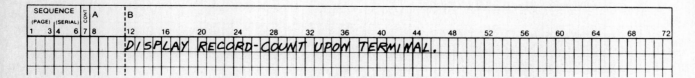

A command that could be used to notify a computer operator whenever a processing error occurs within a program could be written as follows:

The term MESSAGE-DEVICE is a mnemonic that would be defined in the SPECIAL-NAMES paragraph of the ENVIRONMENT DIVISION. The entries that could be used for this purpose are:

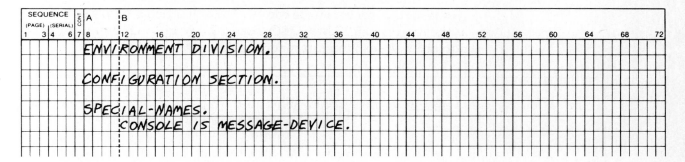

Use of DISPLAY in debugging. In some programs, the use of the DISPLAY command can provide a valuable tool for locating the causes of bugs that occur during program execution.

This can be particularly valuable when applied to programs with large numbers of repetitions of a single module. When erroneous data are presented within such a program, it can be difficult to detect the points and causes of failure. To make the needed corrections, it is necessary to identify when and where the failure occurred. This can be done by using the DISPLAY command to output a record showing the name of the module in which the error occurred and the relevant data value that could not be processed. A command that would cause such an output might look like the example given in Figure 5-3.

```
DISPLAY ''D400-CALCULATE-PAY'', EMP-NBR, EMP-HOURS, EMP-RATE.
        OR
DISPLAY ''SORT STARTED''.
PERFORM SORT-DATA.
DISPLAY ''SORT FINISHED''.
```

Figure 5-3. Use of the DISPLAY command in debugging.

DATA MOVEMENT COMMANDS

It is frequently necessary to move data fields or records within computer memory as part of program processing. For example, an independent field, such as a page number, may have to be moved into a report heading line for output. Accumulated totals may also have to be moved into output summary lines. Many programs also require movement of input records directly to output areas.

One way to accomplish this movement of data is with the MOVE command. This command causes the computer to copy data from one identifier area in memory to a second identifier area, without destroying the original data. The MOVE command accomplishes a copy function.

The basic format of the MOVE command is shown in Figure 5-4. As indicated in this illustration, the programmer has an option of using an identifier or a literal as the data item to be moved. The word MOVE points to the data item to be copied. This identified data item is known as the *sending* field. The COBOL word TO points to the *receiving* location or locations in memory for the move.

MOVE TO *identifier 2* [*Identifier 3*] $\left\{ \begin{array}{l} \textit{identifier-1} \\ \textit{Figuration Constant} \\ \textit{literal} \end{array} \right\}$

Figure 5-4. The MOVE command.

An important rule for use of the MOVE command centers around the PICTURE established in the DATA DIVISION for the receiving area. The rule is that alphanumeric data should not be moved into numeric fields. The classification of the type of move being made—numeric or alphanumeric—depends upon the PICTURE clause describing the receiving area.

Moving Numeric Data

A numeric move is one in which data are transferred into any elementary data item established by a PICTURE clause of 9s. In a numeric move, data entries are copied from the sending field to the receiving field in right-to-left order. Any unfilled positions in the receiving field are filled with leading zeros. Where implied decimal points are included in numeric fields, they provide the focus of alignment. The decimal point assumes its specified position. Alignment then follows this positioning, with zeros placed to fill open positions to both the left and right.

Two examples of numeric MOVE commands are given below:

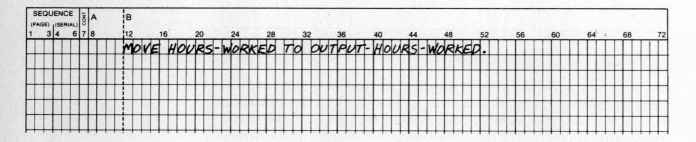

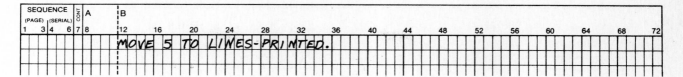

A data move may involve some restructuring of field content. For example, if a field of numeric data is moved to a larger field, leading zeros may be inserted. Figure 5-5 is a table showing some alterations that can occur to numeric data in the course of movement from sending to receiving positions.

EXAMPLE: MOVE A TO B.

BEFORE		AFTER	
A	**B**	**A**	**B**
1 2 3 4	8 0 4 9	1 2 3 4	1 2 3 4
PIC 9(04)	PIC 9(04)		
1 2 3 4	2 1 4 7 3 1 9 2	1 2 3 4	0 0 0 0 1 2 3 4
PIC 9(04)	PIC 9(08)		
1 2 3 4	9 2 7	1 2 3 4	2 3 4
PIC 9(04)	PIC 9(03)		
1 2 3 4	8 9 2 8 9 8	1 2 3 4	0 1 2 3 4 0
PIC 99V99	PIC 9(03)V9(03)		
1 2 3 4	4 7	1 2 3 4	2 3
PIC 99V99	PIC 9V9		

Figure 5-5. Examples of MOVE command executions.

Moving Alphanumeric Data

For alphanumeric data moves, the receiving field must be defined with a PICTURE of Xs. Any valid COBOL character may be moved into an alphanumeric field.

Movement of data into an alphanumeric field begins with the leftmost position and continues in left-to-right order, with unused positions filled with blanks.

Figure 5-6 is a table illustrating several sending-receiving conditions involving alphanumeric moves.

Field sizes in data moves. In any data move, the receiving field must be large enough to accommodate the transferred data. If there is not enough room in the receiving field, the excess data will be *truncated*. This means simply that the excess characters are lost in the receiving field. On numeric moves, truncation is at the left. In alphanumeric moves, truncation is to the right. The final examples in Figures 5-5 and 5-6 show examples of truncation.

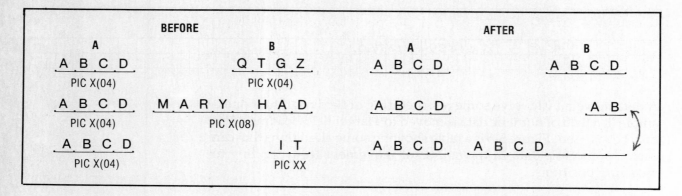

Figure 5-6. Additional examples of MOVE command executions.

CALCULATION COMMANDS

Calculation commands cause the computer to perform arithmetic functions. As a qualification, all calculations must be performed on *elementary* numeric data names that have been defined in a PICTURE clause that consists of 9s.

The commands ADD, SUBTRACT, MULTIPLY, and DIVIDE function in the same manner as pencil-and-paper arithmetic. That is, single functions are performed in a straightforward manner. The COMPUTE command makes more complex calculations possible, including sequences of mathematical functions or the solutions of equations.

ADD Command

The ADD command causes the computer to perform arithmetic summing of numeric data. Addition can be performed upon data names described as numeric, numeric literals, or combinations of numeric fields. However, the result must always be stored in a numeric data name defined by a 9s picture. When ADD commands are executed, results are always stored in the last-named field. The data in the sending (source) fields are not altered by the ADD command. Only the content of the receiving field is changed.

Examples of simple ADD commands include:

Statement	Execution
ADD FIELD-1 TO FIELD-2.	Contents of FIELD-1 are added to FIELD-2 and the sum is placed in FIELD-2.
ADD 1 TO LINE-COUNT.	The literal value of 1 is added to the contents of LINE-COUNT and the sum is placed in LINE-COUNT.
ADD A,B,C TO D.	The values of A, B, C, and D are all added together and the sum is placed in D.

In all of the above commands, the final field named is the receiving field. Thus, the data in the receiving field are altered by the addition process. To perform addition without altering one of the sending fields, a separate receiving area can be set up. This is done through use of the GIVING clause, or option. When this option is used, the sending fields remain unchanged and the result is moved into a new, designated area. Example:

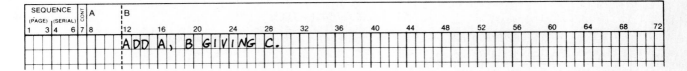

The table in Figure 5-7 shows the sending and receiving fields associated with several types of ADD instructions.

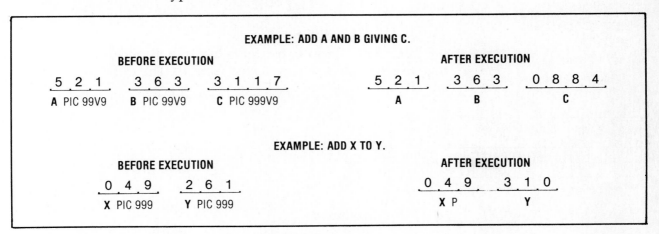

Figure 5-7. Examples of ADD command executions.

SUBTRACT Commands

SUBTRACT commands cause computation of the differences between specified numeric values. Results are stored in the last-named field. In executing commands that involve multiple subtractions, the computer actually adds all of the values to be subtracted, then takes the sum away from the amount in the last field.

The SUBTRACT command can handle data names, literals, or combinations of these types of values. The GIVING option can also be used with the SUBTRACT command. Examples:

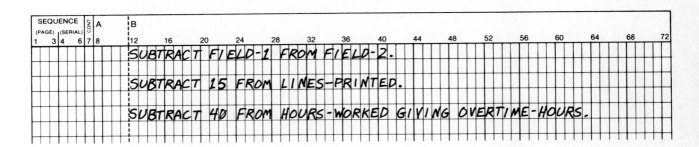

EXAMPLE: SUBTRACT 40 FROM HOURS-WORKED GIVING OVERTIME-HOURS.

BEFORE EXECUTION		AFTER EXECUTION	
5 2 0	0 0 0	5 2 0	1 2 0
PIC 99V9	PIC 99V9	HOURS-WORKED	OVERTIME-HOURS
HOURS-WORKED	OVERTIME-HOURS		

EXAMPLE: SUBTRACT A FROM B.

BEFORE EXECUTION		AFTER EXECUTION	
0 5 3	1 2 8	0 5 3	0 7 5
A PIC 99V9	B PIC 99V9	A	B

Figure 5-8. Examples of SUBTRACT command executions.

Figure 5-8 is a table showing sending and receiving fields for several SUBTRACT operations.

In the following example, the values of A, B, and C would be added together and the sum subtracted from D. The difference would be stored in D.

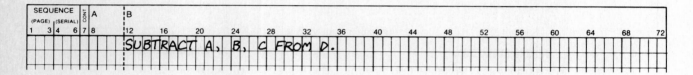

```
SUBTRACT A, B, C FROM D.
```

MULTIPLY Command

The MULTIPLY command causes multiplication of one factor by another with the product stored in the last-named field. The GIVING option may be used with MULTIPLY commands. Examples:

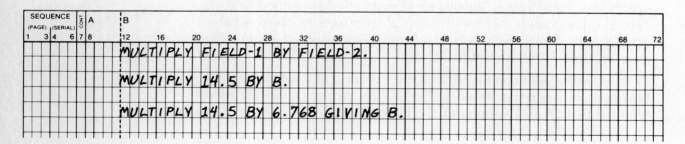

```
MULTIPLY FIELD-1 BY FIELD-2.

MULTIPLY 14.5 BY B.

MULTIPLY 14.5 BY 6.768 GIVING B.
```

The table in Figure 5-9 illustrates sending and receiving results for several MULTIPLY commands.

DIVIDE Command

Because of the basic nature of division, the DIVIDE command has more options than the other simple arithmetic functions. With this command, it is possible to DIVIDE one number BY another number or INTO the

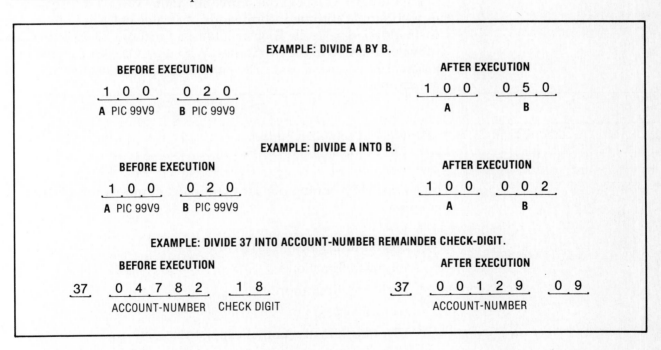

EXAMPLE: MULTIPLY X BY Y.

BEFORE EXECUTION   AFTER EXECUTION

0 1 4   0 5 3   0 1 4   7 4 2
X PIC 999 Y PIC 99   X   Y

EXAMPLE: MULTIPLY A BY B GIVING C.

BEFORE EXECUTION   AFTER EXECUTION

2 3 5   1 8 0   4 8 1 5 3 7   2 3 5   1 8 0   0 4 2 3 0 0
A PIC 99V9 B PIC 99V9 C PIC 9999V99   A   B   C

other number. It is important to be explicit about which kind of division you are doing, since the results of these two operations can be dramatically different, as shown in the illustrations in Figure 5-10. The arithmetic results are not equivalent.

Figure 5-9. Examples of MULTIPLY command executions.

EXAMPLE: DIVIDE A BY B.

BEFORE EXECUTION   AFTER EXECUTION

1 0 0   0 2 0   1 0 0   0 5 0
A PIC 99V9 B PIC 99V9   A   B

EXAMPLE: DIVIDE A INTO B.

BEFORE EXECUTION   AFTER EXECUTION

1 0 0   0 2 0   1 0 0   0 0 2
A PIC 99V9 B PIC 99V9   A   B

EXAMPLE: DIVIDE 37 INTO ACCOUNT-NUMBER REMAINDER CHECK-DIGIT.

BEFORE EXECUTION   AFTER EXECUTION

37   0 4 7 8 2   1 8   37   0 0 1 2 9   0 9
ACCOUNT-NUMBER CHECK DIGIT   ACCOUNT-NUMBER

The GIVING option can be used with the DIVIDE command.

A REMAINDER clause can also be applied, if the application requires saving this value. Otherwise, the remainder is lost.

Results of DIVIDE operations are stored in the last-named data field or in the GIVING field. When a REMAINDER clause is used, only the

Figure 5-10. Examples of DIVIDE command executions.

digits of the remainder are stored in the data name following the word REMAINDER. Examples:

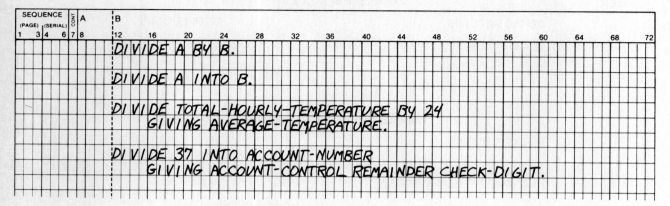

COMPUTE Command

When operations require multiple calculations, the COMPUTE command provides the power to handle the job with a single instruction. By comparison, use of standard calculate commands (ADD, SUBTRACT, etc.) would require a separate instruction for each computation.

For example, consider the simple equation: $x = a + b^2$. To handle this with simple arithmetic commands, the value of b would first have to be multiplied by itself. Then an addition function would be needed to develop the sum of the two values. With the COMPUTE command, the actual equation values can be entered as operational instructions. For example:

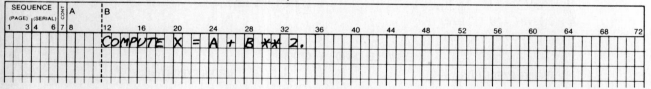

The COMPUTE command uses standard symbols for arithmetic operations:

+ means addition.

– means subtraction.

* means multiplication.

/ means division.

** identifies the function of exponentiation.

( ) indicates the grouping of terms.

= identifies an assignment of value or movement of the result to a data name.

Arithmetic functions processed under the COMPUTE command are always executed in a predetermined order, or precedence. In writing programs, you will have to be aware of this functional sequence so that you can derive the correct result from your calculations. The *order of arithmetic operations* is as follows:

Operations within parentheses are always completed first. For values within parentheses, calculations follow the standard sequence described below.

Exponentiation functions are handled next. Multiplication and division are next in order, followed by addition and subtraction. If operations of the same hierarchical order are present, they are executed from left to right. The assignment operation is processed last, with results stored in the data name to the left of the =.

Examples of COMPUTE commands, as well as a table showing derived results, are presented in Figure 5-11.

EXAMPLE: CONVERTING FAHRENHEIT TEMPERATURE TO CELSIUS.

COMPUTE   TEMP-CELSIUS   =   ((FAHRENHEIT − 32)*5)/9.
          PIC 999V9   PIC 999V9
DATA VALUES   029ˆ4   =   085 ˆ0

EXAMPLE: PAY CALCULATION WITH NO OVERTIME.

COMPUTE GROSS-PAY = HOURS-WORKED * PAY-RATE
  PIC   9(03)V99   99V9   99V9(03)
 (VALUES   877.40   =   40.0   *   21.935)

SYMBOL	MEANING
( )	GROUPING
**	EXPONENTIATION
/	DIVIDE
*	MULTIPLY
−	SUBTRACT
+	ADD

Figure 5-11. Examples of COMPUTE command executions.

The ROUNDED Option

In some situations, it is desirable to *round* the results of calculations. For example, in calculating dollar amounts, it is common to round the third decimal place. If the value of the third decimal place is 5 or more, an extra penny is added in the second decimal place. If the value is four or less, the third place is dropped. The computer can be instructed to round the rightmost needed digit in a calculation through use of the ROUNDED option. For simple arithmetic commands, the ROUNDED instruction is placed at the end of the instruction, after the name of the receiving field. Within COMPUTE instructions, the ROUNDED option is placed after the name of the receiving field identifier, but to the left of the equal sign.

Use of the ROUNDED option is illustrated in Figure 5-12.

ADD	**A**	TO	**B**	*ROUNDED.*		
PIC	99V99		99V9			
VALUES	47.25		23.6		=	70.85
RESULTS	47.25		70.9			
SUBTRACT	**A**	FROM	**B**	*ROUNDED.*		
PIC	99V99		99V9			
VALUES	47.05		63.7		=	16.65
RESULTS	47.05		16.7			
MULTIPLY	**A**	BY	**B**	*ROUNDED.*		
PIC	99V99		9999V9			
VALUES	47.85		0063.0		=	3014.550
RESULTS	47.85		3014.6			
DIVIDE	**A**	INTO	**B**	*ROUNDED.*		
PIC	99		99V99			
VALUES	22		25.25		=	1.1477
RESULTS	22		01.15			

COMPUTE	**A**	*ROUNDED*		**B**	*	**C**	+	(**D** *	**E** / 4)
PIC	9(04)V9		=	99V99		99		9V9	99
VALUES	1297.6		=	25.23		12		8.4	18 4
RESULTS	0340.6		=	25.23		12		8.4	18 4

Figure 5-12. Examples of rounding executions.

Size of Result Fields

When calculation functions are performed, numbers can be generated that are larger than the receiving fields designated to hold them. This is particularly true for multiplications, where the number of digits can increase rapidly. The COBOL language provides a mechanism for reporting on and reacting to oversized results that cause truncation in the receiving fields—the ON SIZE ERROR option.

This option can be entered as an instruction either after or in place of the ROUNDED clause. Following the ON SIZE ERROR clause, an instruction is entered indicating an action to be taken. This usually calls for displaying some sort of error message. For example, the programmer can cause the computer to display a message indicating that the

```
ADD A TO B ON SIZE ERROR    MOVE MESSAGE TO REMARKS.

MULTIPLY A BY B ON SIZE ERROR    ADD 1 TO COUNTER-ONE.

COMPUTE X = A/B*C ON SIZE ERROR    DISPLAY PRINT-LINE.

SUBTRACT A FROM B ON SIZE ERROR   DISPLAY ERROR-MESSAGE.

DIVIDE A INTO B ON SIZE ERROR    MOVE 1 TO INDICATOR.
```

Figure 5-13. Examples of ON SIZE ERROR executions.

output number is greater than the number of positions in the receiving field, as illustrated in Figure 5-13.

Although it does provide a measure of comfort and protection, the ON SIZE ERROR clause is inefficient because it requires a considerable amount of object coding. Therefore, use of this option is discouraged. It is far better to plan ahead and to estimate the size of result fields, and then provide for them in program design. Thus, the size of result fields should always be a point to check during program walkthroughs.

Estimating the size of results is fairly easy and can be done by applying some simple rules of thumb:

- For addition functions, the receiving field should be at least one digit larger than the sending field.
- In subtraction, the sending and receiving fields will be the same length.
- In multiplication, the receiving field should equal the sum of the digits of the factors.
- In division, the quotient will be the same size as the dividend and the remainder will be the same size as the divisor.

Common Programming Errors in Calculation

In writing COBOL programs, you can help improve your quality by anticipating and avoiding typical errors that are committed by many novice programmers. In the calculation area, frequently encountered errors include:

- Instructions may attempt to perform calculations using edited numeric fields. This cannot be done. You cannot calculate on fields that contain dollar signs or actual decimal points. Any decimal fields you use must have the implied (V) decimal point.
- The programmer may fail to include instructions to clear accumulators or counters before use. Any data name into which

values will be added consecutively normally should start at zero. Therefore, if addition or subtraction are to be performed, accumulators or counters normally should be set to zero at the outset.

- Overflow may occur. It is important to anticipate the size of result fields. If truncation occurs in the execution of a program, these errors can be extremely difficult to detect. Therefore, it is worthwhile always to check the size of result fields.

- The TO command may be used improperly. The COBOL compiler does not permit the use of TO in an ADD command that includes a GIVING clause. An incorrect command would be: ADD A TO B GIVING C. The compiler will not execute this command. The statement should read: ADD A, B GIVING C. (Note: The comma is optional.)

- Division by zero (0) is not permitted. Mathematically, division by zero is undefined. Most computers produce unpredictable results when division by zero is attempted. Thus, the divisor should be checked to be sure it is not zero before an attempt is made to execute a divide instruction.

Key Terms

1. verb
2. identifier
3. default
4. mnemonic
5. system printer
6. sending field
7. receiving location
8. truncate
9. elementary data
10. order of arithmetic operations
11. round

Summary

Processing of data within COBOL programs is done under control of a series of commands that initiate input and output, data movement, and calculation functions.

The ACCEPT command initiates input of data defined under a single data name. This command is not appropriate for entry of data files. The ACCEPT command can be followed by a [FROM] clause describing the input device to be used.

The DISPLAY verb causes output of any identified data units up to one complete record. The output can be displayed on many devices within the computer system. An [UPON] clause is used to identify the device upon which the output will be displayed. [*Objective No. 1*]

It is often necessary to move fields of data for processing. One typical application of this capability is the movement of fields into output record areas for printing. This is done through use of the MOVE command. In numeric moves, data are copied into receiving fields in right-to-left order after decimal point alignment. The receiving field must be defined by a PICTURE clause of 9s. In alphanumeric moves, data are written into the receiving fields in left-to-right order. The receiving field must be defined with a picture clause of Xs. [*Objective No. 2.*]

Individual calculations are specified through use of the ADD, SUBTRACT, MULTIPLY, and DIVIDE commands. Multiple calculations in a single operation can be initiated through use of the COMPUTE command. When the COMPUTE command is used, arithmetic functions are always carried out in a set order.

Care should be taken to be sure that the size of the output, or receiving, field is great enough to accept the results of computations. This is particularly important for multiplication, which can lead to output fields that are considerably larger than input fields.

Calculation instructions cannot be applied to edited numeric fields. It is important that any designated accumulators or counters be zeroed before use. The TO and GIVING commands may not be used together in a single ADD instruction. [*Objective No. 3.*]

COBOL Terms

1. ACCEPT
2. [FROM]
3. CONFIGURATION SECTION
4. SPECIAL-NAMES
5. DISPLAY
6. [UPON]
7. MOVE
8. TO
9. ADD
10. GIVING
11. SUBTRACT
12. MULTIPLY
13. DIVIDE
14. BY
15. INTO
16. REMAINDER
17. COMPUTE
18. ROUNDED
19. ON SIZE ERROR

Review/Discussion Questions

1. What conditions must be observed in using the ACCEPT command?

2. What types of data records may and may not be entered under control of an ACCEPT command?

3. What limitations apply to the use of the DISPLAY command?

4. How is an output device identified for use with a DISPLAY command?

5. Why is the DISPLAY command particularly appropriate for the identification of error messages?

6. How is the receiving location identified in the writing of a MOVE command?

7. What requirements apply to the writing of commands for movement of numeric and alphanumeric data?

8. In what situations can the GIVING command be used with calculation functions?

9. With which calculation function is the FROM command used?

10. How are equations presented and solved within COBOL programs?

11. What provisions are made for situations in which output fields will be larger than fields input to calculation functions?

Practice Assignment

A.   The columns below show a source data field, a PICTURE for the source data, and a PICTURE for the field receiving the data. Assume a MOVE command is executed upon the source data. In the column at right, enter the data content for each receiving field.

	Source Data	Source Picture	Receiving Picture	Received Data
1.	12345	9(05)	9(05)	_____
2.	12345	9(04)V9	9(05)	_____
3.	12345	9(03)V99	9(05)	_____
4.	12345	9(02)V9(03)	9(05)	_____
5.	12345	9V9(04)	9(05)	_____
6.	12345	V9(05)	9(05)	_____
7.	12345	9(05)	9(03)	_____
8.	12345	9(05)	9(07)	_____
9.	12345	9(05)	X(05)	_____
10.	12345	9(05)	X(04)	_____
11.	12345	9(03)V99	X(05)	_____
12.	12345	9(05)	X(10)	_____
13.	12345	V9(05)	X(05)	_____
14.	A-TEST	X(06)	X(06)	_____
15.	A-TEST	X(06)	X(10)	_____
16.	A-TEST	X(06)	X(04)	_____
17.	A-TEST	X(06)	9(6)	_____

B.   Show the contents of each field after the specified calculation has been performed.

Data Name	Picture	Before Execution	After Execution

1. ADD ITEM-A TO ITEM-B.

Data Name	Picture	Before Execution	After Execution
ITEM-A	9(04)	2003	_____
ITEM-B	9(04)	6009	_____

2. SUBTRACT ITEM-A FROM ITEM-B.

ITEM-A	9(04)	2003	_____
ITEM-B	9(04)	6009	_____

3. MULTIPLY ITEM-A BY ITEM-B.

ITEM-A	9(04)	1800	_____
ITEM-B	9(06)	000091	_____

4. DIVIDE ITEM-A INTO ITEM-B.

ITEM-A	9(04)	2003	_____
ITEM-B	9(06)	6009	_____

5. COMPUTE ITEM-C = ITEM-A * ITEM-B.

ITEM-A	9(04)	2003	_____
ITEM-B	9(04)	6009	_____

6. ADD ITEM-A ITEM-B GIVING ITEM-C.

ITEM-A	9(04)	2003	_____
ITEM-B	9(04)	6009	_____
ITEM-C	9(06)	012072	_____

7. SUBTRACT ITEM-A FROM ITEM-B GIVING ITEM-C.

ITEM-A	9(04)	2003	_____
ITEM-B	9(04)	6009	_____
ITEM-C	9(06)	012972	_____

8. MULTIPLY ITEM-A BY ITEM-B GIVING ITEM-C.

ITEM-A	9(04)	6829	_____
ITEM-B	9(04)	1294	_____
ITEM-C	9(08)	02934716	_____

9. DIVIDE ITEM-A INTO ITEM-B GIVING ITEM-C.

ITEM-A	9(04)	0974	_____
ITEM-B	9(04)	1948	_____
ITEM-C	9(08)	90911934	_____

10. ADD ITEM-A, ITEM-B, ITEM-C GIVING ITEM-D.

ITEM-A	9(04)	0974	_____
ITEM-B	9(04)	1948	_____
ITEM-C	9(04)	2732	_____
ITEM-D	9(06)	149837	_____

11. SUBTRACT ITEM-A, ITEM-B FROM ITEM-C GIVING ITEM-D.

ITEM-A	9(04)	0974	_____
ITEM-B	9(04)	1948	_____
ITEM-C	9(04)	3162	_____
ITEM-D	9(06)	943413	_____

12. COMPUTE ITEM-D = ITEM-A * ITEM-B/2–ITEM-C.

ITEM-A	9(04)	1047	_____
ITEM-B	9(04)	2931	_____
ITEM-C	9(04)	8726	_____
ITEM-D	9(08)	29134179	_____

Programming Assignments

Two programming assignments are given below. Following directions of your instructor or your own feelings about how much practice you can use, complete either or both of these assignments. For each assignment, make sure all of the following tasks are completed:

1. Review the structure or module hierarchy chart for each assignment.

2. Prepare or complete documentation of processing logic with structured flowcharts *and* pseudocode.

3. Define sample data to be used to test your program logic and prepare expected results for those data.

4. Conduct a walkthrough of your program structure and logical design. Do this by yourself, under guidance of your instructor, or in cooperation with a fellow student.

5. Write, compile, test, and debug the program you have designed.

Problem 1

Purpose: The credit manager of SELLALL Company needs a report on current account balances for all customers.

A structure chart for this application is in Figure 5-14.

Figure 5-14. Structure chart for account balances report. For use in practice assignment.

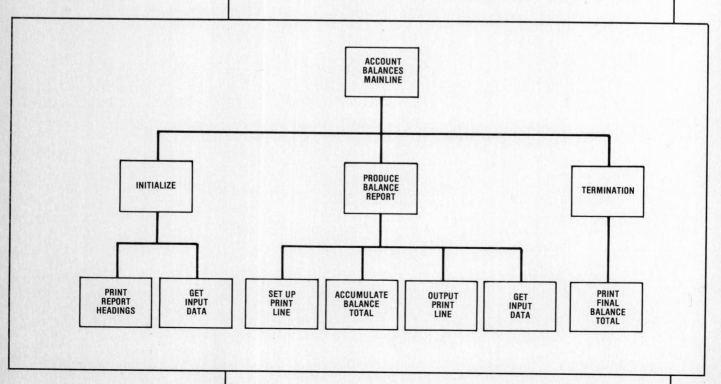

Input: A set of card image records in the following format:

Position	Field
1–7	Customer ID. (numeric)
8–27	Customer Name (alphanumeric)
28–29	Customer Type (RE = retail, WH = wholesale)
30–35	Account Balance (signed, numeric, with two decimal places)

A record layout for this input is shown in Figure 5-15.

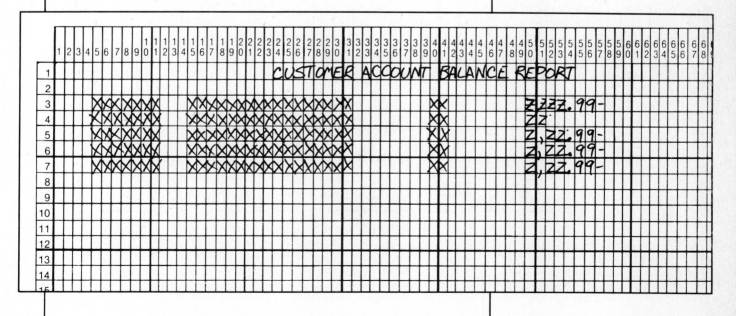

Figure 5-15. Customer account balance input record for use in practice assignment.

Output: A listing of the contents of each record, in the following format:

Print Position	Field
5–11	Customer ID.
15–31	Customer Name
40–41	Customer Type
50–59	Account Balance (Z,ZZ9.99 –)

A report layout for this output is shown in Figure 5-16.

Figure 5-16. Output report layout for account balances report. For use in practice assignment.

144

Processing Requirements: 1) Print one line per input record. 2) Accumulate a total of all account balances after the last input record is printed. Use the following example:

Total account balances ZZZ,ZZ9.99 –

Problem 2

Purpose: Professors Medley and Eaves need help with student grades. For each class, a report is required that will show the results of five quizzes for every student. Also, quiz averages are to be calculated and reported as shown below.

A structure chart for this program is in Figure 5-17.

Figure 5-17. Structure chart for student quiz score report. For use in practice assignment.

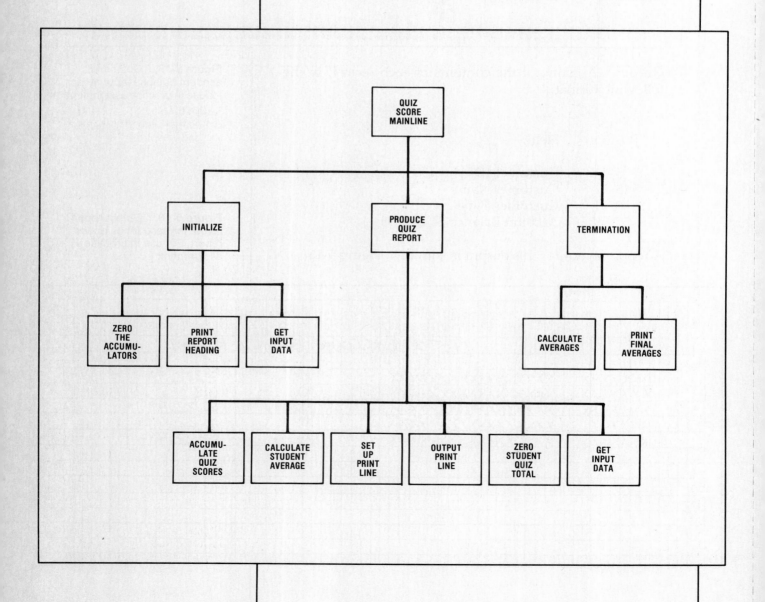

Input: A set of records in the following format:

Position   Field

1–6   Student Number
7–26   Student Name
27–29   Quiz 1 score
30–32   Quiz 2 score
33–35   Quiz 3 score
36–38   Quiz 4 score
39–41   Quiz 5 score

A record layout for this input is given in Figure 5-18.

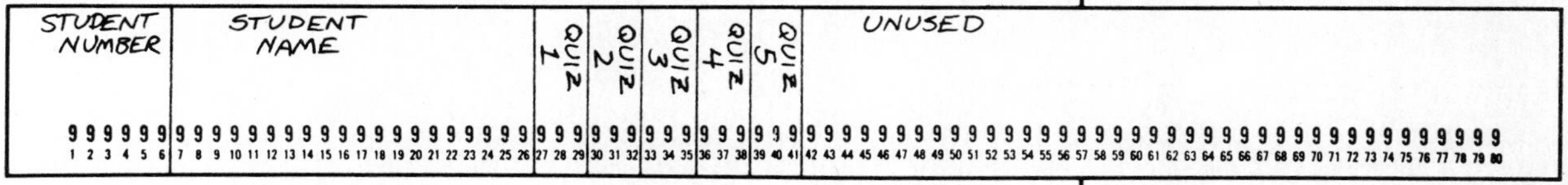

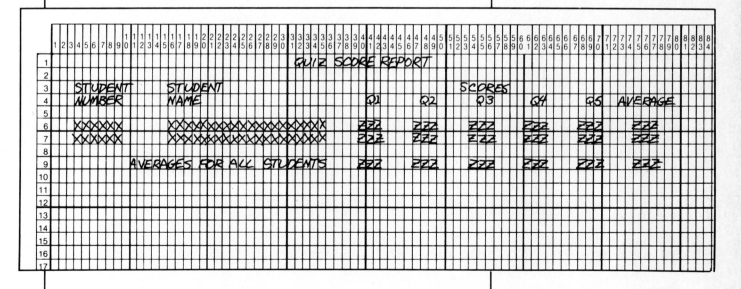

Output: A report in the format shown in Figure 5-19.

Processing: 1) One line per input record. 2) Print column headings. 3) Calculate an average for the five quizzes for each student. 4) Accumulate totals and necessary counts as a basis for calculating and printing an average for all students on each of the quizzes and a final average for all students.

Figure 5-18. Student quiz score input record for use in practice assignment.

Figure 5-19. Output report layout for quiz score report. For use in practice assignment.

Worksheet for Structured Flowchart

Program Name: _____

Prepared By: _____

Worksheet for Pseudocode Specifications

Program Name: _____

Prepared By: _____

Worksheet for Structured Flowchart

Program Name: _____

Prepared By: _____

Worksheet for Pseudocode Specifications

Program Name: _____

Prepared By: _____

COBOL PROGRAM SHEET

System				Punching Instructions		Sheet	of
Program						Identification	
Programmer		Date		Graphic	Card Form #		
		Punch				73]	[80

SEQUENCE		CONT																	
(PAGE)	(SERIAL)		A	B															
1	3 4	6 7 8		12	16	20	24	28	32	36	40	44	48	52	56	60	64	68	72

COBOL PROGRAM SHEET

System		Punching Instructions			Sheet	of
Program		Graphic		Card Form #		Identification
Programmer	Date	Punch			[73]	[80]

COBOL PROGRAM SHEET

System			Punching Instructions			Sheet	of
Program		Graphic		Card Form #			Identification
Programmer	Date	Punch					

SEQUENCE
(PAGE) (SERIAL)

1	3	4	6	7	8	CONT	A	B	12	16	20	24	28	32	36	40	44	48	52	56	60	64	68	72

73]   [80

COBOL PROGRAM SHEET

System				Punching Instructions						Sheet	of

Program			Graphic						Card Form #		Identification

Programmer		Date	Punch								[73] [80]

SEQUENCE						
(PAGE)	(SERIAL)	CONT	A	B		
1 3	4 6	7	8	12 16 20 24 28 32 36 40 44 48 52 56 60 64 68 72		

COBOL PROGRAM SHEET

System				Sheet	of
Program		Punching Instructions			Identification
Programmer	Date	Graphic	Card Form #		73] [80
	Punch			

COBOL PROGRAM SHEET

System				Sheet	of

Program		Punching Instructions		
	Graphic			Identification
Programmer	Date	Punch	Card Form #	[73] [80]

SEQUENCE
(PAGE) (SERIAL)
CONT
A   B
1 3 4 6 7 8 12 16 20 24 28 32 36 40 44 48 52 56 60 64 68 72

COBOL PROGRAM SHEET

System		Punching Instructions			Sheet of
Program			Graphic		Identification
Programmer	Date	Punch		Card Form #	73] [80

SEQUENCE				
(PAGE)	(SERIAL)	CONT	A	B
1 3	4 6	7 8		12 16 20 24 28 32 36 40 44 48 52 56 60 64 68 72

COBOL PROGRAM SHEET

System		
Program		
Programmer		

	Punching Instructions			Sheet	of
Graphic			Card Form #	Identification
Punch				
Date				[73] [80]

SEQUENCE		CONT	A	B																											
(PAGE)	(SERIAL)																														
1 3	4 6	7	8	12	16	20	24	28	32	36	40	44	48	52	56	60	64	68	72											

COBOL PROGRAM SHEET

System		
Program		
Programmer		

		Punching Instructions		Sheet	of
Date	Graphic				
Punch		Card Form #		Identification

SEQUENCE			CONT	A	B
(PAGE)	(SERIAL)				
1	3 4	6 7	8	12 16 20 24 28 32 36 40 44 48 52 56 60 64 68 72	

Identification [73] [80]

COBOL PROGRAM SHEET

System		Punching Instructions		Sheet of

Program		Graphic		Card Form #	Identification
Programmer	Date	Punch			[73] [80]

SEQUENCE		CONT	A	B														
(PAGE)	(SERIAL)																	
1 3	4 6	7	8	12	16	20	24	28	32	36	40	44	48	52	56	60	64	68 72

COBOL PROGRAM SHEET

System				Punching Instructions			Sheet	of	
Program				Graphic				Identification	
Programmer		Date		Punch		Card Form #		[73]	[80]

SEQUENCE								
(PAGE)	(SERIAL)	CONT	A	B				
1 3	4 6	7 8		12 16 20 24 28 32 36 40 44 48 52 56 60 64 68 72				

COBOL PROGRAM SHEET

System					Punching Instructions				Sheet	of
Program								Card Form #		Identification
Programmer		Date			Graphic					[73] [80]
					Punch					

SEQUENCE		CONT	A	B																
(PAGE)	(SERIAL)																			
1 3	4 6	7	8	12	16	20	24	28	32	36	40	44	48	52	56	60	64	68	72	

Vocabulary Building Practice—Exercise 5

Write definitions and/or explanations of the terms listed below.

1. verb _____

   _____

2. default _____

   _____

3. mnemonic _____

   _____

4. system printer _____

   _____

5. sending field _____

   _____

6. receiving location _____

   _____

7. truncate _____

   _____

8. elementary data _____

   _____

9. round _____

   _____

10. IDENTIFICATION DIVISION. _____

    _____

(over, please)

11. **ENVIRONMENT DIVISION.** _____

_____

12. **DATA DIVISION.** _____

_____

13. **WORKING-STORAGE SECTION** _____

_____

14. **PERFORM** _____

_____

15. **ACCEPT** _____

_____

16. **MOVE** _____

_____

17. **RUN** _____

_____

18. **IF. . .THEN. . . ELSE** _____

_____

19. **COMPUTE** _____

_____

20. **ROUNDED** _____

_____

DECISION MAKING, CONTROL, AND REPETITION 6

OBJECTIVES

On completing reading and other learning assignments for this chapter, you should be able to:

1. Define a computer decision and explain the collating sequence upon which data relationships are based.

2. Describe how computer decisions create selection and repetition controls and apply one-way and two-way selection mechanisms.

3. Define and apply COBOL statements for IF. . .THEN. . .ELSE functions.

4. Explain and use the six relational tests: equal to, greater than, less than, not equal to, not greater than, not less than.

5. Explain the principles of the case construct.

6. Describe the use of subroutines in programs.

7. Explain the functions of counters and accumulators and write programs incorporating their use.

DECISION RELATIONSHIPS

Based on instructions in programs, computers can make certain decisions. However, their decision-making abilities are limited and narrowly prescribed.

Some of the tools that programmers may use to help understand decision requirements of a program are decision tables and decision trees. These graphic techniques are covered in Chapter 2. The use of these methods helps the programmer to understand clearly the nature of decisions to be made and the alternative actions to be carried out as a result of decision functions to be incorporated within programs.

165

All *computer decision making* is based on the results of data comparisons. Computers can compare one data item with another. Sophistication comes with human ingenuity—and with the ability of computers to perform these simple comparisons at rates of billions of operations per second.

All computer decision making is based on data relationships. These relationships, in turn, depend upon an established hierarchy of values known as the *collating sequence* (Appendix A). This sequence defines the way in which a given computer will compare the characters it can operate upon. For example, within systems that use Extended Binary Coded Decimal Interchange Code (EBCDIC) characters, the special characters $. / = and others are lower in the comparison hierarchy than letters of the alphabet. Also, all digits (0–9) are higher in the hierarchy than letters.

Thus, the letter "A" would compare higher than an * but lower than the numeral 1. With numbers, the hierarchy value is determined by numeric sequence. The larger number is always higher than the smaller number, and vice versa. For alphabetic data, relationships are based on alphabetic position. B is always higher than A. Z is always higher than X.

With EBCDIC alphanumeric fields, numeric values are always higher than alphabetic values. Within this structure, the blank character is lower than alphabetic values.

In summary, the collating sequence used in comparisons to implement decision-making commands on EBCDIC character systems are, in descending order:

- Numeric characters
- Alphabetic characters
- Special characters
- The blank space.

A table showing the collating sequences of data values for a 64-character subset of the ANSI standard code format (ASCII) is given in Appendix A, Table 2. Figure 6-1 is an abstract highlighting the differences between the EBCDIC and ASCII character collating sequences.

Purpose of Computer Decisions

Computer decisions help to apply controls within computer programs. As described earlier, one of the purposes of controls is to direct the flow of processing within programs. Based on tests applied to the content of data items, the actual sequence of processing can be controlled or directed. The types of controls applied by these computer decisions are selection and repetition. The discussions that follow go into greater depth about the basis for applying these controls.

	ASCII	EBCDIC (IBM)	
HIGH ↓ LOW	LETTERS (A–Z) (upper case) NUMBERS (0–9) SPECIAL CHARACTERS (/, *, #, +, −, etc.) BLANK SPACE	NUMBERS (0–9) LETTERS (A–Z) (upper case) SPECIAL CHARACTERS (/, *, #, +, −, etc.) BLANK SPACE	HIGH ↓ LOW

Figure 6-1. Character collating sequences, ASCII and EBCDIC.

Selection mechanisms in programs are of two types—one-way and two-way. One-way selection involves a decision to execute only one branch of instructions. For example:

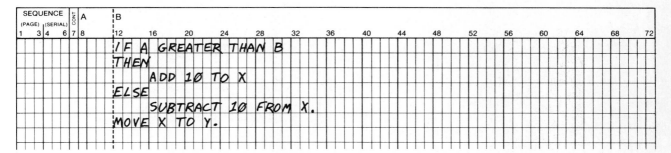

A flowchart for this selection statement is shown in Figure 6-2. In this example, if the value in A is greater than the value in B, the program will cause the computer to add 10 to X. Otherwise, the next statement in the program will be executed. Note that the term NEXT SENTENCE is a reserved word and may be used in either the true or false part of the selection statement.

Two-way selection statements always have explicit commands to be executed in *both* the true and false clauses of the IF statement. As an example, consider the selection statement below and the flowchart in Figure 6-3.

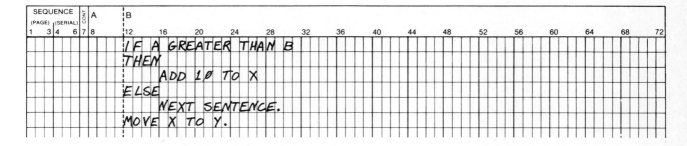

In this example, the value of X will *always* be changed. If A is greater than B, X will increase by 10. But if A is not greater than B, X will decrease by 10.

168

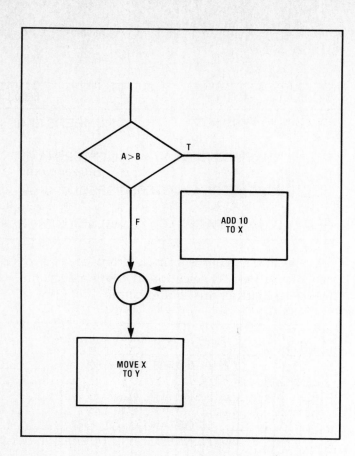

Figure 6-2. Flowchart showing one-way selection.

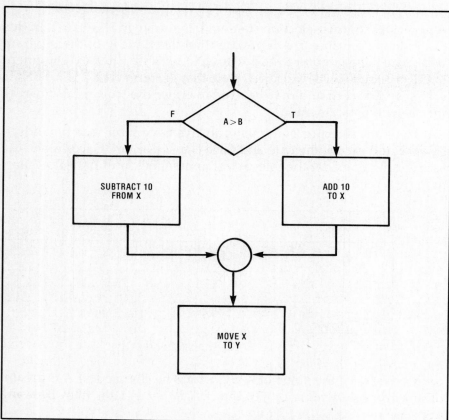

Figure 6-3. Flowchart showing two-way selection.

With these selection statements, the execution of program instructions can be controlled. The one-way selection, in effect, calls for only one alternate instruction or set of instructions before going on to the next command in sequence. The two-way selection mechanism permits execution of *either* of two alternative sets of instructions before resuming the normal sequence of execution.

In addition to controlling the sequence of execution for program instructions, computer-applied decisions are also used to check for the presence of as well as the validity, reasonableness, and accuracy of data items themselves. For example, in a payroll program, the existence of only alphabetic characters in the NAME field would indicate the presence of appropriate data. The presence of the Social Security number with a predetermined number of digits would be a validity check. A check for reasonableness of weekly wages would be written into a program. For example, in an hourly payroll, a limit such as $500 or $750 might be established as an amount not to be exceeded in any single week's paycheck.

Accuracy of the processing of data within programs is achieved through the checking of output records back to input. Control totals or balances are established for input records. These amounts can be established either by machines or by people. After processing, then, the totals developed by the computer are compared with these input controls. Both totals must match before processing can proceed.

COBOL Decision Making

Remember, the flowchart symbol for a program decision is a diamond. A flowchart segment showing use of the diamond symbol to represent a decision is presented in Figure 6-4. In terms of COBOL coding, a diamond is applied by invoking the IF instruction. The general format for an IF instruction is represented as:

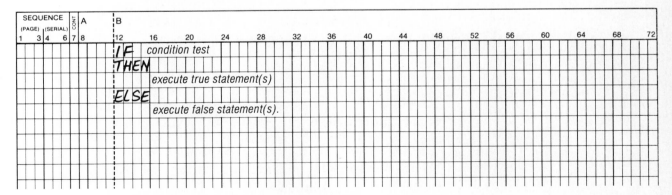

If the result of the comparison can be answered with either of the terms *true* or *yes*, the THEN branch is followed. This, in effect, indicates a positive result from the test. If the condition test is negative, the implied answer is *no* or *false*. A negative decision within the processing stream leads the program into the ELSE branch.

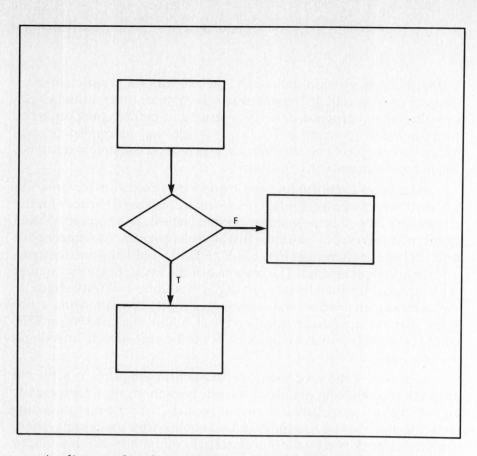

Figure 6-4. Flowchart showing use of decision symbol.

As discussed earlier, either the true or false clause might contain the NEXT SENTENCE clause. This is how one-way or two-way selection is accomplished. The reserved word NEXT SENTENCE causes execution of the program to continue at the instruction immediately following the period at the end of the IF sentence. When used, the NEXT SENTENCE clause must be the only instruction reference for that specific THEN or ELSE condition.

Using the IF instruction, several types, or categories, of computer-applied tests can be used to implement decisions within the processing of COBOL programs. These include:

- Relational tests
- Class tests
- Condition name tests
- Sign tests
- Multilevel (nested ''if'') tests
- Compound condition (AND/OR) tests.

Thus, computer decision making is relatively straightforward to invoke within the COBOL language. The challenge, the sophistication, and whatever complexity enters the picture, result from your application of simple principles.

Relational Tests

Relational tests are based upon logical comparisons of two items of data. The data items may be defined data fields (either alphanumeric or numeric), numeric constants, nonnumeric literals, or figurative constants. As a result of these comparisons, the computer can make one of six determinations about the relationship of the second item to the first item. The second item can be EQUAL TO, GREATER THAN, LESS THAN, NOT EQUAL TO, NOT GREATER THAN, or NOT LESS THAN the first item. The computer can sense any one of these conditions and apply THEN or ELSE options on the basis of condition tests.

For alphanumeric data, relational tests are made using the collating sequence values for each character to be compared. For instance, in Figure 6-2, the following data are compared:

> Let
> A = ''ABCD''
> B = ''ABMK''

The results of the decision will be false and the NEXT SENTENCE clause will be executed. In this example, fields A and B are compared starting with the leftmost character and proceeding rightward until the first unequal condition is sensed or the ends of the fields are reached. The collating sequence value of the first character in field A is compared to the collating sequence value of the character in the first position in B. These are equal. Next, the collating sequence values of the second characters in A and B are compared. They are also equal. When the values in the third position in each field are compared, the first unequal condition is sensed. The computer can now decide if the greater-than test condition is true or false. Since the collating sequence value of a ''C'' is not greater than the value for an ''M,'' the results are false. Thus, the false course is executed.

The IF comparison assumes that the two fields being compared are of the same size. If the sizes of the fields are unequal, the computer makes them equal for purposes of comparison, adding nonsignificant leading and trailing zeros to numeric fields and following blanks to alphanumeric fields.

Relational conditions for numeric data are determined by comparing the algebraic values of the data. The comparison operation aligns the two data items along their respective decimal points and then tests their algebraic values. If the data are not of the same length, nonsignificant zeros are added as needed to make them equal in length. Thus 125 would be compared as equal to 00125. Figure 6-5 shows examples of relational condition tests among numeric data.

Figure 6-6 illustrates implementation of relational tests in COBOL through use of the IF instruction. This instruction is entered in column 12 or beyond on COBOL coding sheets. The COBOL language permits

```
PROCEDURE DIVISION.
          .
          .
          .
IF WS-CURRENT-BALANCE LESS THAN WS-CREDIT-LIMIT
THEN
        PERFORM APPROVAL
ELSE
        PERFORM REJECT.
```

WS-CURRENT-BALANCE	PICTURE	WS-CREDIT-LIMIT	PICTURE	TEST RESULT	MODULE EXECUTED
+0398.55	S9(4)V99	+0500.00	S9)4)V99	TRUE	APPROVAL
+0760.00	S9)4)V99	+0500.00	S9)4)V99	FALSE	REJECT
−0136.73	S9)4)V99	+0500.00	S9)4)V99	TRUE	APPROVAL
+0500.00	S9)3)V99	+0500.00	S9)4)V99	FALSE	REJECT

Note: ˄ indicates implied decimal point.

Figure 6-5. Numeric relation tests.

the optional use of THEN and ELSE clauses as part of the IF instruction. It is recommended that these terms be presented as separate clauses, on individual lines. Further, it is recommended that these clauses be aligned with the IF verb.

In point of fact, the COBOL language does not always *require* use of THEN and ELSE clauses. Use of these clauses is recommended because they represent good structure habits for beginning programmers. Also, program maintenance or revision becomes infinitely easier if persons handling the tasks know automatically to look for certain clauses.

Optionally, however, it is possible to go directly from an IF instruction to a MOVE, PERFORM, or other COBOL statement. When the THEN clause does not appear in program coding, the compiler will automatically apply a default option. In other words, the clause following the IF condition test is assumed to be the true imperative. With the ELSE omitted, the compiler assumes that the NEXT SENTENCE is to be executed as the false imperative. Example:

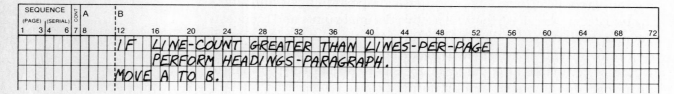

```
IF LINE-COUNT GREATER THAN LINES-PER-PAGE
    PERFORM HEADINGS-PARAGRAPH.
MOVE A TO B.
```

It is also possible, in some logical processing situations to perform tests for negative relationships. This involves use of a NOT clause in an IF command. This form of the command inserts the COBOL word NOT

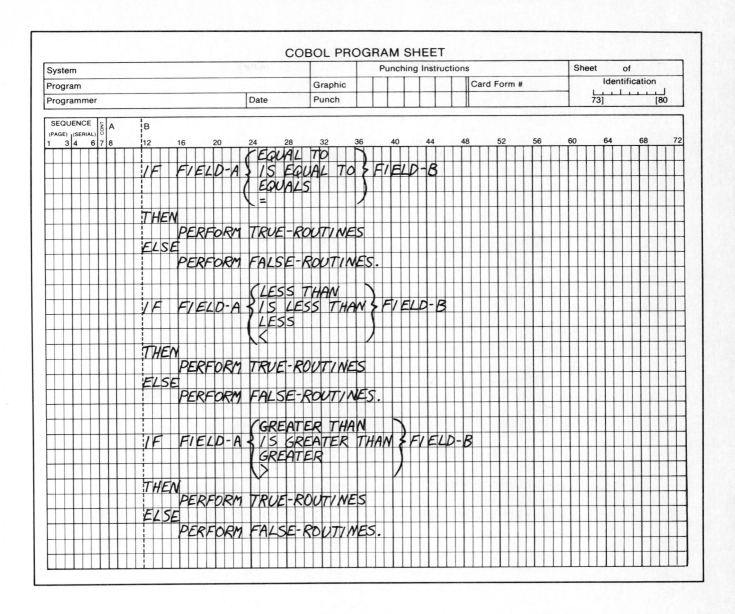

Figure 6-6. Relational tests.

before the condition test clause, as illustrated in Figure 6-7. The computer will then perform tests to determine whether the second item is NOT EQUAL TO, NOT GREATER THAN, or NOT LESS THAN the first item.

The potential use of the NOT clause depends upon the logic requirements of the program being prepared. The COBOL language does not provide a single symbol or term for the algebraic relationships "greater than or equal to ($\geq$)" or "less than or equal to ($\leq$)." Thus, suppose a programmer wants to test to determine if field X is less than or equal to 100. The statement IF X NOT GREATER THAN 100. . . would initiate this test. In such an instance, the IF. . .NOT statement would perform a valuable screening test.

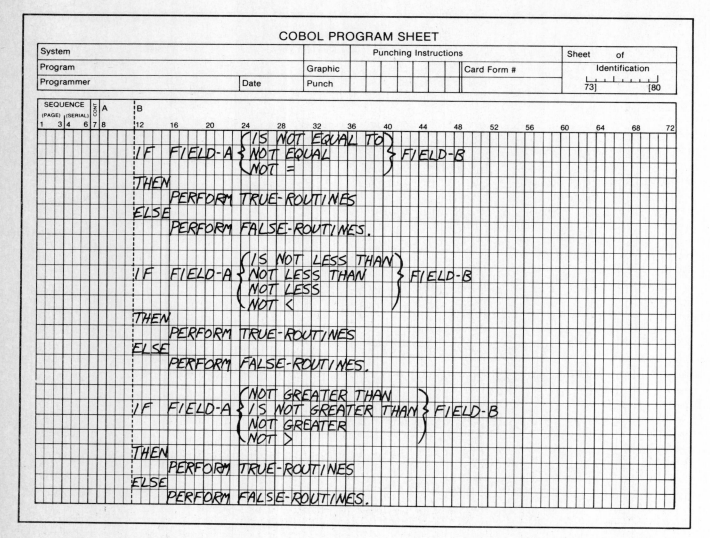

Figure 6-7. Relational tests using the NOT operator.

In writing statements covering relational conditions, it is good programming practice not to use the symbols for greater than (>), less than (<), or equal (=). It is preferable that these statements be spelled out. This is because some COBOL compilers do not accept the symbols. Programs in which the instructions are spelled out will be more transportable among systems and result in more readable, understandable programs.

Class Tests

Class tests perform control functions aimed at assuring the validity of data. It was explained earlier that the computer can perform tests to verify that a field contains numeric or alphabetic data, as appropriate. These tests are performed with an IF instruction.

To illustrate, an instruction can be written to indicate that IF the content of a field for Social Security number is all numeric, program controls should go to the PROCESS-RTN.

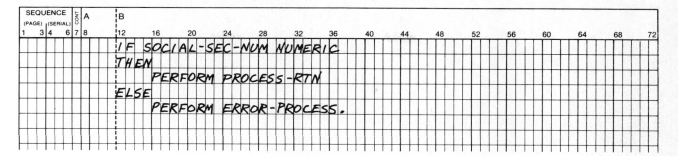

```
IF SOCIAL-SEC-NUM NUMERIC
THEN
        PERFORM PROCESS-RTN
ELSE
        PERFORM ERROR-PROCESS.
```

This same instruction would have an ELSE clause that could trigger an error message if any nonnumeric character appeared in the Social Security number field. Numeric tests will be valid for fields defined as PIC 9s or Xs. The test result will be true only for contents of the digits 0–9. Figure 6-8 presents examples of NUMERIC class tests. Observe the three examples with false results. These are false because of the presence of a blank, a decimal point, and the letter F, which are not numeric.

Similar tests could be made to validate that only alphabetic characters exist in specific fields. For an ALPHABETIC test to be valid, the data field must be defined with a PICTURE of Xs or As. The test will be true if the field contains only the letters A–Z or blank spaces. An example of an ALPHABETIC class test is given in Figure 6-9.

Figure 6-8. Numeric class tests.

```
005010 PROCEDURE DIVISION.
   020    .
   030    .
   040    .
   050 IF  INPUT-PRICE NUMERIC
   060 THEN    PERFORM CALCULATE-COST
   070
   080 ELSE
   090    PERFORM PRICE-ERROR.
```

INPUT-PRICE CONTENTS (PIC 99V99)	CLASS TEST RESULT	STATEMENT EXECUTED
45ˏ67	TRUE	CALCULATE-COST
8ˏ34	FALSE	PRICE-ERROR
08.34	FALSE	PRICE-ERROR
05ˏ1F	FALSE	PRICE-ERROR
00ˏ00	TRUE	CALCULATE-COST

Note: ˏ indicates implied decimal point.

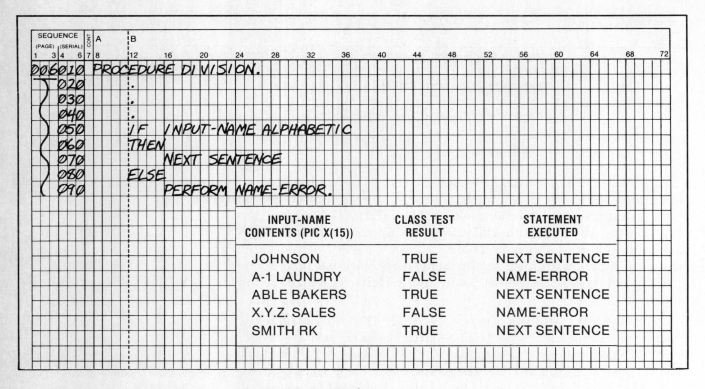

Figure 6-9. Alphabetic class tests.

Condition-Name Tests

The *condition-name condition (test)* is an alternative way of expressing a simple relational condition. The advantage of using condition-name conditions is that they can provide more descriptive documentation.

As an example, consider a personnel record that contains a field for marital status indicator. In the sample below, marital status is a one-digit number whose valid values are 1, 2, or 3. A value of 1 indicates a married person, 2 identifies a single person, and 3 means the individual declined to state a status.

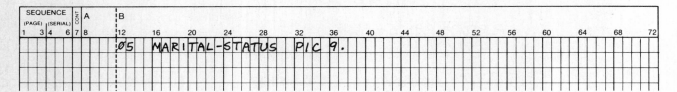

If a program required selection of records for married persons only, the COBOL instruction would be:

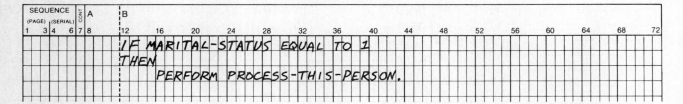

The COBOL program would work correctly. However, if, after several years of use, management decided to change marital status codes, someone would have to go through this program to make the necessary changes. With the IF statement written as above, a maintenance programmer might be hard pressed to remember that the marital status value of 1 is for married persons, not single individuals.

A more readable and more easily understood condition statement would be:

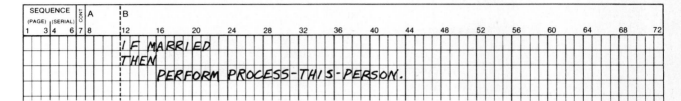

The program, of course, must have some way of knowing what the word MARRIED means. To establish meaning for MARRIED requires special entries in the DATA DIVISION. A new level number (88) must be introduced.

As described in Chapter 4, records are defined with 01 level numbers in the DATA DIVISION. Beneath an 01 record definition, individual fields may be defined at any level number, 2 through 49. The recommended practice, for purposes of this book, was to work in level number intervals of 5.

The level number 88 is used to define the name for a value of the elementary field immediately preceding it. Figure 6-10 shows an example of this. In this illustration, the level 88 entries define program-testable names for specific values of the one-digit MARITAL-STATUS

Figure 6-10. Conditional name definition.

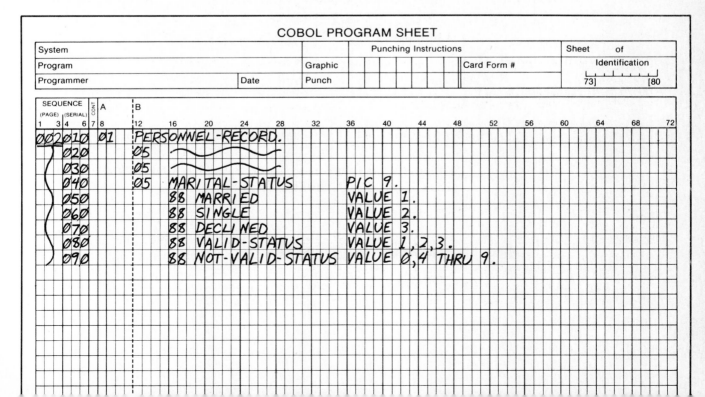

field. In the IF statement above, MARRIED would test as being "true" only if the contents of the MARITAL-STATUS field is a 1. Thus, the VALUE clause in a level 88 entry defines the value for which the condition named will be true.

As shown in Figure 6-10, the VALUE clause of a level 88 entry may contain one value, a range of values, or specific multiple values. The word THRU may also be spelled THROUGH and is used to define a range of values for the condition name. Level 88 entries and the associated value clause may be used in either the WORKING-STORAGE or FILE SECTIONS of the DATA DIVISION.

Any of the condition names defined with level 88 entries may be used in COBOL condition statements. Also, the term NOT may precede the condition name in a condition instruction. This is illustrated in Figure 6-11.

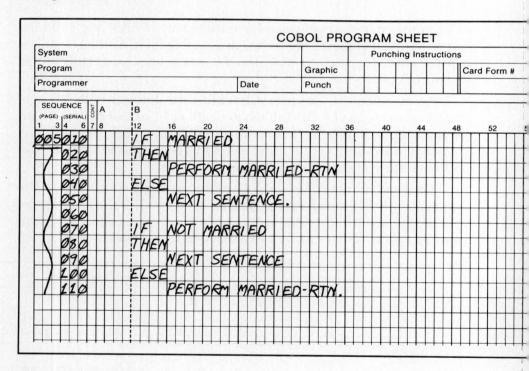

Figure 6-11. Negative condition name tests.

Sign Conditions

Sign tests are applied to signed numeric fields only, as shown below. The conditions that can be encompassed in sign tests are POSITIVE, NEGATIVE, ZERO, and the NOT of each.

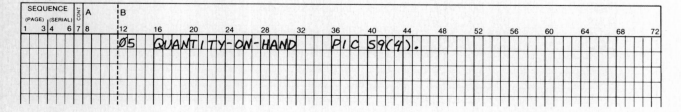

Note that the words for these conditions are used rather than the signs. This is part of the philosophy of the COBOL language—to make COBOL statements as close as possible to English sentences.

Sign tests are applied through IF. . .THEN. . .ELSE instructions, as shown in Figure 6-12. In effect, the computer is told that IF a numeric field has the specified algebraic sign, THEN a stated processing course is followed, ELSE an alternative action is taken.

The test for a value of ZERO is a special case. It is a unique value and is neither positive nor negative. Figure 6-13 presents an example of the results of a sign test.

Multilevel (Nested IF) Tests

The COBOL language permits *multilevel* use of IF. . .THEN. . .ELSE statements in one sentence. Illustrations offered up to this point have involved a single, conditional test. However, as you gain experience

Figure 6-12. General sign tests.

COBOL PROGRAM SHEET

System		Punching Instructions		Sheet of
Program		Graphic		Identification
Programmer	Date	Punch		73] [80

```
005010    IF AMOUNT IS NEGATIVE
   020    THEN
   030        MOVE "CR" TO SIGN-AREA
   040    ELSE
   050        MOVE SPACE TO SIGN-AREA.
   060
   070    IF QUANTITY IS ZERO
   080    THEN
   090        MOVE SPACE TO PRINT-AREA
   100    ELSE
   110        NEXT SENTENCE.
   120
   130    IF COUNT IS POSITIVE
   140    THEN
   150        MOVE COUNT TO FIELD-A
   160    ELSE
   170        MOVE COUNT TO FIELD-B.
   180
   190    IF AMOUNT IS NOT NEGATIVE
   200    THEN
   210        MOVE SPACE TO SIGN-AREA
   220    ELSE
   230        MOVE "CR" TO SIGN-AREA.
```

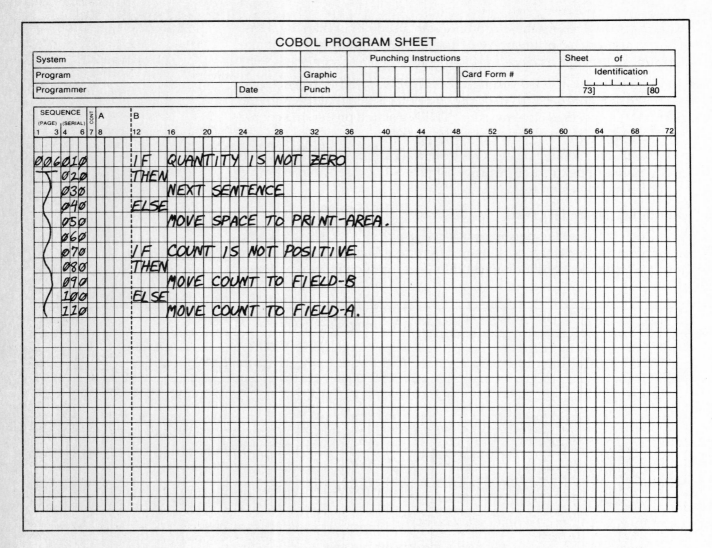

COBOL PROGRAM SHEET		

System

Program

Programmer

Punching Instructions

Graphic

Punch

Card Form #

Sheet   of

Identification

```
006010    IF QUANTITY IS NOT ZERO
   020    THEN
   030        NEXT SENTENCE
   040    ELSE
   050        MOVE SPACE TO PRINT-AREA.
   060
   070    IF COUNT IS NOT POSITIVE
   080    THEN
   090        MOVE COUNT TO FIELD-B
   100    ELSE
   110        MOVE COUNT TO FIELD-A.
```

Figure 6-12. Continued.

in the application of computer logic, and also as you move on to more complex programs, you will find situations in which it makes sense to apply these logical tests on a series basis. In thinking about these possibilities, always bear one rule in mind: multiple IF statements in a sentence must be *nested*. Nesting occurs when an IF instruction is invoked by the THEN or ELSE clauses of another IF instruction. Each level must represent a complete IF. . .THEN. . .ELSE statement.

To illustrate this method of nesting, consider the payroll example in Figure 6-13. The first level of IF tests would be to determine whether HOURS-WORKED are GREATER THAN 40. If the HOURS-WORKED are not GREATER THAN 40, the program would continue processing at the statement following the period at the end of the nested IF sentence. IF the value of HOURS-WORKED is GREATER THAN 40, THEN a test could be performed to determine whether the SALARY-CODE is a 2, indicating a supervision status. IF the record shows the

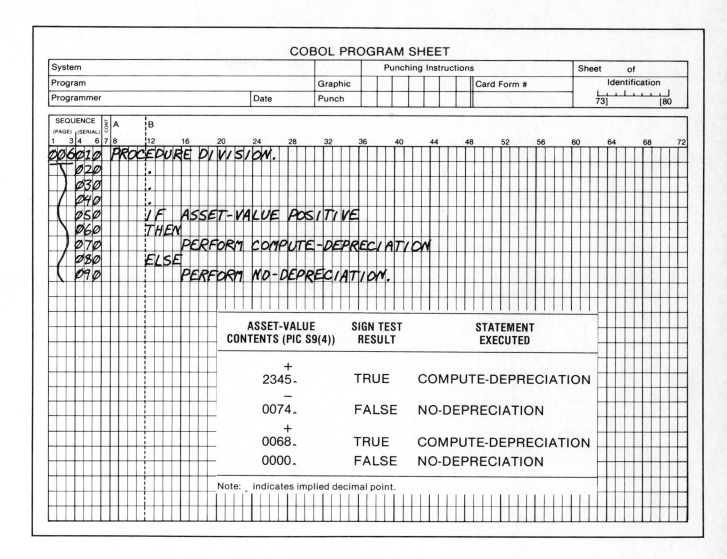

Figure 6-13. Sign tests.

worker is a supervisor, THEN the NEXT SENTENCE clause would point to continued processing, ELSE the OVERTIME-RTN will execute.

Figure 6-14 is a segment of a structured flowchart for this instruction. This illustrates an important point: complexity of processing increases with the complexity of logic.

As indicated in these examples, nested IF statements are basically IFs within IFs, terminated by a single period at the end of the sentence. Understanding the relationships among multiple IFs, ELSEs, and THENs can be difficult. To aid in understanding nested IF statements, indentation is almost always used. Notice the indenting used in the example in Figure 6-14. Each IF. . . THEN. . .ELSE statement is indented from the one preceding. A general model for this approach is shown in Figure 6-15.

Observe that every IF condition includes complete THEN. . .ELSE clauses. This assures proper interpretation by the COBOL compiler and

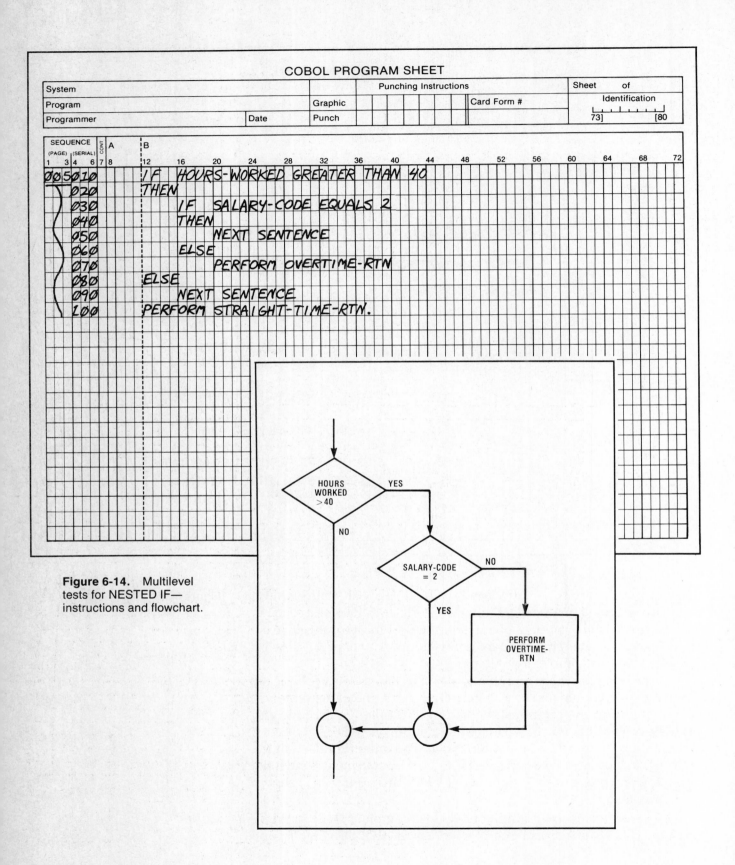

Figure 6-14. Multilevel tests for NESTED IF— instructions and flowchart.

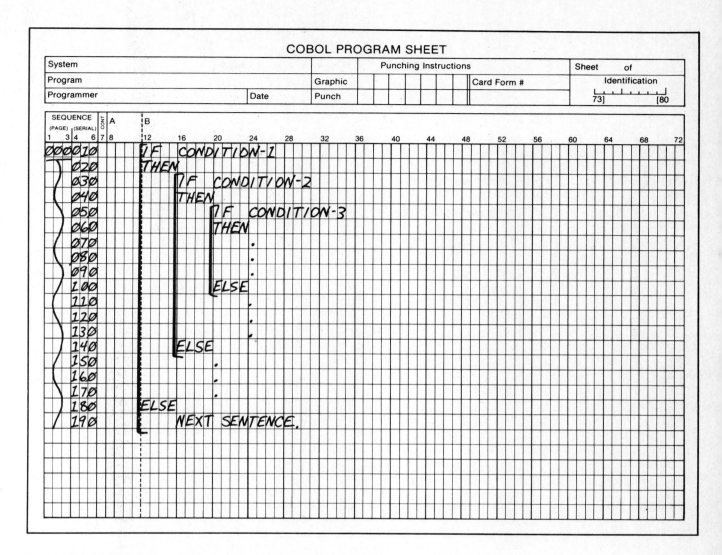

Figure 6-15. Instructions for IFs nested on the true result of a condition test.

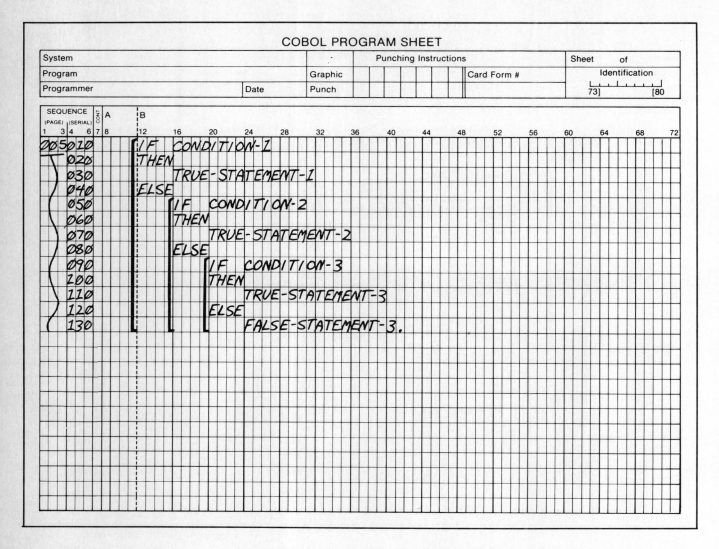

Figure 6-16. Instructions for IFs nested on the false result of a condition test.

represents a good programming practice. In this illustration, the IF clauses are nested on the true part of the preceding IF.

Nesting may also be done on the false part of IF statements, as illustrated in Figure 6-16. The brackets in this example indicate each complete set of IF...THEN...ELSE clauses. Note particularly that there is only one period at the end of the whole nested IF structure. A misplaced period would significantly alter the results of processing. Such errors are often difficult to detect.

In each of these examples, only two or three IF statements are nested. Complexity in understanding and debugging increase rapidly as more IF statements are included. You should generally try to limit the number of nested IF statements to three or four. This will greatly increase your probability of error-free programs.

The nested IF statement is also of special interest in structured COBOL because it represents a convenient method of implementing the structured programming *case construct*. A case construct is a selection mechanism used for controlling the selection of one from among two or more alternative paths of execution. For example, refer back to Figure 6-9, which illustrates the MARITAL-STATUS code value. Program requirements are amended to require the printing of counts of the number of persons within each marital status group and also to print the name of any employee record that has an invalid marital status code. It is necessary, therefore, to have four different procedures that can be executed on the basis of data value in the MARITAL-STATUS field. Condition name entries have already been defined for these values. The COBOL instructions to implement the case construct are:

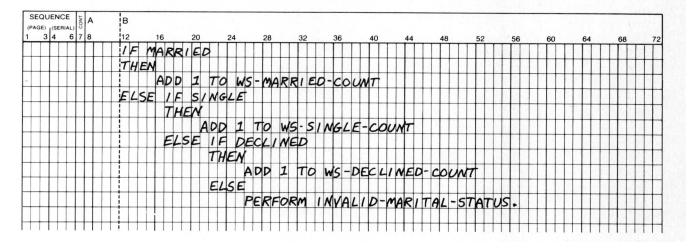

Thus, the nested IF statement has many uses and offers considerable programming flexibility. However, be careful to follow good programming practices whenever you must use nested IF instructions.

Compound Conditional (AND/OR) Tests

Nested IF statements check for multiple conditions dependent upon one another. *Compound conditional* statements, on the other hand, check for relationships among independent data conditions. In effect, these statements make it possible to check for relationships among two or more conditions as a basis for selecting a processing function.

For example, suppose a company wanted to use a computer to check personnel files to identify promotable people. One set of conditions might be that the person have two years of experience with the company AND a college degree as an educational level (level 16). As an alternative (the OR clause), persons might be considered promotable if they had seven years of experience with the company AND two years of college (level 14).

The instruction to execute this review of data, along with its corresponding structured flowchart, is shown in Figure 6-17.

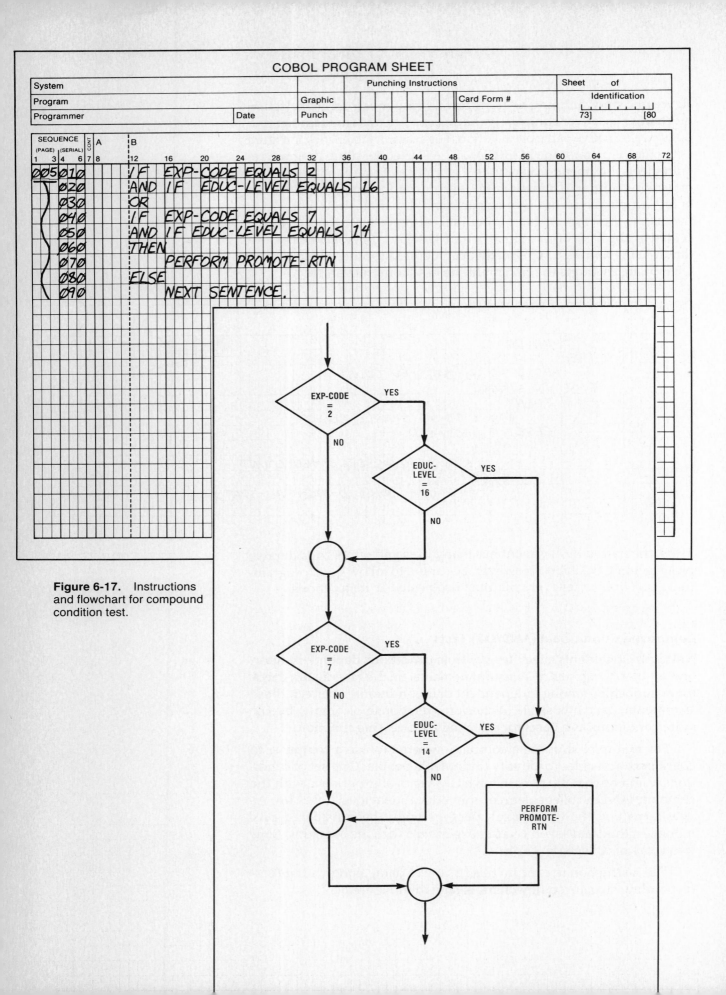

Figure 6-17. Instructions and flowchart for compound condition test.

There is a difference, which must be understood, between the AND and the OR clauses. These clauses serve as *logical operators* that connect two separate conditions. When an AND clause connects two conditions, *both* conditions must be true simultaneously for the true statement to be executed. If either of the two conditions is not true, the false part of the statement will execute.

The OR clause connects conditions so that, each time *either* of the conditions is true, the computer will execute the true statement. When both are false, the combined condition is false.

A compound conditional statement may have any number of *AND/OR* clauses. This simply increases the selection criteria, presumably reducing the number of records that qualify with application of each conditional test. However, the use of multiple conditions connected by AND/OR operators results in a very complex statement that can be extremely difficult to understand and debug. Consider this example:

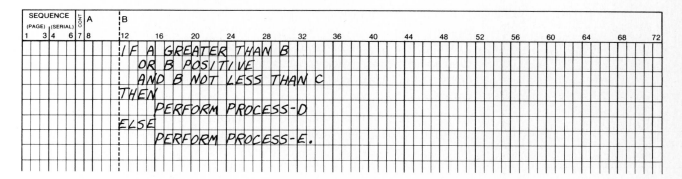

This statement does not give a clear indication of the order in which each condition will be tested. Also, it is not clear whether the first two conditions are in an OR relationship only, or that the first condition is in an OR relationship with the AND relationship between B POSITIVE and B NOT LESS THAN C. COBOL compilers evaluate AND conditions first (left to right), and then evaluate OR conditions (left to right).

Parentheses are permitted in compound condition statements to remove ambiguity, to clarify processing, or to change the normal evaluation sequence. The example below shows the effect of parentheses upon the order of evaluation of the condition.

In this example, the parentheses cause the conditions A GREATER THAN B OR B POSITIVE to be evaluated first. If one of these is true, the AND test is made.

In the example without parentheses, the B POSITIVE AND B NOT LESS THAN C conditions would be tested first. If both are true simultaneously, the program will PERFORM PROCESS-D. If the AND relationship is not true, the A GREATER THAN B relationship would be tested and, if true, PROCESS-D would execute. The PROCESS-E would execute when all three relationships are false.

In summary, if you must write a compound conditional sentence, you should limit the number of AND/OR clauses, simplifying your statement. It is preferable to use multiple, simple sentences to writing long complex statements. Also be sure to use parentheses when they can help you make the meaning of your statements clear.

REPETITIONS IN PROGRAMS

Much of the real power of a computer lies in its ability to repeat operations, over and over, in exactly the same way, until it is told by the program to do something else. The computer does not get bored, distracted, or lose track of what it is doing. Literally millions of records can be acted upon within programs as a result of repeated processing functions.

To illustrate this capability—and also to cause *repetition* to happen within a COBOL program—you can begin by using two key instructions:

- PERFORM
- PERFORM...UNTIL

The PERFORM Command

PERFORM, by itself, is a *sequence control* instruction. That is, it is used within a sequential processing routine to cause a different, or special, set of instructions to be executed at a specific point in the program. All programs, as explained earlier, have an underlying sequence that runs from beginning to end, input to output. Within the established sequence, however, it is sometimes necessary to invoke special processing functions, or modules.

To break out of the straight-line sequence within a program, the PERFORM command uses an *identifier* to tell the computer what to do next. The identifier is the name of a different paragraph or module to which the program will transfer control, or branch, and return following its execution. Thus, the sequence of execution within the program has been altered.

To illustrate, consider the overtime pay example that has been cited in Figure 6-18. A series of records identifying employees and giving the hours worked during the week is presented to the computer for processing. The program is basically sequential. For each employee, the

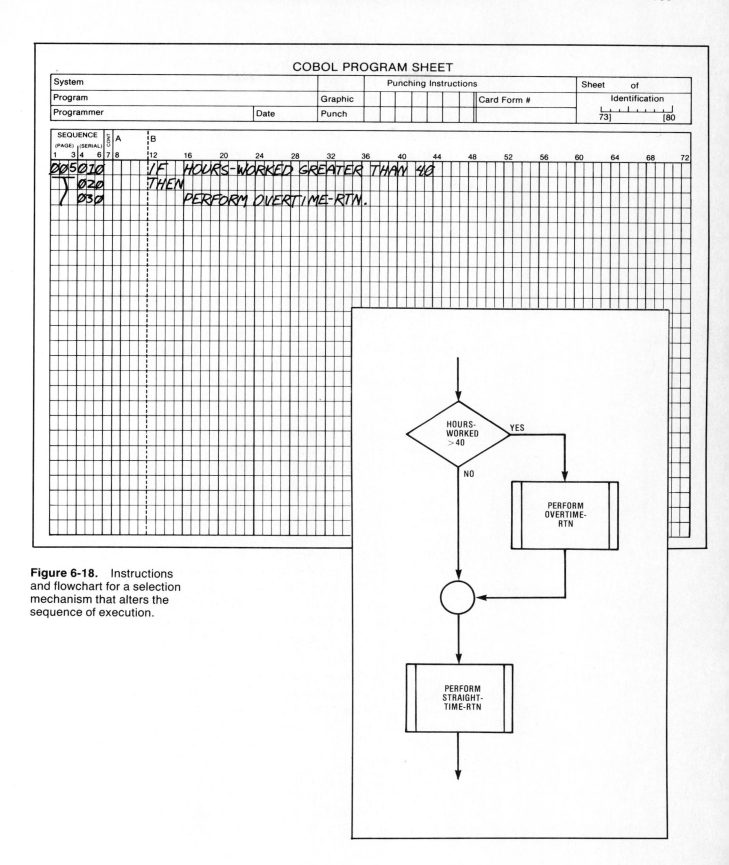

Figure 6-18. Instructions and flowchart for a selection mechanism that alters the sequence of execution.

computer multiplies hours worked by pay rate, computes taxes, determines deductions, computes net pay, then prints a payroll report. The only condition that alters the processing sequence occurs when the HOURS-WORKED field has a value GREATER THAN 40.

The number of hours worked, then, represents the potential condition for changing the sequence of execution. Thus, every record input to the program is put through a test to determine whether the value of HOURS-WORKED is greater than 40. When a value greater than 40 is sensed, a PERFORM command is executed to transfer control to a routine that computes the value of overtime hours. After completing the calculation, control is returned to the instruction following the PERFORM statement.

Subroutines.   The module or paragraph to which control is transferred by a PERFORM statement is sometimes called a *subroutine*. A subroutine is a sequence of instructions that causes a specific processing function or activity to be executed. In many cases, the same set of instructions will be required for execution in different parts of the program. It is an efficient practice to group these common instructions into paragraphs that can be invoked through a PERFORM command. A subroutine has some basic characteristics that are important to business data processing programs. For one thing, a subroutine represents a change from, or branch in, the main sequential processing stream of a program. Another characteristic is that a subroutine is self-contained and can, therefore, be positioned anywhere in a program. Control will be transferred to whatever procedure name is identified in the PERFORM instruction.

Because of the ability to reside anywhere within a set of program instructions, subroutines offer considerable flexibility in program development. A trend is well under way to increase the use of subroutines for general application within business programs. Proponents of this line of thinking see the day when the majority of programs will consist of a collection of subroutines that can be called up from a library and incorporated in programs under development. Thus, the main processing stream of any given program would be a short series of instructions that would invoke each subroutine as needed.

Under this line of thinking, the term *subroutine* is often used interchangeably with the word *module*. A module, as defined earlier, is any segment of a program that can be defined as a box within a structure chart. In effect, available, appropriate subroutines, or modules, can be "plugged into" structure charts. Then, their coding is picked up and incorporated, with only the identifiers changed, into COBOL programs.

The PERFORM. . .UNTIL Command

The PERFORM. . .UNTIL command causes the computer to execute a program *loop*. A loop is a sequence of repetitious processing. That is, the computer performs the same set of instructions continuously—until a conditional test is met. This condition, in turn, causes the program to *exit the loop* and transfer processing to the next instruction in sequence in the program.

The logic of a processing loop is shown graphically in Figure 6-19, which is a segment of a structured flowchart illustrating execution of a loop. In general literature on programming, two terms are used to describe types of loops. They are the DOWHILE loop and the DO-UNTIL loop. This flowchart is an example of the DOWHILE loop structure and is implemented in COBOL with the PERFORM. . .UNTIL statement. The DOUNTIL loop is not implemented directly in COBOL.

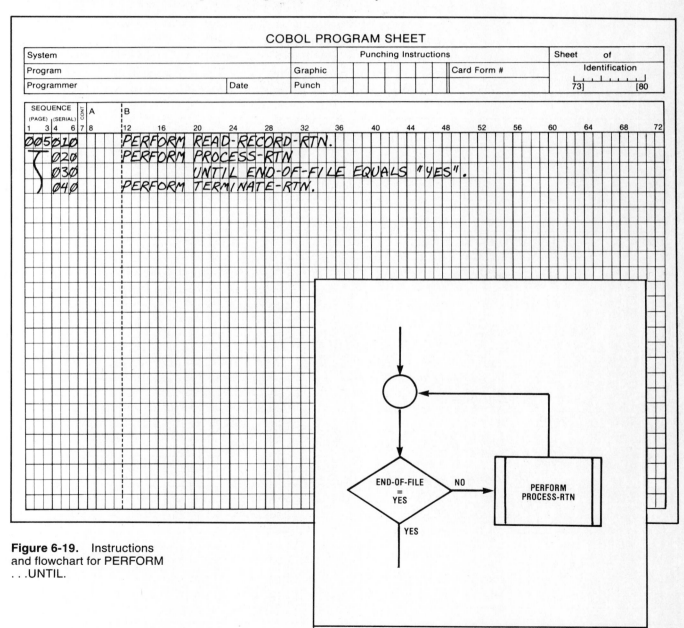

Figure 6-19. Instructions and flowchart for PERFORM . . .UNTIL.

Figure 6-19 also shows the instructions for this processing loop. This illustration shows a portion of a report-generation program. The program simply reads each input record in sequence, testing every one for an end-of-file condition, then processes each record. When an end-of-file condition is sensed, the program exits the processing loop and begins executing its termination procedures.

It is also possible to devise programs that perform loops within loops. Instructions for such a program are given in Figure 6-20. This program could be used for a commercial billing (invoicing) application such as those conducted by credit card plans. The file contains billing items, organized by customer number, for a specific period. The program reads billing items and includes them in the invoice for each customer, executed under the PERFORM WRITE-INVOICE-DETAIL statement. Thus, the basic loop involves reading and printing data records. When a condition test identifies a change in customer number, control is turned over to another processing loop, which causes the

Figure 6-20. Instructions for a loop within a loop.

COBOL PROGRAM SHEET

System	Punching Instructions		Sheet of
Program	Graphic	Card Form #	Identification 73] [80
Programmer Date	Punch		

```
006010     PERFORM READ-RTN.
   020     PERFORM PRODUCE-INVOICES
   030                 UNTIL    END-OF-FILE EQUALS "YES".
   040     PERFORM TERMINATE-RTN.
   050
   060
   070 PRODUCE-INVOICES.
   080     PERFORM WRITE-INVOICE-DETAIL
   090                 UNTIL CUST-NUM GREATER THAN PREV-CUST-NUM.
   100     PERFORM TOTAL-THE-INVOICE.
   110
   120 WRITE-INVOICE-DETAIL.
   130     READ INVOICE-FILE
   140          AT END MOVE "YES" TO WS-EOF-FLAG.
   150     IF  WS-EOF-FLAG EQUALS "NO"
   160     THEN
   170          PERFORM SET-UP-INVOICE-LINE
   180     ELSE
   190          NEXT SENTENCE.
   200 TOTAL-THE-INVOICE.
   210     .
   220     .
   230     .
```

computer to compute and print sales tax and to total the invoice. Following completion of the invoice, control reverts back to the first loop, which continues the reading of data records from the input file.

This example points to a basic characteristic of processing loops. That is, a condition test is included in the procedures for the processing of each record handled within a loop. Further, this test is performed *before the processing is executed,* as a condition on whether to complete the processing or to exit the loop. Since the condition is tested first, the programmer must be careful to initialize the terminating condition to the ''off'' status before entering the loop control command for the first time.

COUNTERS AND ACCUMULATORS

Counters and accumulators are independent data fields set aside in WORKING-STORAGE. These areas are commonly used to support instruction sequence control and also to hold accumulated totals needed for program execution. Example:

```
WORKING-STORAGE SECTION.

01   PRINT-VARIABLES.
     05    LINE-COUNT               PIC 99   VALUE ZERO.
     05    LINES-PER-PAGE           PIC 99   VALUE 56.

PROCEDURE DIVISION.
     .
     .
     .
     IF LINE-COUNT GREATER THAN LINES-PER-PAGE
     THEN
          PERFORM PRINT-HEADINGS.
```

A *counter* is an area of main memory in which a consecutive count is maintained. When a count field is *incremented,* a value of 1 is added for each operation performed. Thus, if the computer was keeping a count of employee records processed in a payroll, each of the records handled would cause the counter to increment by 1. This use of a counter is illustrated in Figure 6-21.

Reporting applications also use the incrementing capability of counters. In the example above, a value for the number of lines on a given report page is entered at the outset. Then, as each line is printed, the count of lines is incremented by 1. When the total count of lines is GREATER THAN the number of lines per page, a condition test causes the transfer of control to a PRINT-HEADINGS routine.

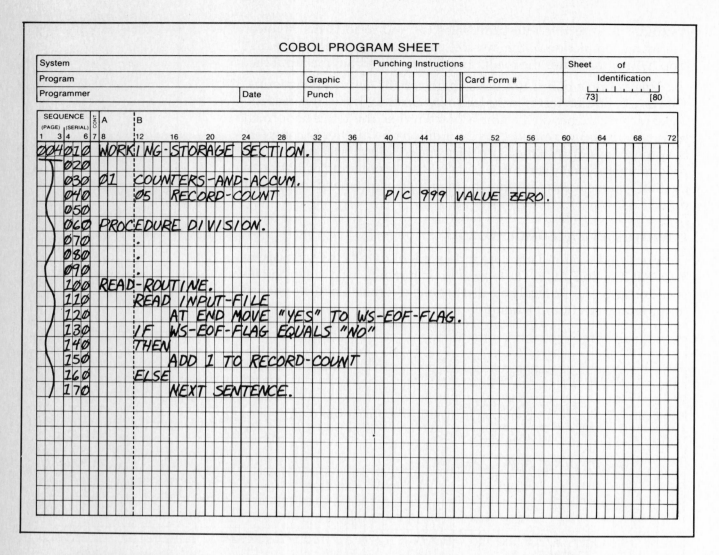

Figure 6-21. Instructions showing use of a counter.

An *accumulator* is a field that retains calculated totals. In effect, the accumulator builds figures representing total values for quantitative fields processed.

One common application using accumulation is the building of running totals for sets of data. For example, in writing invoices, charges for the values of successive purchase items are added together. When the last sales item has been processed, the accumulated total for all charges is printed as a subtotal for the invoice. Taxes can then be computed and added into the same accumulator to arrive at the total amount for the invoice, as shown in Figure 6-22.

As required by individual applications, WORKING-STORAGE entries in the DATA DIVISION can be made that will set up multiple accumulators for a single processing job. For example, a company might want to keep track of total values for all invoices issued, as well as for each invoice. This would require use of two accumulators. If a separate

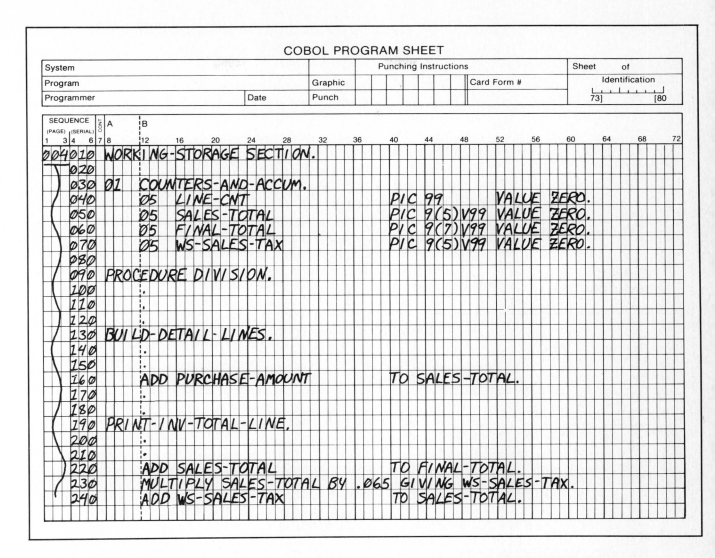

```
COBOL PROGRAM SHEET

System
Program                                          Graphic                Card Form #
Programmer              Date                      Punch

004010  WORKING-STORAGE SECTION.
   020
   030  01  COUNTERS-AND-ACCUM.
   040      05    LINE-CNT          PIC 99      VALUE ZERO.
   050      05    SALES-TOTAL       PIC 9(5)V99 VALUE ZERO.
   060      05    FINAL-TOTAL       PIC 9(7)V99 VALUE ZERO.
   070      05  WS-SALES-TAX        PIC 9(5)V99 VALUE ZERO.
   080
   090  PROCEDURE DIVISION.
   100      .
   110      .
   120      .
   130  BUILD-DETAIL-LINES.
   140      .
   150      .
   160      ADD PURCHASE-AMOUNT          TO SALES-TOTAL.
   170      .
   180      .
   190  PRINT-INV-TOTAL-LINE.
   200      .
   210      .
   220      ADD SALES-TOTAL              TO FINAL-TOTAL.
   230      MULTIPLY SALES-TOTAL BY .065 GIVING WS-SALES-TAX.
   240      ADD WS-SALES-TAX             TO SALES-TOTAL.
```

Figure 6-22. Instructions showing use of an accumulator.

total were needed for taxes collected, a third accumulator could be designated.

An important requirement for the use of accumulators and counters is that, before the first data values are added to them, they must be set to zero. If this is not done, new values will simply add to those already existing in the accumulator area of memory. Thus, as shown in Figures 6-21 and 6-22, the fields are initialized to zero with the VALUE ZERO clause.

FLAGS AND SWITCHES

Flags and switches are signal or control fields identified within programs as a basis for a condition test. The sensing of a flag or switch value affects the processing stream of a program, sometimes causing a transfer of control among modules. The functions of flags and switches are basically the same.

A *flag* or *switch* is a data field containing fixed information inserted by the programmer. The value of the flag is then tested by a conditional statement.

Generally speaking, simple on-off conditions are used as switches. Alternately, individual numbers or letters can be used. For example, the values M and F can be used to designate records for males or females. The values Y and N can be used to designate yes and no; T and F can be used to represent true or false. Condition tests can then be written to respond to the switches. For example, in a payroll application such as that illustrated in Figure 6-23, the value of 1 in the EMP-STATUS-CODE field could be used as a flag to identify active employees. The value 0 would then identify inactive employees. It is necessary to carry inactive employee records until at least the end of the year, when earning statements are issued. However, the company would certainly not want to issue paychecks for inactive employees. This flag acts as a processing control.

Figure 6-23. Instructions showing use of flags.

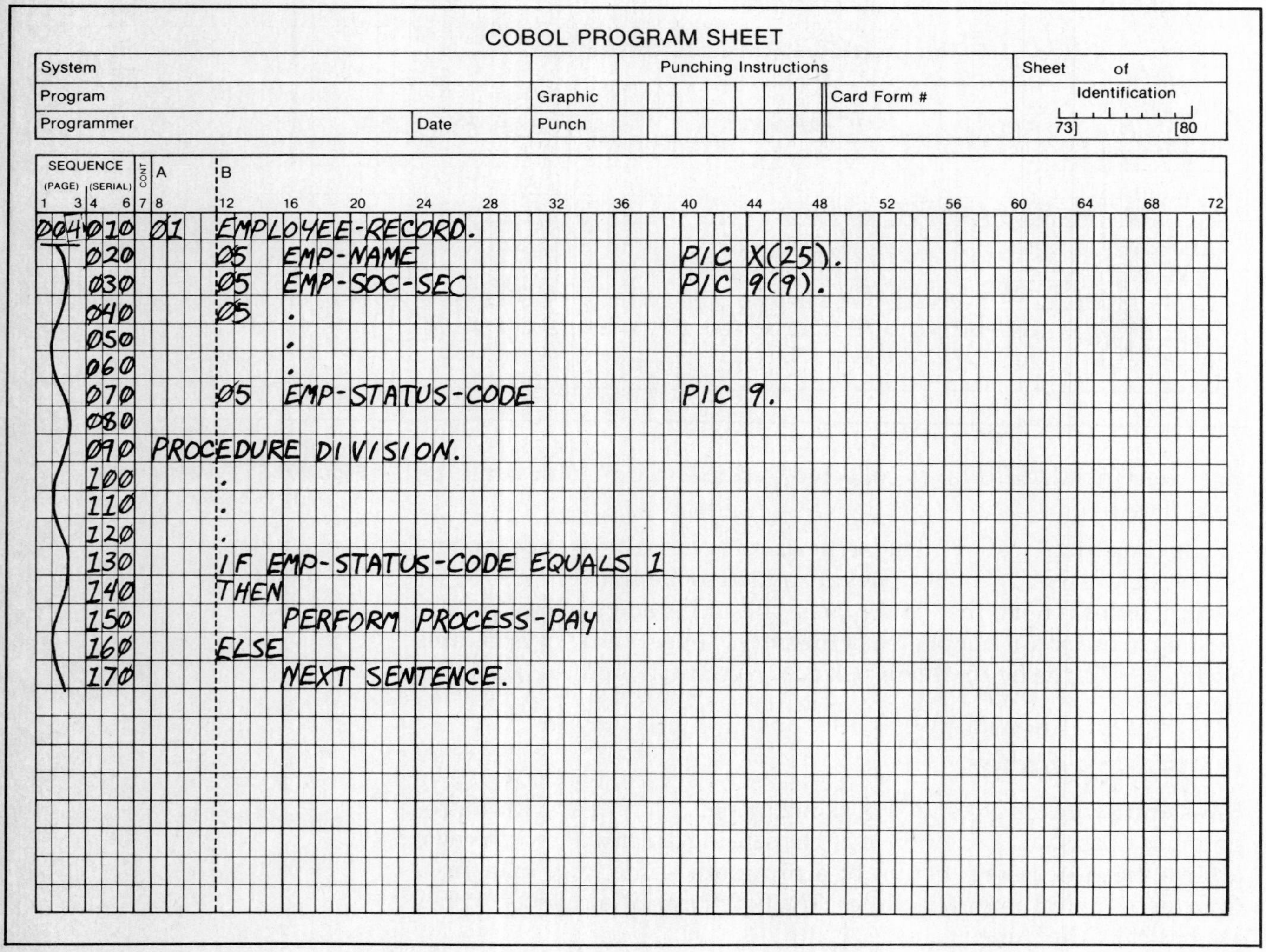
COBOL PROGRAM SHEET

System | Punching Instructions | Sheet of
Program | Graphic | Card Form # | Identification
Programmer | Date | Punch | 73] [80

SEQUENCE (PAGE) (SERIAL) | CONT | A | B

```
ØØ4Ø1Ø Ø1  EMPLOYEE-RECORD.
   Ø2Ø         Ø5  EMP-NAME                  PIC X(25).
   Ø3Ø         Ø5  EMP-SOC-SEC               PIC 9(9).
   Ø4Ø         Ø5    .
   Ø5Ø               .
   Ø6Ø               .
   Ø7Ø         Ø5  EMP-STATUS-CODE           PIC 9.
   Ø8Ø
   Ø9Ø PROCEDURE DIVISION.
   1ØØ         .
   11Ø         .
   12Ø         .
   13Ø         IF EMP-STATUS-CODE EQUALS 1
   14Ø         THEN
   15Ø                 PERFORM PROCESS-PAY
   16Ø         ELSE
   17Ø                 NEXT SENTENCE.
```

Another common example of the use of flags or switches is in the control of the main processing loop of a program. For example:

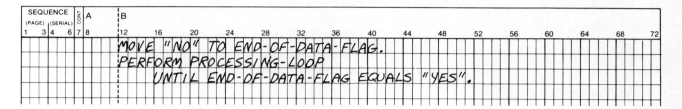

A READ command like that below would commonly be used to set the flag to "YES," thus terminating the processing loop.

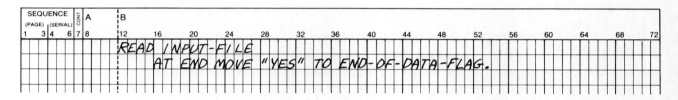

Summary

All computer decision making is based on the results of data comparisons. Values used in data comparisons are based on a series of assigned values for symbols, letters, and numbers. These values are known as the collating sequence. [*Objective No. 1.*]

In individual programs, the actual sequence of processing can be controlled or directed on the basis of tests applied to the content of data items. Programming constructs that can be used to change the normal sequence of execution are selection and repetition. [*Objective No. 2.*]

The selection, or case, construct for controlling program instruction execution is implemented in COBOL with the IF statement. A number of conditions (or selection tests) can be expressed with an IF statement. [*Objective No. 3.*]

Relational condition tests are applied to data items to determine whether one is GREATER THAN, EQUAL TO, or LESS THAN the other. Numeric items are compared on their albegraic values. Alphanumeric data are compared using the collating sequence value of the characters in each item.

Class condition tests may be made to determine if a data item contains only NUMERIC digits or ALPHABETIC characters.

Sign conditions are used to test whether a numeric data field contains algebraic signs, either POSITIVE or NEGATIVE, or whether the field is ZERO.

Key Terms

1. computer decision making
2. collating sequence
3. relational test
4. class test
5. condition name test
6. sign test
7. nested IF test
8. case construct
9. compound conditional
10. AND/OR test
11. logical operator
12. repetition
13. sequence control
14. identifier
15. subroutine
16. module
17. loop
18. exit a loop
19. counter
20. increment
21. accumulator
22. flag
23. switch

Condition name tests are alternative ways of writing relation tests using specially defined, level 88 entries in the DATA DIVISION. A level 88 entry defines a name of the condition for a specific data value.

Multiple conditions can be written in the same IF statement. Two methods are available. Multiple simple conditions can be combined using the logical operators AND or OR. Multiple conditions may also be incorporated in nested IF statements.

In addition to controlling the execution of paths of logic in a program (selection and case), the IF statement plays an important role in helping to validate the accuracy and completeness of data. This validation or editing operation looks at the data from a qualitative viewpoint. [*Objective No. 4.*]

The other important sequence control construct in programs is repetition. The COBOL command PERFORM. . .UNTIL. . . is used to implement the DOWHILE type of loop. In this loop structure, the terminating condition is tested before the procedure named is executed. The PERFORM command is also used as the basis for calling and initiating processing under subroutines. Subroutines make it possible to reuse often-needed program segments conveniently. [*Objectives Nos. 5 and 6.*]

Flags, switches, counters, and accumulators are independent data fields defined in WORKING-STORAGE. These independent data fields are not part of specific input or output records. However, they do play an important role in controlling procedures, holding counts of items processed, and storing totals of important data fields for summary purposes. [*Objective No. 7.*]

Review/Discussion Questions

1. What is a collating sequence and how can this sequence affect program execution?

2. What is the normal ASCII character collating sequence for a blank space, special characters, uppercase alphabetic characters, and numbers?

3. What is a case construct and how is this technique used within COBOL programs?

4. How are computer decision-making techniques used to check for validity, reasonableness, and accuracy of data items?

5. What are relational tests?

6. What are class tests?

7. What are condition name tests? In what situations are they used and what advantages do they offer?

8. What are sign tests?

9. What are nested IF statements and how may they be used in computer decision making?

10. What are the characteristics of AND/OR tests?

11. What is repetition and how is this function controlled in COBOL?

12. What are the differences in application situations that would call for use of the PERFORM and PERFORM. . . UNTIL commands?

13. What is a subroutine and how are subroutines commonly used in COBOL programs?

14. What are the common uses for counters and accumulators within COBOL programs?

Programming Assignments

Two programming assignments are given below. Following directions of your instructor or your own feelings about how much practice you can use, complete either or both of these assignments. For each assignment, make sure all of the following tasks are completed:

1. Prepare or complete a structure or module hierarchy chart.

2. Prepare or complete documentation of processing logic with structured flowcharts *and* pseudocode.

3. Define sample data to be used to test your program logic and prepare expected results for that data.

4. Conduct a walkthrough of your program structure and logical design. Do this by yourself, under guidance of your instructor, or in cooperation with a fellow student.

5. Write, compile, test, and debug the program you have designed.

Problem 1

Purpose: The credit manager of SELLALL Company has requested a report on the current account balances for all customers. In addition to presenting customer balances, the report should indicate separate total balances for all retail and wholesale customer types.

Input: Use the record description for Problem 1 in Chapter 5.

Output: Prepare a report that conforms to the format in Figure 6-24.

Processing Requirements: 1) For each input record, print one detail line, single spaced.

2) If customer type is RE, add account balance to an accumulator for total retail balances.

3) If customer type is WH, add account balance to an accumulator for total wholesale balances.

4) Add every account balance to a grand total.

5) Print headings as specified on the report layout.

6) At the end of input, print the three specified totals.

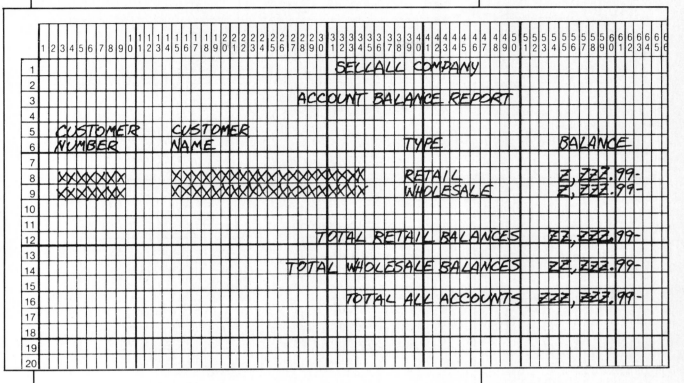

Figure 6-24. Output report layout for account balance report. For use in practice assignment.

Problem 2

Purpose: This program is to produce a product sales report for management.

Input: Prepare a file of approximately 10 data records that conform to the format in Figure 6-25.

Output: Print a sales report that conforms to the format shown in Figure 6-26.

Processing Requirements: 1) Print one detail line per input record.

2) Calculate discount amount (quantity × discount rate).

3) The discount rate depends upon the quantity ordered. The discount schedule is as follows:

Quantity Ordered	Discount Rate
0–99	3%
100–399	4%
400–699	5%
700–or more	6%

202

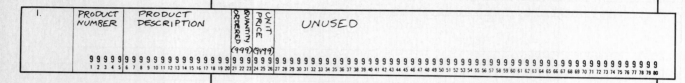

Figure 6-25. Input record layout for product sales record. For use in practice assignment.

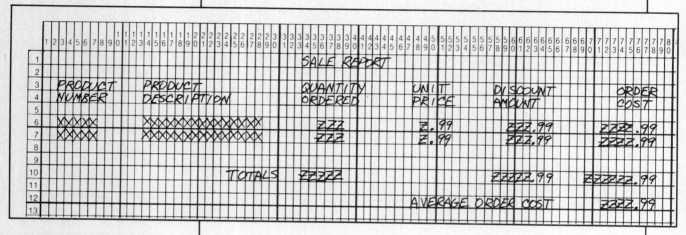

Figure 6-26. Output layout for sales report. For use in practice assignment.

4) When the last input record has been processed, print the accumulated totals for quantity ordered, discount amounts, and order cost.

5) Also calculate and print the average cost per order (total cost ÷ total number of orders).

Worksheet for Structured Flowchart

Program Name: _____

Prepared By: _____

Worksheet for Pseudocode Specifications

Program Name: _____

Prepared By: _____

Worksheet for Structured Flowchart

Program Name: _____

Prepared By: _____

Worksheet for Pseudocode Specifications

Program Name: _____

Prepared By: _____

COBOL PROGRAM SHEET

System		Punching Instructions		Sheet	of
Program				Identification	
Programmer	Date	Graphic	Card Form #		[73] [80]
	Punch				

SEQUENCE		CONT	A	B														
(PAGE)	(SERIAL)																	
1	3 4	6 7	8	12	16	20	24	28	32	36	40	44	48	52	56	60	64	68	72

COBOL PROGRAM SHEET

System				Punching Instructions				Sheet	of
Program			Graphic				Card Form #		Identification
Programmer		Date	Punch					[73]	[80]

SEQUENCE		CONT	A	B																
(PAGE)	(SERIAL)																			
1 3	4 6	7	8	12	16	20	24	28	32	36	40	44	48	52	56	60	64	68	72	

COBOL PROGRAM SHEET

System					Punching Instructions			Sheet	of
Program									
Programmer				Date	Graphic		Card Form #	Identification	
					Punch			73] [80	

SEQUENCE
(PAGE) (SERIAL)
1 3 4 6 7 8 12 16 20 24 28 32 36 40 44 48 52 56 60 64 68 72

CONT A B

COBOL PROGRAM SHEET

System		
Program		
Programmer		

Punching Instructions			
Graphic		Card Form #	
Punch			
Date			

Sheet	of
Identification	
[73]	[80]

SEQUENCE		CONT	A	B																
(PAGE)	(SERIAL)																			
1 3	4 6	7	8	12	16	20	24	28	32	36	40	44	48	52	56	60	64	68	72	

COBOL PROGRAM SHEET

System		Punching Instructions		Sheet of
Program				
Programmer	Date	Graphic	Card Form #	Identification
	Punch			[73] [80]

SEQUENCE
(PAGE) (SERIAL)

1 3	4	6 7	CONT	A	B
			8		12

16 20 24 28 32 36 40 44 48 52 56 60 64 68 72

COBOL PROGRAM SHEET

System		
Program		
Programmer		

Punching Instructions				Sheet	of
Graphic			Card Form #	Identification
Punch				[73] [80]
Date				

SEQUENCE		CONT	A	B															
(PAGE)	(SERIAL)																		
1 3	4 6	7	8	12	16	20	24	28	32	36	40	44	48	52	56	60	64	68	72

COBOL PROGRAM SHEET

System

Program

Programmer

Date

Punching Instructions

Graphic

Punch

Card Form #

Sheet of

Identification
73] [80

SEQUENCE
(PAGE) (SERIAL)
1 3 4 6 7 8

CONT

A B

8 12 16 20 24 28 32 36 40 44 48 52 56 60 64 68 72

COBOL PROGRAM SHEET

System		
Program		
Programmer		

	Punching Instructions		Sheet	of
Graphic				Identification
Punch		Card Form #		
Date				[73] _____ [80]

SEQUENCE																			
(PAGE)	(SERIAL)	CONT	A	B	12	16	20	24	28	32	36	40	44	48	52	56	60	64	68	72
1 3	4 6	7	8																

COBOL PROGRAM SHEET

System		Punching Instructions		Sheet	of

| Program | | | Graphic | | | | | | | |
| Programmer | Date | | Punch | | | Card Form # | | | Identification |

Punching Instructions: Graphic | Punch — Card Form #

Sheet of — Identification 73] [80

SEQUENCE (PAGE) (SERIAL)				CONT	A		B																									
1	3	4	6	7 8			12	16	20	24	28	32	36	40	44	48	52	56	60	64	68	72										

COBOL PROGRAM SHEET

System						Sheet	of
Program			Punching Instructions				
Programmer	Date	Graphic		Card Form #		Identification	[80]
		Punch				[73]	

SEQUENCE		CONT	A	B															
(PAGE)	(SERIAL)																		
1 3	4 6	7	8	12	16	20	24	28	32	36	40	44	48	52	56	60	64	68	72

COBOL PROGRAM SHEET

System		Punching Instructions		Sheet	of
Program		Graphic		Identification	
Programmer	Date	Punch	Card Form #	73]	[80

COBOL PROGRAM SHEET

System					Sheet	of
Program			Punching Instructions			Identification
Programmer			Graphic		Card Form #	[73] [80]
	Date		Punch			

SEQUENCE		CONT	A	B																											
(PAGE)	(SERIAL)																														
1 3	4 6	7	8	12	16	20	24	28	32	36	40	44	48	52	56	60	64	68	72											

Vocabulary Building Practice—Exercise 6

Write definitions and/or explanations of the terms listed below.

1. **collating sequence** _____
    _____

2. **relational test** _____
    _____

3. **class test**_____
    _____

4. **condition name test**_____
    _____

5. **sign test** _____
    _____

6. **nested IF test** _____
    _____

7. **case construct** _____
    _____

8. **compound conditional** _____
    _____

9. **AND/OR test**_____
    _____

10. **logical operator** _____
    _____

(over, please)

11. repetition _____

_____

12. sequence control _____

_____

13. loop_____

_____

14. counter _____

_____

15. increment _____

_____

16. accumulator _____

_____

17. flag _____

_____

18. switch_____

_____

19. PERFORM. . .UNTIL _____

_____

20. DOWHILE_____

_____

COBOL FOR FILES 7

OBJECTIVES

On completing reading and other learning assignments for this chapter, you should be able to:

1. Identify the three COBOL divisions for which statements about files have to be prepared and write appropriate entries for each division.

2. Write file processing statements using the OPEN, CLOSE, READ, and WRITE commands.

3. Describe the use of and prepare a series of carriage control commands for the production of output reports from files.

BUILDING FILES IN COBOL

In this chapter, you learn to use files within the COBOL language. This involves applying an entire series of COBOL statements that are new to you. The new statements involve three of the four divisions of COBOL programs:

- The ENVIRONMENT DIVISION has been blank in most of the previous examples largely because you have not yet used files. Now, in processing files, you will have to prepare a series of ENVIRONMENT DIVISION statements.

- The DATA DIVISION FILE SECTION will be needed to describe files and their records.

- The PROCEDURE DIVISION will require additional statements to direct file processing operations within your programs.

ENVIRONMENT DIVISION

Within a COBOL program, the ENVIRONMENT DIVISION has two formal sections. Each of these sections, in turn, serves a specific purpose in the building of COBOL programs. These ENVIRONMENT DIVISION sections are:

- The CONFIGURATION SECTION describes the physical environment to be used in compiling and executing the program and also provides for the assignment of programmer-defined names for special devices.
- The INPUT-OUTPUT SECTION establishes relationships between the names of files and the equipment upon which they reside.

CONFIGURATION SECTION

Equipment to be used by the COBOL program is defined in the CONFIGURATION SECTION of the ENVIRONMENT DIVISION. The purpose of this section is to identify the computers to be used by the program and special features to be applied.

Within the CONFIGURATION SECTION, two paragraph names are used for computer identification. The first of these paragraph names is SOURCE-COMPUTER. This entry is followed by a designation of the computer on which the program will be compiled.

The second paragraph heading is OBJECT-COMPUTER. This heading is followed by a description of the computer on which the compiled program will be executed.

Usually the SOURCE-COMPUTER and OBJECT-COMPUTER entries are the same. However, there may be situations in which you compile a program on one computer and execute it on another. Usually, this practice is restricted to computers of different sizes within the same family of products from a single manufacturer.

The SOURCE-COMPUTER and OBJECT-COMPUTER paragraphs are treated as comment entries by most COBOL compilers and consequently they are frequently not written into the program. When they are not specifically written, a default, or assumed identification of the computer being used, is inserted.

A third paragraph heading is SPECIAL-NAMES. When included, this paragraph permits use of programmer-defined names that can reference units of equipment within the program. The SPECIAL-NAMES paragraph is also used on some systems to define printer control names and to define special punctuation symbols for foreign currency presentation.

To illustrate, the following sample entries complete a CONFIGURATION SECTION in which a program is to be both compiled and executed on an IBM 370 computer.

```
SEQUENCE  | |A  |B
(PAGE) (SERIAL)| |   |
1    3 4   6 7 8  12   16   20   24   28   32   36   40   44   48   52   56   60   64   68   72
              ENVIRONMENT DIVISION.

              CONFIGURATION SECTION.
              SOURCE-COMPUTER. IBM-370.
              OBJECT-COMPUTER. IBM-370.
              SPECIAL-NAMES.
                  C01 IS TOP-OF-PAGE.
```

INPUT-OUTPUT SECTION

Names of files to be used within a COBOL program are assigned in the
INPUT-OUTPUT SECTION of the ENVIRONMENT DIVISION. These
assignments are made under a paragraph entitled FILE-CONTROL.
Within this paragraph, there must be a SELECT. . . ASSIGN TO statement for each file to be used within the program.

For instance, specific names of an input data file, a printed report
output file, and any other files that a given program might use would
each have to be assigned separately.

Notice in the example below that, following the SELECT entry, the
file to be used is named.

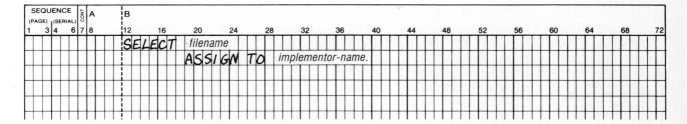

The file name is assigned by the programmer in compliance with all of
the COBOL naming rules. That is, file names may be up to 30 characters
in length, with no imbedded blanks or special characters except the
hyphen. As a sound practice, file names usually describe their contents. Examples: PAYROLL-FILE, ACCOUNTS-RECEIVABLE-FILE,
CUSTOMER-MASTER-FILE.

The ASSIGN TO entry identifies the implementor-name for the external, or secondary storage, device on which the file will be located.

The following are examples of file assignment statements for some
IBM systems:

```
SEQUENCE  | |A  |B
(PAGE) (SERIAL)| |   |
1    3 4   6 7 8  12   16   20   24   28   32   36   40   44   48   52   56   60   64   68   72
              SELECT PAYROLL-DATA-FILE
                  ASSIGN TO SYS007-UR-2540R-S.

              SELECT PAYROLL-REPORT-FILE
                  ASSIGN TO SYS009-UR-1403-S.
```

The meanings of the entries following the ASSIGN TO statements above are as follows:

- The SYS entry identifies the system input/output component by a unique number. This is the device number assigned within the operating system for each installation. The device (SYS) numbers are assigned in the operating system when it is generated by system programmers in preparation for installation. The numbers selected are arbitrary. But each designation must be unique.

- The designation UR indicates that these are unit record devices. This means that the device used is either a card handling or printing device. If a magnetic tape device were to be used, the designation would be UT. If a magnetic disk device were selected, the designation would be DA.

- The entries 2540R and 1403 indicate the model numbers of the peripheral devices to be used.

- The entry S indicates that the data on the file are recorded sequentially.

The examples below are for SELECT. . . ASSIGN TO statements to be compiled and executed on Control Data Corporation (CDC) computers:

```
SEQUENCE        A   B
(PAGE) (SERIAL)
1    3 4    6 7 8   12    16    20    24    28    32    36    40    44    48    52    56    60    64    68    72
            SELECT CUSTOMER-MASTER-FILE
                ASSIGN TO INPUT.

            SELECT BILLING-REPORT-FILE
                ASSIGN TO OUTPUT.
```

Under this system, the assignment of actual physical devices to handle files is done by the operating system.

Other variations are possible for other makes or models of equipment. This section of a COBOL program is highly manufacturer-dependent. Each manufacturer provides reference guides for its own versions of COBOL. They should be consulted in establishing ASSIGN TO designations for different computer systems that you might encounter.

FILE SECTION

Up to this point, you have used only the WORKING-STORAGE SECTION of the DATA DIVISION in your COBOL programs. To use stored files, a new section is needed. This is the FILE SECTION, which must appear immediately following the DATA DIVISION heading.

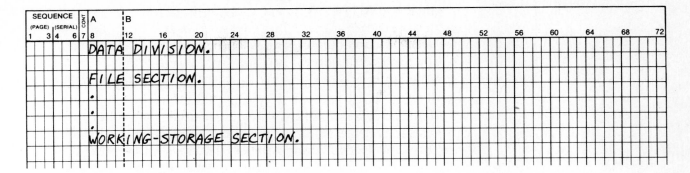

Within the FILE SECTION of the DATA DIVISION, you must include a *file description (FD)*, statement for *each file selected*. The format for a file description (FD) statement is given below. The FD entry begins at the same margin as the division and section entries. This is margin A of your COBOL coding sheet. All other entries to support the FD statement begin in margin B.

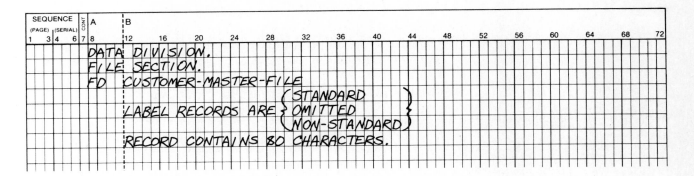

The first line of the FD gives the programmer-assigned, internal name of the file. This *must be identical* with the designation used in the EN-VIRONMENT DIVISION SELECT statement.

In the example above, there is a LABEL RECORDS ARE. . . clause. Label records are used to identify the data contained in the file. When the data in a file can be verified visually, no label record is required or permitted. Examples of this would be card files and printed reports. For these files, the entry would be LABEL RECORDS ARE OMITTED.

When data are stored on a magnetic medium such as a tape or disk, the first record should be a label record that identifies the type of data in that file and the file name. For these types of files, the clause would usually be LABEL RECORDS ARE STANDARD. In some computer installations, labels are the responsibility of the programmer. If this is the case, the entry would be LABEL RECORDS ARE NON-STANDARD.

In many systems, the label clause is optional. To determine how to label files in your programs, check with your instructor or the COBOL reference manual for your particular computer system.

The RECORD CONTAINS. . . clause is an optional entry. However, its use is encouraged. This clause serves two purposes. The first is for better documentation. The second purpose is to assist in defining record length accurately.

The COBOL compiler will always use the sum length of all fields described under the 01 record name that follows the FD sentence. When the RECORD CONTAINS clause is used, the COBOL compiler compares the calculated sum of the field lengths described in the record with the value specified in this clause. If there is a difference, the compiler prints a warning message. This aids in verifying the completeness and accuracy of your data description.

Some formatting notes on FD entries:

- Only the first line, giving the name of the file, is mandatory.

- The LABEL RECORDS and RECORD CONTAINS entries are optional, but recommended strongly. Among other benefits, these entries provide important information in the checking and maintenance of programs.

- Note that there must be a period at the end of the complete FD statement. A complete file definition entry must include both an FD statement and a record description.

A complete file definition entry is illustrated below:

```
FD  CUSTOMER-MASTER-FILE
    LABEL RECORDS ARE OMITTED
    RECORD CONTAINS 80 CHARACTERS.
01  CUSTOMER-RECORD.
    05   CUSTOMER-NUMBER        PIC 9(6).
    05   CUSTOMER-NAME          PIC X(30).
    05   CUSTOMER-BALANCE       PIC 9(4)V99.
    05   FILLER                 PIC X(38).
```

The CUSTOMER-RECORD entry above includes descriptions of each field within the identified record. The descriptions start with the leftmost character in the record and continues rightward. *All* positions, including unused portions of a record, must be accounted for. This technique should be recognizable. It is the same method used to describe records in the WORKING-STORAGE SECTION of the DATA DIVISION.

An alternate method may be used to describe the contents of a data record. This involves an abbreviated record description entry in the

FILE SECTION, supplemented by a detailed description in the WORKING-STORAGE SECTION. If this approach is used, the FILE SECTION entry for the record could be:

```
FD  CUSTOMER-MASTER-FILE
    LABEL RECORDS ARE OMITTED.
01  CUSTOMER-RECORD          PIC X(80).
```

This record defines an 80-character area used by each customer record read into memory. The description represents a minimal entry in the FILE SECTION. This entry is then supplemented with a detailed record description in the WORKING-STORAGE SECTION. The record would then be described in WORKING-STORAGE as follows:

```
01  WS-CUSTOMER-DATA.
    05  CUSTOMER-NUMBER       PIC 9(6).
    05  CUSTOMER-NAME         PIC X(30).
    05  CUSTOMER-BALANCE      PIC 9(4)V99.
    05  FILLER                PIC X(38).
```

The record description rules are the same as those described in Chapter 4. That is, each field is described beginning with the leftmost character position and proceeding rightward through the record.

The advantages of detailing record content in the WORKING-STORAGE SECTION is that the programmer is able to define multiple record formats for a single file and to use the VALUE clause to define contents of specified fields used in output reports. An example illustrating these advantages is given below:

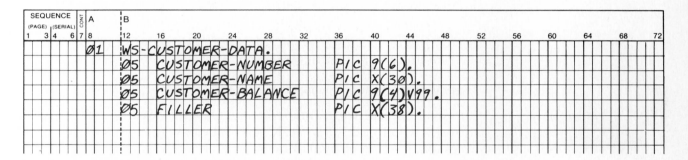

```
WORKING-STORAGE SECTION.

01  COLUMN-HEADING.
    05  FILLER    PIC XXXX    VALUE "NAME".
    05  FILLER    PIC X(31)   VALUE SPACE.
    05  FILLER    PIC X(11)   VALUE "SOC-SEC-NUM".
    05  FILLER    PIC X(8)    VALUE "  DEPT  ".
    05  FILLER    PIC X(13)   VALUE "Y-T-D GROSS  ".
    05  FILLER    PIC X(9)    VALUE "Y-T-D FIT".
```

```
01  REPORT-DETAIL-LINE.
    05  RDL-NAME            PIC X(30).
    05  FILLER             PIC X(5)      VALUE SPACE.
    05  RDL-SOC-SEC        PIC 999/99/9999.
    05  FILLER             PIC XX        VALUE SPACE.
    05  RDL-DEPT           PIC 9(4).
    05  FILLER             PIC XX        VALUE SPACE.
    05  RDL-YTD-GROSS      PIC 9(5).99.
    05  FILLER             PIC XX        VALUE SPACE.
    05  RDL-YTD-FIT        PIC 9(4).99.
```

Except under specific circumstances, as described in Chapter 6, the VALUE clause cannot be used in the FILE SECTION. By using a VALUE clause in the record description within the WORKING-STORAGE SECTION, it becomes possible to designate the contents of areas to be printed between data fields on output reports. In addition, with the VALUE clause, it is possible to assign literals for use as report titles or column headings. Most report-printing operations require the programmer to define and use many print line formats, such as report titles, column headings, detail lines, and summary lines.

Thus, it is more flexible to use the WORKING-STORAGE SECTION for record descriptions, limiting entries in the FILE SECTION to a one-line record description entry.

PROCEDURE DIVISION INSTRUCTIONS

Preparations to select and define the file are made through entries in the ENVIRONMENT DIVISION and the DATA DIVISION. The processing to be performed upon the content of the file must then be defined in the PROCEDURE DIVISION.

The COBOL language provides many instructions for file processing. This text concentrates on the four most important of these instructions: OPEN, CLOSE, READ, and WRITE.

OPEN

Use of the OPEN command establishes a connection between the program and the data file selected for use. In writing an OPEN command, you must decide on what use will be made of the file. Your choices: INPUT or OUTPUT. (Another option, INPUT-OUTPUT, is also available but is beyond the scope of this book.)

OPEN instructions should be written beginning in margin B of COBOL coding sheets. The formats for these instructions are as follows:

```
OPEN INPUT  A-FILE-NAME.
OPEN OUTPUT ANOTHER-FILE-NAME.
```

To illustrate, the PROCEDURE DIVISION instruction that sets up the electronic circuitry to prepare the computer to read and process the CUSTOMER-MASTER-FILE previously identified in the INPUT-OUTPUT SECTION of the ENVIRONMENT DIVISION would be as follows:

Execution of the OPEN statement prepares the program to receive data made available by the READ instruction. The OPEN instruction that would prepare the system to print a report based on the BILLING-REPORT-FILE identified earlier is as follows:

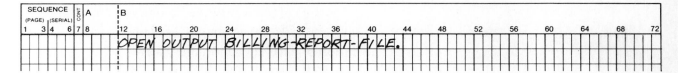

If your program is designed to process multiple files, the OPEN format can be condensed: it is not necessary to prepare two separate OPEN statements. Instead, a single statement can be formatted as follows:

Regardless of the format used, before any file may be accessed it must be appropriately OPENed.

CLOSE

When all records in a file have been processed, activity for that file should be concluded through use of a CLOSE command. This command terminates use of the identified file, making it available for other application programs. In checking your file processing programs prior to compilation, make sure that a CLOSE instruction is executed some time before the STOP RUN command.

The format of the CLOSE command is as follows:

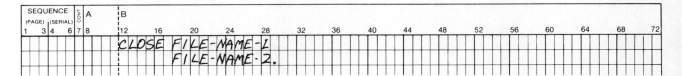

Remember that the CLOSE statement does not use the INPUT or OUT-
PUT designation that is required in the OPEN command. Use of the
INPUT or OUTPUT designation in a CLOSE command will result in
a syntax error upon compilation. An example of the use of this command to close out the file used for the BILLING-REPORT is:

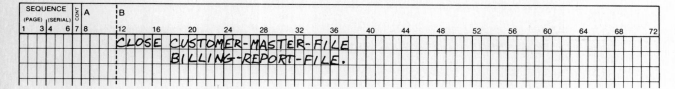

READ

To input file data for processing, the READ command is used within
the PROCEDURE DIVISION. The execution of each READ command
causes the next record in the identified file to be made available in the
01 record description area of the computer's memory. With the record
in memory, the program can then access any field defined in the record.

Prior to execution of a READ command, the file referenced must
have been OPENed for INPUT. Otherwise, the program will terminate
prematurely with an *abend* or *abort* message to the console operator. The
term ''abend'' is an acronym, for ''abnormal ending.''

An example of a READ instruction for the CUSTOMER-MASTER-
FILE is:

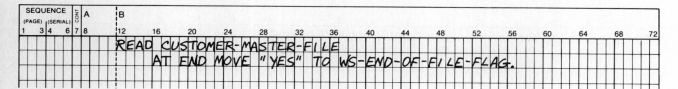

Note that the READ command identifies the file name—not the record
name—even though the command will be executed upon one record
at a time. Each time the READ command is executed, the next available
record within the file is made available in memory. As part of each
READ function, an automatic end-of-file test can be applied. This is accomplished through use of the AT END clause. In the example above,
when no more data are available in the file, the statement(s) following
AT END will be executed. In this case, the literal ''YES'' is moved into
the WORKING-STORAGE SECTION data name called WS-END-OF-
FILE-FLAG.

The *end-of-file* status is sensed when either a predefined sentinal
is present or when an attempt to READ finds no data record available.
To illustrate, on IBM systems, the code /* in columns 1 and 2 of the last
record serve as an end-of-file indicator. When this coding is detected,
the AT END phrase of the READ command is executed and processing of the file is discontinued.

In writing COBOL programs, be aware that, once the AT END phrase has been executed, the READ command cannot be used again on that file, within that program, *unless it is closed and then reopened*. An attempt to read a file after an AT END command has been executed will cause the program to abort, or abend.

Placement of READ Instructions

The placement of the READ instruction within a COBOL program presents a structuring problem. The AT END clause of the READ instruction is very often the source of the main control function in a program. As seen in Figure 7-1, line 0084, the main processing loop is controlled by the WS-END-OF-FILE-FLAG. This flag is changed from ''no'' to ''yes'' by the AT END phrase in the READ statement. The placement of the READ statement within a program, therefore, controls when the main loop will terminate. This, in turn, can affect the accuracy of the data processing results.

Look carefully at the structure of the PRINT-SALESPERSON module in Figure 7-1. The READ instruction is placed at the beginning of the module. The program will produce correct results, except for the last record in the file. The output from this program is shown in Figure 7-2. Notice that the last line of data is printed *twice*. This is a result of the incorrect placement of the READ statement.

When the AT END clause executes, the contents of the 01 record area for the file will contain either the data record previously read or garbage. (Any set of unknown values is considered to be garbage.) In either case, the program continues to execute the instruction in the paragraph. Only when the paragraph has been fully executed will the PERFORM. . .UNTIL statement check the contents of the WS-END-OF-FILE-FLAG, which is now ''yes.'' The main processing loop ends, the files are closed, and the program stops.

Better control of processing occurs when the WS-END-OF-FILE-FLAG is tested immediately after the READ statement is executed. This would involve placing the READ statement at the *bottom* of the main processing loop, as illustrated in Figure 7-3. In this structure, the PERFORM. . .UNTIL instruction would then test the end-of-file-flag contents before attempting to execute the process paragraph again. Under these conditions, when the AT END clause executes, the WS-END-OF-FILE-FLAG does equal ''yes'' and the process paragraph does not get repeated with duplicate or erroneous data. The correct output is shown in Figure 7-4.

The placement of the READ statement at the bottom of the PRINT-SALESPERSON paragraph means that the record that was just read will not be processed until the next iteration of the loop. This is often called ''look ahead'' reading of files. When the program begins execution, the first data record would have to be read *before* the first iteration of the PERFORM. . .UNTIL loop. This preliminary read operation is called a *priming read*, and is executed as part of the INITIALIZATION

```
00001   IDENTIFICATION DIVISION.
00002   PROGRAM-ID.        SALES-REPORT.
00003   AUTHOR.           T.S. DUCK.
00004   DATE-WRITTEN.     SEPTEMBER 1, 1982.
00005   DATE-COMPILED.    FEBRUARY 1, 1983.
00006   *REMARKS.**********************************
00007   *    THIS PROGRAM INPUTS SALESPERSON RECORDS  *
00008   *    AND OUTPUTS ALL SALESPERSONS   WITH      *
00009   *    WITH A BASE SALARY LESS THAN 20,000      *
00010   *    IN A SIMPLE LISTING.                     *
00011   ****.jj***********************************
00012
00013   ENVIRONMENT DIVISION.
00014   CONFIGURATION SECTION.
00015   INPUT-OUTPUT SECTION.
00016   FILE-CONTROL.
00017       SELECT INPUT-FILE ASSIGN TO INPUTS
00018           USE "RT=Z".
00019       SELECT REPORT-FILE ASSIGN TO RPTOUT
00020           USE "PRINTF=YES".
00021 /
00022   DATA DIVISION.
00023   FILE SECTION.
00024
00025   FD INPUT-FILE
00026       LABEL RECORDS ARE OMITTED.
00027   01 INPUT-RECORD              PIC X(43).
00028
00029   FD REPORT-FILE
00030       LABEL RECORDS ARE OMITTED.
00031   01 REPORT-RECORD             PIC X(80).
00032   WORKING-STORAGE SECTION.
00033
00034   01   INPUT-SALES-RECORD.
00035        05  IN-SALESPERSON-NAME     PIC X(20).
00036        05  IN-SALESPERSON-NUMBER   PIC 9(05).
00037        05  IN-EMPLOYMENT-DATE.
00038            10 IN-EMP-YR            PIC 99.
00039            10 IN-EMP-MON-DAY       PIC 9(04).
00040        05  IN-BRANCH-NUMBER        PIC 9(03).
00041        05  IN-TERRITORY-CODE       PIC 9(02).
00042        05  IN-BASE-SALARY          PIC 9(05)V99.
00043
00044   01   OUTPUT-SALESPERSON-RECORD.
00045        05  OT-SALESPERSON-NAME     PIC X(20).
00046        05  FILLER                  PIC X(03).
00047        05  OT-SALESPERSON-NUMBER   PIC 9(05).
00048        05  FILLER                  PIC X(08).
00049        05  OT-EMPLOYMENT-DATE.
00050            10 OT-EMP-MON-DAY        PIC Z9/99/.
00051            10 OT-EMP-YR             PIC 99.
00052        05  FILLER                  PIC X(06).
00053        05  OT-BRANCH-NUMBER         PIC 9(03).
00054        05  FILLER                  PIC X(08).
00055     .  05  OT-TERRITORY-CODE        PIC 9(02).
00056    ``  05  FILLER                  PIC X(06).
00057        05  OT-BASE-SALARY           PIC 9(05).99.
00078 /
00079   PROCEDURE DIVISION.
00080
00081   SALESPERSON-MAINLINE.
00082       PERFORM INITIALIZATION.
00083       PERFORM PRINT-SALESPERSON
00084           UNTIL WS-END-OF-FILE-FLAG = "YES".
00085       PERFORM TERMINATION.
00086       STOP RUN.
00087
00088   INITIALIZATION.
00089       OPEN INPUT INPUT-FILE
00090            OUTPUT REPORT-FILE.
00091       MOVE SPACES  TO OUTPUT-SALESPERSON-RECORD.
00092       PERFORM PRINT-HEADINGS.
```

Figure 7-1. Program example showing READ instruction at the top of the PROCESS module. (Illustration continues.)

```
00093   PRINT-SALESPERSON.
00094       READ INPUT-FILE INTO INPUT-SALES-RECORD
00095           AT END MOVE "YES" TO WS-END-OF-FILE-FLAG.
00096       IF IN-BASE-SALARY LESS THAN 20000
00097       THEN
00098           MOVE IN-SALESPERSON-NAME    TO OT-SALESPERSON-NAME
00099           MOVE IN-SALESPERSON-NUMBER  TO OT-SALESPERSON-NUMBER
00100           MOVE IN-EMP-YR              TO OT-EMP-YR
00101           MOVE IN-EMP-MON-DAY         TO OT-EMP-MON-DAY
00102           MOVE IN-BRANCH-NUMBER       TO OT-BRANCH-NUMBER
00103           MOVE IN-TERRITORY-CODE      TO OT-TERRITORY-CODE
00104           MOVE IN-BASE-SALARY         TO OT-BASE-SALARY
00105           PERFORM OUTPUT-SALESPERSON-LINES
00106       ELSE
00107           NEXT SENTENCE.
00108 /
00109   OUTPUT-SALESPERSON-LINES.
00110       IF LINE-COUNT GREATER THAN 55
00111       THEN
00112           PERFORM PRINT-HEADINGS.
00113       MOVE OUTPUT-SALESPERSON-RECORD TO REPORT-RECORD.
00114       PERFORM WRITE-ONE-LINE.
00115
00116   PRINT-HEADINGS.
00117       MOVE ZEROES                 TO LINE-COUNT.
00118       MOVE HEADING-1              TO REPORT-RECORD.
00119       WRITE REPORT-RECORD
00120           AFTER ADVANCING PAGE.
00121       MOVE SPACES                 TO REPORT-RECORD.
00122       PERFORM WRITE-ONE-LINE.
00123       MOVE HEADING-2              TO REPORT-RECORD.
00124       PERFORM WRITE-ONE-LINE.
00125       MOVE SPACES                 TO REPORT-RECORD.
00126       PERFORM WRITE-ONE-LINE.
00127
00128   WRITE-ONE-LINE.
00129       WRITE REPORT-RECORD
00130           AFTER ADVANCING 1 LINE.
00131       ADD 1 TO LINE-COUNT.
00132   TERMINATION.
00133       DISPLAY " ".
00134       DISPLAY "                            END OF PROCESSING".
00135       CLOSE INPUT-FILE, REPORT-FILE.
```

Figure 7-1. Continued.

```
                              SALES PERSONNEL

    NAME                  NUMBER  EMPLOYEMENT DATE  BRANCH  TERRITORY  BASE SALARY
    JOHN J. SMITH         23456      12/30/80        102       05       19000.00
    DR. THOMAS S DUCK     00001      11/21/79        001       03       19899.00
    JOHN HENRY            12345       5/23/82        176       10       14950.00
    T. J. HOOKER          65897       2/28/78        002       07       15879.99
    DAVID A. JONES        73820      12/31/75        108       20       16000.99
    MANUAL L. PEREZ       66778       8/28/79        102       05       18500.00
    MANUAL L. PEREZ       66778       8/28/79        102       05       18500.00
```

Figure 7-2. Incorrect output resulting from program in Figure 7-1.

```
00001    IDENTIFICATION DIVISION.
00002    PROGRAM-ID.        SALESPERSON.
00003    AUTHOR.            T.S. DUCK.
00004    DATE-WRITTEN.      SEPTEMBER 1, 1982.
00005    DATE-COMPILED.     FEBRUARY 1, 1983.
00006   *REMARKS. *********************************
00007   *     THIS PROGRAM INPUTS SALESPERSON RECORDS  *
00008   *     AND OUTPUTS ALL SALESPERSONS WITH        *
00009   *     A BASE SALARY OF LESS THAN 20,000        *
00010   j`    IN A SIMPLE REPORT. THIS PROGRAM USES A  *
00011   *     PRIMING READ TYPE OF LOGIC.              *
00012   *********************************************
00013
00014    ENVIRONMENT DIVISION.
00015    CONFIGURATION SECTION.
00016    INPUT-OUTPUT SECTION.
00017    FILE-CONTROL.
00018        SELECT INPUT-FILE ASSIGN TO INPUT5
00019            USE "RT=Z".
00020        SELECT REPORT-FILE ASSIGN TO RPTOUT
00021            USE "PRINTF=YES".
00022   /
00023    DATA DIVISION.
00024    FILE SECTION.
00025
00026    FD INPUT-FILE
00027        LABEL RECORDS ARE OMITTED.
00028    01 INPUT-RECORD              PIC X(43).
00029
00030    FD REPORT-FILE
00031        LABEL RECORDS ARE OMITTED.
00032    01 REPORT-RECORD             PIC X(80).
00033    WORKING-STORAGE SECTION.
00034
00035    01  INPUT-SALES-RECORD.
00036        05   IN-SALESPERSON-NAME    PIC X(20).
00037        05   IN-SALESPERSON-NUMBER  PIC 9(05).
00038        05   IN-EMPLOYMENT-DATE.
00039             10 IN-EMP-YR            PIC 9(02).
00040             10 IN-EMP-MON-DAY       PIC 9(04).
00041        05   IN-BRANCH-NUMBER        PIC 9(03).
00042        05   IN-TERRITORY-CODE       PIC 9(02).
00043        05   IN-BASE-SALARY          PIC 9(05)V99.
00044
00045    01  OUTPUT-SALESPERSON-RECORD.
00046        05   OT-SALESPERSON-NAME    PIC X(20).
00047        05   FILLER                 PIC X(03).
00048        05   OT-SALESPERSON-NUMBER  PIC 9(05).
00049        05   FILLER                 PIC X(08).
00050        05   OT-EMPLOYMENT-DATE.
00051             10 OT-EMP-MON-DAY       PIC Z9/99/.
00052             10 OT-EMP-YR            PIC 99.
00053        05   FILLER                 PIC X(06).
00054        05   OT-BRANCH-NUMBER        PIC 9(ps).03
00055        05   FILLER                 PIC X(08).
00056        05   OT-TERRITORY-CODE       PIC 9(02).
00057        05   FILLER                 PIC X(06).
00058        05   OT-BASE-SALARY          PIC 9(05).99.
00059   /
00060    01 HEADING-1.
00061        05 FILLER                    PIC X(28) VALUE SPACES.
00062        05 FILLER                    PIC X(16)
00063                                     VALUE "SALES PERSONNEL".
00064        05 FILLER                    PIC X(44) VALUE SPACES.
00065
00066    01 HEADING-2.
00067        05 FILLER                    PIC X(5) VALUE "NAME".
00068        05 FILLER                    PIC X(18) VALUE SPACES.
00069        05 FILLER                    PIC X(08) VALUE "NUMBER  ".
00070        05 FILLER                    PIC X(16)
00071                                     VALUE "EMPLOYEMENT DATE".
00072        05 FILLER                    PIC X(10) VALUE "  BRANCH  ".
00073        05 FILLER                    PIC X(11) VALUE "TERRITORY  ".
00074        05 FILLER                    PIC X(11) VALUE "BASE SALARY".
00075    01 PRINT-VARIABLES.
00076        05 LINE-COUNT                PIC 9(02) VALUE 00.
00077
00078    01 WS-END-OF-FILE-FLAG           PIC X(03) VALUE "NO ".
```

Figure 7-3. Program structure using the priming read approach. (Illustration continues.)

```
00079 /
00080  PROCEDURE DIVISION.
00081
00082  SALESPERSON-MAINLINE.
00083      PERFORM INITIALIZATION.
00084      PERFORM PRINT-SALESPERSON
00085          UNTIL WS-END-OF-FILE-FLAG >="YES".
00086      PERFORM TERMINATION.
00087      STOP RUN.
00088
00089  INITIALIZATION.
00090       OPEN INPUT INPUT-FILE
00091           OUTPUT REPORT-FILE.
00092      MOVE SPACES             TO OUTPUT-SALESPERSON-RECORD.
00093      READ INPUT-FILE INTO INPUT-SALES-RECORD
00094          AT END MOVE "YES" TO WS-END-OF-FILE-FLAG.
00095      PERFORM PRINT-HEADINGS.
00096  PRINT-SALESPERSON.
00097      IF IN-BASE-SALARY LESS THAN 20000
00098      THEN
00099          MOVE IN-SALESPERSON-NAME    TO OT-SALESPERSON-NAME
00100          MOVE IN-SALESPERSON-NUMBER  TO OT-SALESPERSON-NUMBER
00101          MOVE IN-EMP-YR              TO OT-EMP-YR
00102          MOVE IN-EMP-MON-DAY         TO OT-EMP-MON-DAY
00103          MOVE IN-BRANCH-NUMBER       TO OT-BRANCH-NUMBER
00104          MOVE IN-TERRITORY-CODE      TO OT-TERRITORY-CODE
00105          MOVE IN-BASE-SALARY         TO OT-BASE-SALARY
00106          PERFORM OUTPUT-SALESPERSON-LINES
00107      ELSE
00108          NEXT SENTENCE.
00109      READ INPUT-FILE INTO INPUT-SALES-RECORD
00110          AT END MOVE "YES" TO WS-END-OF-FILE-FLAG.
00109 /
00110  OUTPUT-SALESPERSON-LINES.
00111      IF LINE-COUNT GREATER THAN 55
00112      THEN
00113          PERFORM PRINT-HEADINGS.
00114      MOVE OUTPUT-SALESPERSON-RECORD TO REPORT-RECORD.
00115      PERFORM WRITE-ONE-LINE.
00116
00117  PRINT-HEADINGS.
00118      MOVE ZEROES                 TO LINE-COUNT.
001qy      MOVE HEADING-1              TO REPORT-RECORD.
00120      WRITE REPORT-RECORD
00121          AFTER ADVANCING PAGE.
00122      MOVE SPACES                 TO REPORT-RECORD.
00123      PERFORM WRITE-ONE-LINE.
00124      MOVE HEADING-2              TO REPORT-RECORD.
00125      PERFORM WRITE-ONE-LINE.
00126      MOVE SPACES                 TO REPORT-RECORD.
00127      PERFORM WRITE-ONE-LINE.
00128
00129  WRITE-ONE-LINE.
00130      WRITE REPORT-RECORD
00131          AFTER ADVANCING 1 LINE.
00132      ADD 1 TO LINE-COUNT.
00133  TERMINATION.
00134      DISPLAY " ".
00135      DISPLAY "                            END OF PROCESSING".
00136      CLOSE INPUT-FILE, REPORT-FILE.
```

Figure 7-3. Continued.

```
                              SALES PERSONNEL

        NAME                NUMBER  EMPLOYEMENT DATE  BRANCH  TERRITORY  BASE SALARY

        JOHN J. SMITH       23456      12/30/80        102       05       19000.00
        DR. THOMAS S DUCK   00001      11/21/79        001       03       19899.00
        JOHN HENRY          12345       5/23/82        176       10       14950.00
        T. J. HOOKER        65897       2/28/78        002       07       15879.99
        DAVID A. JONES      73820      12/31/75        108       20       16000.99
        MANUAL L. PEREZ     66778       8/28/79        102       05       18500.00
```

Figure 7-4. Correct output from program in Figure 7-3.

procedures. The main processing loop can now function with valid data present.

READ. . .INTO

When the detailed record description for a file has been placed in the WORKING-STORAGE SECTION, a slightly different format is used for the READ statement:

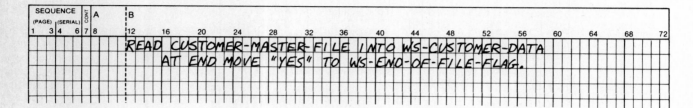

```
READ CUSTOMER-MASTER-FILE INTO WS-CUSTOMER-DATA
    AT END MOVE "YES" TO WS-END-OF-FILE-FLAG.
```

As with the previous READ command, the next record is made available in the 01 record area of memory. In addition, the record is also placed in the WS-CUSTOMER-DATA area in the WORKING-STORAGE SECTION of memory. Thus, the same record is available at two memory areas. The effect of the READ. . .INTO is to READ a record from the file and to MOVE that record to the WS-CUSTOMER-DATA area.

WRITE

When a data record has been read and processed, the WRITE command can be used to cause the results to be copied onto an output device. As with the READ command, a WRITE instruction requires an OPEN statement to be executed first. To print the billing report cited earlier, an OPEN OUTPUT BILLING-REPORT-FILE statement would have to be executed before an attempt is made to write a record.

A WRITE command must then reference the 01 record name associated with the FD entry for the file. An example of the format for the simplest WRITE command is:

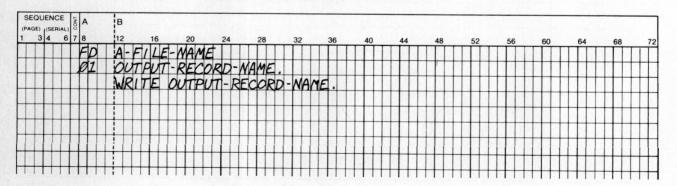

```
FD  A-FILE-NAME
01  OUTPUT-RECORD-NAME.
    WRITE OUTPUT-RECORD-NAME.
```

Execution of this command copies the data in the memory area for the output record onto a device assigned to the file in the INPUT-OUTPUT

SECTION of the ENVIRONMENT DIVISION. Applying this format to the output of the BILLING-REPORT FILE, the command would be:

The exact format of a WRITE statement depends upon the device to which the file is assigned. Alternative formats are discussed later in this chapter. Remember, you READ a file name but WRITE a record name.

WRITE. . .FROM

If a record description is set up in the WORKING-STORAGE SEC-TION, the WRITE statement could include a FROM phrase, which serves a purpose similar to the use of the READ. . .INTO statement. That is, use of the WRITE...FROM command permits placement of a record in both the FILE and WORKING-STORAGE sections of main memory. An example of a WRITE. . .FROM command for the preparation of a billing report is:

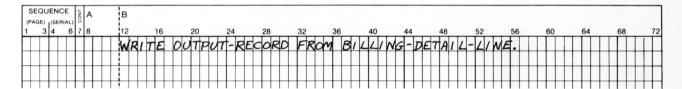

This command has exactly the same effect as would occur through use of separate MOVE and WRITE commands. In other words, the WRITE . . .FROM command effectively performs the following function:

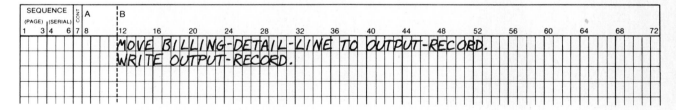

The use of the WRITE. . .FROM statement allows the programmer flexibility in the use of the WORKING-STORAGE SECTION, as described earlier in this chapter.

The discussions above illustrate the relationships of the file specifications and divisions of a COBOL program. In the ENVIRONMENT DIVISION, files are named and assigned to external devices. For each file named in the ENVIRONMENT DIVISION, there must be a file description and an associated record definition (01 level entry) in the DATA DIVISION. These definitions and descriptions must occur in the FILE SECTION. All references to external files in the PROCEDURE DIVISION, such as READ, WRITE, OPEN, or CLOSE, must use the appropriate FILE SECTION entries, although related work areas may be defined in the WORKING-STORAGE SECTION.

Writing Print Files

If data output from a file are to be used to print a report, the program must provide for the *vertical spacing* of print lines on the pages. Options include single- or multiple-line vertical printer spacing—or printing at the top of a page. These vertical spacing functions are called *carriage control.* This control is applied through the placement of specific characters in the leftmost position of print records. This leftmost position is non-printing. That is, entries in this field will not show up on the printed report.

Printers are engineered to use the contents of the leftmost position of a print line to determine vertical spacing requirements. There are many reasons for this. However, this convention is pointed out as a warning. COBOL will *always* use the leftmost position of each print line for carriage control. This means that, if you receive a printed output with the first character of data missing, you have not allocated a place for the carriage control character in your print line description. In the sample below, the one-character FILLER is present specifically for holding the carriage control value.

```
WORKING-STORAGE SECTION.

01  COLUMN-HEADING.
    05  FILLER                  PIC X           VALUE SPACE.
    05  FILLER                  PIC X(4)        VALUE "NAME".
    05  FILLER                  PIC X(31)       VALUE SPACE.
    05  FILLER                  PIC X(11)       VALUE "SOC-SEC-NUM".
    05  FILLER                  PIC X(8)        VALUE "  DEPT  ".
    05  FILLER                  PIC X(13)       VALUE "Y-T-D GROSS  ".
    05  FILLER                  PIC X(9)        VALUE "Y-T-D FIT".

01  REPORT-DETAIL-LINE.
    05  FILLER                  PIC X           VALUE SPACE.
    05  RDL-NAME                PIC X(30).
    05  FILLER                  PIC X(5)        VALUE SPACE.
    05  RDL-SOC-SEC             PIC 999/99/9999.
    05  FILLER                  PIC XX          VALUE SPACE.
    05  RDL-DEPT                PIC 9(4).
    05  FILLER                  PIC XX          VALUE SPACE.
    05  RDL-YTD-GROSS           PIC 9(5).99.
    05  FILLER                  PIC XX          VALUE SPACE.
    05  RDL-YTD-FIT             PIC 9(4).99.
```

The most convenient way of implementing carriage control commands is through the WRITE. . .ADVANCING statement. This command can be used both to identify the record to be written and also to provide vertical spacing instructions for the printer. An example of the format of this command is:

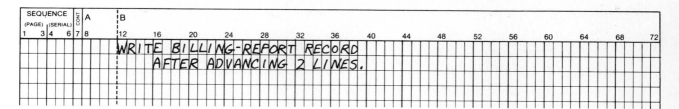

This command will cause the printer to advance one vertical line, then write the contents of one BILLING-REPORT record on the next line.

In formatting printed output reports, you will have several carriage control options available. As one example, spacing can occur either BEFORE or AFTER the print function. You can use either of these options:

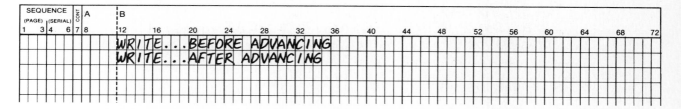

However, it is generally not an acceptable practice to mix these two forms of WRITE commands in the same program. If you mix the formats, you have run the risk of overprinting records that already been imprinted. Therefore, it is best to be consistent. The most common practice is to use the AFTER option.

Another option to be considered is the amount of spacing between print lines. The spacing can be designated by an integer. The most common print patterns used call for spacing of 1, 2, or 3 lines.

A data name in the DATA DIVISION can also be used to establish the integer to be used for vertical spacing control. This definition can then be included in the WRITE command:

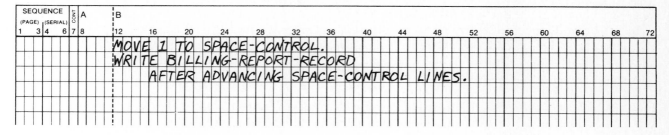

This instruction would call up the contents of SPACE-CONTROL from the WORKING-STORAGE SECTION of the DATA DIVISION. The BILLING-REPORT-RECORD would be printed after the carriage mechanism had advanced one vertical line. A WORKING-STORAGE entry to establish the vertical spacing might read as follows:

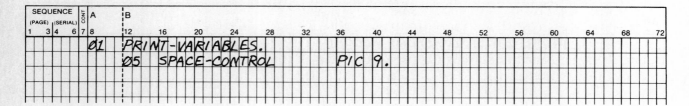

An important advantage in using this variable for vertical line spacing is that you can use one WRITE statement for all printing operations.

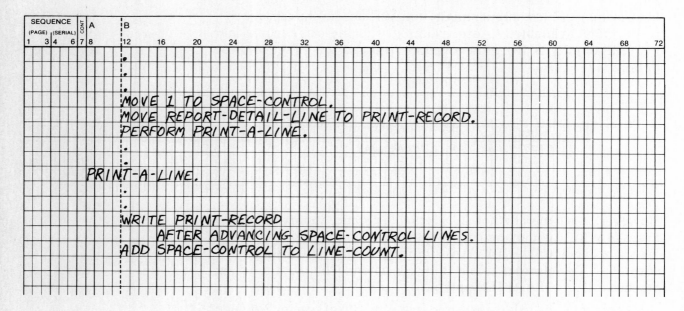

When printing is to begin on the top line of the page, the COBOL reserved word PAGE can be used. An example of this command might be:

```
WRITE PRINT-RECORD RECORD FROM HDG-1
        AFTER ADVANCING PAGE.
```

In this example, the top-of-page title and heading designations for the report would be included in the WORKING-STORAGE SECTION.

The command would cause the HDG-1 records to be moved from WORKING-STORAGE to the PRINT-RECORD area of memory. On executing the command, the printer would feed paper to the top of a new page. Then the heading content would be imprinted. Figure 7-5 illustrates the format of a heading storage record and the resulting imprint.

By applying the lessons of this chapter, you will be able to write COBOL statements that enable you to set up and use files. To increase your knowledge about the building and use of files, Chapter 9 contains additional, important material on the use of files in business information systems.

Figure 7-5. Report title definitions in Working-Storage Section.

```
00049
00050    FD   MACHINE-USE-REPORT
00051         LABEL RECORDS ARE OMITTED.
00052    01   REPORT-RECORD          PIC X(132).
00053
00054    WORKING-STORAGE SECTION.
00055
00056    01   HEADING1.
00057         05 FILLER               PIC X(30) VALUE SPACES.
00058         05 FILLER               PIC X(26)
00059                                 VALUE "MACHINE UTILIZATION REPORT".
00060         05 FILLER               PIC X(14) VALUE SPACES.
00061         05 FILLER               PIC X(05) VALUE "PAGE ".
00062         05 PAGE-NUMBER          PIC    Z9.
00063
00064    01   RUN-DATE.
00065         05 FILLER               PIC X(03) VALUE SPACES.
00066         05 MONTH-RUN            PIC    Z9/.
00067         05 DAY-RUN              PIC    99/.
00068         05 YEAR-RUN             PIC    99.
00069         05 FILLER               PIC X(17) VALUE SPACES.
00070         05 FILLER               PIC X(13) VALUE "WEEK ENDING  ".
00071         05 OUT-MONTH-END        PIC X(09).
00072         05 FILLER               PIC X(01).
00073         05 OUT-DAY-END          PIC X(02).
00074         05 FILLER               PIC X(04) VALUE ", 19".
00075         05 OUT-YEAR-END         PIC X(02).
00076
00077    01   TODAYS-DATE.
00078         05 DATE-YEAR            PIC X(02).
00079         05 DATE-MONTH           PIC X(02).
00080         05 DATE-DAY             PIC X(02).
```

```
                        MACHINE UTILIZATION REPORT         PAGE   1
    4/07/83             WEEK ENDING     JANUARY 26, 1983

  JOB NUMBER          MACHINE TYPE        MACHINE NUMBER        HOURS USED

    BY428               DRILL                28                    8.0
                                             28                    8.0
                                             28                    8.0
                                                      TYPE TOTAL  24.0 *

                        LATHE                54                    2.7
                                                      TYPE TOTAL   2.7 *
```

Key Terms

1. file description
2. end-of-file condition
3. priming read
4. vertical spacing
5. carriage control
6. abend
7. abort

Summary

To use files in COBOL programs, instructions will be required in three divisions, ENVIRONMENT, DATA (FILE SECTION), and PROCEDURE.

In the ENVIRONMENT DIVISION, the CONFIGURATION SECTION is used to identify the computers to be used by the program. The SOURCE-COMPUTER is the one on which the program will be compiled. The OBJECT-COMPUTER is the system to be used for program execution. Also in the ENVIRONMENT DIVISION, the INPUT-OUTPUT SECTION is used to assign file names. Instructions in this section cover selection of files by name and assignment of the system components that will utilize them.

In the DATA DIVISION, the FILE SECTION is used for file description, or FD, entries. These statements describe the content of each record in a file. PICTURE clauses are used to describe each field in a record. The sum length of each record should also be given, using the RECORD CONTAINS clause. [*Objective No. 1.*]

The PROCEDURE DIVISION is used to designate functions to be performed involving files. Available instructions cause COBOL programs to OPEN, CLOSE, READ, and WRITE files. An OPEN instruction prepares the program to receive data to be made available under control of a READ instruction. The OPEN command also designates whether an INPUT or OUTPUT function is to be performed. The CLOSE statement terminates use of a file, making the data available for processing under other programs. Execution of a READ command causes the next available record in a designated file to be placed in computer memory. This gives the program full access to any field in the record. A search for an end-of-file condition takes place as part of each READ command execution. Care is needed to place tests for end-of-file flags or switches so as to avoid dropping or duplicating processing of the final record. WRITE commands cause file records or processing results to be copied to an output device. If outputs are to be printed, special carriage-control instructions are required by most computer systems. [*Objectives Nos. 2 and 3.*]

Review/Discussion Questions

1. What division and section of a COBOL program are used to designate the computers on which the program will be compiled and run?

2. How and where are file handling devices designated within COBOL programs?

3. Where and how are files described within COBOL programs?

4. How are records described in a COBOL program?

5. What are the advantages to be gained from use of the RECORD CONTAINS. . . clause within a COBOL program?

6. What advantages can be gained by detailing record descriptions in the WORKING-STORAGE SECTION of the DATA DIVISION?

7. What functions are executed under control of the OPEN command?

8. Why is it important to use a CLOSE command within COBOL programs?

9. What functions are executed under control of a READ command?

10. What special precautions should be followed in connection with end-of-file conditions?

11. What functions are performed when a WRITE command is executed?

12. What methods are used to accomplish the carriage control functions for the formatting of printed outputs?

COBOL Terms

1. CONFIGURATION SECTION
2. INPUT-OUTPUT SECTION
3. SOURCE-COMPUTER
4. OBJECT-COMPUTER
5. SPECIAL-NAMES
6. FILE-CONTROL
7. SELECT. . . ASSIGN TO
8. FILE-SECTION
9. FD
10. OPEN
11. CLOSE
12. READ
13. WRITE
14. AT END
15. READ. . .INTO
16. WRITE. . .FROM
17. WRITE. . .BEFORE ADVANCING. . .
18. WRITE. . .AFTER ADVANCING. . .
19. PAGE

Programming Assignments

Two programming assignments are given below. Following directions of your instructor or your own feelings about how much practice you can use, complete either or both of these assignments. For each assignment, make sure all of the following tasks are completed:

1. Prepare or complete a structure or module hierarchy chart.

2. Prepare or complete documentation of processing logic with structured flowcharts *and* pseudocode.

3. Define sample data to be used to test your program logic and prepare expected results for those data.

4. Conduct a walkthrough of your program structure and logical design. Do this by yourself, under guidance of your instructor, or in cooperation with a fellow student.

5. Write, compile, test, and debug the program you have designed.

Problem 1

Purpose: South Bay Property Management Company wants you to rewrite the payroll program described in Chapter 1. The input has been modified and a different report format is required.

Input: Develop an input file that conforms to the record layout in Figure 7-6.

Figure 7-6. Payroll input record layout for use in practice assignment.

Output: The payroll report generated by this program should conform to the record layout in Figure 7-7.

Processing Requirements: 1) Single space the report. Print one detail line per employee.

2) Print headings as specified on the output report layout in Figure 7-7.

3) Calculate overtime pay for hours over 40.0 at 1.5 times the employee's regular pay rate.

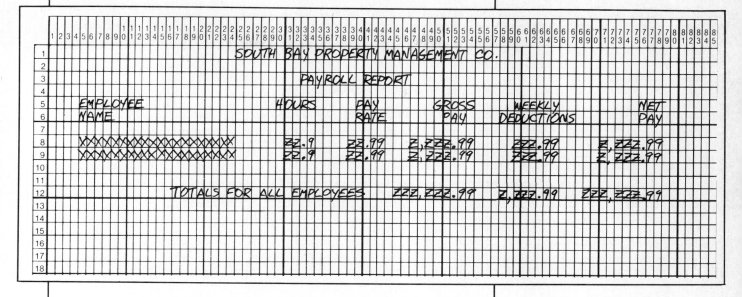

4) At the end of the input file, print the accumulated totals—as shown in the output layout of Figure 7-7.

Figure 7-7. Output layout for payroll report. For use in practice assignment.

5) The calculation for net pay is: Net Pay = Gross Pay − Deductions.

Problem 2

Purpose: The Honest Investment Company wants you to write a program that will calculate the total amount of an investment. The calculation is to be based on application of compound interest.

Input: The input record, depicted in the layout in Figure 7-8, has the following fields and field content.

Position	Field
1—22	Customer name (alphanumeric)
23—28	Principal amount (numeric, integer)
29—32	Interest rate (V9999)
33—35	Compounding factor (numeric, integer)
36—38	Years invested (99V9)
39—45	Unused

Figure 7-8. Investment input record layout for use in practice assignment.

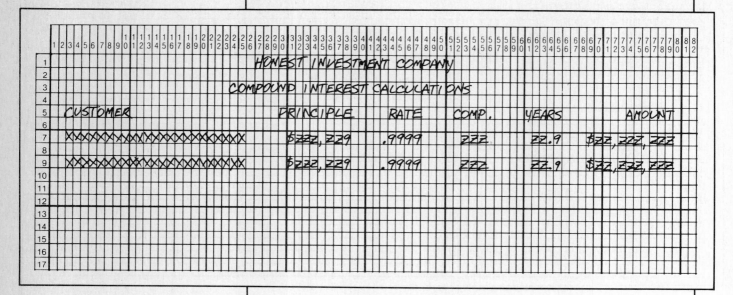

Figure 7-9. Output layout for investment report. For use in practice assignment.

Output: Produce a report that conforms to the record layout in Figure 7-9.

Processing Requirements: 1) Print one line per input record. Use double-spaced printing.

2) Print headings as specified in Figure 7-9.

3) The compounding factor is the number of periods per year in which interest is calculated. Daily compounding would produce a compounding factor of 365, quarterly would be 4, etc.

4) Use the COMPUTE command to write the calculation for the equation:

$$\text{Amount} = \text{Principal} \left(1 + \frac{\text{Interest Rate}}{\text{Compounding Factor}} \right) \text{Years} \times \text{Compounding Factor}$$

Worksheet for Structured Flowchart

Program Name: _____

Prepared By: _____

Worksheet for Pseudocode Specifications

Program Name: _____

Prepared By: _____

Worksheet for Structured Flowchart

Program Name: _____

Prepared By: _____

Worksheet for Pseudocode Specifications

Program Name: _____

Prepared By: _____

COBOL PROGRAM SHEET

System		Punching Instructions			Sheet	of
Program			Graphic			Identification
Programmer	Date		Punch		Card Form #	[73] [80]

SEQUENCE						
(PAGE)	(SERIAL)	CONT	A	B		
1	3 4	6 7	8	12 16 20 24 28 32 36 40 44 48 52 56 60 64 68 72		

COBOL PROGRAM SHEET

System							Sheet	of
Program				Punching Instructions				Identification
Programmer		Date		Graphic		Card Form #		
				Punch				73] [80

SEQUENCE		CONT	A	B																	
(PAGE)	(SERIAL)																				
1 3	4 6	7	8	12	16	20	24	28	32	36	40	44	48	52	56	60	64	68	72		

COBOL PROGRAM SHEET

System		Punching Instructions		Sheet	of
Program		Graphic			Identification
Programmer	Date	Punch	Card Form #		[73] [80]

SEQUENCE
(PAGE) | (SERIAL)

| 1 3 | 4 | 6 7 | 8 CONT A | B 12 | 16 | 20 | 24 | 28 | 32 | 36 | 40 | 44 | 48 | 52 | 56 | 60 | 64 | 68 | 72 |

COBOL PROGRAM SHEET

System			
Program		Punching Instructions	Sheet of
Programmer			Identification

| | Graphic | | Card Form # | [73] [80] |
| Date | Punch | | | |

SEQUENCE
(PAGE) (SERIAL) CONT

1 3 4 6 7 8 A B 12 16 20 24 28 32 36 40 44 48 52 56 60 64 68 72

COBOL PROGRAM SHEET

System				Punching Instructions			Sheet	of
Program		Graphic						Identification
Programmer	Date	Punch		Card Form #				[73] [80]

SEQUENCE			CONT	A	B															
(PAGE)	(SERIAL)																		
1 3	4 6	7 8	8	12	16	20	24	28	32	36	40	44	48	52	56	60	64	68	72

COBOL PROGRAM SHEET

System						Sheet	of
Program		Punching Instructions		Card Form #			
Programmer		Graphic				Identification	
	Date	Punch				[73]	[80]

SEQUENCE			CONT																																			
(PAGE)	(SERIAL)			A		B																																
1 3	4 6	7	8		12	16	20	24	28	32	36	40	44	48	52	56	60	64	68	72																	

COBOL PROGRAM SHEET

System				Punching Instructions			Sheet	of
Program			Graphic			Card Form #	Identification	
Programmer		Date	Punch				73]	[80

SEQUENCE
(PAGE) (SERIAL)
1 3 4 6 7 8 CONT
8 A
B 12 16 20 24 28 32 36 40 44 48 52 56 60 64 68 72

COBOL PROGRAM SHEET

System			
Program		Punching Instructions	Sheet of
Programmer		Graphic	Card Form #
	Date	Punch	Identification [73] [80]

SEQUENCE			
(PAGE)	(SERIAL)	CONT	A B
1 3	4 6	7	8 12 16 20 24 28 32 36 40 44 48 52 56 60 64 68 72

COBOL PROGRAM SHEET

System			Punching Instructions		Sheet	of
Program						Identification
Programmer	Date		Graphic	Card Form #		73] [80
	Punch					

SEQUENCE			CONT	A	B														
(PAGE)	(SERIAL)																	
1 3	4	6 7	8		12	16	20	24	28	32	36	40	44	48	52	56	60	64	68	72

COBOL PROGRAM SHEET

System							Sheet	of
Program				Punching Instructions		Card Form #		Identification
Programmer		Date		Graphic				
				Punch			[73]	[80]

SEQUENCE		CONT	A	B																	
(PAGE)	(SERIAL)																				
1	3 4	6	7	8	12	16	20	24	28	32	36	40	44	48	52	56	60	64	68	72

COBOL PROGRAM SHEET

System		Punching Instructions		Sheet of
Program		Graphic		Identification
Programmer	Date	Punch	Card Form #	[73] [80]

SEQUENCE				
(PAGE)	(SERIAL)	CONT	A	B
1 3	4 6	7 8		12 16 20 24 28 32 36 40 44 48 52 56 60 64 68 72

COBOL PROGRAM SHEET

System		
Program		
Programmer		Date

Punching Instructions			Sheet	of
Graphic		Card Form #	Identification	
Punch			[73] [80]	

SEQUENCE	CONT			
(PAGE) (SERIAL)		A	B	
1 3 4 6 7 8		12 16 20 24 28 32 36 40 44 48 52 56 60 64 68 72		

Vocabulary Building Practice—Exercise 7

Write definitions and/or explanations of the terms listed below.

1. **file description** _____

_____

2. **end-of-file condition** _____

_____

3. **priming read** _____

_____

4. **vertical spacing** _____

_____

5. **carriage control** _____

_____

6. **abend** _____

_____

7. **abort** _____

_____

8. **CONFIGURATION SECTION** _____

_____

9. **INPUT-OUTPUT SECTION** _____

_____

10. **SOURCE-COMPUTER** _____

_____

(over, please)

11. **OBJECT-COMPUTER** _____

_____

12. **SPECIAL-NAMES**_____

_____

13. **FILE-CONTROL** _____

_____

14. **SELECT. . .ASSIGN TO** _____

_____

15. **FD** _____

_____

16. **READ** _____

_____

17. **AT END** _____

_____

18. **READ. . .INTO** _____

_____

19. **WRITE. . .FROM** _____

_____

20. **WRITE. . .BEFORE ADVANCING** _____

_____

PRINTED REPORTS 8

OBJECTIVES

On completing reading and other learning assignments for this chapter, you should be able to:

1. Identify the application objectives satisfied by the four types of reports: detail, summary, exception, and control.

2. Structure output reports by preparing instructions to control generation of headings, detail lines, summary lines, pagination, and totals.

3. Apply effective techniques in defining reports, using the most appropriate instructions to handle such functions as carriage control, indicative information, quantitative information, print field justification, and numeric field editing.

TYPES OF REPORTS

Reports are documents produced by computers from the content of computer-processed files. The reports referred to in this chapter are printed on plain or preprinted continuous-form paper. They contain a concentration of information formatted for ease of use.

Reports are classified into a number of distinct types, based upon the use to which the information will be put. Four types of reports are significant at this point in your learning experience:

- Detail
- Summary
- Exception
- Control.

DETAIL REPORTS

A *detail report* is a listing of records taken directly from a computer-maintained file. Typically, a file record will equate to a line or lines on a report. However, the key characteristic of a detail report is its inclusiveness. No records are skipped; every one is printed.

Some examples of how detail reports may be required as part of routine business data processing applications are:

- The personnel department might have a listing of the names, addresses, and other master record fields for employees of the company. This report would be updated periodically, depending upon the rate of hiring and turnover. Typically, a personnel department might ask that such a report be produced monthly.
- A maintenance shop for an airline might want a listing of parts kept in inventory within a maintenance facility.
- Schools normally produce listings of students, by class, similar to the example in Figure 8-1.

CALIFORNIA STATE POLYTECHNIC UNIVERSITY CLASS L

DATE	COURSE TITLE	DEPT.	DEPT. CODE	INSTRUCTOR	COURSE CODE
04-21-82	SPEC PROB	IS	400	MEDLEY	5140002

STUDENT NAME			MAJOR
JOHNSON,BRET R	130475	2.0	0839
LISCUM,DOUGLAS E	054791	2.0	4734
REID,PAUL JAMES	141334	2.0	0734
THACKER,SCOT HENNING	130413	2.0	0734
VELEZ,CARLOS A	110665	2.0	0734
-- TOTAL STUDENTS -- 5		10.0	

Figure 8-1. Detail report.

SUMMARY REPORTS

A *summary report* is one in which information is consolidated so that a single line represents more than one detail record from the file.

Summary reports are commonly used to provide status information for managers. Some examples are:

- A sales manager might want to know total sales for a given period, such as one week, for each salesperson, for every product. These reports would be summarized from detail records of orders turned in by salespeople.

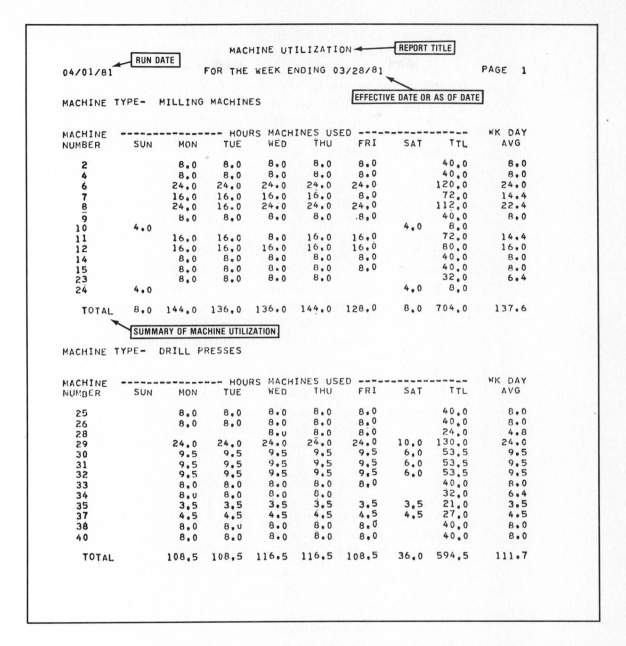

MACHINE UTILIZATION ◄——— REPORT TITLE

04/01/81 ◄— RUN DATE   FOR THE WEEK ENDING 03/28/81   PAGE 1

EFFECTIVE DATE OR AS OF DATE

MACHINE TYPE- MILLING MACHINES

MACHINE									WK DAY
NUMBER	SUN	MON	TUE	WED	THU	FRI	SAT	TTL	AVG
2		8.0	8.0	8.0	8.0	8.0		40.0	8.0
4		8.0	8.0	8.0	8.0	8.0		40.0	8.0
6		24.0	24.0	24.0	24.0	24.0		120.0	24.0
7		16.0	16.0	16.0	16.0	8.0		72.0	14.4
8		24.0	16.0	24.0	24.0	24.0		112.0	22.4
9		8.0	8.0	8.0	8.0	.8.0		40.0	8.0
10	4.0						4.0	8.0	
11		16.0	16.0	8.0	16.0	16.0		72.0	14.4
12		16.0	16.0	16.0	16.0	16.0		80.0	16.0
14		8.0	8.0	8.0	8.0	8.0		40.0	8.0
15		8.0	8.0	8.0	8.0	8.0		40.0	8.0
23		8.0	8.0	8.0	8.0			32.0	6.4
24	4.0						4.0	8.0	
TOTAL	8.0	144.0	136.0	136.0	144.0	128.0	8.0	704.0	137.6

SUMMARY OF MACHINE UTILIZATION

MACHINE TYPE- DRILL PRESSES

MACHINE									WK DAY
NUMBER	SUN	MON	TUE	WED	THU	FRI	SAT	TTL	AVG
25		8.0	8.0	8.0	8.0	8.0		40.0	8.0
26		8.0	8.0	8.0	8.0	8.0		40.0	8.0
28			8.0	8.0	8.0			24.0	4.8
29		24.0	24.0	24.0	24.0	24.0	10.0	130.0	24.0
30		9.5	9.5	9.5	9.5	9.5	6.0	53.5	9.5
31		9.5	9.5	9.5	9.5	9.5	6.0	53.5	9.5
32		9.5	9.5	9.5	9.5	9.5	6.0	53.5	9.5
33		8.0	8.0	8.0	8.0	8.0		40.0	8.0
34		8.0	8.0	8.0	8.0			32.0	6.4
35		3.5	3.5	3.5	3.5	3.5	3.5	21.0	3.5
37		4.5	4.5	4.5	4.5	4.5	4.5	27.0	4.5
38		8.0	8.0	8.0	8.0	8.0		40.0	8.0
40		8.0	8.0	8.0	8.0	8.0		40.0	8.0
TOTAL		108.5	108.5	116.5	116.5	108.5	36.0	594.5	111.7

- A manufacturing manager might want to know the total hours of usage for each machine in the factory. This report would be summarized from detail machine utilization records. An example is shown in Figure 8-2.

- An airline president might want to know total seats sold for flights based on time of day, day of week, or by week. This would be a summary report based upon detail records from the company's reservation system. In summarizing the data, percentages would be computed that reflected the number of seats sold as compared with all seats available.

Figure 8-2. Annotated summary report.

Summary reports are sometimes called *tabulations*. This terminology comes from the name of the machine, a tabulator, on which this type of report was prepared during the punched card era. For the same reason, detail reports are often called *detail listings*. This reflects the former practice of printing a line for each punched card, rather than accumulating totals and summarizing them as in a tabulation.

EXCEPTION REPORTS

An *exception report* is one that contains records selected for their content. This is done through program-controlled selection of records that meet or fail certain tests or conditions. An *exception*, in these terms, is any situation defined as unusual or abnormal. The boundaries of acceptability or normalcy are written into computer programs. Then, any records that fall outside these limits are included on the report.

Most business application systems use exception processing and reporting. Any application system typically encompasses several programs. One of the first operations in a system is usually a data validation program used to check the accuracy and completeness of transactions to be processed.

An important type of exception reporting involves the screening of raw input data for accuracy and completeness. This process is known as *editing*, or *validating*. In a program for validating data, every input record is tested to verify the accuracy and completeness of characters, fields, and of the record as a whole. Figure 8-3 is an example of this type of report.

Character testing involves the use of the *class* and *sign* conditions described in Chapter 6. The characters in a given field could be tested to determine whether they are all NUMERIC or ALPHABETIC, as appropriate. Numeric data may be tested further for the presence of algebraic signs, either POSITIVE or NEGATIVE.

Validating the accuracy and completeness of data fields can also involve tests of reasonableness, range, limits, presence or absence, dates, and many others.

A *reasonableness test* might check the content of the NUMBER-OF-DEPENDENTS field in a payroll file. This test could determine whether the number of dependents is less than some selected value, such as 12 or 15.

Range checks are often used to determine if a data value lies between some minimum and maximum value. For instance, in an inventory control application, the master records contain data about the level at which items should be reordered (often called safety stock or reorder point). As inventory transaction records are input, they might cause the master records to be tested to determine whether the quantity on hand is GREATER THAN the safety stock (minimum) value and LESS THAN 10 times the safety stock value (a maximum).

```
   02-08-83     INVALID SALES AND RETURN TRANSACTIONS    PAGE    1

 TRAN  ------------------- *INDICATES ERROR FIELDS -------------------
 CODE     REF NO      DATE     BR SLSMN    CUST      QTY      PART    AUTH

 C1    BAD SAL  1   *790228    04   333    12004    00040    10200
 C1    BAD SAL  2   *821328    04   333    12004    00040    10200
 C1    BAD SAL  3   *820232    04   333    12004    00040    10200
 C1    BAD SAL  4    820228   *00   333    12004    00040    10200
 C1    BAD SAL  5    820228   *26   333    12004    00040    10200
 C1    BAD SAL  6    820228    04  *...    12004    00040    10200
 C1    BAD SAL  7    820228    04   333   *.....    00040    10200
 C1    BAD SAL  8    820228    04   333    12004   *.....    10200
 C1    BAD SAL  9    820228    04   333    12004    00040   *.....
 C1    BAD SAL 10   *800228    04   333    12004    00040   *70999
 C1    BAD SAL 11   *791332   *!!  *"""   *&&&&&   *=====   */////
 C2    BAD RET  1   *790331              13005    00050    10500    AAAA
 C2    BAD RET  2   *820031              13005    00050    10500    AAAA
 C2    BAD RET  3   *820300              13005    00050    10500    AAAA
 C2    BAD RET  4    820331             *00000    00050    10500    AAAA
 C2    BAD RET  5    820331              13005   *00000    10500    AAAA
 C2    BAD RET  6    820331              13005    00050   *00000    AAAA
 C2    BAD RET  7    820331              13005    00050    10500   *9999
 C2    BAD RET  8   *000000             *&&&&&   *=====   */////
 C3    BAD ???    ??????   ??   ???    ?????    ?????    ?????    ????
 X1    BAD UPDCOD ??????   ??   ???    ?????    ?????    ?????    ????
```

Figure 8-3. Validation report.

A *limit test* is usually used to determine if data are above or below some selected value. For example, in this same inventory application, the system designer may decide that the only exception condition to be concerned with is when quantity on hand is LESS THAN the safety stock value. Safety stock, therefore, becomes a lower limit and no check is made against a maximum.

In many applications, certain data fields must always be *present* before correct processing of a record can take place. In a personnel file, every employee must have a Social Security number. The following statement could be used in a validation program to test for the above condition.

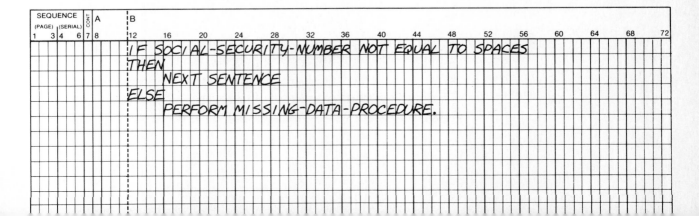

Similarly, the IF. . .EQUAL TO SPACES statement can check for the *absence* of data when that situation is appropriate.

In the example below, a credit check process would approve a purchase if the customer account was not delinquent.

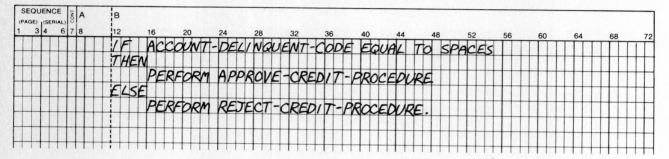

Testing the contents of date fields is really a type of range check. However, *date checks* are often done and sometimes exist as a separate subroutine available in a library of programs. In checking dates, the programmer is concerned with verifying that the month number is between 1 and 12, the day number between 1 and 28, 29, 30, or 31; and that the year number is appropriate. Each of these tests is represented by separate IF. . .THEN. . . ELSE statements.

Validation programs may also test whole records for completeness or accuracy. One of the common *record tests* that is conducted is to check the record type field and then to determine whether all fields are present as specified for a given type of code.

Data editing and validation processes are very important to computer information systems. They basically serve two important functions. First, as discussed above, these tests help to verify the accuracy and completeness of data. The other function is to present exception information for management review.

Exception reports, as management tools, are designed to focus attention on situations that require decisions or corrections. The following are examples:

- Many payroll systems produce reports listing unusually large checks. For example, on an hourly payroll, any checks drawn for more than $750 might be listed for management review before they are issued.

- If an individual employee works more than 60 hours per week for three weeks in a row, the personnel manager may want to know about this. If so, these conditions can be included in the payroll program and exception reports prepared to reflect this information.

- A common use of exception reports is for reordering of inventory items. A portion of a report of this type is illustrated in Figure 8-4. Each item in the file is assigned a reorder point and/or an economic

```
                          PRODUCTS INVENTORY STATUS

    DATE    05/10/81                                          PAGE    1


    PROD
    NO        DESCRIPTION              QTY ON   REORDER
                                       HAND     POINT       EOQ    MAKE


    1174      WURP                       900     1,040     1,000    YES
    1286      MAZZLE                     425       300        86
    1297      GRICKER                    260       260       162    YES
    1358      CRATCHERT                  500       420       117
    1379      THISTEW                  1,000       538       734
    1401      STURF                      667       735       132    YES
    1453      LIMU                        63-      600     3,387    YES
    1460      VIVOMY                               360     1,077    YES
    1515      BLISTOW                  7,214       256       743
    1527      CALOSTAY                 2,105       300       162
    1589      DIRCH                       36        75        97    YES
    1600      XENOTHITE                  786       148       131
    1601      XENOTHOL                   815       655        37
    1662      ASYMTICK                 2,561     3,160       553    YES
    1694      FIXO                     6,293     1,770       594
    1727      SCREECHER                2,700     1,512       995
    1836      GUMP                     1,700     1,760       156    YES
    1863      NEVERDO                  1,040       440       161
    1888      OMNIRAY                  2,000     2,280       164    YES
    1905      RESTOGRUNGE              4,180     1,260       794
    1917      YEARTHY                  2,673     1,020       229
    1944      FUZZLE                      32-    2,880     1,958    YES
    1947      SLIPSOWELL                 120     1,560     1,400    YES
    1952      UNDROX                   9,218       784       385
    1953      BIGELSASS                8,379     3,722       279
    1979      CHIGORICAL                 134       560       177    YES
    2164      VELLOW                   2,891     1,120       423
    2318      MYSTIFOR                 3,365     1,260       247
    2320      PECULARISM               9,637       975       556
    2396      UNSTIR                   1,558     1,960       289    YES
    2400      RASTOFUR                    10       725       440    YES
    2411      KAROO                      450       360       500
    2496      ZEBAR                      212        80        93
    3178      FLISTOL                    130       130       173    YES
    3207      POLUMA                     246       158       248
    3284      GORGRIST                   505       133       367
    3333      MULL                       342       330       255
    3339      IBENSALUKYEY                         600       860    YES
    3470      AFFULEEZE                  153       260     1,095    YES
    3522      BATNANZIZU               3,707        82       769
    3535      FORTICKLEY                  15        40       172    YES
    3561      NEVOGATH                    72        75        98    YES
    3606      NATCHPULL                  385        62        65
    3657      GROSSPLATH                 417       380        73
    3698      LIMURE                   1,339     1,040       548
    3743      SENTICULAR               3,147       580       605
    3829      RANDOCULL                1,468       478       496
    3840      FISTICULE                1,800     1,860     1,225    YES
    3914      AMBILOTHUS                 950     1,200       125    YES
```

Figure 8-4. Exception report.

order quantity. Each time the master record for that inventory item is processed, the stock on hand is compared with the reorder point. If the stock on hand is below the established minimum (reorder point), the item is included on an exception report as a candidate for stock replenishment.

• Bank data processing systems regularly report closed accounts or accounts on which normal transaction limits have been overridden by a manager. It is also commonplace, in banks, to report large dollar-amount transactions and transactions on accounts that have been dormant for a number of years.

CONTROL REPORTS

A *control report* is a quality control tool within a computer information system. Extensive controls are built into each programmed system to assure that the processing of data is complete, accurate, and reliable. To do this, a number of control techniques can be invoked, including:

- One technique would be to accumulate a balance for all the amounts in a batch of checks being processed in a bank before the data are input to a computer. Generally, this is done as part of imprinting the dollar amount on the bottom of the check through use of a device called a proof machine. This batch control total is created before the checks are entered into the computer and is recorded on

Figure 8-5. Update report.

```
                          PRODUCTS INVENTORY UPDATE

        05/09/81                                              PAGE    1


        PROD        TYPE
         NO         UPDATE      -------------- RESULTS OF PROCESSING ---------


        1056        ADD         RECORD ADDED

        1453        CHANGE      UNIT COST CHANGED
                                CARRYING COST % CHANGED
                                AVG DAILY USAGE CHANGED
                                SAFETY STOCK CHANGED

        1460        DELETE      RECORD DELETED

        1527        ADD         *ERROR  RECORD ALREADY ON FILE

        1590        CHANGE      *ERROR  NO MATCHING PRODUCT ON MASTER

        1682        DELETE      *ERROR  DELETE HAS NON-BLANK FIELDS
                                *ERROR  NO MATCHING PRODUCT ON MASTER

        1730        ADD         *ERROR  UNIT COST ZERO OR NOT NUMERIC
                                *ERROR  CARRYING COST % ZERO OR NOT NUMERIC
                                *ERROR  ANNUAL QTY NEEDED ZERO OR NOT NUMERIC
                                *ERROR  COST TO PRODUCE ZERO OR NOT NUMERIC
                                *ERROR  LEAD TIME ZERO OR NOT NUMERIC
                                *ERROR  AVG DAILY USAGE ZERO OR NOT NUMERIC
                                *ERROR  SAFETY STOCK ZERO OR NOT NUMERIC

        1863        CHANGE      *ERROR  SAFETY STOCK ZERO OR NOT NUMERIC

        1952        DELETE      *ERROR  QTY ON HAND NOT ZERO

        2400        X           *ERROR  INVALID UPDATE CODE

        3787        ADD         RECORD ADDED

        3787        CHANGE      ANNUAL QTY NEEDED CHANGED
                                COST TO PRODUCE CHANGED
                                LEAD TIME CHANGED

        3787        DELETE      RECORD DELETED

        3985        CHANGE      *ERROR  NO CHANGES SPECIFIED

        4950        ADD         RECORD ADDED
```

a batch ticket used as an input document. Then, when the checks are read into the computer, a separate control total is prepared and printed out on a report, along with the control total recorded on the batch ticket. The two totals must be equal. That is, the totals must *balance* before processing proceeds. Similar balance and control techniques are used at every point within many computer information systems that process data on dollar amounts.

- Another type of control report is the *update report*. Typically, this is used to review alterations of master files. Fields are established on the report to list, for easy comparison, the control field, the transaction type, and a message describing the action taken.

- Any errors encountered during processing are listed. Examples would include attempts to add duplicate records or to change or delete a nonexistent record. A control report of this type is shown in Figure 8-5.

REPORT STRUCTURES

No matter what type of report is to be produced, there are certain fundamental structural requirements to be met. Report structure information is usually given to the programmer in the form of a *print layout* diagram like the one shown in Figure 8-6. A checklist of these requirements is given below, followed by discussions of how these report structure elements are implemented:

- Headings
- Detail lines
- Summary lines
- Pagination
- Totals.

HEADINGS

Two types of *headings* must be provided for in the structuring of a report:

- Report headings
- Columnar headings.

Report Headings

Report headings (refer back to Figure 8-2) are printed at the top of each page of the report. Information presented in these headings includes the title of the report, the page number, and the effective date of the information presented. A second date, the day on which the report is run, may also be given in the heading.

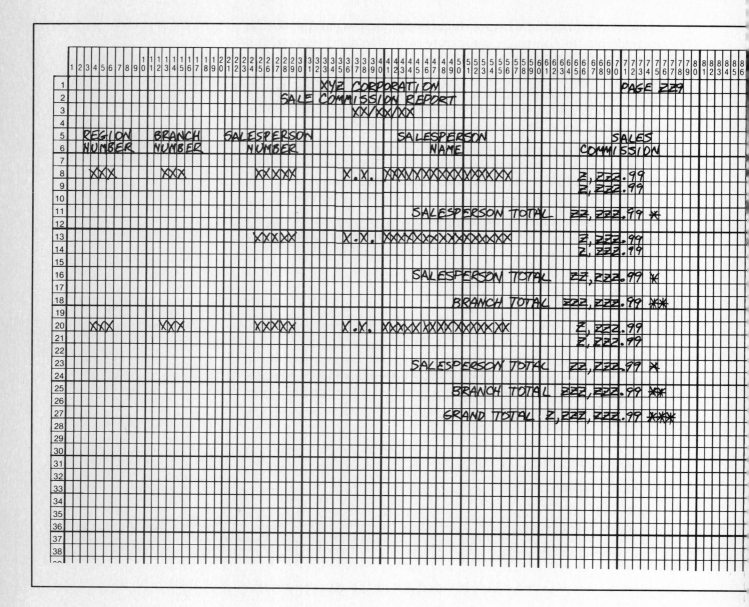

Figure 8-6. Print layout form.

The report title may be provided in specifications for the program or may have to be composed as part of the programming job. The report title can occupy one or more lines, though single-line titles are most common. Report titles are usually centered at the top of each page.

Titles of reports should be as simple and as descriptive as possible. Examples: *Monthly Sales Report, Payroll Register,* and *Inventory Status Report.*

The consecutive numbering of report pages should be provided for within the program. A counter can be used to increment the number of pages as they are printed. To do this, the programmer must set up a command to activate the counter. To print the *page numbers* on the report, the contents of the counter are usually moved to a print line area to edit out the leading zeros normally maintained in the counter.

The *effective date* for a report reflects the control date for the information provided. For example, a report printed this Thursday reflects payroll status as of the previous Friday. Thus, last Friday is the effective date.

The *run date* is the day on which the report is actually prepared. This date can be entered automatically through use of an ACCEPT instruction that causes the operating system to input the date. (See Chapter 5.) The operating system for each make and model of computer has some facility for carrying date and time information. The COBOL language has instructions that can access these data as needed. Specific instructions on formats vary with make and model of computer. Check the reference manuals for your equipment or check with your instructor.

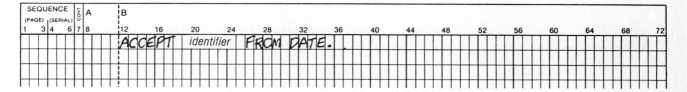

The value for the current date returned by the operating system is in the form of YYMMDD, where the YY field contains the last two digits representing the year, MM represents the month, and DD is the day.

In the example below, the ACCEPT instruction would retrieve the current date and store it in the field WS-TODAYS-DATE.

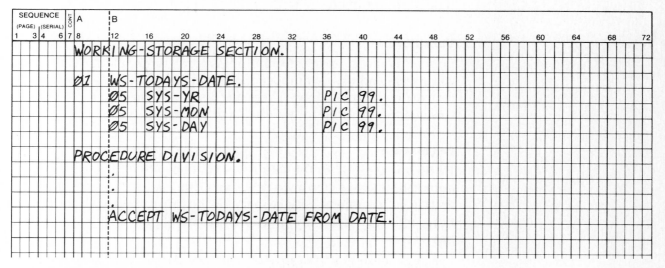

Another item of information sometimes found in report headings is a report number. This is used for control of report distribution and for ease of identification for reference purposes.

Columnar Headings

Columnar headings, as the name implies, are placed at the tops of columns of information. They should be written so that they describe accurately the information content below the headings. Both the columns and their respective headings should be spaced for readability, with the positions of the headings corresponding with the alignment of data within the columns.

For some types of corresponding columnar information, it is best to center the headings over the data provided. This occurs when the field of data is of fixed length and longer than the column heading. If the width of data entries in a column will be variable, the headings should be placed right or left justified for greatest clarity in identifying the information. For example, a Name column might be 30 characters wide. The column will contain entries of varying widths. Thus, greatest clarity is achieved by placing the heading toward the left of the column.

Conversely, if a column of data contains numerical information, entries will be aligned to the decimal point or to the right. If the heading is shorter than the width of the column, it should be placed toward the right of the column.

If multiple words are needed in a heading, a standard practice is to use two or more lines. If this is done, it is necessary to arrange the lines on a print layout diagram—and structure the commands that execute the layout—so that the multiple-line headings are correctly aligned.

To make reports readable, it is a standard practice to skip a line between the report title and the first line of the columnar headings. Also, it is standard practice to leave a blank line between the last line of the columnar headings and the first detail line of the report. This is done with a printer instruction for entry of a blank line.

Detail Lines

Detail lines are set up in columns to fall clearly under the corresponding columnar headings. A number of commands and practices apply to the formatting of detail lines. These are discussed later, in the section of this chapter devoted to report design practices.

Pagination

In printing reports, the COBOL language does not cause forms automatically to eject from the bottom of one page to the top of the next. *Pagination* provisions must be made by the programmer. These instructions are based upon design criteria covering page length and conditions for advancing forms.

Pagination practices are based on some commonly used standards throughout the computer information systems field. The most common standard for the spacing of reports, for example, is six vertical lines per inch. (Optionally, spacing can be eight lines per inch.)

There is also a standard for page length—11 inches. Thus, an 11-inch-long form spaced six lines to the inch will have a maximum of 66 print lines. Standards also call for top and bottom margins on reports, typically six lines at the top and four at the bottom. This leaves 56 lines for actual printing on an 11-inch-long form.

Thus, a common practice is to instruct the computer to move to the top of the next page and imprint appropriate headings when the line count for a current page reaches some predetermined number, such as 54, 56, or 58. These figures, of course, apply to reports that are single spaced. If double spacing is used, either the test values would be cut in half or the value 2 would be added to the line counter each time a line is printed.

When the established line limit is reached, the heading procedure, which includes advancing the paper to the top of the next page, is invoked. This is accomplished through use of the WRITE. . .AFTER ADVANCING PAGE, as described in Chapter 7. If a report segment ends before a complete page is used, a command can be inititated that will move the paper automatically to the top of the next page and invoke the heading.

Any time the heading routine is invoked, of course, the line counter must be reset to zero. A program subroutine for pagination is shown in Figure 8-7.

Totals

Totals can be developed for any numeric column in a report. When they are printed, the totals should be lined up under the columns for which their values have been accumulated. However, care must be taken in placing the totals, since these amounts are usually considerably larger than the detail entries. One method is to space the column so that there is enough room to accommodate the totals. If this is impossible or undesirable, multiple lines can be used for totals, thus providing room to present the totals in alignment with the detail entries with which they correspond. This is illustrated in Figure 8-8.

Some reports require totals at the bottom of each page. These are known as page totals, or *footings*. Provision is made for footings in the same way as for headings. That is, specific positions must be provided in report layouts for entry of footings. Footing output routines are then established, to be invoked by line counts in much the same way as the heading routines.

Reports may also include multiple levels of totals, which may be identified by level numbers or by designations such as minor, intermediate, major, and final.

Different levels of totals are invoked by some change in detail information presented to a report. For example, a change in department numbers in the input information stream may invoke a minor total and cause the program to paginate. When a lower level total is printed, the

COBOL PROGRAM SHEET

System		Punching Instructions								Sheet	of
Program		Graphic							Card Form #	Identification	
Programmer	Date	Punch								73] [80	

```
005010 PROCEDURE DIVISION.
   020           .
   030           .
   040           .
   050           PERFORM PRINT-DETAIL-LINE.
   060           .
   070           .
   080           .
   090
   100      PRINT-DETAIL-LINE.
   110           IF WS-LINE-COUNT GREATER THAN WS-LINE-LIMIT
   120           THEN
   130               PERFORM PRINT-HEADINGS.
   140           MOVE WS-DETAIL-LINE TO REPORT-RECORD.
   150           MOVE 1 TO LINE-SPACING.
   160           PERFORM PRINT-A-LINE.
   170
   180      PRINT-HEADINGS.
   190           MOVE ZERO TO WS-LINE-COUNT.
   200           ADD 1 TO WS-PAGE-COUNT.
   210           MOVE WS-PAGE-COUNT TO RPT-PAGE-NUMBER.
   220           MOVE WS-HEADING-1 TO REPORT-RECORD.
   230           PERFORM PRINT-TOP-OF-PAGE.
   240           MOVE WS-HEADING-2 TO REPORT-RECORD.
   250           MOVE 2 TO LINE-SPACING.
   260           PERFORM PRINT-A-LINE.
   270           MOVE WS-HEADING-3 TO REPORT-RECORD.
   280           MOVE 1 TO LINE-SPACING.
   290           PERFORM PRINT-A-LINE.
   300           MOVE SPACES TO REPORT-RECORD.
   310           PERFORM PRINT-A-LINE.
   320
   330      PRINT-A-LINE.
   340           WRITE REPORT-RECORD
   350               AFTER ADVANCING LINE-SPACING LINES.
   360           ADD LINE-SPACING TO WS-LINE-COUNT.
   370
   380      PRINT-TOP-OF-PAGE.
   390           WRITE REPORT-RECORD
   400               AFTER ADVANCING PAGE.
```

Figure 8-7. Sample pagination instructions.

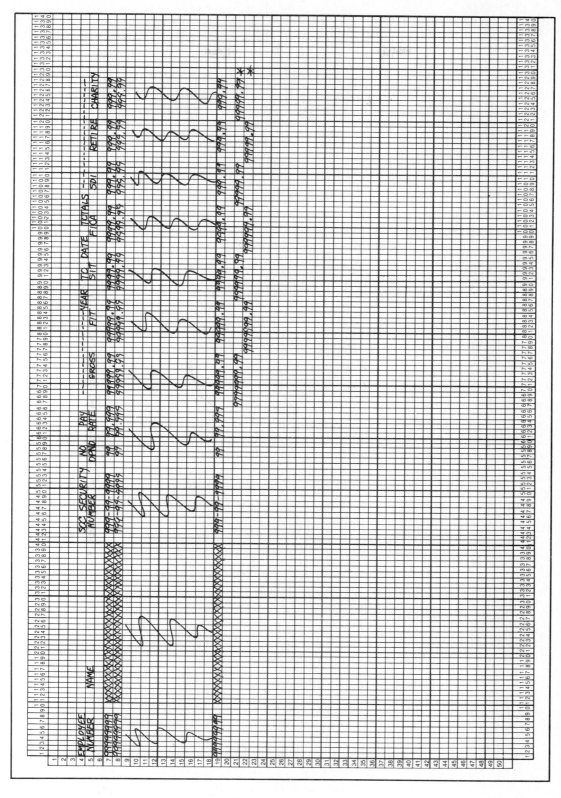

Figure 8-8. Sample print layout with multiple total lines.

accumulator for that total must be set to zero. At the same time, however, the total is rolled (added) forward into the accumulator for the next highest level of total.

Thus, totals are maintained on a running basis. For example, a minor total for a department might be carried forward into a store total. Store totals may be carried forward into regional totals. Regional totals, in turn, can be carried forward into totals for the chain as a whole. Throughout this buildup, all totals are maintained at the most minor level, rolling forward as totalling procedures are invoked. This concept of multiple totals is covered in greater depth in Chapter 11.

Reports are generally formatted to identify totals and their significance. This is usually done with an imprint of a symbol, usually an * (asterisk) to the right of the rightmost entry on the line. A single asterisk might identify a minor total, two asterisks an intermediate total, three asterisks a major total, and so on.

REPORT DESIGN PRACTICES

No matter what type of report is prepared or how it is structured, certain design requirements must be observed. To format reports effectively the programmer must be familiar with a number of practices and options. These are reviewed in the discussion that follows.

Carriage Control

Carriage control encompasses the instructions transmitted to the printer for vertical spacing of output reports. These instructions include single spacing, double spacing, triple spacing, or ejecting to a new page. Refer to Chapter 7 for a review of these concepts.

Indicative Information

Indicative, or *descriptive*, information provides identifiers for detail lines. These identifiers usually do not change with the production of new reports. Typical examples of identifiers might be name, Social Security number, part number, and so on.

A sound practice to follow is to place all indicative information to the left on detail lines on reports. This is a generally accepted convention that information users are conditioned to accept. Consider standard catalogues, telephone books, or other directories. It is a common practice for indicative information to be on the left, quantitative or variable information on the right.

Quantitative Information

Quantitative, or *variable*, information is usually positioned to the right of indicative information on report detail lines. The reasoning for this practice is explained above.

Print Field Justification

Numeric data should be justified to the right of the fields in which they are printed. When a decimal point is used, the data should be justified to the decimal position. If decimal points are eliminated, it is assumed that they are at the right of the units position in numeric fields. Alignment is to the units position.

All other fields should be aligned to the left, including both alphabetic and alphanumeric fields.

These practices should be followed unless special instructions are received to override them.

Dollar Signs

It can be highly desirable to identify those fields of a computer-produced report that present dollar values. However, use of the dollar sign within printed reports can be cumbersome and can cause problems. These problems relate to the varying field widths encountered in detail lines and between detail lines and total lines.

As a general practice, therefore, it is best never to include dollar signs in detail lines. It is still permissible, though the practice is declining, to use dollar signs in total lines. A more common technique is to include a dollar sign in the header line for a column that presents monetary information.

Algebraic Signs

Numeric values can be positive or negative. In most business data processing reports, the numeric fields presented have positive values. By convention, numeric values are assumed to be positive unless otherwise indicated.

However, COBOL provides the ability to indicate positive, negative, credit, and debit conditions for numeric fields. The signs used are +, −, CR, and DB.

In general, a - (hyphen) imprinted alongside a numeric field means that an account has been overdrawn or that a negative balance exists. This sign can be printed either to the left or to the right of the field.

Negative data can also be indicated with the designations CR and DB. These indicate accounting credits and debits. Both these symbols can indicate negative balances, depending upon whether the value given is an asset or a liability on the books of account. For a refresher on edit symbols, refer to Chapter 4. This book will not get into the principles of accounting statements. If these value signs are required in reports you are asked to prepare, be sure to get specific instructions from a qualified accountant.

Commas in Numeric Fields

Traditionally, commas are used in the decimal numbering system to indicate values of three digits (thousands) or multiples of thousands.

In producing computer output reports, it is becoming an accepted practice not to include commas in numeric fields unless the numbers involved are relatively large—into the hundreds of thousands or millions. For shorter numeric fields, commas simply take up space and do not add significant meaning.

Decimal Points

Decimal points are frequently used in numeric fields with dollar values because they impart a specific meaning to the data. In editing output fields for printing, it is necessary to review data content to make sure that, when appropriate, zeros are printed in the first decimal position.

On many reports, it may be both acceptable and desirable to print a decimal point and two zeros in the cents field even if no values under a dollar are imprinted. This formatting practice indicates to the user of the report that an action has been taken on the field and that the values are, in fact, zero.

The decimal point and zero decimal values can be suppressed in output reports through use of the BLANK WHEN ZERO clause.

In the data description below, if the content of ORDER-QUANTITY equals zero, the field would be printed as blanks. The BLANK WHEN ZERO clause may follow any numeric PICTURE description.

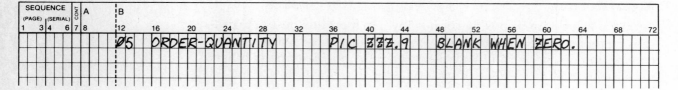

Caution should be exercised when considering the use of BLANK WHEN ZERO. This clause should be used only when the blank field does a better job of fulfilling the requirements of the user of the report.

REPORT FORMAT DEFINITIONS

In defining outputs for reports, the most effective way to specify content is through use of the WORKING-STORAGE SECTION of the DATA DIVISION. Each of the formats to be used—headings, detail lines, and total lines—can be outlined in a record description entry within the WORKING-STORAGE SECTION. Report lines are then formatted within this section of the COBOL program. After lines are formatted, they are transferred to the FILE SECTION of the DATA DIVISION for printing at the appropriate time in the program.

Summary

Reports are printed outputs produced from the content of computer-processed files. Four common types of reports are described.

A detail report is a listing of records taken directly from files. Often, each file record is represented by a single line on a report.

A summary report consolidates information from mutiple file records into individual report lines.

An exception report presents records selected on the basis of their content. Exception conditions, based on values within the records, identify situations requiring management decisions or corrective actions. Exception sensing techniques are also used in the editing, or validating, of data records to assure accuracy and reliability of computer-produced results. Data validation techniques include character tests, reasonableness tests, range checks, limit tests, date checks, and record tests.

A control report checkpoints the completeness, accuracy, and reliability of processing within computer programs. Control reports provide the basis for balancing inputs to outputs to assure validity of processing. Update reports assure retention of control following execution of programs that alter computer files. [*Objective No. 1.*]

For any type of report, the programmer must provide instructions that structure and format the presentation of information. Provision must be made for report headings, columnar headings, detail lines, pagination, and totals or footings. [*Objective No. 2.*]

Report design specifications must be received or prepared by the programmer. Instructions must then be prepared to apply carriage control, presentation of indicative information, positioning of quantitative information, print field justification, dollar signs, value indicator signs, commas in numeric fields, and decimals, as appropriate. [*Objective No. 3.*]

Key Terms

1. report
2. detail report
3. summary report
4. tabulation
5. exception report
6. exception
7. editing
8. validating
9. character testing
10. class condition
11. sign condition
12. reasonableness test
13. range check
14. limit test
15. present data check
16. absent data check
17. date check
18. record test
19. control report
20. update report
21. print layout
22. report heading
23. page number
24. effective date
25. run date
26. columnar heading
27. detail line
28. pagination
29. footing
30. indicative information
31. descriptive information
32. quantitative information
33. variable information

Review/Discussion Questions

1. What is the usual relationship between records in a file and the contents of detail reports?

2. What are some typical applications for detail reports?

3. What are the main differences in content and purpose between detail and summary reports?

4. What are some typical applications for summary reports?

5. How are exception-sensing techniques used to edit, or validate, the completeness, accuracy, and reliability of processing?

6. What are some typical applications for exception reports?

7. How are character, reasonableness, and limit tests applied?

8. What are the purposes and applications of control reports?

9. What are the major rules that apply to the structuring of report headings?

10. What standards or recommended procedures should be followed for report pagination?

11. What are typical levels for report totals and how are levels determined and identified?

12. What differences and relationships exist between indicative and quantitative information?

Programming Assignment

A programming assignment is given below. Following directions of your instructor, complete this assignment, making sure that all of the following tasks are completed:

1. Prepare or complete a structure or module hierarchy chart.

2. Prepare or complete documentation of processing logic with structured flowcharts *and* pseudocode.

3. Define sample data to be used to test your program logic and prepare expected results for that data.

4. Conduct a walkthrough of your program structure and logical design. Do this by yourself, under guidance of your instructor, or in cooperation with a fellow student.

5. Write, compile, test, and debug the program you have designed.

Purpose: Screen payroll input records. Before raw payroll input data can be processed to produce employee paychecks, they must be edited and validated. This means each payroll record must be screened for accuracy and completeness.

Input: Create an input file of employee payroll records to conform to the format defined in Figure 8-9.

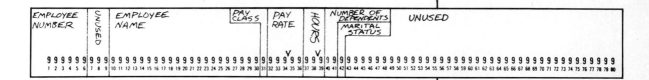

Output: The output is to be a report that conforms to the layout in Figure 8-10.

Figure 8-9. Input record layout for payroll. For use in practice assignment.

Processing Requirements: 1) Print one line per input record.

2) Print the current date as part of the heading, following the format in the report layout.

3) Apply the following validation rules:

- Employee number must be numeric and greater than 0.

- Pay class must be H for hourly or S for salaried. If pay class is invalid, do not test pay rate and hours.

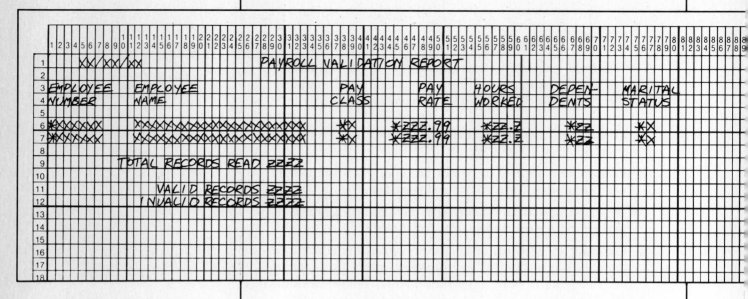

Figure 8-10. Output layout for validation report. For use in practice assignment.

- Pay rate must be numeric and a range check must be performed for hourly personnel. Valid hourly pay is 3.50 to 25.00. No range check should be applied for salaried personnel.

- Hours must be numeric and greater than 0 and less than 65.0 for hourly employees.

- For salaried employees, hours must be blank.

- Dependents must be numeric and less than 21.

- Marital status must be M, S, or D.

4) Print an asterisk (*) to the left of each invalid field.

5) At end of file of input data, print control totals as specified in output layout.

Programming Technique Note: To suppress printing of the decimal point on the hours field for salaried employees, use BLANK WHEN ZERO clause after the PICTURE of the output field. Then move zeros to that field when a valid condition is detected.

Worksheet for Structured Flowchart

Program Name: _____

Prepared By: _____

Worksheet for Pseudocode Specifications

Program Name: _____

Prepared By: _____

Worksheet for Structured Flowchart

Program Name: _____

Prepared By: _____

Worksheet for Pseudocode Specifications

Program Name: _____

Prepared By: _____

COBOL PROGRAM SHEET

System					Sheet	of

Punching Instructions

Program			Graphic		Card Form #	Identification

| Programmer | Date | | Punch | | | [73] [80] |

SEQUENCE		CONT	A	B																
(PAGE)	(SERIAL)																			
1 3	4 6	7	8	12	16	20	24	28	32	36	40	44	48	52	56	60	64	68	72	

COBOL PROGRAM SHEET

System			Sheet	of

	Punching Instructions			
Program	Graphic		Card Form #	Identification
Programmer	Date	Punch		[73] [80]

SEQUENCE			CONT	A	B																											
(PAGE)	(SERIAL)																															
1 3	4 6	7	8	12	16	20	24	28	32	36	40	44	48	52	56	60	64	68	72												

COBOL PROGRAM SHEET

System		Punching Instructions		Sheet	of
Program					
Programmer	Date	Graphic		Identification	
	Punch	Card Form #			73] [80

SEQUENCE (PAGE) (SERIAL)			CONT	A	B																			
1	3 4	6 7	8		12	16	20	24	28	32	36	40	44	48	52	56	60	64	68	72			

COBOL PROGRAM SHEET

System			Punching Instructions				Sheet	of
Program			Graphic			Card Form #		Identification
Programmer		Date	Punch					[73] [80]

SEQUENCE			CONT	A	B																		
(PAGE)	(SERIAL)																						
1 3	4 6	7	8	12	16	20	24	28	32	36	40	44	48	52	56	60	64	68	72				

COBOL PROGRAM SHEET

System				Punching Instructions			Sheet	of
Program								
Programmer			Date	Graphic		Card Form #		Identification
				Punch				73] [80

SEQUENCE					
(PAGE)	(SERIAL)	CONT	A	B	
1	3 4	6 7	8	12	16 20 24 28 32 36 40 44 48 52 56 60 64 68 72

COBOL PROGRAM SHEET

System			Punching Instructions			Sheet	of
Program				Graphic		Card Form #	Identification
Programmer		Date		Punch			[73] [80]

SEQUENCE		CONT	A	B																	
(PAGE)	(SERIAL)																				
1 3	4 6	7	8	12	16	20	24	28	32	36	40	44	48	52	56	60	64	68	72		

COBOL PROGRAM SHEET

System				Punching Instructions			Sheet	of
Program				Graphic		Card Form #		Identification
Programmer			Date	Punch				

SEQUENCE					
(PAGE)	(SERIAL)	CONT	A	B	
1 3	4 6	7 8		12 16 20 24 28 32 36 40 44 48 52 56 60 64 68 72	73] [80

COBOL PROGRAM SHEET

System				Sheet	of

Program			Punching Instructions			Card Form #		Identification

Programmer		Date	Graphic					[73] [80]
			Punch					

SEQUENCE		CONT	A	B														
(PAGE)	(SERIAL)																	
1 3	4 6	7	8	12 16 20 24 28 32 36 40 44 48 52 56 60 64 68 72														

COBOL PROGRAM SHEET

System			Punching Instructions		Sheet	of
Program						
Programmer	Date	Graphic			Identification	
	Punch		Card Form #			

SEQUENCE (PAGE) (SERIAL)	CONT	A	B														
1 3 4 6 7 8			12	16	20	24	28	32	36	40	44	48	52	56	60	64	68	72

73] [80]

COBOL PROGRAM SHEET

System				Sheet	of
Program		Punching Instructions		Identification	
Programmer	Date	Graphic	Card Form #	[73]	[80]
		Punch			

SEQUENCE		CONT	A	B																
(PAGE)	(SERIAL)																			
1 3	4 6	7	8	12	16	20	24	28	32	36	40	44	48	52	56	60	64	68	72	

COBOL PROGRAM SHEET

System			
Program			
Programmer		Date	Punch

Punching Instructions		
Graphic		
	Card Form #	

Sheet	of
Identification	
73]	[80

SEQUENCE		CONT	A	B																
(PAGE)	(SERIAL)																		
1 3	4 6	7 8		12	16	20	24	28	32	36	40	44	48	52	56	60	64	68	72

COBOL PROGRAM SHEET

System					Sheet	of
Program		Punching Instructions		Card Form #	Identification	
Programmer	Date	Graphic			[73]	[80]
		Punch				

SEQUENCE		CONT	A	B																	
(PAGE)	(SERIAL)																				
1 3	4 6	7	8	12	16	20	24	28	32	36	40	44	48	52	56	60	64	68	72		

Vocabulary Building Practice—Exercise 8

Write definitions and/or explanations of the terms listed below.

1. detail report _____

_____

2. summary report _____

_____

3. tabulation _____

_____

4. exception report _____

_____

5. validating _____

_____

6. character testing _____

_____

7. class condition _____

_____

8. sign condition _____

_____

9. reasonableness test _____

_____

10. range check _____

_____

(over, please)

11. limit test _____

_____

12. present data check _____

_____

13. absent data check _____

_____

14. date check _____

_____

15. record test _____

_____

16. control report _____

_____

17. update report _____

_____

18. print layout _____

_____

19. report heading _____

_____

20. effective date _____

_____

FILE PRINCIPLES AND MANAGEMENT 9

OBJECTIVES

On completing reading and other learning assignments for this chapter, you should be able to:

1. Describe the makeup of files as sets of related records and identify an organization's set of files as a database.
2. Explain the four basic methods under which files are organized for processing, covering the features, advantages, and disadvantages of each.
3. Explain the methods used to sort and organize sequential, indexed sequential, and direct records, including the roles of record keys.
4. Describe the characteristics of types of files structured to support applications, including master, transaction, log, historic, archival, and backup files.
5. Describe the structure, intended use, and method of writing and reading data for different types of storage media, including punched cards, magnetic tape, magnetic disk, printers, and microfilm.
6. Describe and apply procedures for sequential file processing, including creating, sorting or merging, and maintaining files.

MAKEUP OF FILES

One of the basic strengths of the COBOL language—indeed, one of the reasons for developing the COBOL language initially—lies in the ability to create, manage, and use data in files stored within computer systems. This book has already established the need for files within COBOL programs. Chapter 4 describes the basic structures of characters, fields, records, and files. Chapter 7 provides an introduction to and practice in the use of COBOL instructions for the handling and use of files.

305

Up to this point in your programming experience, you have been using files that were constructed in advance by someone else. You have not yet had to deal with the building and managing of files. That is the purpose and topic of this chapter.

To review, records are formed from fields of related data. For example, a vendor record might contain name, street address, city, state, and zip code. A payroll record might consist of department number, occupation classification code, employee name, address, date hired, Social Security number, and fields for pay rates and earnings.

The underlying makeup of a data record, then, is a series of data fields recorded contiguously to provide related data values normally processed as a single unit. Thus, a file is a collection of related records, one or more for each entity in the set. For example, a payroll file might consist of the set of all time cards for a company, one for each employee.

The collection of files that support a computer information system within an organization is known as a *database*. In addition to consisting of computer-processable records, a database also includes a plan of organization and management for the accumulation and use of data. Most organizations have multiple databases. Each database is controlled under a common management system that has its own approach and philosophy, known as a *database management system (DBMS)*.

FILE ORGANIZATION METHODS

To be useful within computer information systems, files must be organized according to some structure that makes it possible to write and read records for processing by programs. Four basic techniques are used in recording files for computer processing:

- Serial

- Sequential

- Indexed sequential

- Direct.

Serial

Serial files consist of records recorded one after another, in the sequence in which they are received by the recording device. Thus, the only plan of organization in a serial file is the chronological order of recording.

To illustrate, data entry operators may record data as orders or other documents are presented to them. The resulting files will be in serial order, as the entries are made. Similarly, many computer systems use a technique called *electronic journaling*. This, simply, is a logging of all transactions into a computer system that provides on-line service.

These logging entries are recorded on computer files in chronological order, as transactions occur. Thus, the only common denominator that ties the records together is the time of occurrence.

Sequential

Sequential files are also written one record after another. However, the ordering of sequential files is based on a logical plan. The order of records within a sequential file is determined by some unique attribute, or content item, within the records. This content item is known as a *record key*.

To illustrate, payroll files may be recorded by using employee name, Social Security number, employee number assigned by a company, or other unique identifier as the record key.

In some situations, the sequencing of records may be based upon two or more record keys. For example, one record key for a payroll file may be department number. Then, within department number, sequencing may be according to employee number. As another example, some banks organize their checking account files in sequence by branch number, then by customer account number within branches.

When two or more record keys are used to sequence files, they are usually referred to as the *major key* and *minor keys*. The major key is the first one used in sorting and organizing files. Minor keys follow the major key.

Sequencing of records within files can be either in ascending or descending order. The process of arranging records in a prescribed order for sequential files is known as *sorting*.

Four separate options can be used in sorting records into a desired sequence:

- The data may be sorted manually. However, the normal volume of data processed by computers makes this option impractical.

- The programmer can write an algorithm to handle the sorting. This option is used only infrequently because of the greater convenience of standardized tools described below.

- Sorting can be done through use of the SORT verb within the COBOL language. This is an advanced topic that will not be treated in this beginning book.

- Standard programs provided by computer manufacturers can be used for sorting records. These are known as sort *utilities*. When sorting is done under utility programs, this function is completed outside of application programs. To use sort utilities, consult a special manual from the computer manufacturer.

In summary, sequential files are distinguished by a logical organization in which records are ordered according to the content of specific fields.

Indexed Sequential

An *indexed sequential* file is a sequential file with an index added to identify record locations. An index, in turn, is a list of record keys and their corresponding storage location addresses.

The use of an indexed sequential organization permits processing of a file either sequentially or through individual access to records without regard to the order in which they are stored. For example, an indexed sequential file of inventory records might be processed sequentially to produce a stock status report of all products. However, the same file could, in an order entry application, be accessed to provide quantity-on-hand information for individual products.

With this choice of access and processing methods, the indexed sequential file organization makes possible a high degree of flexibility in the use of data.

Direct

Direct files are organized under a system in which record keys are used to determine storage location. The records themselves are not stored in any particular logical sequence or order. Rather, records are stored in address order, as determined by an address-generating algorithm.

The main difference between direct and other types of file organizations lies in the way their records are accessed by a computer system. Serial and sequential records must be read in order, as they are recorded. In direct files, records can be read or written individually, or randomly, as needed by an application.

This ability to locate and process records randomly is a major advantage of direct files.

To illustrate, persons using automatic teller machines at banks follow procedures that cause their account records to be updated automatically. To provide this service, the computer must be able, in a short time while the customer is waiting, to find the record, determine whether there are sufficient funds in the account to process the transaction, then update the account and provide the requested customer service. This type of service could not be provided if the computer had to search, in sequence, the millions of records that might be contained in the computer files of a large bank.

FILE TYPES

Files are organized according to the processing requirements of computer applications and equipment. File types, on the other hand, are determined by the application needs involved, or the use to which the data will be put. There are many types of files used within computer systems. The most common, and those which you will encounter in learning to develop application programs, include:

- Master files
- Transaction files
- Log files
- History files
- Archival files
- Backup files.

Master Files

Master files are relatively permanent in nature and include comprehensive data about a given subject. The data involved are usually basic to business patterns or functions of the organization maintaining the files. For example, most businesses have customer files. Customers are regarded as necessary to the conduct of the business. Content of this customer file generally would include all data that a business needs about each customer, such as name, address, accounting data, credit history, and payment history. Therefore, these files are used and re-used continually in the processing of business transactions by computers. Other examples of master files include:

- Account files at banks
- Inventory files for items stocked by a company
- Social Security files maintained by the Social Security Administration in Baltimore, MD
- Taxpayer files maintained by the Internal Revenue Service
- Vendor, or supplier, files that contain records of organizations with which an entity does business.

Transaction Files

A *transaction* is the result of an act of doing business. It takes place over a short period of time and is then concluded. Files of transaction data are temporary. They are generally used to update master files to reflect current information. Then, most transaction records become part of history files, as described below.

Examples of transaction items include time cards to be used in processing a weekly payroll, checks drawn upon bank accounts, bills issued to customers, shipping and receiving records, sales slips in stores, or any other record created as a by-product of the act of doing business.

Log Files

Log files were described earlier, in the discussion of serial files. Log files are always serial. They represent a continuous recording of activity within a computer system, in order of occurrence. There are two kinds of computer system activities for which logging is important. One such activity is to record when programs are executed. A second activity is to log transactions as they are processed.

Log files play important control, recovery, and security roles in the management of modern computer installations. Control stems from the fact that there is a permanent record of all transactions handled within a computer. Thus, the computer, through its log files, provides the same kind of protection as traditional, paper-based accounting systems. That is, there is a record that can be referenced at any time to determine exactly what transactions were processed on a computer, and at what time.

Log files are used to reestablish computer service if there is an interruption due to accident or disaster. The log files may be processed as though they were new input, updating the last version of files that were created by the computer before service was interrupted.

Log files also play a security role in that they are always present as a means of monitoring assets controlled through computer processing. For example, a continuing security concern for computer users lies in the issuing of checks by machines. Log files indicate the time, sequence, and occurrence of the execution of check-writing programs. Thus, any unauthorized use of the computer for distribution of a company's assets would be recorded in the log file for security reference.

History Files

History files are chronological records covering the use of files by computer systems. In effect, a history file is like a log file—except that the data recorded deal only with access to the file, rather than detailing all transactions processed through the entire computer system.

For example, if a customer uses an automatic teller machine to withdraw money, there would be separate records in the log file and also in the history file for that account. The log file would record the fact that access to a given account was made from a specific machine, at a specific time, on a given day. The history file for that application system would record the specifics of the individual account accessed and the transactions completed. However, if the password entered by the customer was incorrect and the money withdrawal transaction was not authorized, there would be no history record, but the attempted access would be recorded in the log.

Archival Files

Archival files are generally permanent, or long-term, copies of records that must be retained for legal or other references. For example, at the end of each year, a company processes its payroll records and creates an archival file that contains year-to-date earnings records for all employees. These records must be kept for a minimum of seven years.

As another example, master records covering life insurance policies must be recorded in archival files and kept permanently. Potential implications for these records can run into centuries.

In most cases, archival files are recorded on magnetic tape because of the economies involved and the high-density recording that is possible. Usually, archival files are stored away from the computer site, in a vault facility that specializes in the storage of vital records.

Backup Files

Backup files are special-purpose collections of records that are designed to assure continuity of the computer information system's function—and of the organization that entrusts its records to that function. There is always the possibility that files developed and maintained by computers will be destroyed by operational problems, fire, flood, or other disaster. There have actually been companies that have been forced to go out of business because they could not reconstruct these vital business records.

Backup files are prior versions or copies of actual working data maintained on computers. Backup copies of files are made at specific points in time—such as daily, weekly, or monthly. They may be produced at times when the computer center is not normally busy, perhaps in the middle of the night. More commonly, however, backup files are produced as part of the normal processing in an application system.

Backup files contain complete copies of files with current data. They also contain copies of all operating system and application software. Copies of backup files are created at regular intervals and, periodically, replace old backup files. Backup files are stored away from the computer facility, in the same manner as archival files.

The procedure used to rebuild a computer information system through use of backup files is known as *recovery*.

FILE STORAGE MEDIA

The structure, intended use, and method of storage applied for computer-maintained files are interdependent factors. That is, certain types of files require certain types of storage devices. Similarly, certain applications require certain types of files and also certain types of storage devices.

To illustrate, the automatic teller machine application must be able to access any account record within the bank's computer system in a very short period of time. This application requires a random access file. The most commonly used device for random access files is the magnetic disk drive.

The relationships among type of file, application, and storage method can be illustrated by reviewing the capabilities and functions of several common types of storage media:

- Punched cards
- Magnetic tape
- Magnetic disk
- Printers
- Computer output microfilm (COM) and computer input microfilm (CIM).

Punched Cards

Punched cards maintain *unit records* of data. They are handled in groups, or decks. Within these decks, cards can be sorted or sequenced for processing. In processing, cards are read in serial order only, as presented to a computer input device. Because of the nature of processing that takes place, punched cards can be used only for serial or sequential files.

Magnetic Tape

Magnetic tape is a long ribbon of material that presents a recording surface. Records are encoded consecutively on magnetic tape. Thus, processing runs serially, from the beginning of a tape reading operation through to the end. Magnetic tape devices are also limited in the applications they can support. Only serial or sequential files may be recorded on or read from magnetic tape.

Magnetic Disk

Magnetic disk drives are random access devices. That is, these units are designed so that a computer can find any individual records stored on the disk on a direct basis, without serial or sequential reading. However, this capability does not preclude the recording of data on disk devices in serial or sequential order. Thus, disk drives can support all types of file organization—serial, sequential, or random. The ability to find records at random in computer files is known as *direct access*. This means, simply, that the computer can go to and retrieve any record directly, without processing all records within a file.

Printers

Printers are the most commonly used output devices in any computer installation. Therefore, computer printouts are the most commonly used file reference methods. Printed documents or reports are often created when people must use data. Thus, printers serve users who support the computer installation. Printed reports are among the chief reasons for the very existence of computer centers. Data are presented to printers by computer systems in serial order. Each record, in turn, is printed as it is received.

Many installations are seeking to reduce the amount of printed output from their computers. Visual display output to CRT terminals is becoming increasingly common.

Microform Media

Microform is a term used to describe any kind of microimage recorded on film. Both *computer-output microfilm (COM)* and *computer-input microfilm (CIM)* applications use microform techniques. Images formed from computer files are recorded on film either in rolls or on sheets measuring approximately four by six inches that contain large numbers of page-like images. Film provided in rolls is called *microfilm*. Sheets of film used for microimages are called *microfiche* or just plain *fiche*.

The chief reason for using microform output from computers is to reduce the amount of paper generated by traditional printing techniques. A single roll of microfilm can replace hundreds of pounds of paper. Thus, storage and reference become far more convenient.

Operationally, microfilm devices operate in much the same way as printers. That is, records are presented serially to the recording devices.

In the past few years, microform applications have taken on a new dimension. Computer input microfilm (CIM) makes it possible to read data from microimages into computer systems. Thus, microforms become file devices that can enter data into computer files as well as receive data from computer files.

FILE PROCESSING

Virtually every application written in COBOL will require creation or processing of files. Many business applications use sequential files. In this first programming text, your work centers around four fundamental sequential file processes:

- Creating files
- Sorting or merging files
- Maintaining files
- Reporting.

Virtually all business applications using COBOL will require one or more of these processes. One of the critical application areas, reporting, is covered in Chapter 8. The discussions that follow deal with the major problems and techniques for applying the other three processes.

CREATING SERIAL FILES

Any group, or batch, of data—or any collection of individual transactions entered through terminals—must be incorporated into a file if the data are to undergo further processing. The basic procedure for data

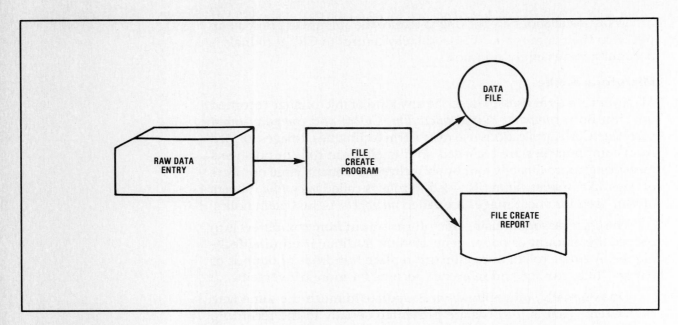

Figure 9-1. Steps in creating a serial file.

entry and file creation is diagrammed in the flowchart in Figure 9-1. This shows, simply, that raw data are entered into a computer for processing under a file creation program. Outputs from this processing include the recording of a file on magnetic media, and, optionally, the printing of the results on a report.

The file creation program used to implement a procedure like the one in Figure 9-1 can come from either of two sources. First, the programmer can write his or her own special programs for this operation. Alternatively, the job can be done with the aid of a system utility provided by the computer manufacturer. Such utilities are generally available as part of each operating system software package. Capabilities of operating system utility packages generally include the ability to copy:

- A file captured in punched cards onto magnetic tape or disks
- Magnetic tape or disk to punched cards
- A disk file to another disk file
- A disk file to magnetic tape
- A magnetic tape file to another tape
- Any file to printed output—known as a *file dump* operation.

File Creation Program

A program that creates a serial file uses a processing loop, or iterative processing, to read the input, write the output, then return for another record—until an end-of-file sentinel is encountered in the input data. At this point, the file is created and the program goes through its termination sequence.

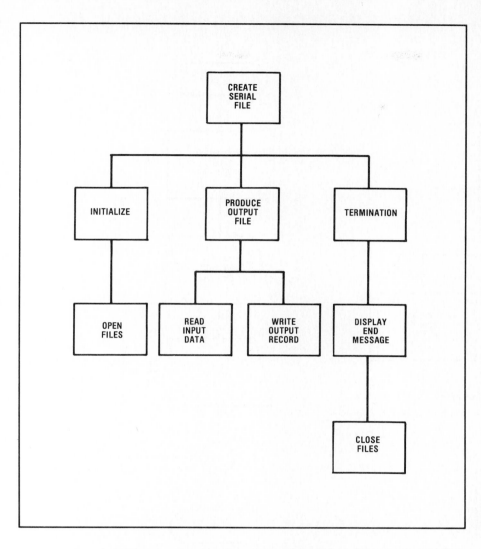

Figure 9-2. Structure chart for serial file creation program.

A structure chart showing a file creation program is presented in Figure 9-2.

Figure 9-3 is a structured flowchart for the same program.

Figure 9-4 shows source coding of the PROCEDURE DIVISION for this program.

Many programmers actually create routines of this type and keep them in their own working libraries for use as needed. It can actually be more convenient to call up and modify a standard routine than to implement a system utility.

With the coding in place in a computer program library, it is necessary only to modify the SELECT and ASSIGN clauses and also the READ and WRITE statements to run the program for any application. There are many standard functions within business applications for which these techniques apply. Experienced programmers tend to build their own libraries of reusable modules in this way.

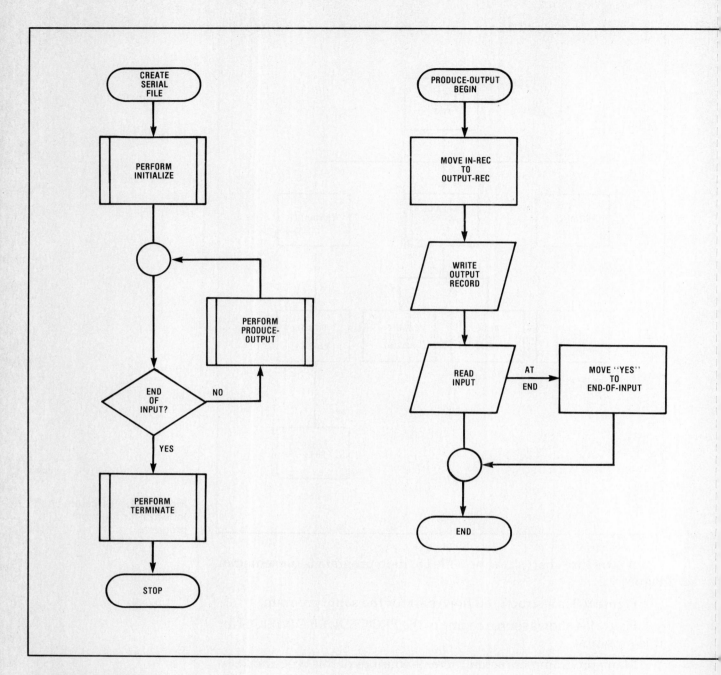

Figure 9-3. Structured flowchart for serial file creation program.

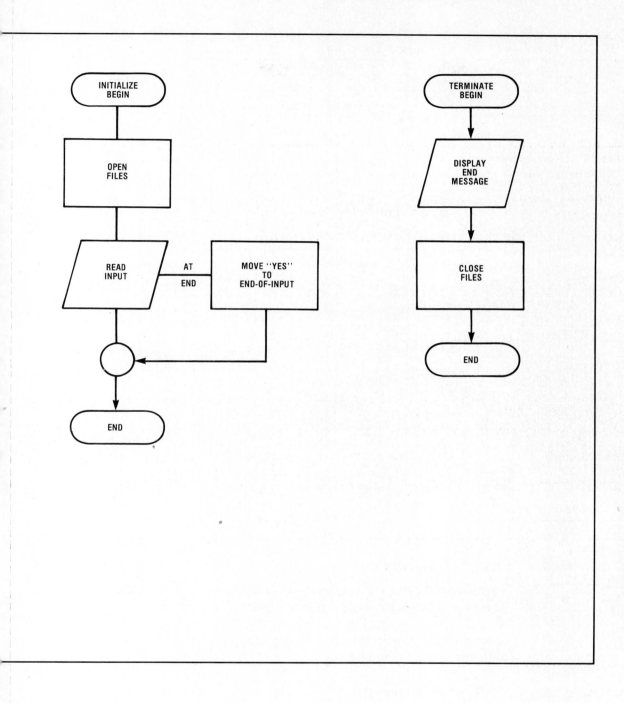

```
COBOL PROGRAM SHEET

System                                    Punching Instructions      Sheet    of
Program                          Graphic                  Card Form #    Identification
Programmer              Date     Punch                                   73]          [80
```

```
SEQUENCE    CONT  A    B
(PAGE)(SERIAL)
1   3 4  6 7 8      12   16   20   24   28   32   36   40   44   48   52   56   60   64   68   72

Ø Ø 5 Ø 1 Ø  PROCEDURE DIVISION.
     Ø 2 Ø  CREATE-SEQ-FILE.
     Ø 3 Ø      PERFORM INITIALIZE.
     Ø 4 Ø      PERFORM PRODUCE-OUTPUT
     Ø 5 Ø          UNTIL END-OF-INPUT EQUALS "YES".
     Ø 6 Ø      PERFORM TERMINATE.
     Ø 7 Ø      STOP RUN.
     Ø 8 Ø
     Ø 9 Ø  INITIALIZE.
     1 Ø Ø      OPEN INPUT INPUT-DATA-FILE
     1 1 Ø          OUTPUT NEW-SEQ-FILE.
     1 2 Ø      READ INPUT-DATA-FILE
     1 3 Ø          AT END MOVE "YES" TO END-OF-INPUT.
     1 4 Ø
     1 5 Ø  PRODUCE-OUTPUT.
     1 6 Ø      MOVE IN-RECORD TO OUTPUT-RECORD.
     1 7 Ø      WRITE OUTPUT-RECORD.
     1 8 Ø      READ INPUT-DATA-FILE
     1 9 Ø          AT END MOVE "YES" TO END-OF-INPUT.
     2 Ø Ø
     2 1 Ø  TERMINATE.
     2 2 Ø      DISPLAY "FILE CREATION ENDED".
     2 3 Ø      CLOSE INPUT-DATA-FILE, NE-SEQ-FILE.
```

Figure 9-4. COBOL source code for serial file creation program.

FILE SORTING AND MERGING

The basic structure of sequential files is described earlier in this chapter. That is, records within these files are ordered according to one or more record keys. Ordering or sequencing of records can be done either in ascending or descending order. Sequencing can be numeric, alphabetic, or alphanumeric.

The role of the sort function is also discussed earlier in this chapter. Typically, input records are recorded as they are presented. This creates serial files. Serial files are then sorted into the desired sequence.

Merging is a procedure for bringing together corresponding contents from two or more separate sequential files, forming a single, combined file. The merging process is diagrammed in Figure 9-5. In this example, records are sequenced according to the employee number field at the left of the record format. This meets one of the requirements

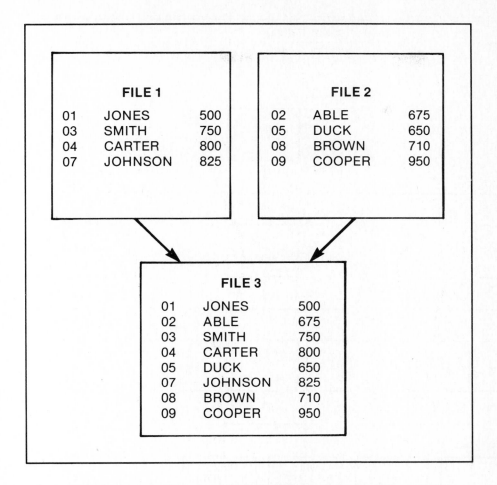

Figure 9-5. File merge procedure.

of a merge function. That is, multiple files to be merged must be sequenced according to the same rules, using the same record keys. In other words, the files must be in corresponding sequences.

A program for merging files is considerably more complex than for creating a new file, as indicated through the structure chart shown in Figure 9-6.

To review the actual procedures for file merging, consider the sequence of modules aligned under the MERGE THE FILES leg of the structure chart of Figure 9-6. The concept used in merging is to designate an *active key* for the merge function. The active key, basically, is the key with the lowest value among those currently being processed. Thus, the active key is a dynamic value, changing with each iteration of the merge process. A WORKING-STORAGE area is set up for the active key. When record key values are compared, the value of the lowest key is moved into the active key. To trace the processing steps in the selection of the active key, look at the module entitled CHOOSE-ACTIVE-KEY in the pseudocode for this program, which is listed in Figure 9-7.

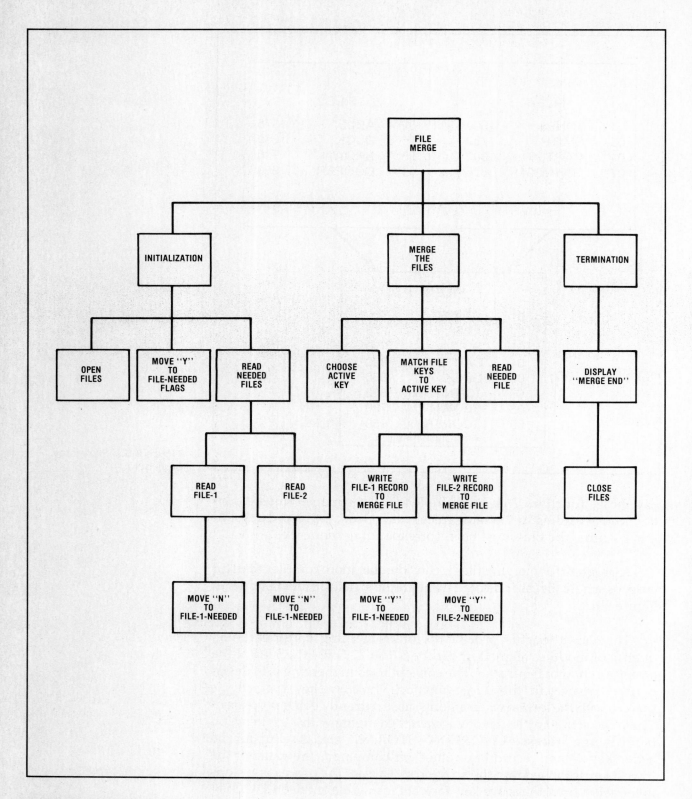

Figure 9-6. Structure chart
for a two-file merge program.

000-MERGE-CONTROL.
    Perform Initialization.
    Perform Merge-the-Files until Active-Key = High-Values.
    Perform Termination.
    STOP RUN.

INITIALIZATION.
    Open Input File-1, File-2.
    Open Output Merge-File.
    Move ''Y'' to File-1-Needed
          File-2-Needed.
    Perform Read-Needed-File.

TERMINATION.
    Display ''MERGE ENDED''.
    Close File-1, File-2, Merge-File.

MERGE-THE-FILES.
    Perform Choose-Active-Key
    Perform Match-Files-to-Active-Key
    Perform Read-Needed-File.

CHOOSE-ACTIVE-KEY.
    If File-1 key less than File-2 key
    Then Move File-1 key to Active-Key
    Else Move File-2 key to Active-Key.

MATCH-FILES-TO-ACTIVE-KEY.
    If File-1 key = Active-Key
    Then Move File-1-Record to Merge-Record
        Perform Write-Merge-Record
        Move ''Y'' to File-1-Needed.
    If File-2 key = Active-Key
    Then Move File-2-Record to Merge-Record
        Perform Write-Merge-Record
        Move ''Y'' to File-2-Needed.

READ-NEEDED-FILE.
    If File-1-Needed = ''Y''
    Then Perform Read-File-1
        Move ''N'' to File-1-Needed.
    If File-2-Needed = ''Y''
    Then Perform Read-File-2
        Move ''N'' to File-2-Needed.

READ-FILE-1.
    READ File-1.
        At end Move High-Values to File-1 key.
            Move ''N'' to File-1-Needed.

READ-FILE-2.
    READ File-2.
        At end Move High-Values to File-2 key.
            Move ''N'' to File-2 Needed.

WRITE-MERGE-RECORD.
    WRITE Merge-Record.

Figure 9-7. Pseudocode for a two-file merge program.

After the active key is chosen, each file key is again compared with the active key, which, in this function, serves as an *activity directing item* within the program. When a *match,* or *equal condition,* occurs between the active key and one of the record keys, that record is written to the output merge file. The next file key is also compared with the active key. If a second match occurs, that record is also written out. If not, processing proceeds to the next module in the program. The pseudocoding for this matching function appears under the module heading MATCH-FILES-TO-ACTIVE-KEY module in Figure 9-7.

Because the record keys from the two source files are matched against the value of an active key before records are merged into the output file, this process is sometimes called a *match/merge.*

SEQUENTIAL FILE MAINTENANCE

The term *file maintenance* describes the procedure for modifying, or *updating,* master files to reflect the content of transaction files. As transactions occur, these records should be processed against the corresponding master file records to change either status or content of those master records.

Master files are primary information resources for any company. Updating is necessary to keep them accurate, complete, and current. In effect, then, master files contain the records that reflect the status and condition of the organization. Because of this, file maintenance is an extremely important information system function. All qualified programmers should understand and know how to handle file maintenance operations.

The actual programming of file maintenance is an advanced topic, beyond the scope of this book. However, an introduction to the process itself is important at this point in your learning experience. To illustrate what happens in a file maintenance operation, Figure 9-8 is a data flow diagram for this function. As shown, the processing is applied to two separate files, a customer master file and a set of customer transactions. Both these files are in corresponding sequential order—probably customer number order in this example. The output from this process is a new file, known as the updated customer master file, as well as a report of the update activity.

In file maintenance processes, the master records each contains a unique record key. For each such unique record key there is one—and only one—master record. On the other hand, this record key may exist in none of the transaction records, in one of the transaction records, or in any number of transaction records. Thus, it is possible for multiple transaction records—or none at all—to impact a given record in the master file. A variety of records may exist within the transaction file. These can include new records to be added to the master file, records that change or modify the content of existing master records, or transaction records that cause master records to be deleted from the file.

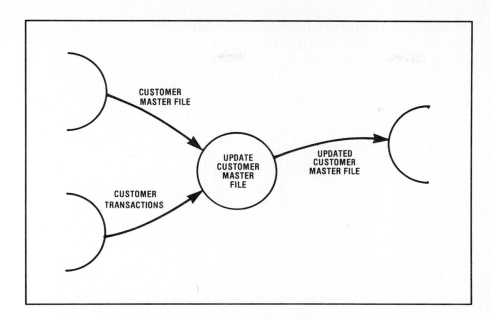

Figure 9-8. Data flow diagram for file update program.

After all of the records in the transaction file have been processed, an updated master file exists. This may have new, additional records inserted that were not in the original master file. Some records may have been modified while others were deleted. When completed, the new master file represents the current state of that phase of the organization's business activities.

In practice, the logic of file updating is a modification, or an extension, of basic match/merge procedures. The chief difference is that multiple types of functions may be performed, rather than simply bringing records together.

This chapter has discussed the principles and procedures associated with the creation and management of sequential files. This basic knowledge about the structure and handling of files will, in turn, provide the basis for the learning that follows.

Summary

Files consist of sets of records grouped according to related data values normally processed together. The collection of files used by a computer information system makes up its database. [*Objective No. 1.*]

Four basic organization methods are used in recording files for computer processing: serial, sequential, indexed sequential, and direct.

In serial files, records are recorded in chronological sequence, as they are presented to the computer.

Sequential records are also written consecutively, one after the other, in a specified order. Record sequences are determined by the content of one or more keys within each record. Ordering of records can be according to relative values and importance of one, two, or more

Key Terms

1. database
2. database management system (DBMS)
3. serial file
4. electronic journal
5. record key
6. sequential file
7. major key
8. minor key
9. sorting
10. indexed sequential file
11. direct file
12. master file
13. transaction file
14. log file
15. history file
16. archival file
17. backup file
18. recovery
19. punched card
20. unit record
21. magnetic tape
22. magnetic disk
23. direct access
24. printer
25. microform
26. computer-output microfilm (COM)
27. computer-input microfilm (CIM)
28. microfilm
29. microfiche
30. file dump
31. merging
32. active key

record keys. The most important is the major key. Others are known as minor keys. The ordering of records within a file is known as sorting.

Indexed sequential files are recorded in order, in the same manner as sequential files. In addition, these files have indexes that make it possible to look up the addresses of and to access individual records. Thus, indexed sequential files may be processed in order as they are recorded or can be used to support applications requiring references to individual records.

In direct files, an algorithm using the record key determines the storage position of each record. This makes it possible to access records individually and directly. [*Objectives Nos. 2 and 3.*]

For use in business application programs, files are classified according to types. Common types of files include master, transaction, log, history, archival, and backup. [*Objective No. 4.*]

Media used for recording and handling of files include punched cards, magnetic tape, magnetic disk, printers, and microforms (microfilm and microfiche used for output and input). [*Objective No. 5.*]

Processing of files is done through standard techniques applied for creating, sorting or merging, maintaining, or reporting from files.

File creation uses iteration techniques to enter and record data under the specified organization structure.

Sorting is the procedure for arranging records in a desired sequence. Merging is the technique for ordering sets of sequenced records from two or more files into a single file arranged according to record key values.

Maintenance is the updating of master files to reflect addition, change, or deletion activity. [*Objective No. 6.*]

Review/Discussion Questions

1. What characteristics identify serial files?

2. What are the primary applications of serial files?

3. What are the differences in structuring and principal applications between serial and sequential files?

4. What are the identifying features and primary advantages of random access files, as compared with sequential files?

5. What are typical contents and purposes of master files?

6. What type of structure is used and what purpose is typically served by log files?

7. What are the relationships among history, archival, and backup files?

8. What types of files can be stored on magnetic tape. What are the special features and advantages of this medium?

9. What types of files can be stored on magnetic disk media? What are the special features and advantages of this medium?

10. What are the relative advantages and disadvantages of printer and microfilm output?

11. What requirements must be met and which procedures followed in the merging of files?

12. What are the purposes of file maintenance and what is the importance of this processing technique?

33. match
34. match/merge
35. file maintenance
36. updating

Practice Assignment

1. Do a structured walkthrough of the pseudocode in Figure 9-7. For this assignment, use the data in Figure 9-5. Follow each record through the logic of the match/merge functions of the pseudocode.

2. After you are satisfied with the pseudocode in Figure 9-7—correcting the pseudocode as necessary—write the COBOL source code to implement this program. Compile the program. Then test and debug it with the data in Figure 9-5—or other data that may be provided.

Worksheet for Structured Flowchart

Program Name: _____

Prepared By: _____

Worksheet for Pseudocode Specifications

Program Name: _____

Prepared By: _____

COBOL PROGRAM SHEET

System			
Program			
Programmer			

Punching Instructions		Sheet	of
Graphic			Identification
Punch	Card Form #		[73] [80]

Date	

SEQUENCE
(PAGE) (SERIAL)

1 3 4	6 7 8	CONT	A	B	12	16	20	24	28	32	36	40	44	48	52	56	60	64	68	72

COBOL PROGRAM SHEET

System						Punching Instructions				Sheet	of
Program					Graphic			Card Form #		Identification	
Programmer			Date		Punch					[73]	[80]

SEQUENCE		CONT																	
(PAGE)	(SERIAL)		A	B															
1 3	4 6	7	8	12	16	20	24	28	32	36	40	44	48	52	56	60	64	68	72

COBOL PROGRAM SHEET

System								Punching Instructions			Sheet	of
Program								Graphic				
Programmer				Date				Punch		Card Form #		Identification

SEQUENCE		CONT															
(PAGE)	(SERIAL)		A	B	16	20	24	28	32	36	40	44	48	52	56	60	64	68	72
1	3 4	6 7 8	12															

73] [80

COBOL PROGRAM SHEET

System				
Program		Punching Instructions		Sheet of
Programmer	Date	Graphic	Card Form #	Identification
		Punch		[73] [80]

SEQUENCE			CONT	A	B																		
(PAGE)	(SERIAL)																						
1 3	4	6	7	8	12	16	20	24	28	32	36	40	44	48	52	56	60	64	68	72			

COBOL PROGRAM SHEET

System		Punching Instructions		Sheet	of
Program		Graphic		Identification	
Programmer	Date	Punch	Card Form #	73]	[80]

SEQUENCE
(PAGE) (SERIAL)
1 3 4 6 7 8 CONT A B
12 16 20 24 28 32 36 40 44 48 52 56 60 64 68 72

Vocabulary Building Practice—Exercise 9

Write definitions and/or explanations of the terms listed below.

1. database _____
   _____

2. serial file _____
   _____

3. electronic journal_____
   _____

4. record key _____
   _____

5. sequential file _____
   _____

6. major key _____
   _____

7. minor key _____
   _____

8. sorting _____
   _____

9. indexed sequential file _____
   _____

10. master file _____
    _____

(over, please)

11. transaction file _____

_____

12. backup file _____

_____

13. recovery _____

_____

14. direct access file _____

_____

15. computer-output microfilm (COM) _____

_____

16. file dump _____

_____

17. merging _____

_____

18. active key _____

_____

19. match/merge _____

_____

20. updating _____

_____

USING SECONDARY STORAGE 10

OBJECTIVES

On completing reading and other learning assignments for this chapter, you should be able to:

1. Explain how data are recorded on and read from magnetic tape by tape drives or transports.

2. Describe the recording patterns, densities, and blocking patterns used in recording data on magnetic tape.

3. Explain how data are recorded on and read from magnetic disk media by fixed- and removable-disk drives.

4. Describe the recording patterns, densities, and access times related to typical operating features of fixed- and removable-disk drives.

5. Compare and describe relationships among logical and physical records, files, and volumes.

SECONDARY STORAGE DEVICES

Secondary storage devices—magnetic tape and magnetic disk units—represent the primary media for maintaining files for use with computer information systems. This chapter, following presentations in two earlier chapters, completes the information you will need to build, use, and control files on these secondary storage devices.

Chapter 9 covers the basic principles of the organization of information within files. Chapter 7 introduces the basic COBOL statements for creation and use of files. However, Chapter 7 limits its examples to card input and printer output applications. This chapter provides the basis for extending your knowledge and experience into the areas of tape and disk operations.

MAGNETIC TAPE RECORDING

The magnetic tape used in computer applications is a half-inch wide ribbon of highly stable plastic material that has been coated on one side with a ferrous oxide material that can be magnetized to record data bit patterns. The most common form of use for magnetic tape is in 2400-foot reels. Shorter reels are available for special applications, such as key-to-tape input devices. However, the 2400-foot reel is considered to be an industry standard.

To use magnetic tape in a program, the SELECT statement must indicate a tape device assignment. To illustrate, the statement below assigns a file for storage on a tape device within an IBM system.

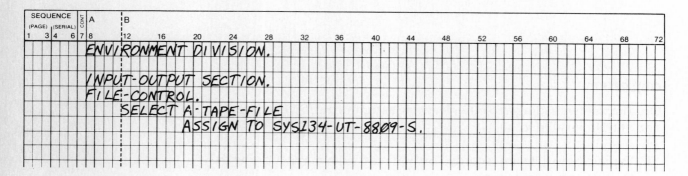

Recording Devices

Data are recorded on and read from reels of tape processed on machines known as *tape drives*, or *tape transports*.

The mechanism of a typical tape drive is shown in Figure 10-1. As indicated, there are two positions for tape reels. One of these, shown at the left in the illustration, is known as the *file reel*. On some devices, the file reel may be at the right. In any case, the important thing about this reel is its function. It contains either a recorded tape to be read or raw tape on which data are to be written. The second reel, the *machine reel*, or *take-up reel*, serves only to hold the tape that is unwound from the file reel. When processing is completed, tape is rewound onto the file reel for future storage and handling.

Tapes are recorded or read at extremely high speeds on tape drives. Therefore, a series of mechanisms is necessary to keep tension on the tape. This tension serves to maintain close, necessary contact between the tape and the magnetic heads that do the actual reading, writing, or erasing of data in preparation for writing. The rotary devices that feed the tape and maintain tension are called *capstans*. Typically, some type of loop containing slack tape is maintained on both the feeding and take-up sides of tape drives. This provides a buffer, or holding area, for the feeding of tape, avoiding stress that could tear the tape. As tape passes over the read or write heads of the tape drive, data are either sensed or recorded. When data are written on tape, any previously

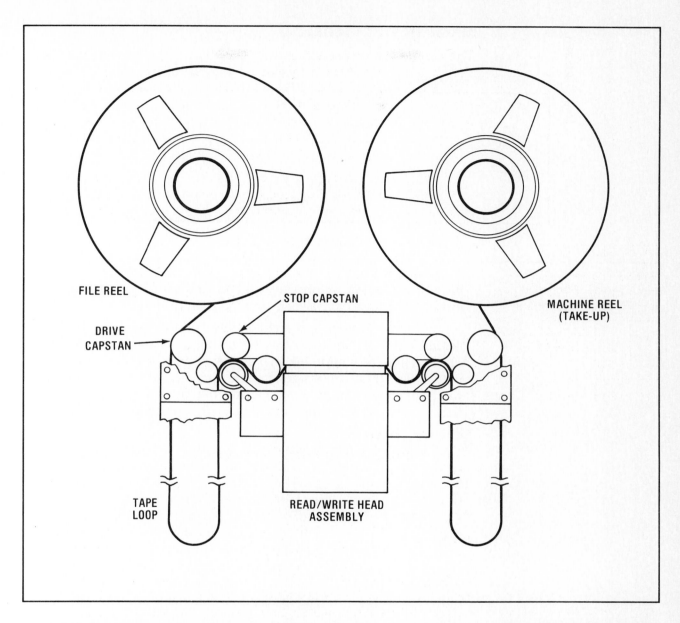

FILE REEL

STOP CAPSTAN

DRIVE
CAPSTAN

MACHINE REEL
(TAKE-UP)

TAPE
LOOP

READ/WRITE HEAD
ASSEMBLY

recorded data are simply written over. This procedure is known as *destructive writing.* The term describes the fact that any existing data are obliterated by the new recordings.

Figure 10-1. Tape transport mechanism.

In *reading* functions, the tape devices simply sense data that have already been recorded on tape. The data are transferred rapidly into computer memory in a nondestructive process. That is, after reading, the data exists both on the tape file and also in computer memory.

Recording Patterns

Virtually all tape drives now being delivered record data in nine *tracks,* or *channels,* as shown in Figure 10-2. Recording patterns representing numbers, letters, or special symbols are recorded across the width of

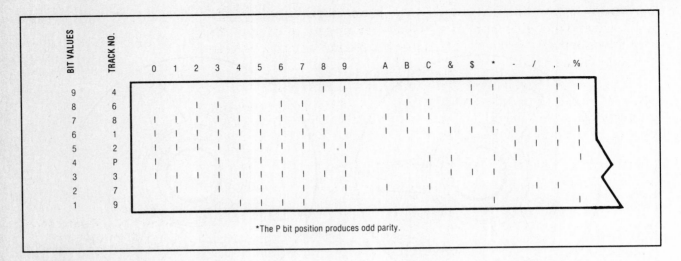

Figure 10-2. Recording pattern for nine-channel tape.

the tape. Specific positions are assigned for the values of these bits, with individual tracks or channels representing these values.

In a nine-channel tape, eight of the positions usually represent data values. These are known as *binary digit*, or *bit*, values. Within the coding systems used by computers, eight bit positions constitute a *byte* of data. Byte values, then, are assigned to the numbers, letters, or symbols that can be encoded. As shown in Figure 10-2, the value of a given byte is determined by the arrangment of the ''on,'' or positively magnetized, bits.

The fourth channel in the magnetic tape recording pattern is used for a *parity bit*, or *check bit*. This position in the recording pattern is used for automatic checking of the accuracy of recording or reading operations. For example, the recording pattern in Figure 10-2 uses what is known as *odd parity*. Other systems may use *even parity*. Whichever approach is used, the computer checks itself as it writes or reads data using tape. Depending on the parity scheme used, the computer must sense either an odd or even number of bits in each byte. If the proper number of bits is not sensed in a given byte, the computer will attempt either to rewrite or reread the data, whichever is appropriate. Several tries will be made to reprocess the data. After a given number of attempts, the computer will abort processing and signal that an input/output error has taken place.

Recording Densities and Record Blocking

COBOL programs designate the length of data records in terms of numbers of characters, or bytes. COBOL programs automatically control the writing of data onto tape within these format constraints. Remember, the basic data processing cycle runs from input, to processing, to output. Magnetic tapes on computer systems move only when an input or output operation actually occurs. Between records, the tape drive leaves a blank space, known as an *interrecord gap*. The gap, in effect, is the space needed for the starting or stopping of the tape before or after an input or output operation. Gap spaces vary depending upon the make and model of tape drive, usually ranging between one-half and three-quarters of an inch. The pattern of records and gaps is illustrated in Figure 10-3.

The closeness, or spacing, of bit positions on tape in recording patterns is known as *recording density*. Magnetic tape provides a high-density means of storing data. Three standard recording densities are now used on tape drives. These are 800, 1,600, and 6,250 characters per

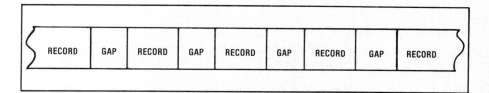

Figure 10-3. Relationships of interrecord gaps and records on magnetic tape.

inch. Thus, a 2,400-foot reel of tape can, potentially, hold millions of characters of data.

The actual amount of data that can be recorded on a reel of tape will vary widely with the file structure plan that is used. For example, the illustration in Figure 10-3 shows a series of records interspersed with gaps that serve to identify the records. Suppose, now, that this was a continuous input file involving 80-character records. If the recording density is 800 characters per inch, each record occupies one-tenth of an inch. However, the gap between records must be at least one-half inch. Thus, the gaps take up five times as much room as the data. This isn't an efficient way of recording data, particularly if large files are involved. For example, if a 2,400-foot reel of tape were recorded entirely with 80-character data records, the total space occupied by the data would be a maximum of 480 feet. Thus, 1,920 feet of the 2,400-foot reel would be blank. This type of recording pattern would make poor use of the storage medium—and also slow down the computer's processing capability significantly.

To get around these problems, it is possible to group a series of records together into a *block*. A block of records, simply, is a series of records that are grouped together when they are written on tape. Gaps, then, can be inserted between blocks, instead of between individual records, as shown in Figure 10-4.

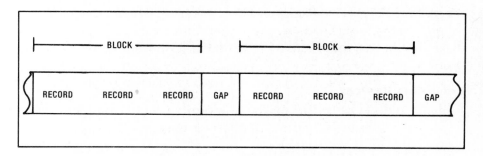

Figure 10-4. Blocking of logical records on magnetic tape.

The number of records included in any given block can vary. The specific number of records in a block is called a *blocking factor*. For example, records recorded as shown in Figure 10-4 would have a blocking factor of 3. This means that there are three logical records per block. Actual blocking factors are limited by the amount of temporary storage available in main memory of the computer system. Thus, it is theoretically possible to have hundreds of records per block. Within a COBOL program, the blocking factor is defined within an FD statement. Example:

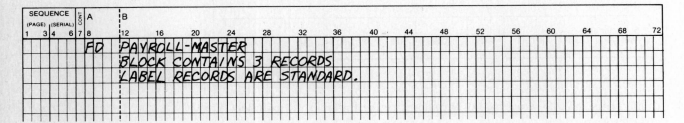

The BLOCK CONTAINS clause is used by the COBOL compiler and also by the operating system software. However, the PROCEDURE DIVISION commands for use of the files would not change at all. When the operating system senses a BLOCK CONTAINS clause, an area known as a *buffer* is set up in main memory. This area is large enough to hold one block of data. Thus, in the example given above, the buffer zone would be large enough to hold three 80-character records.

Blocking is handled through capabilities of the operating system, in response to COBOL commands. Normally, the processing logic of the PROCEDURE DIVISION is to follow the sequence of READ, PROCESS, WRITE output for one logical record at a time. Blocking occurs through the response of the operating system to COBOL instructions. When the operating system senses a COBOL read command, it causes the system to remove one record at a time from a block and to present this to the 01 record name area of the FILE SECTION. When it senses a command to WRITE blocked records, the operating system transfers the contents of one record from the FILE SECTION to the output buffer area.

MAGNETIC DISK RECORDING

Magnetic disks present flat, plate-like surfaces for the recording of data. Magnetic read/write heads are positioned above the surfaces of rotating disks. The heads, then, sense or record data as the disks rotate beneath them.

Recording Devices

Individual disks or sets of disks are mounted on peripheral devices known as *disk drives*. The disks themselves may be either *rigid* or *flexible (floppy)*.

Rigid disks have metal (usually an aluminum alloy) bases or *substrates*. These substrates, then, are coated with a thin layer of iron oxide material like that used for coating magnetic tape.

Floppy disks use substrates of flexible plastic sheeting, also coated with thin layers of iron oxide. Floppy disks are usually smaller and have lower capacities than rigid disks. Most floppy disks are used with microcomputers or data entry devices.

Disk recording media may be either *removable* or *fixed*. Removable media may contain one or several disks, or *platters*. A removable unit with a single platter is known as a *disk cartridge*. Devices with multiple platters are called *disk packs*. In either case, the removable packages are mounted on disk drives for access by movable read/write heads. Figure 10-5 shows the data access mechanism for a disk pack drive.

Fixed disks are not removable. They usually offer extremely large storage capacities. Also, fixed disks tend to operate at higher speeds than devices handling removable media. This is because fixed disks often have a separate read/write head over every recording position on the disk surface. Thus, any data record can be accessed within one rotation of the disk device. By contrast, access devices that process removable media usually have a single head per surface, as shown in Figure 10-5. This single read/write head must then move across the surface of the disk for access operations.

Recording Patterns

Data are recorded on magnetic disk surfaces in concentric circles. That is, there is a series of circles beginning near the center, or hub, of the disk surface and moving outward. The circles are not connected in spiral fashion as they are with phonograph records. Rather, each circle is independent and complete in itself. These concentric circles for

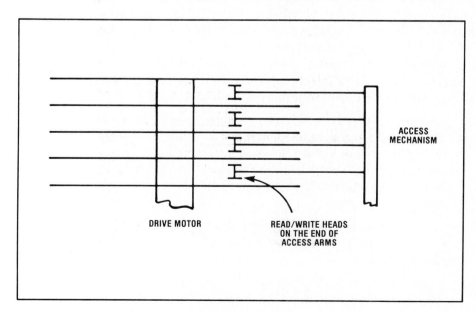

Figure 10-5. Disk access mechanism.

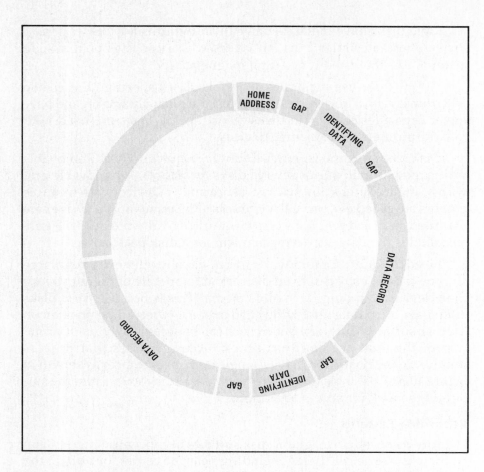

Figure 10-6. Disk track format.

data recording are called *tracks*. The pattern for the recording of data on a disk track is illustrated in Figure 10-6. As shown, each track has a beginning location. The starting point for a track is known as its *home address*. Following this identification point, data records are recorded around the track in patterns much like those for magnetic tape. That is, after the home address, there is a gap. Then there is an *identification field*, followed by another gap. Gaps and identification fields are interspersed between data records. Recording patterns for specific disk devices vary with individual manufacturers.

Another variable in disk recording patterns is that some equipment units divide tracks into a fixed number of segments of equal size. These track segments are known as *sectors*. When a sector system is used, records begin and end within the sectors. Typical sector designations include eight, 16, and 32 sectors per track.

Still another variable lies in the number of tracks per recording surface. Diskettes may have as few as 40 tracks per recording surface. Rigid disk systems, on the other hand, typically have between 200 and 800 tracks per surface.

On devices that use disk packs, the alignment of tracks is identical for all recording surfaces within a pack. This correspondence of track positions is necessary because all of the read/write heads within a disk pack, as shown in Figure 10-5, operate as a unit. That is, all of the read/write heads move together. Thus, all heads are positioned over the same track on each disk at any given time. For this reason, recording patterns are established for vertical sets of tracks within any given disk pack. Thus, read/write operations would, typically, go from top to bottom, through an entire disk pack, as a single recording sequence. These multiple-track positions that correspond within disk pack arrangements are called *cylinders*. For emphasis: a cylinder is a set of tracks in the identical position on multiple disks within a single pack. The organization of disk packs into cylinders is illustrated graphically in Figure 10-7.

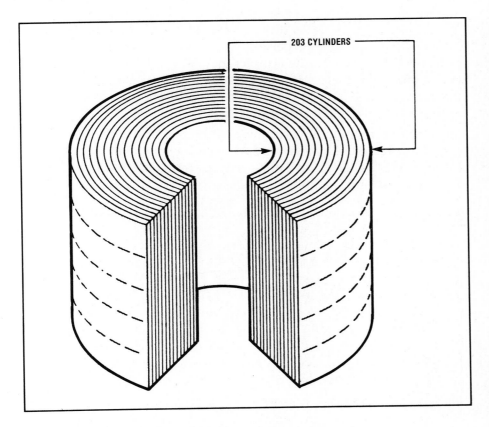

203 CYLINDERS

Figure 10-7. Disk cylinder format.

Recording of data on disk devices is in linear patterns. That is, instead of aligning data in columns and rows as is done on tape, the bits of characters entered onto disk files are in continuous sequence, one bit after another and one character after another. However, records are still formed and blocked through use of patterns much the same as those for magnetic tape. The concept of blocking records on disks is the same as it is for tape. That is, the use of blocking techniques increases recording density and also improves file processing productivity, or *throughput*. Recording density actually varies from track to track. This is because recording is done at a fixed timing rate by read/write heads while the actual rotation speed of the tracks varies according to position on the disk. The principle is simple: as a disk rotates, the outer tracks move farther, thus turning faster than the inner ones. Recording density varies with this speed factor, as illustrated in Figure 10-8.

Capacities for disk recording devices vary widely, reflecting differences in recording densities and numbers of tracks available. For diskettes, capacities range from approximately 100,000 characters to 1.2 million characters. For rigid disks, the range is from approximately 5 million to some 2.4 billion characters of data.

An important factor in evaluating the performance of disk devices is *access time,* the elapsed time between the initiation of a read or write command and the completion of the function. Access times for different disk devices vary widely on the basis of three basic factors. The first factor is rotation speed. Most disk devices rotate at speeds ranging from 1,500 to 2,500 revolutions per minute. Obviously, the faster the rotation speed, the shorter the access time will be. Other factors include the number of cylinders in a disk device and the movement speed of the access arm. (Disk devices that have a read/write head on each track will access records in a single revolution of the disk.)

Depending upon the position of the access arm at the time a command is executed, the actual access time can vary widely, usually ranging from as short as about 5 milliseconds (thousandths of a second) to as long as 100 milliseconds.

Figure 10-8. Variable recording densities on different disk tracks.

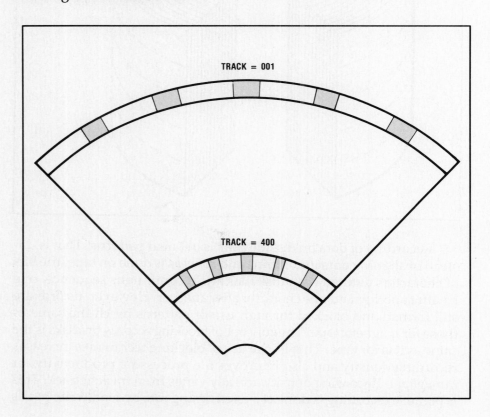

Using Disk Files

A major advantage of disk devices is that they permit direct access to individual records. Disk devices can be directed to find records on any cylinder, track, or sector within an entire system, even when multiple disk drives are used. This direct access, also known as random access, is essential to the implementation of on-line or interactive systems in which users working at terminals can enter or access data directly and rapidly from computer files.

In addition, files stored on disk devices can be organized and processed in sequential order, much as though they were written and stored on magnetic tape. Thus, disk devices provide complete flexibility for support of computer information system applications.

COBOL techniques for random access processing of disk files are an advanced topic. These skills will be acquired in a later course.

Sequential file processing for data stored on disk devices uses the same COBOL instructions as for tape processing, discussed earlier. The only significant difference is in the file assignment clause of the SELECT statement. To illustrate, the statement below assigns a file for storage on a disk device within an IBM system.

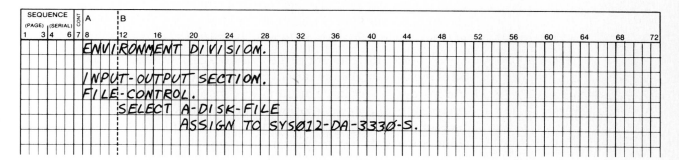

Logical and Physical Data

To this point, data have been viewed in terms of how they are used and described in programs. This is a logical approach to data description. The three logical units of data are the field, the logical record, and the file.

Definitions of these terms in earlier portions of this text have not been concerned with methods for recording or storage. A file has been defined simply as a set of related logical records. Therefore, the collection of all payroll records in an organization forms a payroll file.

The term *logical record* has been regarded as a collection of a set of fields relating to a single subject or data entity. The name, address, department number, etc., fields for one employee thus constitute a payroll record.

A field, in turn, is regarded as the space allocated to hold specific attributes of records. For example, a person's name is an attribute, department number is an attribute of an employee, and any specific, descriptive type of data recorded about each employee is considered an attribute. Therefore, each attribute stored is called a field in a record.

These descriptions are concerned with the uses, rather than the physical storage characteristics, of data. *Physical characteristics* of data depend upon the storage medium and the specific input or output devices used.

The three terms used to describe physical data are *character position, physical record,* and *volume.*

Figure 10-9 illustrates the relationship between physical and logical data.

One of the more common methods used to store a character of a field is to represent that character as a byte. As discussed earlier, a byte is a physical storage unit that represents a data character using eight binary digits (eight bits), plus one parity bit. On physical storage devices, a character position is often the smallest unit of data that can be referenced. In this case, a character position is a byte.

As discussed earlier, a block, or physical record, is composed of one or more logical records. The physical record is then transferred to or from a secondary storage medium as a whole unit of data. This physical record is, in fact, composed of data concerning several different logical entities, such as persons, dollars, or things.

When writing an entire file to a storage medium, it is possible that all of the data for the file cannot fit onto one unit of the storage medium. For instance, very large master files for some companies would not fit on one reel of magnetic tape or onto one disk pack. Therefore, many reels of tape or multiple disk packs could be required. In other organizations, some data files may be small enough to place two, three, or more files on one magnetic tape reel.

Individual, physical units of secondary storage media are called *volumes.* One reel of magnetic tape is a volume. One magnetic disk pack is also a volume. If three reels of magnetic tape are used to hold a large file, they would be identified as Volume 1, Volume 2, and Volume 3 of the file.

Summary

The primary devices for secondary storage of data are magnetic tape and magnetic disk.

Magnetic tape consists of half-inch ribbons of plastic coated with an iron oxide material that can be magnetized. Tapes are handled on drives, or transports. Reels on which files are recorded or are to be written feed tape across the drive's read, write, and erase heads. Tapes are wound onto take-up reels within the drives, then rewound following processing. [*Objective No. 1.*]

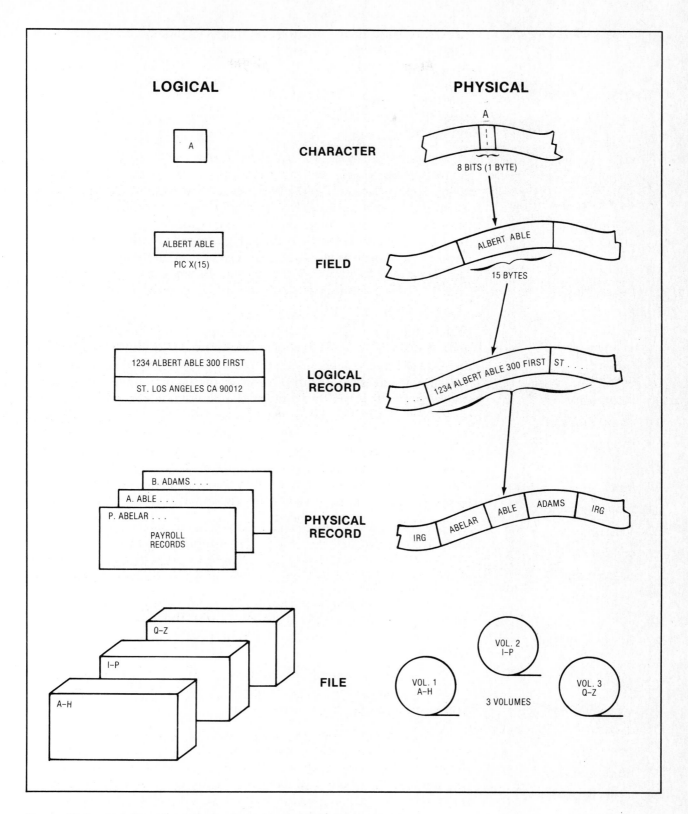

Figure 10-9. Relationships between logical and physical data records.

Key Terms

1. tape drive
2. tape transport
3. file reel
4. machine reel
5. take-up reel
6. capstan
7. destructive writing
8. reading
9. track (tape)
10. channel
11. binary digit
12. bit
13. byte
14. parity bit
15. check bit
16. odd parity
17. even parity
18. interrecord gap
19. recording density
20. block
21. blocking factor
22. disk drive
23. rigid disk
24. flexible disk
25. floppy disk
26. substrate
27. removable disk
28. fixed disk
29. platter
30. disk cartridge
31. disk pack
32. track (disk)
33. home address
34. identification field
35. sector

Data characters are recorded on magnetic tapes in nine-bit byte pattern positions across the width. Each bit position of a byte is called a channel, or track. Eight of the nine bits in a byte are used to code the data. The ninth bit, known as the parity bit or check bit, is used to validate the accuracy of recording and reading. This checking is based on determination that all bytes contain either an odd or an even number of bits, depending on the validation method that is used.

Recording densities for magnetic tape are 800, 1,600, and 6,250 bits per inch. Records are usually grouped into blocks within recording patterns. Blank spaces, or gaps, between records or blocks allow for the starting and stopping of drives during processing. The number of records in a block is determined, in large part, by computer memory capacity—the number of records that can be stored for processing. The number of records assigned to each block is called the blocking factor. The blocking factor for a COBOL program is specified with a BLOCK CONTAINS command in the FD entry. [*Objective No. 2.*]

When magnetic disks are used, data are recorded in concentric circles on disk surfaces. Disks may be rigid or flexible (floppy). Rigid disks have iron oxide coatings on metal bases, or substrates. Floppy disks have flexible acetate substrates. Disk drives may be either fixed or removable. Devices with removable media may have a single disk (platter) or a set of platters. Single-disk removable modules are called cartridges. Multiple-platter media are called disk packs. [*Objective No. 1.*]

The circular recording path on a disk surface is called a track. Each track has a starting, or base, point known as its home address. Individual disk surfaces may have anywhere from 40 to 800 tracks. Tracks, in turn, may be subdivided into sectors.

Data are stored in linear fashion on disks, with bit streams recorded continuously. Records and blocks are interspersed by gaps and identification fields. Otherwise, record and block formatting are similar to the methods used on tape files. [*Objective No. 2.*]

On disk packs, recording patterns are set up for continuous use of track positions on multiple surfaces. That is, the identical tracks on all disk surfaces in a pack are used as a unit, called a cylinder. [*Objective No. 3.*]

Performance capabilities, or throughput, of disk devices is measured in terms of access time, the period between initiation of an access command and delivery of data to memory. [*Objective No. 4.*]

For design purposes, physical requirements and constraints of file storage media must be compared with the content and format of records that have been designed from a logical perspective. That is, records that have been formatted on the basis of their logical content must be organized for optimum storage and processing configurations. [*Objective No. 5.*]

Review/Discussion Questions

1. What are file reels and take-up reels and what are their functions?

2. What recording patterns are used in storing data on magnetic tape?

3. What are parity bits and how are they used?

4. What is an interrecord gap and what purpose does it serve?

5. What is recording density?

6. Why are records blocked?

7. What is the blocking factor and how is it invoked in COBOL programs?

8. What are the types and structures of magnetic disk devices?

9. What are tracks, sectors, and cylinders and how are they related?

10. What is throughput and how is it measured?

11. What is access time and how is it measured?

36. cylinder
37. throughput
38. access time
39. logical record
40. physical characteristic
41. character position
42. physical record
43. volume

COBOL Terms

1. BLOCK CONTAINS

Vocabulary Building Practice—Exercise 10

Write definitions and/or explanations of the terms listed below.

1. file reel _____
_____

2. machine reel _____
_____

3. capstan _____
_____

4. destructive writing _____
_____

5. reading _____
_____

6. tape track _____
_____

7. channel _____
_____

8. bit _____
_____

9. byte _____
_____

10. parity bit _____
_____

(over, please)

11. **check bit** _____

_____

12. **odd parity** _____

_____

13. **even parity** _____

_____

14. **interrecord gap** _____

_____

15. **recording density** _____

_____

16. **block** _____

_____

17. **disk track** _____

_____

18. **home address** _____

_____

19. **identification field** _____

_____

20. **throughput** _____

_____

CONTROL BREAK REPORTS 11

OBJECTIVES

On completing reading and other learning assignments for this chapter, you should be able to:

1. Define and describe control break reports.

2. Design and code programs to produce one-, two-, or three-level control break reports.

3. Use control break options in programs you prepare, including detail line suppression, group indicating, and significance indication.

4. Conduct structured walkthroughs to check and review the quality of program design.

CHARACTERISTICS OF CONTROL BREAK REPORTS

A *control break report* is a type of summary report. Summary reports, described in Chapter 8, print lines summarizing the content of portions of a file or group of records. These summary, or total, lines are positioned intermittently within the body of the report itself. Control break reports are special types of summary reports that react to the content of specific, selected keys within the records of a file being processed. The name, control break report, comes from the fact that summarizing of data is triggered by a change (break) in the content of the control key.

The record key that triggers a control break is known as the *control field*. This may be one or more fields that appear within every record in a given file. For example, in a customer master file, every record would have a customer account number. In an inventory file, every record would have a product number. It is also possible to process on the basis of multiple control fields. For example, summary totals may be initiated on the basis of changes in invoice date fields for successive account numbers. Thus, in a sales summary, it may be desirable to total the amounts of all business done with every customer, each month. Within this report, it may also be desirable to have a control break for the specific purchases made within the month. In this case, the major control key would be the customer account number, while a minor control key would be the invoice date. Each time the invoice date changed, the summary of business transacted to date would be printed out.

Figure 11-1 shows a typical control break report. Data in this report cover activities in a manufacturing plant. The object is to determine manufacturing time utilization for the basic types of machines in the factory. There are three kinds of machines—drill presses, lathes, and milling machines. For each type of machine, the report lists all of the jobs processed and time utilized. Each time the record key for machine type changes, the report produces a summary line totaling machine time utilization.

The report in Figure 11-1 is annotated to show the important characteristics of file organization for this type of reporting. One characteristic is that files are organized in sequence according to a control field value. Organization is usually in ascending order. As long as the value in the control field of each new record presented for processing equals the control field of the previous record, data accumulation continues. When a record is presented with a control field that has a value greater than the previous control field value, a break occurs. At the control break, the accumulated total is printed, summed to the next

Figure 11-1. Annotated output report from a single-level control break program.

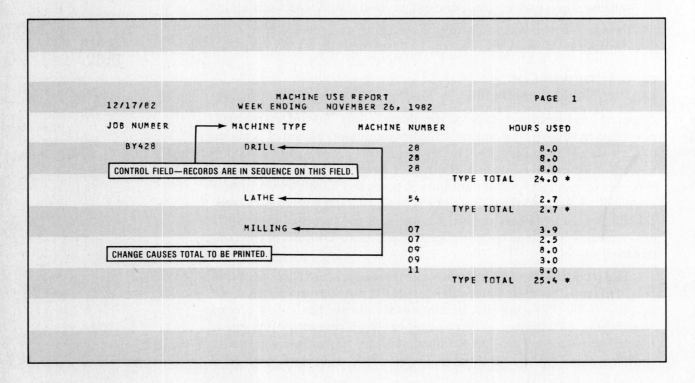

control level, and the accumulators are reset to zero. Then processing continues, with a new accumulation beginning for the values of the current record.

The file structure needed to support multiple-level control break processing and reports is a sequential file with records arranged in sequence based upon multiple record keys. The use of multiple record keys to determine file sequence is discussed in Chapter 9. In the case of control break reports, the major key would represent the highest level of report totals and each minor key would represent intermediate or minor report totals.

PREPARATION OF CONTROL BREAK REPORTS

The example in Figure 11-1 shows what is known as a single-level control break report. That is, all of the breaks are based upon the content of a single control field. It is also possible to use multiple control fields to identify report breaks. For example, a two-level control break report is illustrated in the report layout shown in Figure 11-2. This report forms the basis for the case study that follows.

Figure 11-2. Output layout for monthly commission summary report.

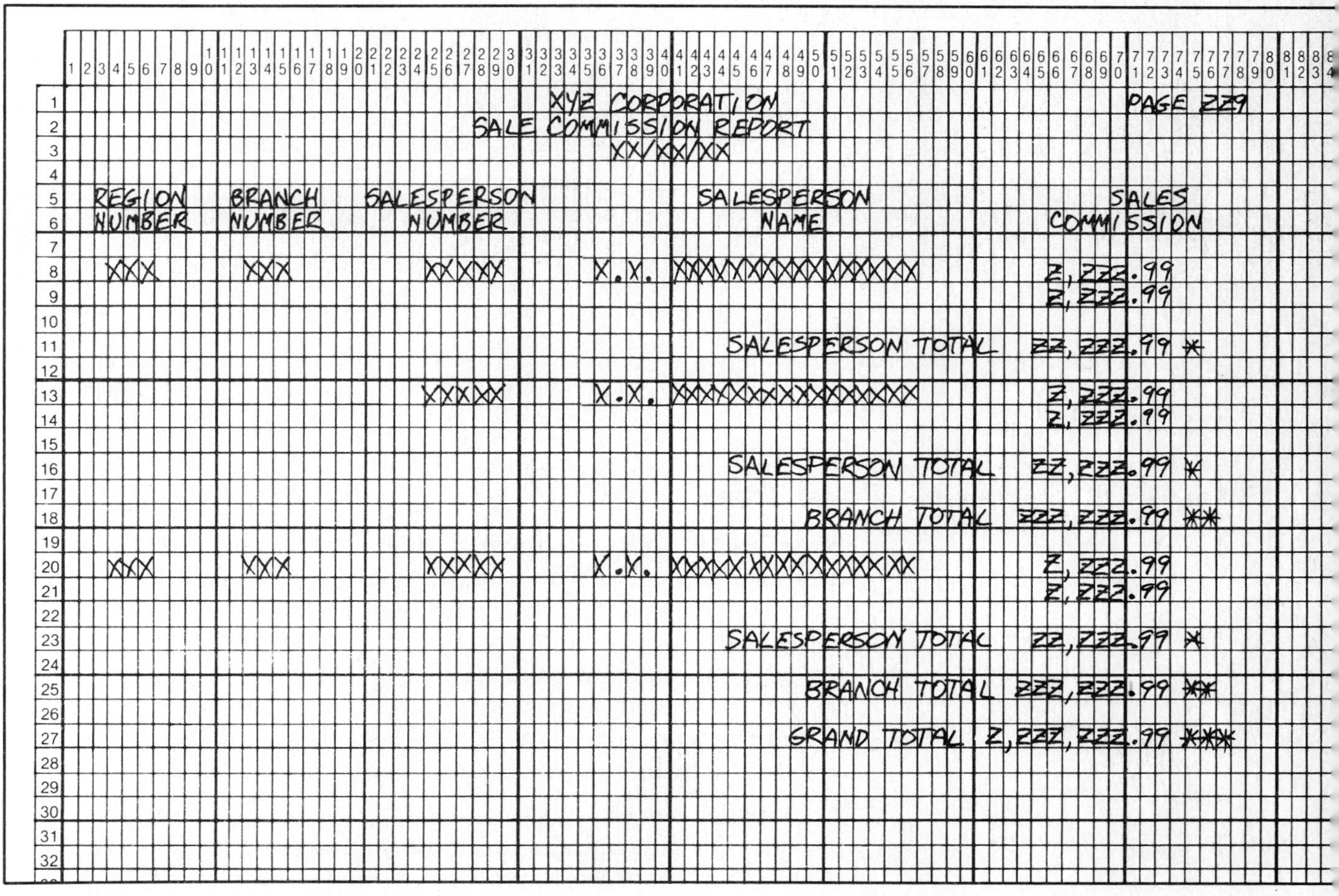

```
                      MONTHLY COMMISSION REPORT                    PAGE   1
                            1/28/83
        REGION    BRANCH    SALESPERSON           SALESPERSON       SALES
        NUMBER    NUMBER      NUMBER                  NAME         COMMISSION

         100       010        12345        BAKER        A. N.        95.90
         100       010        12345        BAKER        A. N.        51.25
         100       010        12345        BAKER        A. N.        64.00
                                               SALESPERSON TOTAL    211.15 *

         100       010        13466        DAVIS        T. H.        82.50
         100       010        13466        DAVIS        T. H.        12.35
                                               SALESPERSON TOTAL     94.85 *

                                                  BRANCH TOTAL      306.00 **

         100       020        12544        KWAN         M. M.        80.00
                                               SALESPERSON TOTAL     80.00 *

         100       020        16678        JOHNSON      B. C.       203.30
         100       020        16678        JOHNSON      B. C.        30.57
                                               SALESPERSON TOTAL    233.87 *

                                                  BRANCH TOTAL      313.87 **

         200       010        15387        MORALES      P. L.       185.08
         200       010        15387        MORALES      P. L.     2,056.05
         200       010        15387        MORALES      P. L.        29.88
                                               SALESPERSON TOTAL  2,271.01 *

                                                  BRANCH TOTAL    2,271.01 **

         300       026        10974        SMITHE       K. B.     1,064.53
         300       026        10974        SMITHE       K. B.     3,092.22
                                               SALESPERSON TOTAL  4,156.75 *

                                                  BRANCH TOTAL    4,156.75 **

         300       034        29763        PICCOLO      F. A.        68.84
         300       034 ``     29763        PICCOLO      F. A.     1,000.00
                                               SALESPERSON TOTAL  1,068.84 *

                                                  BRANCH TOTAL    1,068.84 **

                                                   GRAND TOTAL    8,116.47 ***
```

Figure 11-3. Output report for two-level commission control break program.

CASE STUDY

Figure 11-3 is a report showing commissions paid to salespersons, within branch offices. Thus, the salesperson number is the minor key for this control break report. The major key is the branch office number. A final total, output on the sensing of the end of the file, is a grand total of all sales commissions paid within the company. The problem for this case study is to read in sales records and to produce a report summarizing monthly sales commissions to be paid. The report is to summarize commissions by branch number and by salesperson within each branch.

Consider this report as an output, an end product resulting from application of the program development process described in Chapter 2. Recall that this process involves five steps, completed in sequence.

The first step in program development is to analyze the problem. One of the products of this analysis is a description of the end product, or output, to be produced. One method of identifying the required output is through preparation of a report layout like the one shown in Figure 11-2. Another analysis tool is an input record layout. A sample input record layout for this application is shown in Figure 11-4.

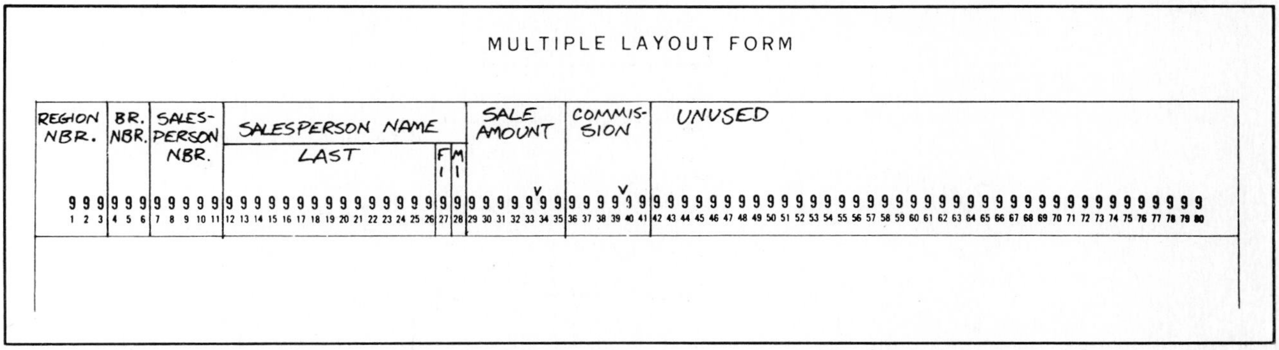

MULTIPLE LAYOUT FORM

Figure 11-4. Input record layout for sales commission report with two-level control breaks.

The second step in the program development process calls for designing the program structure. That is, the programmer must decide what processing must be applied to the input records to produce the desired output. In doing this, the programmer decomposes the overall problem into a series of parts. This is done by following a top-down approach to identifying the components, or modules, of the program needed to solve the stated problem. Another way of describing the top-down approach is to say that the programmer applies *stepwise refinement* to the overall identified program to go from this general problem statement to the specific steps needed to process the data and to produce the identified output. The result of the work in this phase of the program development process is a program structure chart like the one shown in Figure 11-5.

The third step in the program development process is to design the processing to be done. Flowcharts and pseudocoding are two commonly used program development tools. These are alternate methods for specifying the step-by-step functions to be performed by the computer in processing the data and producing the required results. To illustrate the output of this phase of the program development process, Figure 11-6 shows the psuedocode for the program needed to produce the commission report. Figure 11-7 presents structured flowcharts for this same application.

The fourth step in program development is to write the program itself. Coding for the commission report program is given in Figure 11-8.

The fifth and final step in program development, then, is to debug and test the program. This involves compiling, clearing up any syntax errors identified by the compiler, then testing the program with a file of test data like the one shown in Figure 11-9. Each time the program

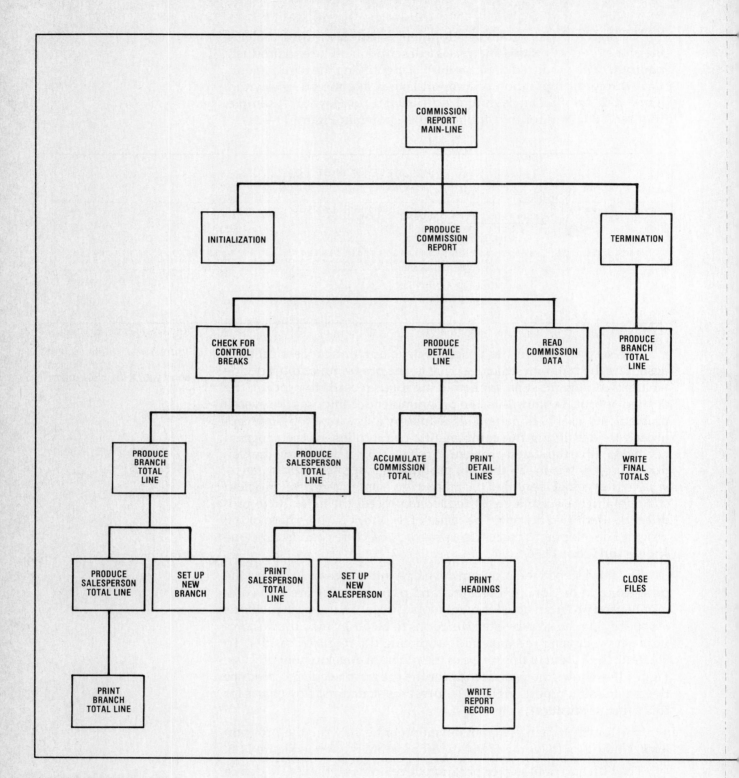

Figure 11-5. Structure chart for program to produce two-level control break commission report.

REPORT MAINLINE.
   Perform Initialization.
   Perform Produce-Commission-Report
      Until End-of-File.
   Perform Termination.
   STOP.

INITIALIZATION.
   Open Input file, Output file.
   Perform Print-Headings.
   Perform Read-Commission-Data.
   Move In-Salesperson-Nbr to Prev-Sales-Nbr.
   Move In-Branch-Nbr to Prev-Branch-Nbr.

PRODUCE-COMMISSION-REPORT.
   If In-Branch-Nbr not = Prev-Branch-Nbr
      Perform Write-Branch-Total-Lines
   Else
      If In-Salesperson-Nbr not = Prev-Sales-Nbr
         Perform Write-Salesperson-Total Lines.
   Perform Write-Detail-Lines.
   Perform Read-Commission-Data.

WRITE-DETAIL-LINE.
   Add In-Commission-Amount to Total-Commission-Amount.
   Move space to Detail-Line.
   Move each input field to Detail-Line.
   Perform Print-A-Line.

WRITE-BRANCH-TOTAL-LINES.
   Perform Write-Salesperson-Total-Line.
   Move Branch-Total-Commission to Out-Br-Total.
   Add Branch-Total-Commission to Grand-Total-Commission.
   Move Prev-Branch-Nbr to Out-Branch-Nbr.
   Move Branch-Total-Line to Print-Record.
   Perform Print-Double-Spaced.
   Move zeros to Branch-Total-Commission.
   Move In-Sequence-Fld to Prev-Sequence-Fld.

WRITE-SALESPERSON-TOTAL-LINES.
   Move Total-Commission-Amount to Out-Total-Commission.
   Add Total-Commission-Amount to Branch-Total-Commission.
   Move Prev-Sales-Nbr to Out-Sales-Nbr.
   Move Salesperson-Total-Line to Print-Record.
   Perform Print-Double-Spaced.
   Move zeros to Total-Commission-Amount.
   Move In-Salesperson-Nbr to Prev-Sales-Nbr.

Figure 11-6. Pseudocode for program to produce two-level control break commission report. (Illustration continues.)

362

PRINT-A-LINE.
    If Line-Count > Max-Lines-Per-Page
        Perform Print-Headings.
    Move Detail-Line to Print-Record.
    Write Print-Record after advancing 1 line.
    Add 1 to Line-Count.

READ-COMMISSION-DATA.
    Move "Not Sure" to Good-Record-Flag.
    Perform Get-Next-Record
        Until Good-Record-Flag = "Yes".

GET-NEXT-RECORD.
    Read Commission-File.
        At end move "Yes" to End-of-Data Flag.
    Move High-Values to In-Salesperson-Nbr.
    If In-Sequence-Fld < Prev-Sequence-Fld
        Display Sequence-Error-Message.
    Else
        Move "Yes" to Good-Record-Flag.

PRINT-HEADINGS.
    Add 1 to Page-Count.
    Move Page-Count to Rpt-Page-Number.
    Move zeros to Line-Count.
    Move Rpt-Title-Line to Print-Record.
    Write Print-Record after advancing page.
    Move Column-Head-1 to Print-Record.
    Perform Print-Double-Spaced.
    Move Column-Head-2 to Print-Record.
    Perform Print-Single-Spaced.
    Move Spaces to Detail-Line.
    Perform Print-A-Line.

TERMINATION.
    Perform Write-Branch-Total-Lines.
    Move Grand-Total-Commission to Out-Gr-Total.
    Move Grand-Total-Summary-Line to Print-Record.
    Perform Print-Double-Spaced.
    Close Input file, Output file.

Figure 11-6. Continued.

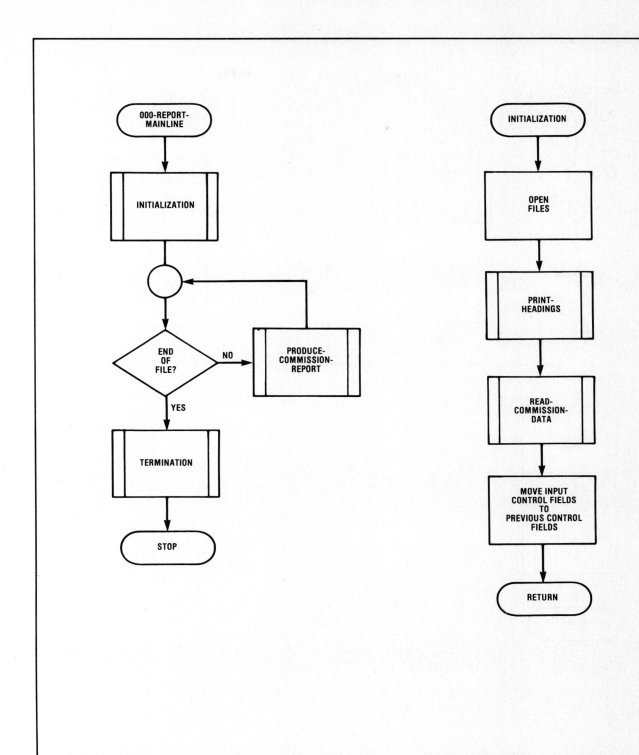

Figure 11-7. Flowchart for program to produce two-level control break commission report. (Illustration continues.)

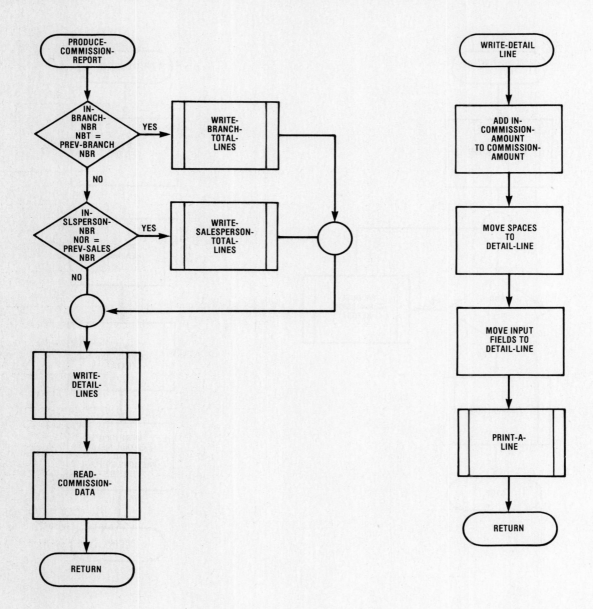

Figure 11-7. Continued.

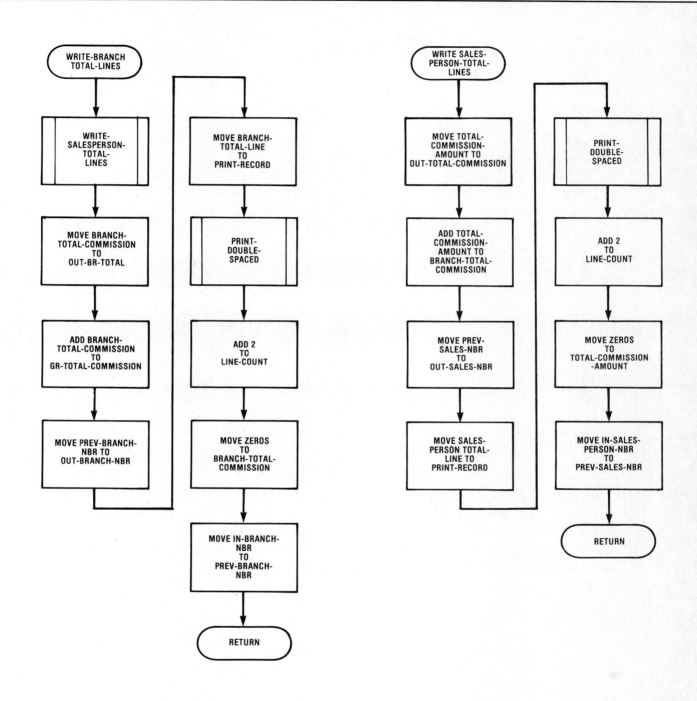

Figure 11-7. Continued.

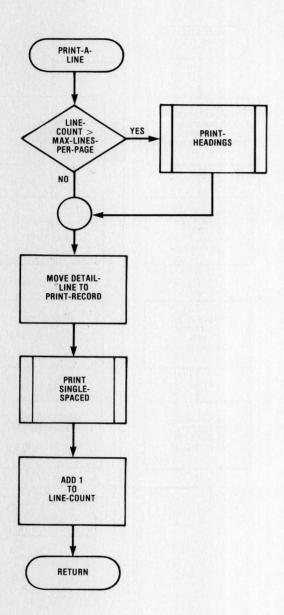

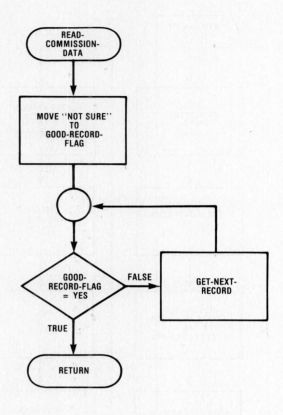

Figure 11-7. Continued.

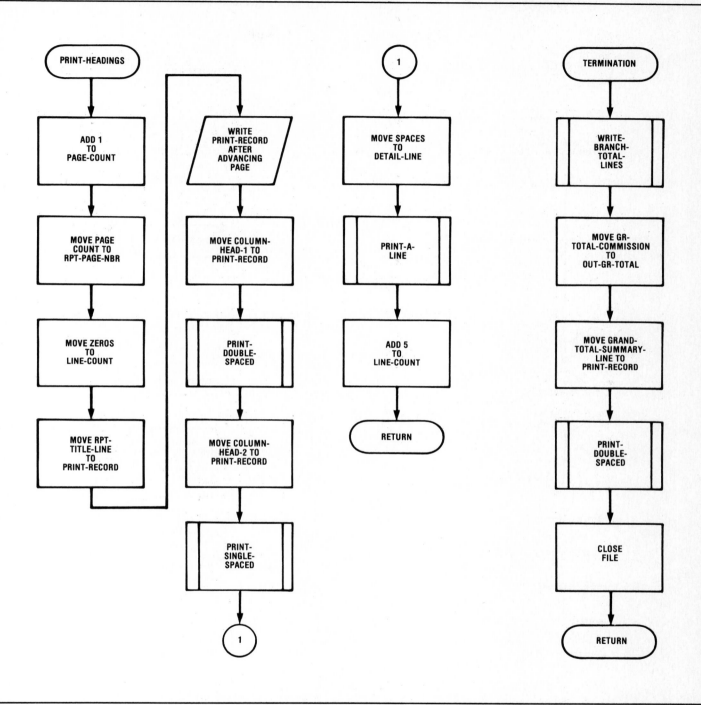

Figure 11-7. Continued.

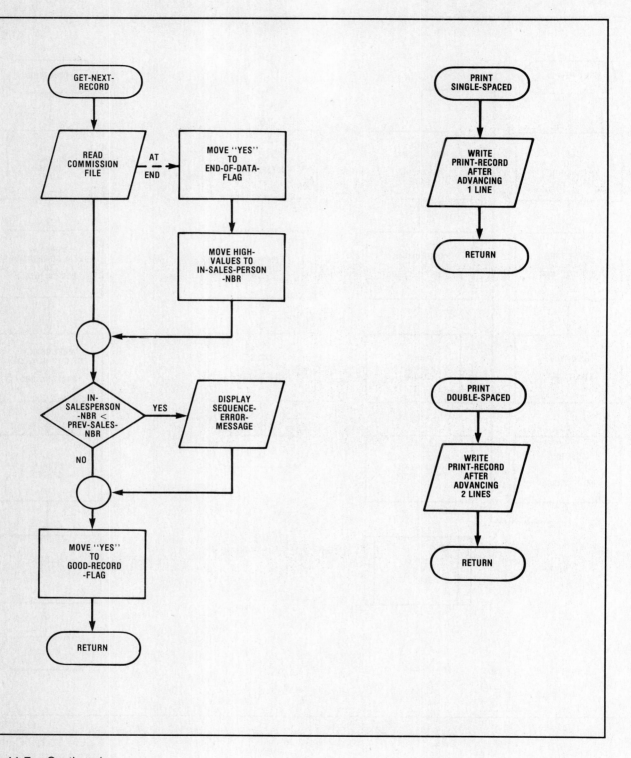

Figure 11-7. Continued.

```
00001   IDENTIFICATION DIVISION.
00002   PROGRAM-ID.      COMRPT.
00003   AUTHOR.          T.S. BUCK
00004   DATE-WRITTEN.    DECEMBER 15, 1982
00005   DATE-COMPILED.   FEBRUARY 1, 1983.
00006  *REMARKS. ****************************************************
00007  *    THIS PROGRAM IS A 2-LEVEL CONTROL BREAK REPORT.       *
00008  *    INPUT IS FROM SALES COMMISSION DATA.                  *
00009  *    OUTPUT IS THE SALES COMMISSION REPORT.                *
00010  * THE FILE IS SEQUENCED ON REGION NUMBER,BRANCH NUMBER, AND *
00011  * SALESPERSON NUMBER WITHIN BRANCH. TOTALS ARE PRODUCE FOR  *
00012  * SALESPERSON WITHIN BRANCH.                               *
00013  ****************************************************************
00014
00015   ENVIRONMENT DIVISION.
00016   CONFIGURATION SECTION.
00017   INPUT-OUTPUT SECTION.
00018   FILE-CONTROL.
00019       SELECT COMMISSION-FILE  ASSIGN TO INPTCOM
00020          USE "RT=Z".
00021       SELECT REPORT-FILE       ASSIGN TO RPTOUT
00022          USE "PRINTF=YES".
00023  /
00024   DATA DIVISION.
00025   FILE SECTION.
00026   FD  COMMISSION-FILE
00027       LABEL RECORDS ARE OMITTED.
00028   01  COMMISSION-RECORD.
00029       05 IN-SEQUENCE-FLD.
00030          10 IN-REGION-NBR      PIC 9(03).
00031          10 IN-BRANCH-NBR      PIC 9(03).
00032          10 IN-SLSPERSON-NBR   PIC 9(05).
00033       05 IN-SLSPERSON-NAME.
00034          10 IN-LAST-NAME       PIC X(15).
00035          10 IN-FIRST-INT       PIC X.
00036          10 IN-MID-INT         PIC X.
00037       05 IN-SALES-AMOUNT       PIC S9(05)V99.
00038       05 IN-COMMISSION         PIC S9(04)V99.
00039
00040   FD  REPORT-FILE
00041       LABEL RECORDS ARE OMITTED.
00042
00043   01 PRINT-RECORD             PIC X(80).
00044
00045  /
00046   WORKING-STORAGE SECTION.
00047
00048   01  RPT-TITLE-LINE.
00049       05 FILLER               PIC X(22) VALUE SPACES.
00050       05 FILLER               PIC X(25)
00051                               VALUE "MONTHLY COMMISSION REPORT".
00052       05 FILLER               PIC X(23) VALUE SPACES.
00053       05 FILLER               PIC X(4)  VALUE "PAGE".
00054       05 RPT-PAGE-NBR         PIC ZZ9.
00055
00056
00057   01  RPT-TITLE-DATE.
00058       05  FILLER              PIC X(30) VALUE SPACES.
00059       05  RPT-DATE.
00060          10 RPT-MON-DAY       PIC Z9/99/.
00061          10 RPT-YR            PIC 99.
00062   01  COLUMN-HEAD-1.
00063       05 FILLER               PIC X(08) VALUE " REGION".
00064       05 FILLER               PIC X(09) VALUE "  BRANCH".
00065       05 FILLER               PIC X(14) VALUE "   SALESPERSON".
00066       05 FILLER               PIC X(15) VALUE SPACES.
00067       05 FILLER               PIC X(11) VALUE "SALESPERSON".
00068       05 FILLER               PIC X(11) VALUE SPACES.
00069       05 FILLER               PIC X(05) VALUE "SALES".
00070
00071   01  COLUMN-HEAD-2.
```

Figure 11-8. Complete source program to produce two-level control break commission report. (Illustration continues.)

```
00072        05 FILLER                    PIC X(08) VALUE "  NUMBER".
00073        05 FILLER                    PIC X(09) VALUE "  NUMBER".
00074        05 FILLER                    PIC X(12) VALUE "     NUMBER".
00075        05 FILLER                    PIC X(20) VALUE SPACES.
00076        05 FILLER                    PIC X(04) VALUE "NAME".
00077        05 FILLER                    PIC X(13) VALUE SPACES.
00078        05 FILLER                    PIC X(11) VALUE "COMMISSION ".
00079 /
00080  01   DETAIL-LINE.
00081        05 FILLER                    PIC X(04) VALUE SPACES.
00082        05 DT-REGION-NBR             PIC 9(03).
00083        05 FILLER                    PIC X(06) VALUE SPACES.
00084        05 DT-BRANCH-NBR             PIC 9(03).
00085        05 FILLER                    PIC X(08) VALUE SPACES.
00086        05 DT-SLSPERSON-NBR          PIC 9(05).
00087        05 FILLER                    PIC X(12) VALUE SPACES.
00088        05 DT-SLSPERSON-NAME.
00089           10 DT-LAST-NAME           PIC X(15).
00090           10 DT-FIRST-INT           PIC X.
00091           10 FILLER                 PIC X(02) VALUE ". ".
00092           10 DT-MID-INT             PIC X.
00093           10 FILLER                 PIC X(02) VALUE ". ".
00094        05 FILLER``                  PIC X(05) VALUE SPACES.
00095        05 DT-COMMISSION             PIC Z,ZZZ.99.
00096
00097  01   SALESPERSON-TOTAL-LINE.
00098        05 FILLER                    PIC X(47) VALUE SPACES.
00099        05 FILLER                    PIC X(17)
00100                                     VALUE "SALESPERSON TOTAL".
00101        05 FILLER                    PIC X(02) VALUE SPACES.
00102        05 OUT-COMMISSION            PIC ZZ,ZZZ.99.
00103        05 FILLER                    PIC X(02) VALUE " *".
00104
00105  01   BRANCH-TOTAL-LINE.
00106        05 FILLER                    PIC X(51) VALUE SPACES.
00107        05 FILLER                    PIC X(14) VALUE "BRANCH TOTAL  ".
00108        05 OUT-BR-TOTAL              PIC ZZZ,ZZZ.99.
00109        05 FILLER                    PIC X(03) VALUE " **".
00110
00111  01   GRAND-TOTAL-LINE.
00112        05 FILLER                    PIC X(50) VALUE SPACES.
00113        05 FILLER                    PIC X(13) VALUE "GRAND TOTAL  ".
00114        05 OUT-GR-TOTAL              PIC Z,ZZZ,ZZZ.99.
00115        05 FILLER                    PIC X(04) VALUE " ***".
00116 /
00117  01   ACCUMULATORS.
00118        05 TOTAL-COMMISSION-AMOUNT   PIC S9(05)V99 VALUE ZERO.
00119        05 BRANCH-TOTAL-COMMISSION   PIC S9(06)V99 VALUE ZERO.
00120        05 GRAND-TOTAL-COMMISSION    PIC S9(07)V99 VALUE ZERO.
00121
00122
00123  01   PRINT-VARRIABLES.
00124        05 LINE-COUNT                PIC 9(02) VALUE 66.
00125        05 MAX-LINES-PER-PAGE        PIC 9(02) VALUE 55.
00126        05 PAGE-COUNT                PIC 9(02) VALUE ZERO.
00127
00128  01   CONTROL-FLAGS.
00129        05 WS-END-OF-FILE-FLAG       PIC X(03) VALUE "NO".
00130           88 END-OF-FILE VALUE bYES".
00131        05 WS-NEED-SLSPERSON-NBR     PIC X.
00132        05 WS-NEED-BRANCH-NBR        PIC X.
00133        05 WS-NEED-REGION-NBR        PIC X.
00134        05 WS-GOOD-RECORD-FLAG       PIC X(08) VALUE "NOT SURE".
00135
00136  01   SEQUENCE-CHECK-FIELDS.
00137        05 PREV-SEQUENCE-FLD.
00138           10 PREV-REGION-NBR        PIC 9(03).
00139           10 PREV-BRANCH-NBR        PIC 9(03).
00140           10 PREV-SLSPERSON-NBR     PIC 9(05).
00141
00142  01   SEQUENCE-ERROR-MESSAGE.
00143        05 FILLER                    PIC X(10) VALUE SPACES.
00144        05 FILLER                    PIC X(30) VALUE
00145                "INPUT FILE OUT OF SEQUENCE".
00146
00147  01   TODAYS-DATE.
00148        05 SYS-YR                    PIC 99.
00149        05 SYS-MON-DAY               PIC 9(04).
00150
```

Figure 11-8. Continued.

```
00151 /
00152   PROCEDURE DIVISION.
00153   000-REPORT-MAINLINE.
00154       PERFORM INITIALIZATION.
00155       PERFORM PRODUCE-COMMISSION-REPORT
00156           UNTIL END-OF-FILE.
00157       PERFORM TERMINATION.
00158       STOP RUN.
00159
00160   INITIALIZATION.
00161       OPEN INPUT  COMMISSION-FILE
00162            OUTPUT REPORT-FILE.
00163       ACCEPT TODAYS-DATE FROM DATE.
00164       MOVE SYS-YR TO RPT-YR.
00165       MOVE SYS-MON-DAY TO RPT-MON-DAY.
00166       PERFORM PRINT-HEADINGS.
00167       PERFORM READ-COMMISSION-DATA.
00168       MOVE IN-SEQUENCE-FLD TO PREV-SEQUENCE-FLD.
00169
00170   PRODUCE-COMMISSION-REPORT.
00171       IF IN-BRANCH-NBR NOT EQUAL TO PREV-BRANCH-NBR
00172       THEN
00173           PERFORM WRITE-BRANCH-TOTAL-LINES
00174       ELSE
00175           IF IN-SLSPERSON-NBR NOT EQUAL TO PREV-SLSPERSON-NBR
00176           THEN
0017w               PERFORM WRITE-SALESPERSON-TOTAL-LINES.
00178       PERFORM WRITE-DETAIL-LINES.
00179       PERFORM READ-COMMISSION-DATA.
00180
00181   WRITE-DETAIL-LINES.
00182       ADD IN-COMMISSION TO TOTAL-COMMISSION-AMOUNT.
00183       MOVE IN-REGION-NBR TO DT-REGION-NBR.
00184       MOVE IN-BRANCH-NBR TO DT-BRANCH-NBR.
00185       MOVE IN-SLSPERSON-NBR TO DT-SLSPERSON-NBR.
00186       MOVE IN-LAST-NAME TO DT-LAST-NAME.
00187       MOVE IN-FIRST-INT TO DT-FIRST-INT.
00188       MOVE IN-MID-INT TO DT-MID-INT.
00189       MOVE IN-COMMISSION TO DT-COMMISSION.
00190       PERFORM PRINT-A-LINE.
00191
00192   WRITE-SALESPERSON-TOTAL-LINES.
00193       MOVE TOTAL-COMMISSION-AMOUNT TO OUT-COMMISSION.
00194       ADD  TOTAL-COMMISSION-AMOUNT TO BRANCH-TOTAL-COMMISSION.
00195       MOVE SALESPERSON-TOTAL-LINE TO PRINT-RECORD.
00196       PERFORM PRINT-SINGLE-SPACED.
00197       ADD 2 TO LINE-COUNT.
00198       MOVE SPACES TO PRINT-RECORD.
00199       PERFORM PRINT-SINGLE-SPACED.
00200       MOVE ZEROS TO TOTAL-COMMISSION-AMOUNT.
00201       MOVE IN-SLSPERSON-NBR TO PREV-SLSPERSON-NBR.
00202
00203   WRITE-BRANCH-TOTAL-LINES.
00204       PERFORM WRITE-SALESPERSON-TOTAL-LINES.
00205       MOVE BRANCH-TOTAL-COMMISSION TO OUT-BR-TOTAL.
00206       ADD  BRANCH-TOTAL-COMMISSION TO GRAND-TOTAL-COMMISSION.
00207       MOVE BRANCH-TOTAL-LINE TO PRINT-RECORD.
00208       PERFORM PRINT-DOUBLE-SPACED.
00209       MOVE SPACES TO PRINT-RECORD.
00210       PERFORM PRINT-SINGLE-SPACED.
00211       ADD 2 TO LINE-COUNT.
00212       MOVE ZEROS TO BRANCH-TOTAL-COMMISSION.
00213       MOVE IN-SEQUENCE-FLD TO PREV-SEQUENCE-FLD.
00214
00215
00216   READ-COMMISSION-DATA.
00217       MOVE "NOT SURE" TO WS-GOOD-RECORD-FLAG.
00218       PERFORM GET-NEXT-RECORD
00219           UNTIL WS-GOOD-RECORD-FLAG EQUALS 'YES'.
00220
00221   GET-NEXT-RECORD.
00222       READ COMMISSION-FILE
00223           AT END MOVE "YES" TO WS-END-OF-FILE-FLAG
00224               MOVE HIGH-VALUES TO IN-SLSPERSON-NBR.
00225       IF IN-SEQUENCE-FLD LESS THAN PREV-SEQUENCE-FLD
00226       THEN
00227           DISPLAY SEQUENCE-ERROR-MESSAGE
00228       ELSE
00229           MOVE "YES" TO WS-GOOD-RECORD-FLAG.
```

Figure 11-8. Continued.

Figure 11-8. Continued.

```
00230
00231   PRINT-A-LINE.
00232       IF LINE-COUNT GREATER THAN MAX-LINES-PER-PAGE
00233       THEN
00234           PERFORM PRINT-HEADINGS.
00235       MOVE DETAIL-LINE TO PRINT-RECORD.
00236       PERFORM PRINT-SINGLE-SPACED.
00237       ADD 1 TO LINE-COUNT.
00238
00239   PRINT-SINGLE-SPACED.
00240       WRITE PRINT-RECORD
00241           AFTER ADVANCING 1 LINES.
00242
00243   PRINT-DOUBLE-SPACED.
00244       WRITE PRINT-RECORD
00245           AFTER ADVANCING 2 LINES.
00246
00247   PRINT-HEADINGS.
00248       ADD 1 TO PAGE-COUNT.
00249       MOVE PAGE-COUNT TO RPT-PAGE-NBR.
00250       MOVE ZEROS TO LINE-COUNT.
00251       MOVE RPT-TITLE-LINE TO PRINT-RECORD.
00252       WRITE PRINT-RECORD
00253           AFTER ADVANCING PAGE.
00254       MOVE RPT-TITLE-DATE TO PRINT-RECORD.
00255       PERFORM PRINT-SINGLE-SPACED.
00256       MOVE COLUMN-HEAD-1 TO PRINT-RECORD.
00257       PERFORM PRINT-DOUBLE-SPACED.
00258       MOVE COLUMN-HEAD-2 TO PRINT-RECORD.
00259       PERFORM PRINT-SINGLE-SPACED.
00260       MOVE SPACES TO PRINT-RECORD.
00261       PERFORM PRINT-SINGLE-SPACED.
00262       ADD 5 TO LINE-COUNT
00263
00264   TERMINATION.
00265       PERFORM WRITE-BRANCH-TOTAL-LINES.
00266       MOVE GRAND-TOTAL-COMMISSION TO OUT-GR-TOTAL.
00267       MOVE GRAND-TOTAL-LINE TO PRINT-RECORD.
00268       PERFORM PRINT-DOUBLE-SPACED.
00269       CLOSE   COMMISSION-FILE, REPORT-FILE.
00270
```

Figure 11-9. Input data file for two-level control break commission report.

```
10001012345BAKER          AN0095900009590
10001012345BAKER          AN0051250005125
10001012345BAKER          AN0064000006400
10001013466DAVIS          TH0082500008250
10001013466DAVIS          TH0012345001235
10002012544KWAN           MM0080000008000
10002016678JOHNSON        BC0203300020330
10002016678JOHNSON        BC0030566003057
20001pq5387MORALES        PL0185075018508
20001015387MORALES        PL0056050205605
20001015387MORALES        PL0002988002988
30002610974SMITHE         KB0064532106453
30002610974SMITHE         KB0092223309222
30003429763PICCOLO        FA0006884006884
30003429763PICCOLO        FA1000050100000
```

is modified in response to debugging and testing, the procedures are repeated, until accurate and reliable results are output.

The result of application of the program development process to the sales commission reporting application is the report shown in Figure 11-3.

Compare this final report with the supporting documentation in Figures 11-2 through 11-9.

Analysis of Case Study

For a closer review of development of the commission report case, consider the pseudocoding in Figure 11-6. Pseudocoding for a program provides an excellent basis for a structured walkthrough, or a review of the basic design, for a program. Reviewing pseudocoding is a good habit to get into. This is where mistakes can be avoided before they are built into programs.

Note the entries under the INITIALIZATION module in Figure 11-6. Within this module, input and output files are opened, headings are printed, and the first data record is read into the computer. The computer is then instructed to move the salesperson number to the memory area for the previous salesperson number. Likewise, the branch number is moved to the location for the previous branch number. This sets up the basis for control break comparisons—the heart of processing the file to produce the report.

Next, notice the pseudocoding for the module entitled PRODUCE-COMMISSION-REPORT. This is the main processing leg of the program. Functions within this module are repeated until the end-of-file indicator is sensed.

The first instruction under PRODUCE-COMMISSION-REPORT is an IF statement that causes a comparison between the input branch number and the previous branch number. This is to detect a major control break that is triggered by a difference between the input and previous records of branch numbers. If the numbers are different, the module that causes the program to print a major total is invoked.

A second IF statement is included in the same module. This calls for comparison of the current salesperson number with the previous salesperson number. Again, if a difference is sensed, a module is invoked to generate a minor total.

Whenever a control break occurs, all lower level totals will have to be generated. Thus, a major control key change will generate a minor total, then the major total. A final total procedure will cause the minor totals to be printed, followed by major totals, then the final (grand) total.

As this program is structured, it is impossible to produce output totals for the first records. This is because the initialization module forced an equal comparison by moving the current values of the control fields to the positions for the previous values.

When the current and previous values of the control keys match, the program will execute the PERFORM WRITE-DETAIL-LINE instruction. The last instruction in the PRODUCE-COMMISSION-REPORT module is the statement to read in the next commission record.

The next module is labeled WRITE-DETAIL-LINE. This causes the commission value from the new input record to be added to an accumulator for total commissions (TOTAL-COMMISSION-AMOUNT). As part of the same module, detail lines are formatted and printed.

The two modules, illustrated in Figure 11-10, cause the program to write totals for the branch and for the salesperson. As described, these modules are invoked when control break conditions are sensed for either branch number or salesperson number. Note the relationships between the modules for the writing of branch and salesperson totals. A feature has been built into the pseudocoding that is known as a *rolling total*. That is, when a control break for salesperson occurs, the program, in addition to printing the accumulated record, will also cause the total to be added into the amount for the branch. After this has been done, the accumulator for the salesperson record will be zeroed. When totals are rolled in this way, accumulation begins at the lowest level in the report hierarchy. When a control break occurs, it causes the printing of this first-level total and the balance is transferred to the next highest level. This continues to occur until all of the control breaks have been satisfied and all levels of the report have been printed—including the final, or grand, total.

Figure 11-10. Instructions for salesperson and branch-total modules of two-level control break commission report.

```
WRITE-BRANCH-TOTAL-LINES.
    Perform Write-Salesperson-Total-Line.
    Move Branch-Total-Commission to Out-Br-Total.
    Add Branch-Total-Commission to Grand-Total-Commission.
    Move Branch-Total-Line to Print-Record.
    Perform Print-Double-Spaced.
    Move zeros to Branch-Total-Commission.
    Move In-Sequence-Fld to Prev-Sequence-Fld.


WRITE-SALESPERSON-TOTAL-LINES.
    Move Total-Commission-Amount to Out-Total-Commission.
    Add Total-Commission-Amount to Branch-Total-Commission.
    Move Salesperson-Total-Line to Print-Record.
    Perform Print-Double-Spaced.
    Move zeros to Total-Commission-Amount.
    Move In-Sequence-Fld to Prev-Sequence-Fld.
```

Now note the module entitled READ-COMMISSION-DATA, in Figure 11-8. The purpose of this module is to access and bring into memory the next record in proper sequence for processing. In the process, this module uses a technique often called *defensive programming*. That is, a *sequence check* is applied to be sure that the next record accepted for processing is, in fact, in proper sequential order. If so, the first instruction under this module will set a flag to permit the processing to go forward. If a record presented to the program has a value lower than the previous record, the processing flag will not be set and that record will be ignored. In addition, a sequence-error message will be displayed for later action by the user.

This offers an excellent example of how quality control features are built into computer programs. The programmer who prepared this pseudocoding reasoned that the program was being designed to process data from a file in which records were sequenced in ascending order according to a given control field. Given this program specification, a programmer should be naturally concerned with all errors that can occur within input and processing for the program under development. An obvious potential input error lies in out-of-sequence records. Such records would destroy the validity of the data being processed. Therefore, a safeguard has to be built into the program to assure that such records cannot be processed. Similarly, the file of test data for this program should include out-of-sequence records to test this feature.

Actual reading of records from the input files is under control of the module titled GET-NEXT-RECORD. The module reads in one record at a time and compares the value of the control fields with that of a previous record. If the value of the new record is less than that of the previous record, this indicates an out-of-sequence condition and an appropriate error-handling activity is executed. A choice of actions can be built into the program at this point. Either processing can be aborted when an out-of-sequence record is sensed, or it may be decided to ignore the improperly placed record and continue with processing. This is a design specification decision that is implemented by the programmer. The programmer should not try to make these decisions, but should ask for proper specifications from the system designer. If succeeding records are equal to or greater than previous records, processing continues normally.

Now note the content of the TERMINATION module. The key feature of this module is that, before the grand total is printed, the previous rolling totals for salesperson and branch are printed and the accumulators are zeroed. At the conclusion of this module, input and output files are closed.

OPTIONS FOR
CONTROL BREAK REPORTS

Through selective printing options, control break reports can be tailored to specific needs of individual users.

One such option centers around a decision on whether to print detail lines on control break reports. The case study of the commission report used detail lines. This meant that every commissionable sale, by each salesman, was listed on the final report. As an option, a decision could have been made to suppress the printing of the detail lines, producing a report that consisted of control break totals only. The finished document would be considerably shorter than the one that incorporates detail lines. However, significant managment information would still have been included. An example of a report printed under control of a program using this option is shown in Figure 11-11.

```
                    MONTHLY COMMISSION REPORT                    PAGE   1
                          5/03/83

REGION     BRANCH    SALESPERSON            SALESPERSON            SALES
NUMBER     NUMBER    NUMBER                 NAME                   COMMISSION

 100        010       12345        BAKER          F. A.           211.13 *

 100        010       13466        DAVIS          T. H.            94.85 *


                                               BRANCH TOTAL       306.00 **

 100        020       12544        KWAN           M. M.            80.00 *

 100        020       16678        JOHNSON        B. C.           233.87 *


                                               BRANCH TOTAL       313.87 **

 200        010       15387        MORALES        P. L.         2,271.01 *


                                               BRANCH TOTAL     2,271.01 **

 300        026       10974        SMITHE         K. B.         4,156.75 *


                                               BRANCH TOTAL     4,156.75 **

 300        034       29763        PICCOLO        F. A.         1,068.841*


                                               BRANCH TOTAL     1,068.84 **


                                               GRAND TOTAL     8,116.47 ***
```

Figure 11-11. Commission report with summary data only.

Another available option is known as *group indicating.* Under this approach, only the first occurrence of a control field value is printed on the report. On subsequent occurrences, the printing of the control field value is suppressed. Thus, using this option, only the first detail line for each salesperson would include that salesperson's number. Similarly, in Figure 11-12, only the first line indicating a new job number or machine type would include those values. On subsequent lines for which those fields are the same, blanks are printed in those field locations. The value of group indicating lies in clarity of presentation. Rather than repeating numbers that would clutter the report with repetitive information, the identification lines stand out through this formatting.

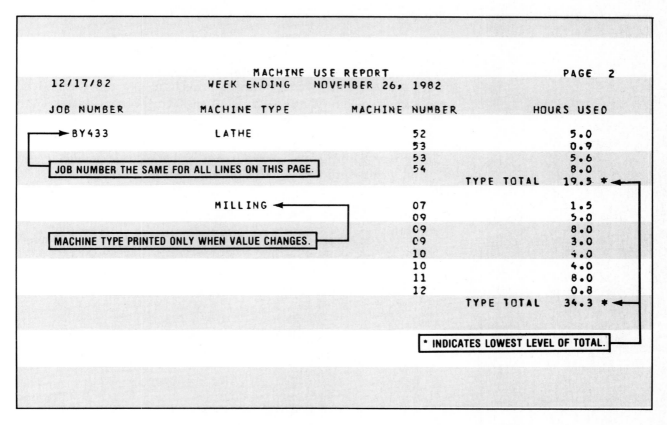

Another option available on control break reports is the use of indicators to mark the significance of control break totals. This has been done also in the report in Figure 11-3. Note that an asterisk (*) has been printed to the right of the rightmost character on the lines totaling salesperson commissions. The lines presenting major totals, for branches, have two asterisks to the right of the rightmost character. If still another level of control break were added to this program, there would be three asterisks to the right of the rightmost total. Any desired symbol can be used to identify the significance of control breaks. However, the asterisk is most commonly used.

Figure 11-12. Group indicated report.

Key Terms

1. control break report
2. control field
3. stepwise refinement
4. structured walkthrough
5. rolling total
6. defensive programming
7. sequence check
8. group indicating

Summary

A control break report is a summary report in which the printing of total lines is triggered by changes in content for selected fields within records being processed. The fields that cause the printing of total lines are called control fields. These can be any fields that occur uniformly in all records within a file. Usually, control fields are numeric and uniformly structured, with values assigned in ascending order. The contents of specified fields are accumulated for all records with identical control fields. Totals are printed when the control field value of an input record is greater than that of the previous record.

When one control field is designated, the result is a single-level report. Multiple control fields can be designated. Use of two control fields produces a two-level report, and so on. [*Objective No. 1.*]

Control break programs use sets of accumulators. Values are entered into detail line accumulators and also into accumulators for each control break level. When a control break is sensed, the total in the lowest-level accumulator is printed. At this time, the total is rolled forward into the next higher-level accumulator. The procedure repeats for each level, generating a grand total when an end-of-file condition is sensed. [*Objective No. 2.*]

Selective printing options that are available include detail line suppression, group indicating, and significance indication through use of asterisks. [*Objective No. 3.*]

Control break techniques are illustrated through presentation of a case study. [*Objectives Nos. 2 and 4.*]

Review/Discussion Questions

1. What are the uses of a control break report?

2. What is a control field and what are its characteristics?

3. What are control break levels and how are they established?

4. What is a structured walkthrough and what role does this task play in program development?

5. What initializing functions should be included in the structured design of a control break report?

6. What iteration loops are used in control break report programs and what results do they produce?

7. Define the term *rolling total* and describe how this technique is implemented.

8. What special termination procedures should be included in control break programs?

9. What are the benefits of group indicating and how is this option implemented?

Practice Assignment

Refer back to the layout for the sales commission report (Figure 11-2) developed in the case study. Note that, in addition to fields identifying salesperson number and branch number, there is also a field that identifies the region in which the branch is located. This field is called REGION-NUMBER.

Your assignment is to modify the program developed in the case study. Expand the two-level control break report program to produce a three-level control break report. The new major control field in your program will be for region number. The branch number control field becomes an intermediate level of control break. The salesperson number remains as the minor control break field.

In addition to totaling sales commissions, expand the report to produce totals of sales amounts. (See input record layout in Figure 11-4.)

Retain the final, grand total for this report. Suppress detail lines, printing only minor, intermediate, major, and final totals. Use the group indication option as well.

Figure 11-9 contains the test data for this program.

Worksheet for Structured Flowchart

Program Name: _____

Prepared By: _____

Worksheet for Pseudocode Specifications

Program Name: _____

Prepared By: _____

COBOL PROGRAM SHEET

System				Punching Instructions		Sheet	of
Program			Graphic		Card Form #		Identification
Programmer			Date	Punch		73]	[80

SEQUENCE			CONT	A	B																
(PAGE)	(SERIAL)																				
1 3	4 6	7	8		12	16	20	24	28	32	36	40	44	48	52	56	60	64	68	72	

COBOL PROGRAM SHEET

System		
Program		
Programmer		

	Punching Instructions			Sheet	of
	Graphic		Card Form #	Identification	
Date	Punch			[73] [80]	

SEQUENCE		CONT																	
(PAGE)	(SERIAL)		A	B															
1 3	4 6	7	8	12	16	20	24	28	32	36	40	44	48	52	56	60	64	68	72

COBOL PROGRAM SHEET

System

Program

Programmer

Date

Punching Instructions

Graphic

Punch

Card Form #

Sheet   of

Identification

73]   [80

SEQUENCE

(PAGE)   (SERIAL)

CONT

A   B

1   3 4   6 7 8   12   16   20   24   28   32   36   40   44   48   52   56   60   64   68   72

COBOL PROGRAM SHEET

System				Sheet	of
Program		Punching Instructions		Identification	
Programmer		Card Form #		[73] [80]	
	Graphic				
	Date	Punch			

SEQUENCE		CONT	A	B	16	20	24	28	32	36	40	44	48	52	56	60	64	68	72
(PAGE)	(SERIAL)		8	12															
1 3	4 6	7																	

COBOL PROGRAM SHEET

System					Punching Instructions		Sheet	of
Program				Graphic				Identification
Programmer		Date		Punch		Card Form #		73] [80

SEQUENCE			CONT																
(PAGE)	(SERIAL)			A	B	16	20	24	28	32	36	40	44	48	52	56	60	64	68	72
1	3 4	6 7	8	12																

COBOL PROGRAM SHEET

System				Punching Instructions			Sheet	of
Program						Card Form #		Identification
Programmer		Date		Graphic				
				Punch			73]	[80

SEQUENCE		CONT																		
(PAGE)	(SERIAL)		A	B																
1 3	4 6	7 8	12	16	20	24	28	32	36	40	44	48	52	56	60	64	68	72		

Vocabulary Building Practice—Exercise 11

Write definitions and/or explanations of the terms listed below.

1. **control break report** _____

   _____

2. **control field** _____

   _____

3. **stepwise refinement** _____

   _____

4. **structured walkthrough** _____

   _____

5. **rolling total** _____

   _____

6. **defensive programming** _____

   _____

7. **sequence check** _____

   _____

8. **group indicating** _____

   _____

9. **blocking factor** _____

   _____

10. **disk cartridge** _____

    _____

(over, please)

11. sector _____

_____

12. cylinder _____

_____

13. access time _____

_____

14. logical record _____

_____

15. physical characteristic _____

_____

16. character position _____

_____

17. physical record _____

_____

18. volume _____

_____

19. archival file _____

_____

20. unit record _____

_____

TABLES 12

OBJECTIVES

On completing reading and other learning assignments for this chapter, you should be able to:

1. Define and design single-level tables for use in COBOL programs.
2. Develop programs that incorporate use of static single-level tables.
3. Develop programs that incorporate use of dynamic single-level tables.
4. Develop programs that access single-level tables through use of the subscript technique.
5. Develop programs that access single-level tables through use of the index technique.
6. Describe and be able to apply the binary search technique to appropriately structured tables.

TABLES: WHAT THEY ARE AND WHY THEY ARE USED

A *table* is an area defined in computer memory to hold repeated occurrences of a particular data item. For example, almost everyone is familiar with paying sales taxes on purchases. The card used by salespersons to look up the amount of tax on a purchase is a type of table. There are two sets of data in sales tax tables: the amount of purchase and the corresponding amount of sales tax.

Thus, tables are a means of describing relationships among sets of data. The ability to describe and use data on the basis of relationships can be extremely economical and efficient as a programming tool. This is because, in some situations, data items are repeated and can assume a number of values. Instead of having to create individual records for each possible combination of data fields, it is easier to write a short, repeated series of instructions that will enable the computer to process all needed data from a stored table.

To illustrate, a simple, single-dimension table is presented in Figure 12-1. This is a typical pricing table. In the column at the left are product numbers. In the column at the right are prices for these items. The advantage of using this pricing table is that it is not necessary to store the price as part of the product master record. It is much more efficient and convenient, when prices are changed, to modify only one data item located in a table.

In a table of this type, the left column is called the *argument,* while the right column is called the *function.* The argument is a unique value used to locate a data item in the table. The function is the usable data. In the price table referred to above, the product number is the argument and the price is the function. In the sales tax example, the dollar amount of purchase is the argument and the amount of sales tax is the function.

It is also possible to have more than one function per argument, as shown in Figure 12-2. This is the type of table that would be used in a typical retailing or wholesaling application. The product number from an input record could be used as the argument to locate the appropriate table entry. Locating the table entry makes available a product description and price to the program.

Consider what would happen in a retailing environment. Without a tabling capability of this type, the salesperson would have to enter product descriptions and pricing for each item sold. Transaction processing at the cash register would take many times as long as a simple

Figure 12-1. Single-level table with one argument and one function.

PRICING TABLE	
PRODUCT NUMBER	PRICE
1234	$217.42
1329	18.95
1476	117.20
2001	86.50
2941	9.95
3649	100.99
4319	4.75
5640	29.95
6715	3.76
7171	18.94
7290	643.19
8333	31.13
8427	75.00
9119	229.31

PRICING TABLE

PRODUCT NUMBER	PRICE	DESCRIPTION
1234	$217.42	BLENDER
1329	18.95	4 × 8 PLYWOOD
1476	117.20	TOASTER OVEN
2001	86.50	SHOES
2941	9.95	NECKTIE
3649	100.99	LAWN MOWER
4319	4.75	CAP
5640	29.95	ICE CRUSHER
6715	3.76	GLOVES
7171	18.94	CAN OPENER
7290	643.19	DINING ROOM TABLE
8333	31.13	SHOVEL
8427	75.00	ROBE
9119	229.31	COMPACTOR
ARGUMENT	FUNCTION 1	FUNCTION 2

Figure 12-2. Single-level table with multiple functions.

entry of an item number. If the product price table is available in a computerized point-of-sale system, the salesperson must enter only the product number for each item sold. The computer program will retrieve and print the description and price on the sales slip and accumulate a total for the sale.

Because of the convenience and potential savings made possible by tables, they have become standard tools within business application programs. In developing programs calling for data repetitions, you may also encounter the term *array*. This, in effect, is the correct mathematical term for a table. An array, simply, is a display of numeric values showing the relationships among those values.

DEFINING TABLES

Tables to be used within COBOL programs are defined within the DATA DIVISION. The great majority of tables are set up in the WORKING-STORAGE SECTION. In a few special situations, the FILE SECTION may also be used.

Tables can be defined to COBOL programs as:

* *Static* tables have both arguments and functions defined during the writing of the program. These values, then, are imbedded within the program itself when it is compiled.

- *Dynamic* tables are defined as the program is written and compiled. The actual data contents of the table are loaded from an external storage medium such as magnetic tape or disk when the program executes.

Static tables, as their name implies, are fixed and unchanging. By contrast, dynamic tables can use different values with each separate execution of the program. Definition of tables, either static or dynamic, is done through use of the OCCURS clause. Using the OCCURS clause, the programmer names a table entry, gives the number of times it repeats within the program, then presents a picture of the data.

To illustrate, consider the sample entry in Figure 12-3. This is a classic data table used in business programs. Within the WORKING-STORAGE SECTION, the 01 entry identifies the stored values as a MONTH-NAME-TABLE. Subsequent code lines indicate that the data table is for MONTH-NAME and that it occurs (repeats) 12 times within the program. The PICTURE for this data is X(9).

This entry means that a data table is being established for identification of the month name within a date field. The PICTURE for this table entry is specified for nine positions of alphanumeric data. This provides enough area in memory to spell out September, the month with the largest number of letters.

In total, this entry has reserved in memory 12 locations of nine characters each, for a total of 108 characters of memory. At this point, no data have been entered to occupy these memory positions. These entries can then be done either dynamically from outside sources or statically through the use of the REDEFINE command.

Figure 12-3. Sample OCCURS clause.

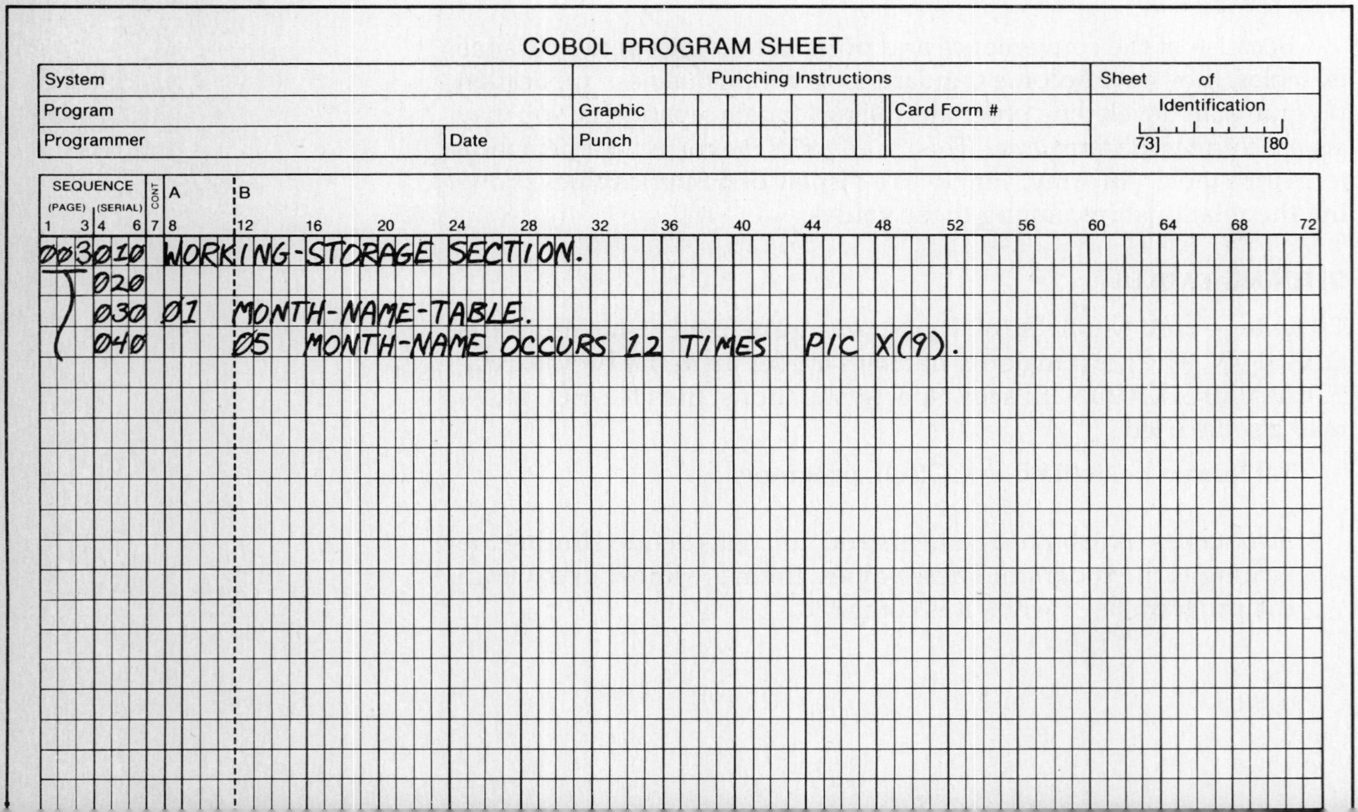

COBOL PROGRAM SHEET

```
003010  WORKING-STORAGE SECTION.
   020
   030  01  MONTH-NAME-TABLE.
   040      05  MONTH-NAME OCCURS 12 TIMES  PIC X(9).
```

STATIC TABLES

Definition of static tables requires a special technique. This method, in effect, helps the programmer to get around a limitation placed upon the OCCURS clause. That is, the OCCURS clause may not be used in the same sentences as a VALUE clause.

Therefore, for multiple entries in a static table, definitions using the VALUE clause are prepared separately within the WORKING-STORAGE SECTION. These values are then REDEFINEd in terms of the areas they will occupy through use of the OCCURS clause.

This practice is illustrated in Figure 12-4. A section of the table is identified as containing month-name values. Below this, each of the 12 months is identified as an 05 FILLER and given a specific value, along with a PICTURE.

In the 01 entry that follows, the MONTH-NAME-VALUES data name is then redefined as the MONTH-NAME-TABLE with an OCCURS clause identifying 12 entries within the table.

Figure 12-4. Use of REDEFINES to create a static table.

COBOL PROGRAM SHEET

```
003010 WORKING-STORAGE SECTION.
   020
   030 01 MONTH-NAME-VALUES.
   040    05 FILLER                PIC X(9)  VALUE "  JANUARY".
   050    05 FILLER                PIC X(9)  VALUE " FEBRUARY".
   060    05 FILLER                PIC X(9)  VALUE "    MARCH".
   070    05 FILLER                PIC X(9)  VALUE "    APRIL".
   080    05 FILLER                PIC X(9)  VALUE "      MAY".
   090    05 FILLER                PIC X(9)  VALUE "     JUNE".
   100    05 FILLER                PIC X(9)  VALUE "     JULY".
   110    05 FILLER                PIC X(9)  VALUE "   AUGUST".
   120    05 FILLER                PIC X(9)  VALUE "SEPTEMBER".
   130    05 FILLER                PIC X(9)  VALUE "  OCTOBER".
   140    05 FILLER                PIC X(9)  VALUE " NOVEMBER".
   150    05 FILLER                PIC X(9)  VALUE " DECEMBER".
   160
   170 01 MONTH-NAME-TABLE REDEFINES MONTH-NAME-VALUES.
   180    05 MONTH-NAME           PIC X(9)
                                  OCCURS 12 TIMES.
```

The previous discussion covers the creation of simple, single-level, static tables. Note that the data content of the table is fixed as the table is defined. This is not very flexible. Another approach would be to define the storage positions for the tables in your program but not assign the data values until the program executes.

ACCESSING TABLE DATA

The name in the OCCURS statement is the single data name that will be used to reference any of the items in a table. To locate and withdraw individual values from the table, two methods are used—subscripting and indexing.

A *subscript* provides a value for the occurrence number of the table entry to be referenced. For example, consider the entry: MONTH-NAME (05). The number in parentheses is the subscript identifying which month value is to be referenced. When this clause is executed under the COBOL language, the program will select the fifth MONTH-NAME entry, or May.

A subscript may be either a positive numeric integer value or a data name for a positive integer field. Subscript values may be entered either through an external source, such as a data record, or they may result from direct calculation in the program. Use of a fixed numeric value for a subscript identifies only one specific table entry. On the other hand, greater flexibility is available if the subscript is a variable data name. Use of a number means that only the specific field in the table can be referenced. Use of a variable name means that any of the 12 names in the table can be accessed with one COBOL statement. Consider the following two COBOL sentences:

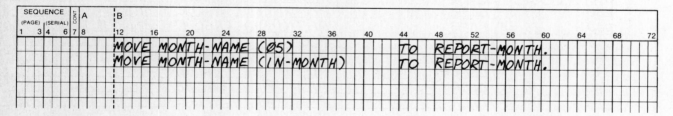

In the first sentence, it would be possible to move *only* the fifth month (May) to the report-month location. Every time the program executed, it would be necessary to use the same month name. However, in the second sentence, the subscript is a variable called IN-MONTH. This might be a field within an input record. In this case, the command would select the appropriate month from the set of 12 names, depending on the specific value in IN-MONTH.

Subscripts are written within parentheses immediately following the referenced name for the table. There must be at least one space between the left parenthesis of the subscript and the name that it follows. However, the subscript must be the entry immediately following the accompanying name. Subscripts must be numeric. They must be positive integers. The value of a subscript must be at least 1 and may be no larger than the maximum occurrence in the table itself.

The second way of accessing data in tables is through the use of *indexes.* Indexes are similar to subscripts in that they are numeric values that are used to make specific references to individual table entries. As far as the programmer is concerned, the differences between subscripts and indexes are in efficiencies of use and in the ability to use a new COBOL instruction, SEARCH, covered later in this chapter.

To define a table that uses indexing as opposed to subscripting, the INDEXED BY clause is used. Figure 12-5 presents a table using this clause.

When using indexing, the data name of the index is defined with the INDEXED BY clause. The index data name *must not be* the subject of any other definition statements. An index data name may not be used in any MOVE or arithmetic statements.

Figure 12-5. Use of INDEXED BY clause.

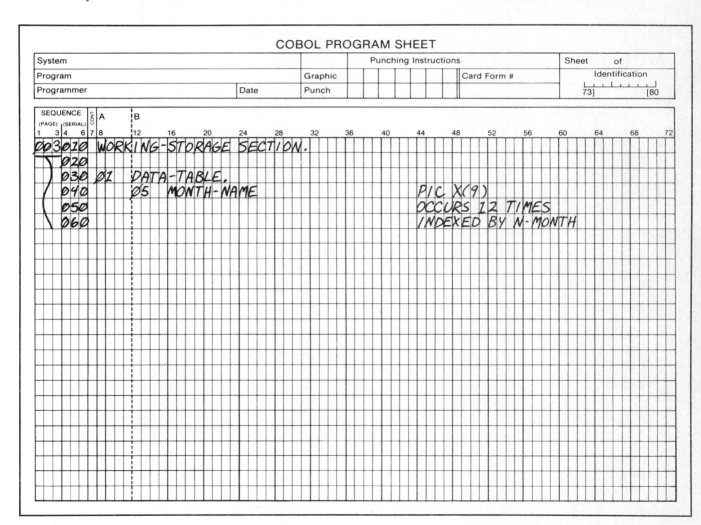

Figure 12-6. General format of SET instruction.

COBOL PROGRAM SHEET

System				Punching Instructions				
Program				Graphic				Card Form #
Programmer		Date		Punch				

```
SET {INDEX-NAME-1}  TO {INDEX-NAME-2}.
    {DATA-NAME-1}      {DATA-NAME-2}
                       {LITERAL-1   }
```

Figure 12-7. Use of SET instructions.

COBOL PROGRAM SHEET

System				Punching Instructions				Sheet	of
Program				Graphic			Card Form #	Identification	
Programmer		Date		Punch				73] [80	

```
004010  WORKING-STORAGE SECTION.
   020
   030  01   DATE-FIELD.
   040       05   SYS-DATE-YEAR          PIC 99.
   050       05   SYS-DATE-MONTH         PIC 99.
   060       05   SYS-DATE-DAY           PIC 99.
   070
   080  01   MONTH-NAME-VALUES.
   090       05   FILLER      PIC X(9)   VALUE "  JANUARY".
   100       05   FILLER      PIC X(9)   VALUE " FEBRUARY".
   110       05   FILLER      PIC X(9)   VALUE "    MARCH".
   120       05   FILLER      PIC X(9)   VALUE "    APRIL".
   130       05   FILLER      PIC X(9)   VALUE "      MAY".
   140       05   FILLER      PIC X(9)   VALUE "     JUNE".
   150       05   FILLER      PIC X(9)   VALUE "     JULY".
   160       05   FILLER      PIC X(9)   VALUE "   AUGUST".
   170       05   FILLER      PIC X(9)   VALUE "SEPTEMBER".
   180       05   FILLER      PIC X(9)   VALUE "  OCTOBER".
   190       05   FILLER      PIC X(9)   VALUE " NOVEMBER".
   200       05   FILLER      PIC X(9)   VALUE " DECEMBER".
   210
   220  01   MONTH-NAME-TABLE REDEFINES MONTH-NAME-VALUES.
   230       05   MONTH-NAME     PIC X(9)
   240                           OCCURS 12 TIMES
   250                           INDEXED BY N-MONTH.
   260
   270  PROCEDURE DIVISION.
   280
   290
   300      ACCEPT DATE-FIELD FROM DATE.
   310
   320
   330      SET N-MONTH              TO  SYS-DATE-MONTH.
   340
   350
   360      MOVE MONTH-NAME (N-MONTH)  TO  REPORT-MONTH.
   370
   380
```

To establish or change the value in an index, the SET instruction is used. The general form of the SET instruction is shown in Figure 12-6.

An illustration of accessing table data using indexing is shown in Figure 12-7.

DYNAMIC TABLES

In Figure 12-8, the product price table illustrated in Figure 12-1 is defined. This definition only *reserves* storage locations for the 50 products and their corresponding prices. No actual data are in the table as yet. PROCEDURE DIVISION commands would be required to cause appropriate data to be read in and placed in the table locations before the tables can be used.

In many applications, table data values are volatile. That is, the values are subject to changes in content, additions of new values, or deletions. Under these circumstances, it is more efficient to store these data on an external file that is then loaded into the tables each time the program is run.

Maintenance of the table data stored on secondary storage devices requires file updating procedures. Methods for maintaining and updating files are discussed in Chapter 9. Methods for updating and storing tables on secondary storage devices would be the same as for any file maintenance activity.

The instructions needed to load data into the product price table (Figure 12-8) are shown in Figure 12-9. This load procedure assumes that there is one product number/price record for each table entry. The MOVE-DATA-TO-TABLE module checks the SUBSCRIPT value to determine if the end of the table has been reached. If not, the product number and price values are moved into the table area of WORKING-STORAGE. If the end of the table is reached before the input PRICE-DATA-FILE is finished, a table overflow message is displayed. This is

Figure 12-8. Product price table and variables.

```
COBOL PROGRAM SHEET

003010  WORKING-STORAGE SECTION.
   020
   030  01  PRICE-DATA.
   040      05  PRODUCTS OCCURS 50 TIMES.
   050          10  PRODUCT-NUMBER          PIC 9(4).
   060          10  PRODUCT-PRICE           PIC 9(3)V99.
   070
   080  01  TABLE-VARIABLES.
   090      05  WS-TABLE-SIZE               PIC 9(2)    VALUE 50.
   100      05  SUBSCRIPT                   PIC S9(2).
   110      05  WS-TABLE-LOADED-FLAG        PIC X(3).
```

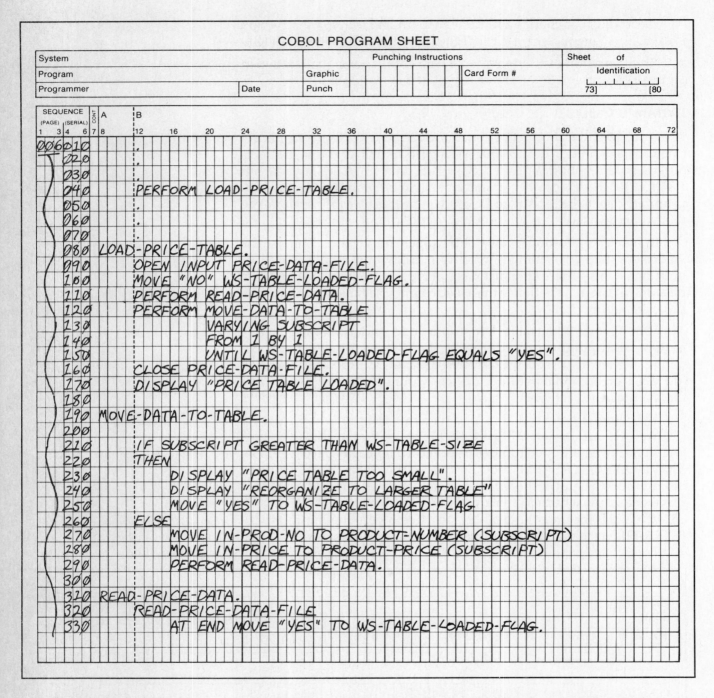

```
006010        .
     020      .
     030      .
     040      PERFORM LOAD-PRICE-TABLE.
     050      .
     060      .
     070      .
     080  LOAD-PRICE-TABLE.
     090      OPEN INPUT PRICE-DATA-FILE.
     100      MOVE "NO" WS-TABLE-LOADED-FLAG.
     110      PERFORM READ-PRICE-DATA.
     120      PERFORM MOVE-DATA-TO-TABLE
     130          VARYING SUBSCRIPT
     140          FROM 1 BY 1
     150          UNTIL WS-TABLE-LOADED-FLAG EQUALS "YES".
     160      CLOSE PRICE-DATA-FILE.
     170      DISPLAY "PRICE TABLE LOADED".
     180
     190  MOVE-DATA-TO-TABLE.
     200
     210      IF SUBSCRIPT GREATER THAN WS-TABLE-SIZE
     220      THEN
     230          DISPLAY "PRICE TABLE TOO SMALL".
     240          DISPLAY "REORGANIZE TO LARGER TABLE"
     250          MOVE "YES" TO WS-TABLE-LOADED-FLAG.
     260      ELSE
     270          MOVE IN-PROD-NO TO PRODUCT-NUMBER (SUBSCRIPT)
     280          MOVE IN-PRICE TO PRODUCT-PRICE (SUBSCRIPT)
     290          PERFORM READ-PRICE-DATA.
     300
     310  READ-PRICE-DATA.
     320      READ-PRICE-DATA-FILE
     330      AT END MOVE "YES" TO WS-TABLE-LOADED-FLAG.
```

Figure 12-9. Instruction format for loading a dynamic table.

a table processing programming practice that should always be followed. Attempting to exceed the limit of the table size can cause extremely serious errors in your program.

This load table subroutine uses a new version of the PERFORM. . . UNTIL instruction. The PERFORM. . .VARYING instruction provides a convenient mechanism for controlling subscripts and indexes and is discussed later in this chapter.

Once the creation of tables is understood, the next requirement is to determine a way to get data out of the table and onto a document or report.

REFERENCES TO TABLES

The discussion above deals with how to access an individual value in a table. The next logical topic deals with how to determine which table entry is needed or desired. There are two common methods for determining which table element to access. One method is by determining the *position* of the data within a table. The other is to *search* for a specific argument value in the table.

In the MONTH-NAME example, a program might input a data record. Within that record, there would be a field containing a date of employment. The month digits in that date could be used as the subscript or index value to extract the corresponding name of the month from the table. Thus, access to the table is by position of the data element. The subscript or index number is the position value. Searching the table by argument value is also known as *table lookup,* or *table search.*

TABLE LOOKUP TECHNIQUES

Suppose a search was needed for a single employee within a large collection of data covering all employees in a company. This type of search, or lookup, would be needed, for example, to determine the commission rate due to an employee as part of a program for recording a sale. The search could be based upon the employee number. The search would be conducted through use of a technique known as a *sequential search.*

One way to implement table lookup functions is with the aid of the PERFORM. . .UNTIL instruction, which is explained in Chapter 6. By adding the VARYING clause to that instruction, it becomes an efficient mechanism for supporting table access. The format for the PERFORM . . .VARYING instruction is:

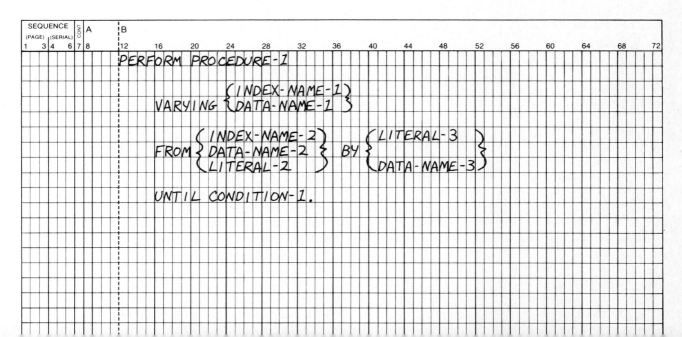

Sequential Search

To conduct a sequential search in an array of data, the specific argument for the needed commission rate is used. In this instance, the argument would be the employee number. The purpose of the search would be to find the corresponding function, the applicable commission rate. Figure 12-10 illustrates this technique.

To conduct this lookup procedure, the employee number (search argument) is compared with the table argument at subscript location (1). If a match occurs, the lookup is ended. If no match is found, the subscript is incremented by 1 and the process repeats. Every table argument value is consecutively compared with the search argument until a match is found or the end of the table is encountered.

Using this sequential table lookup or searching technique can sometimes be inefficient. At the very least, a sequential search of this type opens the possiblity that the comparison function will have to be

Figure 12-10. Instruction format for sequential table search.

COBOL PROGRAM SHEET

```
006010
  020    MOVE "NO" TO WS-END-OF-LOOKUP
  030                WS-ENTRY-FOUND.
  040    PERFORM LOOKUP-RATES
  050        VARYING TBL-SUB
  060        FROM 1 BY 1
  070        UNTIL WS-END-OF-LOOKUP EQUALS "YES".
  080    IF WS-ENTRY-FOUND EQUALS "YES"
  090    THEN
  100        SUBTRACT 1 FROM TBL-SUB
  110        MOVE TBL-COMMISSION-RATE (TBL-SUB) TO RPT-COM-OUT
  120    ELSE
  130        MOVE ZEROS TO RPT-COM-OUT.
  140
  150 LOOKUP-RATES.
  160        IF TBL-SUB NOT LESS THAN TBL-SIZE
  170    THEN
  180        MOVE "YES" TO WS-END-OF-LOOKUP
  190    ELSE
  200        IF IN-EMPL-NBR EQUALS TBL-EMPL-NBR (TBL-SUB)
  210        THEN
  220            MOVE "YES" TO WS-ENTRY-FOUND
  230                        WS-END-OF-LOOKUP
  240        ELSE
  250            NEXT SENTENCE.
```

applied to every entry in the array—for each incoming detail record to be processed. This can be extremely wasteful of computer time if the table is large or if there is a large volume of input data.

Binary Search

If a table to be searched encompassed 100 employees, the shortest search procedure under the sequential search method would occur when the needed value was located in the first position of the table. The longest search time would be encountered when the needed value was in the last position. On the average, then, it would require 50 accesses or comparisons to locate a specific employee number in the table if the sequential method were used.

If the table were 10 times larger, holding data on 1,000 employees, it would take 10 times as many comparisons, on the average, to locate any specific commission rate. Thus, the number of accesses to the table is in direct relation to table size when sequential lookup is applied. The average number of accesses under sequential techniques will be half the total size of the table.

An alternative technique for searching tables is the *binary search*. This method, quite simply, reduces data searching times by iteratively discarding half of the table. Take an entire table, for example. Divide that table in half. There is now a 50 percent chance that the needed value will be in either half.

The binary search method flowcharted in Figure 12-11 does just this. Instructions are entered identifying the size of the tables to be searched. An algorithm is applied that divides the data array in half and looks at the midpoint location. If the needed value is not found in the initial search, the remaining table is cut in half and searched. If a third try is needed, whatever data remain are still cut in half and searched. Each time, if the search argument is not found, half of the table is discarded. In this type of search, the needed value will be found following comparisons with substantially less than 100 percent of the table arguments.

This principle can be illustrated through a simple example that you can test at any time, almost as though it were a game. Assume that someone is asked to select a page in a textbook. The idea is to find the selected page on a minimum number of tries, with only minimum guidance from the person who made the selection. The person who knows the page to be found can only answer the same questions that a computer can deal with in making comparisons. That is, questions can be answered only with a yes or no response. These answers will indicate comparison conditions only: greater than, less than, or equal to. Suppose the page selected is number 380 of a 501-page book.

In this situation, a typical initial question would be: ''Is the page number greater than 251?'' The response would be positive.

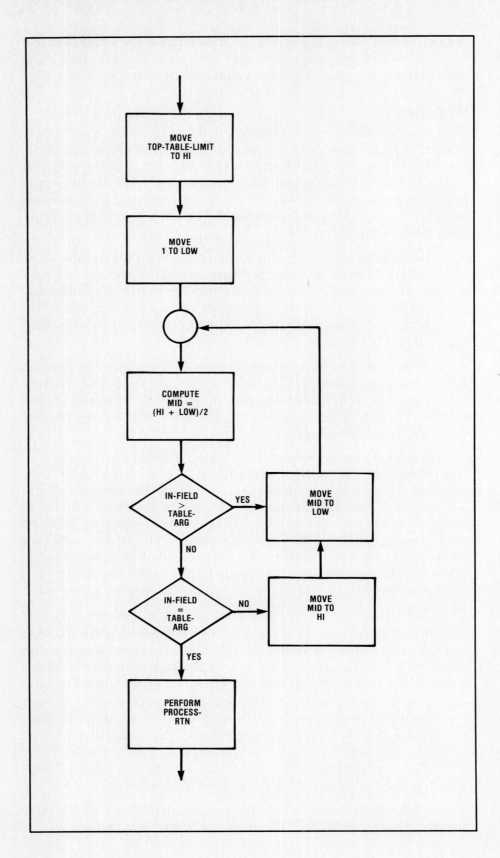

Figure 12-11. Flowchart for binary search program.

Succeeding questions would divide the remaining half of the book in half and, repeating the process, in half again until the specific page number was identified. In this case, as shown in the table in Figure 12-12, page 380 would be identified on the ninth comparison—substantially sooner than going page by page.

SELECTED PAGE IS 380					
HI	LOW	CALCULATION	MID	> MID	= MID
501	1	(501 + 1)/2	251	Y	
501	251	(501 + 251)/2	376	Y	
501	376	(501 + 376)/2	438	N	N
438	376	(438 + 376)/2	407	N	N
407	376	(407 + 376)/2	391	N	N
391	376	(391 + 376)/2	383	N	N
383	376	(383 + 376)/2	379	Y	
383	379	(383 + 379)/2	381	N	N
381	379	(381 + 379)/2	380	N	Y

Figure 12-12. Operation listing for binary search execution.

As a rule of thumb, the maximum number of searches to find a value in a table is related to the power of 2 closest to the table size. For example, the number 2 raised to the ninth power is 512. Thus, the number of comparisons to locate an item in an array of up to 512 elements would be nine.

These two searching techniques are discussed here as an aid to understanding of table processes. The COBOL language provides single-statement instructions to implement these two techniques. The SEARCH instruction executes a sequential search of a table and the SEARCH ALL statement initiates a binary search. Detailed discussion of these instructions is left for a more advanced book.

In the successive functions of the binary search, the computer compares data relationships for conditions of equal to, greater than, and less than to eliminate half of the set of possible data values. This implies that the data in the table must be arranged in some known sequence. Therefore, a condition for use of binary search techniques is that data must be arranged in a predetermined order.

The most practical way to meet this need is to set up tables in a known sequential order or under a known sequential hierarchy. It is possible to read data into tables on a random basis initially. This is most likely to happen with dynamic tables, since static tables would be built and loaded in their desired sequence. However, even if dynamic tables are loaded randomly, it might be necessary to sort tabled data into a known sequential order. This can be done by applying sort routines like those discussed in Chapter 9 (a topic not dealt with in this book).

SEARCH Instructions

One table search method, the sequential technique, has already been reviewed. Another method for sequential searching of a table involves the use of the SEARCH instruction. Using this instruction, a complete table search routine can be invoked by a single sentence of coding. The program instructions in Figure 12-13 illustrate the search of a commission rate table. Note that, in this example, the SET statement is invoked just prior to the SEARCH instruction. The SEARCH instruction will cause a sequential search, element by element, for the specified search argument. However, programming must establish the beginning reference point from which the search will proceed. The SET instruction is used to establish that beginning reference point.

The AT END clause specifies what action is to be taken when the end of the table is encountered prior to finding a match for the search argument. In this example, the FOUND-SWITCH is made equal to "NO" when the AT END is encountered. The use of the AT END

Figure 12-13. Formats for SET and SEARCH instructions.

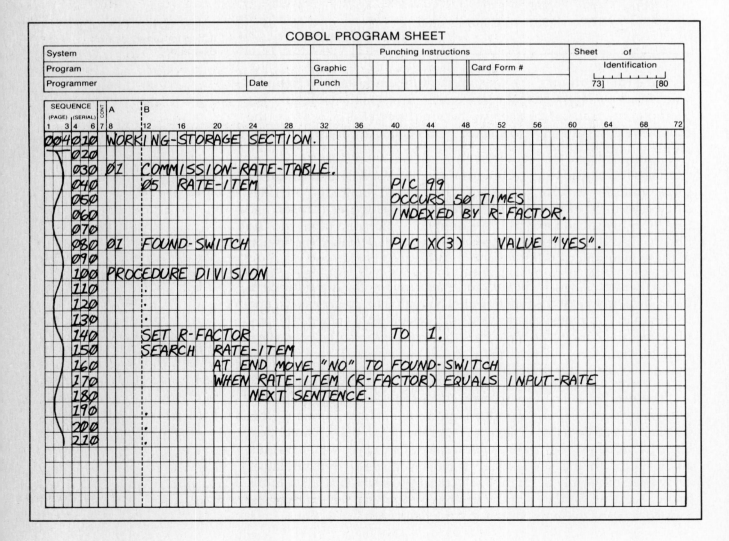

clause is optional. If omitted, the compiler will assume that the next sentence is to be executed when the end of the table is sensed.

The WHEN clause specifies the condition to be tested in the search. It is like a relational test statement. In the example in Figure 12-13, the search argument INPUT-EMPLOYEE-NUMBER is compared with the table entry TBL-EMPLOYEE-NUMBER. When these two data items are equal, the appropriate TBL-COMMISSION-RATE value is moved from the table to a calculation field.

SEARCH ALL Instruction

Just as the SEARCH instruction is a single sentence replacement for an entire sequential search procedure, the SEARCH ALL instruction is a single sentence version of a binary search. There are, however, some important differences in the two instructions. With the SEARCH instruction, the programmer must provide the beginning index value, using the SET instruction. The SEARCH ALL instruction computes its own first index value.

A second important difference between SEARCH and SEARCH ALL is that the SEARCH ALL instruction requires that the table data be arranged in ASCENDING or DESCENDING order. Figure 12-14 illustrates the SEARCH ALL instruction. In this PRODUCT-PRICE search example, the corresponding price of an input product number is to be looked up and retrieved from the table. The use and structure of the AT END and WHEN clauses is the same as those for the SEARCH instruction, as described previously.

MULTIPLE-LEVEL TABLES

The tables, or arrays, of data described so far in this chapter have all had a single level. That is, the tables presented have had a single OCCURS clause in the definition. In practice, tables sometimes require more than a single level of data.

In an insurance company, tables of premium rates are often published for use by the sales staff. Premiums for life insurance are generally based upon the type of policy as well as on the age and sex of the insured. To build premium rate tables for a COBOL program would require that the programmer be able to access a rate amount on the basis of specific values of policy type, insured's age, and insured's sex. The table in Figure 12-15 illustrates a two-level table. To access a specific premium amount, it is necessry to provide separate subscript, or index, values for age group and policy type.

Many tables used within COBOL programs have two or more levels—with a maximum of three arguments available for any given table. You will learn how to build and use multi-level tables in your future work with COBOL. At this point, an initial familiarity with tables—coupled with an ability to build and use single-level tables is important to your progress.

COBOL PROGRAM SHEET

System
Program
Programmer   Date

Punching Instructions
Graphic
Punch
Card Form #

Sheet   of
Identification
73]   [80

SEQUENCE (PAGE) (SERIAL)	CONT	A B																

```
004010  WORKING-STORAGE SECTION.
   020
   030  01  PRICE-DATA.
   040      05  PRODUCTS            OCCURS 500 TIMES
   050                             ASCENDING KEY IS PRODUCT-NUMBER
   060                             INDEXED BY PRICE-FACTOR.
   070          10  PRODUCT-NUMBER          PIC 9(4).
   080          10  PRODUCT-PRICE           PIC 9(3)V99.
   090
   100  01  FOUND-SWITCH                    PIC X(3)    VALUE "YES".
   110
   120
   130  PROCEDURE DIVISION.
   140      .
   150      .
   160      .
   170      SEARCH ALL PRODUCTS
   180          AT END MOVE "NO" TO FOUND-SWITCH
   190          WHEN PRODUCT-NUMBER (PRICE-FACTOR) EQUALS IN-PRODUCT
   200              NEXT SENTENCE.
   210      .
   220      .
   230      .
```

Figure 12-14. Formats for SEARCH ALL instructions.

Figure 12-15. Instructions for two-level table.

COBOL PROGRAM SHEET

System
Program
Programmer   Date

Punching Instructions
Graphic
Punch
Card Form #

Sheet   of
Identification
73]   [80

SEQUENCE (PAGE) (SERIAL)	CONT	A B																

```
004010  WORKING-STORAGE SECTION.
   020
   030  01  PREMIUM-RATE-TABLE.
   040      05  INSURED-AGE-GROUPS   OCCURS 5 TIMES.
   050          10  POLICY-TYPE       OCCURS 3 TIMES.
   060              15  FEMALE-PREMIUM        PIC 9(3)V99.
   070              15  MALE-PREMIUM          PIC 9(3)V99.
```

Summary

A table is an area defined in computer memory to hold repeated occurrences of a particular data item. Tables are used as a means of describing relationships among sets of data. Within tables, arguments are unique values used to locate data items. A function within a table is a usable item of data. [*Objective No. 1.*]

Tables may be static or dynamic. A static table is one for which all values of the arguments and functions are defined within a program. A dynamic table is one in which the arguments and functions for a table are defined within a program but the values are maintained on an external storage medium. Dynamic table data are then loaded into the table at the time of program execution. Table structures are defined in WORKING-STORAGE through statements that include OCCURS clauses. Such basic definitions can then be applied to either static or dynamic tables.

To build static tables, data definitions established in the WORKING-STORAGE SECTION through use of VALUE clauses are then related to their specific table locations through use of the REDEFINE clause. [*Objective No. 2.*]

Table data can be accessed through the use of either subscripts or indexes. Subscripts define the occurrence number of a table element. Subscripts may be either numeric literals or data names that represent numeric integers. Indexes are data names representing numeric integers whose contents are defined by the computer. The major difference between these methods is that the SEARCH command must use an index.

When dynamic tables are used, PROCEDURE DIVISION commands are needed to load data into the table when the program begins execution. The PERFORM. . .VARYING instruction is a convenient method for loading data into a dynamic table. [*Objective No. 3.*]

Table lookups or searches can be performed with either sequential search or binary search techniques.

In a sequential search, the computer looks at the argument for each entry in a table, in sequence, until the needed entry is found. If the identified entry is not found, the program will either follow an AT END instruction if one is provided or process the next sentence. There is a potential for having to reference 100 percent of the items in a table. On average, 50 percent of the data items in a table will be reviewed in a sequential search. [*Objectives Nos. 4 and 5.*]

The binary search technique is based on the principle that, with each access to the table, one-half of the remaining items can be discarded. Thus, a binary search starts at the value of the midpoint item in the table. This item is tested to determine whether it is greater than

Key Terms

1. table
2. argument
3. function
4. array
5. static tables
6. dynamic tables
7. subscript
8. index
9. position reference
10. search
11. table lookup
12. table search
13. sequential search
14. binary search

COBOL Terms

1. OCCURS
2. REDEFINE
3. SEARCH
4. INDEXED BY
5. SET
6. PERFORM. . . VARYING
7. SEARCH ALL
8. AT END
9. WHEN

the value of the item being referenced. The result of this test makes it possible to discard 50 percent of the data items. The process is iterated with the remaining table items until a match occurs, or until an AT END activity is processed. [*Objective No. 6.*]

Review/Discussion Questions

1. What are tables and what purposes do they serve?
2. How do tables save both programming and computer processing times?
3. What are the similarities and differences between static and dynamic tables?
4. How are static tables defined within a COBOL program?
5. What methods are used to access table data and what are the similarities and differences among them?
6. How is a subscript used to find a desired table item?
7. How is an index used to find a desired table item?
8. What instructions are used within COBOL programs for the loading of data into dynamic tables?
9. What is a sequential search and how is it implemented?
10. What problems can be encountered in the execution of sequential searches?
11. What is a binary search and how is it implemented?
12. Why is a binary search executed in fewer processing operations than a sequential search?

Programming Assignments

Two programming assignments are given below. Following directions of your instructor or your own feelings about how much practice you can use, complete either or both of these assignments. For each assignment, make sure all of the following tasks are completed:

1. Prepare or complete a structure or module hierarchy chart.

2. Prepare or complete documentation of processing logic with structured flowcharts *and* pseudocode.

3. Define sample data to be used to test your program logic and prepare expected results for that data.

4. Conduct a walkthrough of your program structure and logical design. Do this by yourself, under guidance of your instructor, or in cooperation with a fellow student.

5. Write, compile, test, and debug the program you have designed.

Problem 1

Purpose: The Gee Whiz Computer Company is considering salary raises for all salespersons employed before January 1, 1982, who now have a base salary of less than $25,000 per year. You have been asked to write a program to extract these records from the sales personnel file and to print the report. A static table for branch office names will be required.

Input: Input is from the sales personnel file. A record layout for this file is shown in Figure 12-16.

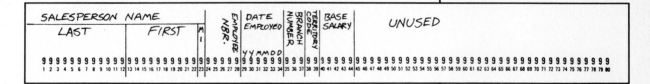

Output: The output is to be a report that conforms to the layout in Figure 12-17.

Figure 12-16. Input layout for salary eligibility report program. For use in practice assignment.

Processing Requirements: 1) Read the input file and select sales personnel records for those employed earlier than January 1, 1982. Note date is in the YYMMDD format (820101).

2) If the selected record also has base salary of less than $25,000, print record in detail line as specified.

412

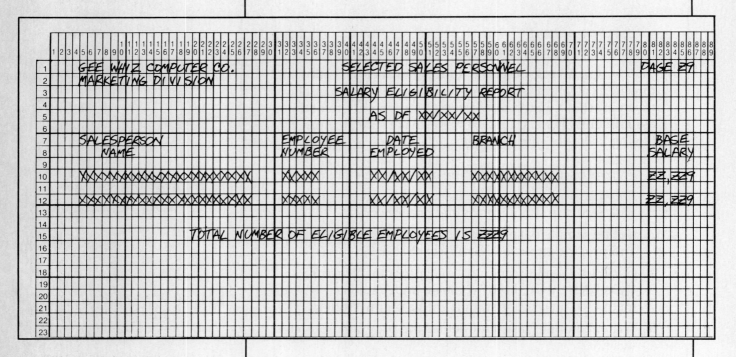

Figure 12-17. Output layout for salary eligibility report. For use in practice assignment.

3) Headings are to be printed on each page of the report.

4) Double space detail line printing with 25 lines per page.

5) Use the input branch number to look up the corresponding branch name in a static table defined in WORKING-STORAGE. The table to use is given below. If the branch number is not found in the table, print "UNKNOWN" in the branch name field for that record.

Branch	Name Table
100	Los Angeles
200	Seattle
300	Chicago
400	Dallas
500	New York
600	Boston
700	Atlanta

6) At the end of the input file, print a count of the number of eligible salespersons whose records have been printed.

Problem 2

Purpose: The management of the Rare Imports Company has requested a printout of prices for the company's products. The highest and lowest prices must also be printed at the bottom of the report.

Input: Use the data found in Figure 12-2 or create your own. The record layout to be used is shown in Figure 12-18.

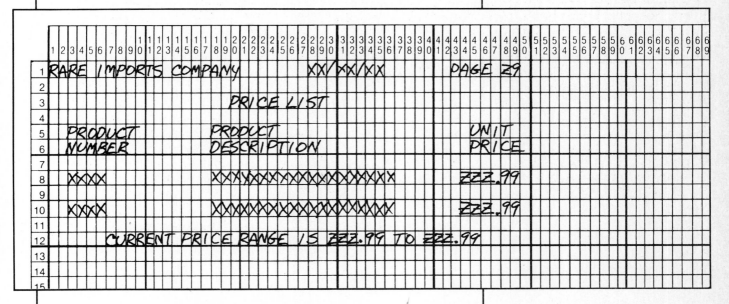

Output: Produce a price list that conforms to the record layout in Figure 12-19.

Figure 12-18. Input layout for price table data records. For use in practice assignment.

Figure 12-19. Output layout for price table records. For use in practice assignment.

Processing Requirements: 1) Using subscripting, load the table data dynamically into a table in your program.

2) After the table is loaded completely, print the price list in the required format. Use double-space printing and print only 10 items per page.

3) Obtain the current date from the system and print this as an entry in the first heading line.

4) Determine the part numbers of the highest- and lowest-price items.

5) When the price list has been printed, print the lowest and highest prices as specified on the report layout.

Worksheet for Structured Flowchart

Program Name: _____

Prepared By: _____

Worksheet for Pseudocode Specifications

Program Name: _____

Prepared By: _____

Worksheet for Structured Flowchart

Program Name: _____

Prepared By: _____

Worksheet for Pseudocode Specifications

Program Name: _____

Prepared By: _____

COBOL PROGRAM SHEET

System	
Program	
Programmer	

	Punching Instructions			Sheet of

Date	Graphic		Card Form #	Identification
	Punch			73] [80

COBOL PROGRAM SHEET

System				Punching Instructions			Sheet	of
Program			Graphic			Card Form #		Identification
Programmer		Date	Punch					[73] [80]

SEQUENCE																								
(PAGE)	(SERIAL)	CONT	A	B																				
1 3	4 6	7	8	12	16	20	24	28	32	36	40	44	48	52	56	60	64	68	72					

COBOL PROGRAM SHEET

System		
Program		
Programmer	Date	

Punching Instructions			
Graphic			Sheet of
Punch		Card Form #	Identification
			73] [80

SEQUENCE
(PAGE) (SERIAL)
1 3 4 6 7 8 | CONT | A | B
12 16 20 24 28 32 36 40 44 48 52 56 60 64 68 72

COBOL PROGRAM SHEET

System					Sheet	of

Program			Punching Instructions		Card Form #	Identification
Programmer	Date		Graphic			[73]
			Punch			[80]

SEQUENCE		CONT	A	B															
(PAGE)	(SERIAL)																		
1 3	4 6	7	8	12	16	20	24	28	32	36	40	44	48	52	56	60	64	68	72

COBOL PROGRAM SHEET

System

Program

Programmer

Date

Punching Instructions		Sheet	of
Graphic		Identification	
Punch	Card Form #	73]	[80

SEQUENCE
(PAGE) (SERIAL)
1 3 4 6 7 8 CONT

A B

12 16 20 24 28 32 36 40 44 48 52 56 60 64 68 72

COBOL PROGRAM SHEET

System		Punching Instructions		Sheet	of
Program			Graphic		Card Form #	Identification
Programmer	Date		Punch			[73] [80]

SEQUENCE		CONT	A	B																
(PAGE)	(SERIAL)																		
1 3	4 6	7	8	12	16	20	24	28	32	36	40	44	48	52	56	60	64	68	72

COBOL PROGRAM SHEET

System		
Program		
Programmer		

	Punching Instructions		Sheet of
Date	Graphic	Card Form #	Identification
Punch			[73] [80]

SEQUENCE						
(PAGE)	(SERIAL)	CONT	A	B		
1	3 4	6 7	8	12	16	20 24 28 32 36 40 44 48 52 56 60 64 68 72

COBOL PROGRAM SHEET

System				Sheet	of
Program		Punching Instructions		Identification	
Programmer	Date	Graphic	Card Form #		
		Punch		[73]	[80]

SEQUENCE			CONT	A	B															
(PAGE)	(SERIAL)																		
1	3	4 6	7	8	12	16	20	24	28	32	36	40	44	48	52	56	60	64	68	72

COBOL PROGRAM SHEET

System					Punching Instructions			Sheet	of
Program					Graphic		Card Form #	Identification	
Programmer			Date		Punch			73]	[80

SEQUENCE																		
(PAGE)	(SERIAL)	CONT	A	B	12	16	20	24	28	32	36	40	44	48	52	56	60	64	68	72
1	3 4	6 7 8																

COBOL PROGRAM SHEET

System					Punching Instructions		Sheet	of

Program

Programmer

Graphic

Punch

Date

Punching Instructions

Card Form #

Identification

[80

73]

SEQUENCE
(PAGE) (SERIAL)
CONT
1 3 4 6 7 8

A

B

12 16 20 24 28 32 36 40 44 48 52 56 60 64 68 72

Vocabulary Building Practice—Exercise 12

Write definitions and/or explanations of the terms listed below.

1. table _____

_____

2. argument _____

_____

3. function _____

_____

4. array _____

_____

5. static _____

_____

6. dynamic _____

_____

7. subscript _____

_____

8. index _____

_____

9. position reference _____

_____

10. search _____

_____

(over, please)

11. **table lookup** _____

_____

12. **table search** _____

_____

13. **sequential search** _____

_____

14. **binary search** _____

_____

15. **OCCURS** _____

_____

16. **REDEFINE** _____

_____

17. **INDEXED BY** _____

_____

18. **SET** _____

_____

19. **PERFORM. . . VARYING** _____

_____

20. **AT END** _____

_____

COLLATING SEQUENCES A

ASCII CHARACTER SET COLLATING SEQUENCE.

COLLATING SEQUENCE DECIMAL/OCTAL		ASCII GRAPHIC SUBSET	DISPLAY CODE	ASCII CODE	COLLATING SEQUENCE DECIMAL/OCTAL		ASCII GRAPHIC SUBSET	DISPLAY CODE	ASCII CODE
00	00	blank	55	20	32	40	@	74	40
01	01	!	66	21	33	41	A	01	41
02	02	,,	64	22	34	42	B	02	42
03	03	#	60	23	35	43	C	03	43
04	04	$	53	24	36	44	D	04	44
05	05	%	63†	25	37	45	E	05	45
06	06	&	67	26	38	46	F	06	46
07	07	'	70	27	39	47	G	07	47
08	10	(	51	28	40	50	H	10	48
09	11	)	52	29	41	51	I	11	49
10	12	*	47	2A	42	52	J	12	4A
11	13	+	45	2B	43	53	K	13	4B
12	14	,	56	2C	44	54	L	14	4C
13	15	–	46	2D	45	55	M	15	4D
14	16	.	57	2E	46	56	N	16	4E
15	17	/	50	2F	47	57	O	17	4F
16	20	0	33	30	48	60	P	20	50
17	21	1	34	31	49	61	Q	21	51
18	22	2	35	32	50	62	R	22	52
19	23	3	36	33	51	63	S	23	53
20	24	4	37	34	52	64	T	24	54
21	25	5	40	35	53	65	U	25	55
22	26	6	41	36	54	66	V	26	56
23	27	7	42	37	55	67	W	27	57
24	30	8	43	38	56	70	X	30	58
25	31	9	44	39	57	71	Y	31	59
26	32	:	00†	3A	58	72	Z	32	5A
27	33	;	77	3B	59	73	[	61	5B
28	34	<	72	3C	60	74	\	75	5C
29	35	=	54	3D	61	75	]	62	5D
30	36	>	73	3E	62	76	^	76	5E
31	37	?	71	3F	63	77	__	65	5F

† In installations using a 63-graphic set, the % graphic does not exist. The : graphic is display code 63.

EBCDIC 64-CHARACTER SUBSET COLLATING SEQUENCE

COLLATING SEQUENCE DECIMAL/OCTAL		GRAPHIC	EBCDIC PUNCH	DISPLAY CODE	EBCDIC CODE
00	00	blank	no punch	55	40
01	01	.	12-8-3	57	4B
02	02	<	12-8-4	72	4C
03	03	(	12-8-5	51	4D
04	04	+	12-8-6	45	4E
05	05	|	12-8-7	66	4F
06	06	&	12	67	50
07	07	$	11-8-3	53	5B
08	10	*	11-8-4	47	5C
09	11	)	11-8-5	52	5D
10	12	;	11-8-6	77	5E
11	13	¬	11-8-7	76	5F
12	14	-	11	46	60
13	15	/	0-1	50	61
14	16	,	0-8-3	56	6B
15	17	%	0-8-4	63	6C
16	20	—	0-8-5	65	6D
17	21	>	0-8-6	73	6E
18	22	?	0-8-7	71	6F
19	23	:	8-2	00	7A
20	24	#	8-3	60	7B
21	25	@	8-4	74	7C
22	26	'	8-5	70	7D
23	27	=	8-6	54	7E
24	30	"	8-7	64	7F
25	31	¢	12-8-2/12-0	61	4A
26	32	A	12-1	01	C1
27	33	B	12-2	02	C2
28	34	C	12-3	03	C3
29	35	D	12-4	04	C4
30	36	E	12-5	05	C5
31	37	F	12-6	06	C6

EBCDIC 64-CHARACTER SUBSET COLLATING SEQUENCE (Contd)

COLLATING SEQUENCE DECIMAL/OCTAL		GRAPHIC	EBCDIC PUNCH	DISPLAY CODE	EBCDIC CODE
32	40	G	12–7	07	C7
33	41	H	12–8	10	C8
34	42	I	12–9	11	C9
35	43	!	11–8–2/11–0	62	5A
36	44	J	11–1	12	D1
37	45	K	11–2	13	D2
38	46	L	11–3	14	D3
39	47	M	11–4	15	D4
40	50	N	11–5	16	D5
41	51	O	11–6	17	D6
42	52	P	11–7	20	D7
43	53	Q	11–8	21	D8
44	54	R	11–9	22	D9
45	55	none	0–8–2	75	E0
46	56	S	0–2	23	E2
47	57	T	0–3	24	E3
48	60	U	0–4	25	E4
49	61	V	0–5	26	E5
50	62	W	0–6	27	E6
51	63	X	0–7	30	E7
52	64	Y	0–8	31	E8
53	65	Z	0–9	32	E9
54	66	0	0	33	F0
55	67	1	1	34	F1
56	70	2	2	35	F2
57	71	3	3	36	F3
58	72	4	4	37	F4
59	73	5	5	40	F5
60	74	6	6	41	F6
61	75	7	7	42	F7
62	76	8	8	43	F8
63	77	9	9	44	F9

B RESERVED WORDS

ACCEPT
ACCESS
ACTUAL-KEY
ADD
ADDRESS
ADVANCING
AFTER
ALL
ALPHABET
ALPHABETIC
ALPHANUMERIC
ALPHANUMERIC-EDITED
ALSO
ALTER
ALTERNATE
AND
ANY
APOSTROPHE
APPLY
ARE
AREA
AREAS
ASCENDING
ASSIGN
AT
AUTHOR
BEFORE
BEGINNING
BITS
BLANK
BLOCK
BOOLEAN
BOOLEAN-AND
BOOLEAN-EXOR
BOOLEAN-OR
BOTTOM
BY
CALL
CANCEL
CD
CF
CH
CHARACTER
CHARACTERS
CLOCK-UNITS
CLOSE
COBOL
CODE
CODE-SET
COLLATING
COLUMN
COMMA
COMMON-STORAGE
COMMUNICATION
COMP
COMP-1
COMP-2
COMP-3
COMP-4
COMPUTATIONAL
COMPUTATIONAL-1

COMPUTATIONAL-2
COMPUTATIONAL-3
COMPUTATIONAL-4
COMPUTE
CONFIGURATION
CONTAINS
CONTINUE
CONTROL
CONTROLS
CONVERSION
COPY
CORR
CORRESPONDING
COUNT
CURRENCY
DATA
DATE
DATE-COMPILED
DATE-WRITTEN
DAY
DAY-OF-WEEK
DE
DEADLOCK
DEBUG-CONTENTS
DEBUG-ITEM
DEBUG-LINE
DEBUG-NAME
DEBUG-NUMERIC-CONTENTS
DEBUG-SUB-1
DEBUG-SUB-2
DEBUG-SUB-3
DEBUGGING
DECIMAL-POINT
DECLARATIVES
DELETE
DELIMITED
DELIMITER
DEPENDING
DESCENDING
DESTINATION
DETAIL
DIRECT
DISABLE
DISPLAY
DIVIDE
DIVISION
DOWN
DUPLICATES
DYNAMIC
EGI
ELSE
EMI
ENABLE
END
END-IF
END-OF-PAGE
END-PERFORM
END-SEARCH
ENDING
ENTER
ENVIRONMENT

EOP
EQUAL
EQUALS
ERROR
ESI
EVERY
EXCEEDS
EXCEPTION
EXIT
EXTEND
EXTERNAL
FALSE
FD
FILE
FILE-CONTROL
FILES
FILLER
FINAL
FIRST
FOOTING
FOR
FROM
GENERATE
GIVING
GO
GREATER
GROUP
HASHED-VALUE
HASHING
HEADING
HIGH-VALUE
HIGH-VALUES
I-O
I-O-CONTROL
IDENTIFICATION
IF
IN
INDEX
INDEXED
INDICATE
INITIAL
INITIALIZE
INITIATE
INPUT
INPUT-OUTPUT
INSPECT
INSTALLATION
INTO
INVALID
IS
JUST
JUSTIFIED
KEY
LABEL
LAST
LEADING
LEFT
LENGTH
LESS
LIMIT
LIMITS

LINAGE
LINAGE-COUNTER
LINE
LINE-COUNTER
LINES
LINKAGE
LOCK
LOW-VALUE
LOW-VALUES
MEMORY
MERGE
MESSAGE
MODE
MODULES
MOVE
MULTIPLE
MULTIPLY
NATIVE
NEGATIVE
NEXT
NO
NOT
NUMBER
NUMERIC
NUMERIC-EDITED
OBJECT-COMPUTER
OBJECT-PROGRAM
OCCURS
OF
OFF
OMITTED
ON
OPEN
OPTIONAL
OR
ORDER
ORGANIZATION
OTHER
OUTPUT
OVERFLOW
PAGE
PAGE-COUNTER
PERFORM
PF
PH
PIC
PICTURE
PLUS
POINTER
POSITION
POSITIVE
PRINTING
PROCEDURE
PROCEDURES
PROCEED
PROGRAM
PROGRAM-ID
PURGE
QUEUE
QUOTE
QUOTES

RANDOM
RD
READ
REALMS
RECEIVE
RECORD
RECORDING
RECORDS
REDEFINES
REEL
REFERENCES
RELATIVE
RELEASE
REMAINDER
REMOVAL
RENAMES
REPLACE
REPLACING
REPORT
REPORTING
REPORTS
RERUN
RESERVE
RESET
RETURN
REVERSED
REWIND
REWRITE
RF
RH
RIGHT
ROUNDED
RUN
SAME
SD
SEARCH
SECONDARY-STORAGE
SECTION
SECURITY
SEGMENT
SEGMENT-LIMIT
SELECT
SEND
SENTENCE
SEPARATE
SEQUENCE
SEQUENTIAL
SET
SIGN
SIZE
SORT
SORT-MERGE
SOURCE
SOURCE-COMPUTER
SPACE
SPACES
SPECIAL-NAMES
STANDARD
STANDARD-1
START
STATUS

STOP
STRING
SUB-SCHEMA
SUB-QUEUE-1
SUB-QUEUE-2
SUB-QUEUE-3
SUBTRACT
SUM
SUPERVISOR
SUPPRESS
SUSPEND
SYMBOLIC
SYNC
SYNCHRONIZED
TABLE
TALLYING
TAPE
TERMINAL
TERMINATE
TEST
TEXT
THAN
THEN
THROUGH
THRU
TIME
TIMES
TO
TOP
TRACE—ON
TRACE—OFF
TRAILING
TRUE
TYPE
UNEQUAL
UNIT
UNSTRING
UNTIL
UP
UPON
USAGE
USE
USING
VALUE
VALUES
VARYING
WHEN
WITH
WORD-ADDRESS
WORDS
WORKING-STORAGE
WRITE
ZERO
ZEROES
ZEROS

+   **
—   >
*   <
/   =

COBOL LANGUAGE SUMMARY–ABRIDGED C

The following summary of COBOL format, while not complete, includes the COBOL features used in this text. This language subset contains the COBOL formats that the average student will require in the first programming course.

COBOL FORMAT NOTATION

NOTATION	EXAMPLE	MEANING
Uppercase words underlined	**ADD**	Required reserved word
Uppercase words (not underlined)	IS	Optional reserved word
Lowercase words	identifier	Word or entry must be supplied by programmer
Brackets	[**ROUNDED**]	Optional feature
Braces	{BEFORE} {AFTER}	Alternatives
Elipses	. . .	Repetition may occur at user option
Punctuation		
Period	.	Required period
Comma	,	Optional punctuation
Semicolon	;	Optional punctuation

FORMAT NOTATION USAGE

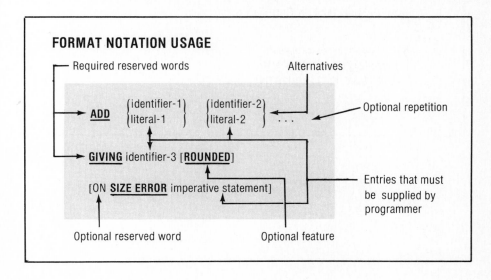

Required reserved words — Alternatives — Optional repetition

ADD {identifier-1} {identifier-2} . . .
{literal-1} {literal-2}

GIVING identifier-3 [**ROUNDED**]

[ON **SIZE ERROR** imperative statement]

Optional reserved word — Optional feature — Entries that must be supplied by programmer

General Format for IDENTIFICATION DIVISION

IDENTIFICATION DIVISION.
PROGRAM-ID. *program-name.*
[AUTHOR. [*comment-entry*] . . .]
[INSTALLATION. [*comment-entry*] . . .]
[DATE-WRITTEN. [*comment-entry*] . . .]
[DATE-COMPILED. [*comment-entry*] . . .]
[SECURITY. [*comment-entry*] . . .]
[REMARKS.* [*comment-entry*] . . .]

* Although no longer part of COBOL, REMARKS is still recognized by many compilers.

General Format for ENVIRONMENT DIVISION

ENVIRONMENT DIVISION.
CONFIGURATION SECTION.
SOURCE-COMPUTER. *computer-name.*
OBJECT-COMPUTER. *computer-name.*
  [SPECIAL-NAMES.
    [*implementor-name IS mnemonic*] . . .].
  [INPUT-OUTPUT SECTION.
FILE CONTROL.
    (*file-control-entry*)].

General Format for File Control Entry

SELECT *file-name*
  ASSIGN TO *implementor-name*
  [ORGANIZATION IS SEQUENTIAL]
  [ACCESS *MODE IS* SEQUENTIAL].

General Format for DATA DIVISION

DATA DIVISION.
  [FILE SECTION.
   FD file-name
  [BLOCK CONTAINS integer-1 RECORDS]
    LABEL {RECORD IS   } {STANDARD}
        {RECORDS ARE} {OMITTED }.
  record-description-entry].
  [WORKING-STORAGE SECTION.
  record-description-entry . . .]

General Format for Data Description Entry

FORMAT 1

level-number {data-name-1}
         {FILLER   }
[REDEFINES data-name-2]
[{PICTURE} IS character-string]
 {PIC   }
[OCCURS integer-2 TIMES
[{ASCENDING } KEY IS data-name-3
 {DESCENDING}
  INDEXED BY index-name-1]
[BLANK WHEN ZERO]
[VALUE IS literal].

FORMAT 2

88 condition-name {VALUE IS } literal-1 [{THROUGH} literal-2]
           {VALUES ARE}   [{THRU   }   ] . . .

COBOL COMMAND FORMATS

<u>ACCEPT</u> *data-name* [<u>FROM</u> *mnemonic-name*]

<u>ADD</u> $\begin{Bmatrix} data\text{-}name\text{-}1 \\ literal\text{-}1 \end{Bmatrix}$ $\begin{bmatrix} data\text{-}name\text{-}2 \\ literal\text{-}2 \end{bmatrix}$ . . . <u>TO</u> *data-name-m* [<u>ROUNDED</u>]

[*data-name-n* <u>ROUNDED</u>] . . .]

[ON <u>SIZE ERROR</u> *Cobol-command*]

<u>ADD</u> $\begin{Bmatrix} data\text{-}name\text{-}1 \\ literal\text{-}1 \end{Bmatrix}$ $\begin{Bmatrix} data\text{-}name\text{-}2 \\ literal\text{-}2 \end{Bmatrix}$ $\begin{bmatrix} data\text{-}name\text{-}3 \\ literal\text{-}3 \end{bmatrix}$ . . .

<u>GIVING</u> *data-name-m* [<u>ROUNDED</u>]

[*data name-n* [<u>ROUNDED</u>]] . . .

[ON <u>SIZE ERROR</u> *Cobol-command*]

<u>ADD</u> $\begin{Bmatrix} \underline{CORRESPONDING} \\ \underline{CORR} \end{Bmatrix}$ *data-name-1* <u>TO</u> *data-name-2* [<u>ROUNDED</u>]

[ON <u>SIZE ERROR</u> *Cobol-command*]

<u>CLOSE</u> *file-name-1* [*file-name-2*] . . .

<u>COMPUTE</u> *data-name-1* [<u>ROUNDED</u>]

[*data-name-2* [<u>ROUNDED</u>] . . .]

= *arithmetic-expression* [ON <u>SIZE ERROR</u> *Cobol-command*]

<u>DISPLAY</u> $\begin{Bmatrix} data\text{-}name\text{-}1 \\ literal\text{-}1 \end{Bmatrix}$ $\begin{bmatrix} data\text{-}name\text{-}2 \\ literal\text{-}2 \end{bmatrix}$ . . . (<u>UPON</u>*mnemonic-name*]

<u>DIVIDE</u> $\begin{Bmatrix} data\text{-}name\text{-}1 \\ literal\text{-}1 \end{Bmatrix}$ <u>INTO</u> *data-name-2* [<u>ROUNDED</u>]

[*data-name-3* [<u>ROUNDED</u>]] . . .

[ON <u>SIZE ERROR</u> *Cobol-command*]

<u>DIVIDE</u> $\begin{Bmatrix} data\text{-}name\text{-}1 \\ literal\text{-}1 \end{Bmatrix}$ <u>INTO</u> $\begin{Bmatrix} data\text{-}name\text{-}2 \\ literal\text{-}2 \end{Bmatrix}$ <u>GIVING</u> *data-name-3* [<u>ROUNDED</u>]

[*data-name-4* [<u>ROUNDED</u>]] . . .

[ON <u>SIZE ERROR</u> *Cobol-command*]

<u>DIVIDE</u> $\begin{Bmatrix} data\text{-}name\text{-}1 \\ literal\text{-}1 \end{Bmatrix}$ <u>BY</u> $\begin{Bmatrix} data\text{-}name\text{-}2 \\ literal\text{-}2 \end{Bmatrix}$ <u>GIVING</u> *data-name-3* [<u>ROUNDED</u>]

[*data-name-4* [<u>ROUNDED</u>]] . . .

[ON <u>SIZE ERROR</u> *Cobol-command*]

<u>DIVIDE</u> $\begin{Bmatrix} data\text{-}name\text{-}1 \\ literal\text{-}1 \end{Bmatrix}$ <u>INTO</u> $\begin{Bmatrix} data\text{-}name\text{-}2 \\ literal\text{-}2 \end{Bmatrix}$ <u>GIVING</u> *data-name-3* [<u>ROUNDED</u>]

<u>REMAINDER</u> *data-name-4* [ON <u>SIZE ERROR</u> *Cobol-command*]

<u>DIVIDE</u> $\begin{Bmatrix} data\text{-}name\text{-}1 \\ literal\text{-}1 \end{Bmatrix}$ <u>BY</u> $\begin{Bmatrix} data\text{-}name\text{-}2 \\ literal\text{-}2 \end{Bmatrix}$ <u>GIVING</u> *data-name-3* [<u>ROUNDED</u>]

<u>REMAINDER</u> *data-name-4* [ON <u>SIZE ERROR</u> *Cobol-command*]

IF *condition-test* $\begin{Bmatrix} Cobol\text{-}command(s) \\ \underline{NEXT\ SENTENCE} \end{Bmatrix}$ $\begin{bmatrix} \underline{ELSE} \begin{Bmatrix} Cobol\text{-}command(s) \\ \underline{NEXT\ SENTENCE} \end{Bmatrix} \end{bmatrix}$

PROCEDURE DIVISION FORMAT

<u>PROCEDURE DIVISION</u>.
[*section-name* <u>SECTION</u>.]
paragraph-name.
   Cobol-command
   [*Cobol-command*] . . .
[*paragraph-name.*
   Cobol-command
   [*Cobol-command*] . . .]

FORMATS FOR TEST-CONDITIONS

Relational condition:

$$
\begin{Bmatrix} \textit{data-name-1} \\ \textit{literal-1} \\ \textit{arith-expression-1} \end{Bmatrix}
\begin{Bmatrix}
\text{IS } [\underline{\text{NOT}}] \; \underline{\text{GREATER}} \text{ THAN} \\
\text{IS } [\underline{\text{NOT}}] \; \underline{\text{LESS}} \text{ THAN} \\
\text{IS } [\underline{\text{NOT}}] \; \underline{\text{EQUAL TO}} \\
\text{IS } [\underline{\text{NOT}}] > \\
\text{IS } [\underline{\text{NOT}}] < \\
\text{IS } [\underline{\text{NOT}}] =
\end{Bmatrix}
\begin{Bmatrix} \textit{data-name-2} \\ \textit{literal-2} \\ \textit{arith-expression-2} \end{Bmatrix}
$$

Class condition:

data-name IS [<u>NOT</u>] $\begin{Bmatrix} \underline{\text{NUMERIC}} \\ \underline{\text{ALPHABETIC}} \end{Bmatrix}$

Sign condition:

$\begin{Bmatrix} \textit{data-name} \\ \textit{arith-expression} \end{Bmatrix}$ IS [<u>NOT</u>] $\begin{Bmatrix} \underline{\text{POSITIVE}} \\ \underline{\text{NEGATIVE}} \\ \underline{\text{ZERO}} \end{Bmatrix}$

Condition-name condition:

condition-name

Combined Relational Condition:

relation-condition $\begin{Bmatrix} \underline{\text{AND}} \\ \underline{\text{OR}} \end{Bmatrix}$ [<u>NOT</u>] [*relational-operator*] *object* . . .

<u>MOVE</u> $\begin{Bmatrix} \textit{data-name-1} \\ \textit{literal} \end{Bmatrix}$ <u>TO</u> *data-name-2* [*data-name-3*] . . .

<u>MULTIPLY</u> $\begin{Bmatrix} \textit{data-name-1} \\ \textit{literal} \end{Bmatrix}$ <u>BY</u> *data-name-2* [<u>ROUNDED</u>]
   [*data-name-3* [<u>ROUNDED</u>]] . . .
   [ON <u>SIZE ERROR</u> *Cobol-command*]

<u>MULTIPLY</u> $\begin{Bmatrix} \textit{data-name-1} \\ \textit{literal-1} \end{Bmatrix}$ <u>BY</u> $\begin{Bmatrix} \textit{data-name-2} \\ \textit{literal-2} \end{Bmatrix}$ <u>GIVING</u> *data-name-3* [<u>ROUNDED</u>]
   [*data-name-4* [<u>ROUNDED</u>]] . . .
   [ON <u>SIZE ERROR</u> *Cobol-command*]

<u>OPEN</u> [<u>INPUT</u> *file-name-1* [*file-name-2*] . . .]
    [<u>OUTPUT</u> *file-name-3* [*file-name-4*] . . .]

<u>PERFORM</u> *procedure-name-1*
<u>PERFORM</u> *procedure-name-1* <u>UNTIL</u> *condition*
<u>PERFORM</u> *procedure-name-1*

$$\underline{\text{VARYING}} \begin{Bmatrix} \textit{data-name-1} \\ \textit{index-name-1} \end{Bmatrix} \underline{\text{FROM}} \begin{Bmatrix} \textit{data-name-2} \\ \textit{index-name-2} \\ \textit{literal-1} \end{Bmatrix} \underline{\text{BY}} \begin{Bmatrix} \textit{data-name-3} \\ \textit{literal-2} \end{Bmatrix} \underline{\text{UNTIL}} \textit{ condition-1}$$

$$\left[\underline{\text{AFTER}} \begin{Bmatrix} \textit{data-name-4} \\ \textit{index-name-3} \end{Bmatrix} \underline{\text{FROM}} \begin{Bmatrix} \textit{data-name-5} \\ \textit{index-name-4} \\ \textit{literal-3} \end{Bmatrix} \underline{\text{BY}} \begin{Bmatrix} \textit{data-name-6} \\ \textit{literal-4} \end{Bmatrix} \underline{\text{UNTIL}} \textit{ condition-2} \right.$$

$$\left. \underline{\text{AFTER}} \begin{Bmatrix} \textit{data-name-7} \\ \textit{index-name-5} \end{Bmatrix} \underline{\text{FROM}} \begin{Bmatrix} \textit{data-name-8} \\ \textit{index-name-6} \\ \textit{literal-5} \end{Bmatrix} \underline{\text{BY}} \begin{Bmatrix} \textit{data-name-9} \\ \textit{literal-6} \end{Bmatrix} \underline{\text{UNTIL}} \textit{ condition-3} \right]$$

$\underline{\text{READ}}$ *file-name* RECORD [$\underline{\text{INTO}}$ *record-name*] [AT $\underline{\text{END}}$ *Cobol-command*]

$\underline{\text{SEARCH}}$ *data-name-1* $\left[\underline{\text{VARYING}} \begin{Bmatrix} \textit{data-name-2} \\ \textit{index-name-1} \end{Bmatrix} \right]$ [AT $\underline{\text{END}}$ *Cobol-command-1*]

$$\underline{\text{WHEN}} \textit{ condition-1} \begin{Bmatrix} \textit{Cobol-command-2} \\ \underline{\text{NEXT SENTENCE}} \end{Bmatrix} \left[\underline{\text{WHEN}} \textit{ condition-2} \begin{Bmatrix} \textit{Cobol-command-3} \\ \underline{\text{NEXT SENTENCE}} \end{Bmatrix} \right] \ldots$$

$\underline{\text{SEARCH ALL}}$ *data-name* [AT $\underline{\text{END}}$ *Cobol-command-1*] $\underline{\text{WHEN}}$ *condition* $\begin{Bmatrix} \textit{Cobol-command-2} \\ \underline{\text{NEXT SENTENCE}} \end{Bmatrix}$

$\underline{\text{SEARCH ALL}}$ *data-name-1* [AT $\underline{\text{END}}$ *Cobol-command-1*]

$$\underline{\text{WHEN}} \textit{ data-name-1} \begin{Bmatrix} \text{IS } \underline{\text{EQUAL}} \text{ TO} \\ \text{IS } = \end{Bmatrix} \begin{Bmatrix} \textit{data-name-2} \\ \textit{literal-1} \\ \textit{arith-expression-1} \end{Bmatrix}$$

$$\left[\underline{\text{AND}} \textit{ data-name-2} \begin{Bmatrix} \text{IS } \underline{\text{EQUAL}} \text{ TO} \\ \text{IS } = \end{Bmatrix} \begin{Bmatrix} \textit{data-name-3} \\ \textit{literal-2} \\ \textit{arith-expression-2} \end{Bmatrix} \right] \ldots$$

$$\begin{Bmatrix} \textit{Cobol-command-2} \\ \underline{\text{NEXT SENTENCE}} \end{Bmatrix}$$

$$\underline{\text{SET}} \begin{Bmatrix} \textit{data-name-1 } [\textit{data-name-2}] \ldots \\ \textit{index-name-1 } [\textit{index-name-2}] \ldots \end{Bmatrix} \underline{\text{TO}} \begin{Bmatrix} \textit{data-name-n} \\ \textit{index-name-n} \\ \textit{integer} \end{Bmatrix}$$

$$\underline{\text{SET}} \textit{ index-name-1} [\textit{index-name-2}] \ldots \begin{Bmatrix} \underline{\text{UP BY}} \\ \underline{\text{DOWN BY}} \end{Bmatrix} \begin{Bmatrix} \textit{data-name} \\ \textit{integer} \end{Bmatrix}$$

$$\underline{\text{STOP}} \begin{Bmatrix} \underline{\text{RUN}} \\ \textit{literal} \end{Bmatrix}$$

$$\underline{\text{SUBTRACT}} \begin{Bmatrix} \textit{data-name-1} \\ \textit{literal-1} \end{Bmatrix} \left[\begin{matrix} \textit{data-name-2} \\ \textit{literal-2} \end{matrix} \right] \ldots \underline{\text{FROM}} \textit{ data-name-m} [\underline{\text{ROUNDED}}]$$

[*data-name-n* [$\underline{\text{ROUNDED}}$] . . . [ON $\underline{\text{SIZE ERROR}}$ *Cobol-command*]

$$\underline{\text{SUBTRACT}} \begin{Bmatrix} \textit{data-name-1} \\ \textit{literal-1} \end{Bmatrix} \left[\begin{matrix} \textit{data-name-2} \\ \textit{literal-2} \end{matrix} \right] \ldots \underline{\text{FROM}} \begin{Bmatrix} \textit{data-name-m} \\ \textit{literal-m} \end{Bmatrix}$$

$\underline{\text{GIVING}}$ *data-name-n* [$\underline{\text{ROUNDED}}$]

[*data-name-p* [$\underline{\text{ROUNDED}}$]] . . .

[ON $\underline{\text{SIZE ERROR}}$ *Cobol-command*]

$\underline{\text{WRITE}}$ *record-name* [$\underline{\text{FROM}}$ *data-name-1*]

$$\left[\begin{Bmatrix} \underline{\text{BEFORE}} \\ \underline{\text{AFTER}} \end{Bmatrix} \text{ADVANCING} \begin{Bmatrix} \textit{data-name-2 } \text{LINES} \\ \textit{integer } \text{LINES} \\ \textit{mnemonic-name} \end{Bmatrix} \right]$$

$$\left[\begin{Bmatrix} \underline{\text{BEFORE}} \\ \underline{\text{AFTER}} \end{Bmatrix} \text{ADVANCING} \begin{Bmatrix} \textit{data-name-2} \\ \textit{integer} \\ \textit{mnemonic-name} \\ \underline{\text{PAGE}} \end{Bmatrix} \left[\begin{matrix} \text{LINE} \\ \text{LINES} \end{matrix} \right] \right]$$

GLOSSARY

A

abend Message indicating an ''abnormal ending'' to a program execution. *See also* abort.

abort Message indicating that a programming error has caused the program to terminate prematurely.

absent data check Part of a data validation program that checks for the missing items.

access time The elapsed time between the initiation of a read or write command and completion of the function. Access times for disk devices vary according to rotation speed, number of tracks or cylinders, and movement speed of the access arm holding the read/write head(s).

accumulator A memory area used in building running totals for use within a program.

active key The key with the lowest value among those currently being processed in the merging or updating of sequential files. This low key value serves as an activity director to control sequential file merging on updating.

algorithm A ''recipe,'' or series of steps, that describes the solution to a problem. An algorithm establishes the sequence of instructions to be followed in a computer program.

alphabetic Data consisting only of the letters A-Z and blank spaces, indicated in COBOL data definitions by the symbol A. *See also* numeric and alphanumeric.

alphanumeric Data consisting of letters, numbers, and/or special characters, indicated in COBOL data definitions by the symbol X. *See also* alphabetic and numeric.

ALU *See* arithmetic logic unit (ALU).

American National Standards Institute (ANSI)   National organization that establishes and recommends standards for the computer industry.

ANSI   *See* American National Standards Institute (ANSI).

application   An information processing job to be performed with the aid of a computer.

application program   A computer program, written in a language such as COBOL, that follows an algorithm to solve some phase of an identified user problem.

archival file   A permanent copy of records that must be retained for legal or other long-term reference purposes. Storage is usually at a site remote from the computer center.

argument   A unique value used to identify and locate a data item in a table.

arithmetic logic unit (ALU)   Area within a computer processor that performs computations and comparison operations.

array   *See* table.

assembler language   A programming language in which alpha-numeric codes are used to represent computer instructions and addresses. Also called assembly language.

authorization   A processing control function that permits or forbids the acceptance of data.

B

backup file   A copy of a current working file, updated at regular intervals and usually stored in a separate location, to be used for rebuilding the system if the original file is destroyed. Backup files contain complete copies of all current data, as well as copies of all operating system and application software, so that the entire computer information system can be rebuilt from the ground up if

balancing   A type of processing control that compares a computed value with an independent value entered specifically for control purposes.

binary digit   The value represented in one position of a binary number. May have a value of 0 or 1. Also called a bit.

binary search   A type of search in which a sequentially ordered table is iteratively divided in half to search for a given value. If the search is unsucessful, half the remaining table is searched. The dividing of the remaining table is repeated until the target item is located.

bit   *See* binary digit.

black box   The concept of a computer or other processing device whose internal components and functioning can be ignored by the programmer.

block   A series of logical records that are grouped together on magnetic tape or disk for processing efficiency. Term is synonymous with a physical record.

blocking factor   The number of logical records included in a block.

bubble   A circle used to represent a processing step in a data flow diagram.

buffer   An area set up in main memory that is large enough to hold a physical record in readiness for processing.

bug   A program statement or command that violates syntax requirements or rules of logic. *See also* syntactical error and logical error.

byte   A group of bits representing a number, letter, or other character. Most commonly, a byte consists of eight data bits and one parity bit, or check bit.

C

capstan   A rotary device within a tape drive that friction-feeds the tape for reading or writing.

carriage control   Printer-control function that establishes the pattern of vertical line spacing in a printed report.

case construct   A control structure within a structured program used for the selection of one from among two or more processing alternatives.

central processing unit (CPU)   A portion of a computer's processor containing the control unit and the arithmetic logic unit.

channel   A magnetic path along the length of a magnetic tape that can be magnetized in bit patterns to represent data. *See also* track (tape).

character   The smallest unit of data that can be presented to a COBOL program; a letter, numeral, or special symbol.

character position   The amount of physical storage used for one character.

character set   The letters, numbers, and special characters acceptable for input, processing, and output by a COBOL program.

character testing   A validating process that tests whether input characters are acceptable for processing and/or storage.

check bit   *See* parity bit.

CIM   *See* computer input microfilm (CIM).

class condition   The presence within a field of data of wholly numeric or alphabetic characters.

class test   In a COBOL selection statement, a condition test within a program aimed at ensuring the integrity of data by verifying that only numeric or alphabetic data are present, as specified in programs.

clause   One part or element of a program sentence, or statement.

COBOL (COmmon Business Oriented Language)   The high-level programming language most commonly used in computer solutions to business problems.

COBOL program sheet   Coding sheet used in the writing of COBOL instructions.

CODASYL (COnference on DAta SYstems Languages)   Conference convened by the Department of Defense to develop a business data processing language, led to the creation of COBOL.

code   The source instructions that the computer will follow in compiling a program to process an application.

collate   Program routine to merge records from two correspondingly ordered sequential files into a single file sequence that follows the same rules for ordering records.

collating sequence   An established hierarchy of values for valid characters that are applied in setting processing or data sequencing rules.

columnar heading   Heading at the top of a column of information on a printed report that identifies content of the column.

COM   *See* computer output microfilm (COM).

command   An instruction within a computer source program. Term is synonym for instruction.

comment line   A descriptive, informative entry within a source program represented by an asterisk in column 7 of a COBOL programming sheet. Comments are not to be translated by the compiler.

compilation   The translation of source instructions by the compiler to generate a machine-language object program.

compiler   A program that translates source code instructions into machine language commands.

compound conditional test   A complex condition test that determines whether two or more conditions are true simultaneously (AND) or whether any one of two or more conditions is true (OR). Also called an AND/OR test.

computer   A series of interconnected devices that accepts raw facts, performs processing, and delivers usable information continuously and under control of sets of instructions known as programs.

computer decision making   The routine for comparing one data item with another and then selecting a processing alternative on the basis of the outcome.

computer input microfilm (CIM)   A system for data input from microimages recorded on film.

computer output microfilm (COM)   Computer output in the form of microimages recorded on rolls or sheets of film.

computer system Components of hardware and software, integrated to accept inputs, process data, and produce information, and also to store and retrieve files of data and information.

condition name condition A condition test that determines whether a user-defined descriptive term is true for a value or set of values that apply to the data item under consideration.

constant A fixed data item that does not change in the course of processing.

control break report A report with subtotals and totals produced on the basis of the content of control fields.

control field A data item that triggers a control break, causing a total to be printed in an output report.

control report An interim report used to check the accuracy, completeness, and reliability of processed data.

control unit A portion of a computer processor that evaluates and carries out program instructions.

counter An area of main memory in which a consecutive count of data items is maintained.

CPU *See* central processing unit (CPU).

cylinder A set of tracks occupying the same position on multiple disk surfaces within a disk pack, over which all read/write heads are positioned at the same time.

D

data Basic facts, represented by letters, numbers, symbols, and spaces, that are the raw material of data processing and of computer information systems.

database The collection of files that support computer information systems within an organization.

database management system (DBMS) A software system that incorporates a plan of structure and management that controls the accumulation and use of data within an organization.

data definition In programming, a description required for each data item, such as a field or a record.

data element A basic unit of data.

data field *See* field.

data file *See* file.

data flow diagram Systems analysis tool used to document the flow and transformation of data as they are processed through a system. In a data flow diagram, circles, or bubbles, represent processing activities. Data being processed are represented by arrows. Open rectangles represent stores of data (files)

data format   The organizational arrangement of data for input, processing, storage, or output.

data record   *See* record.

date check   Part of a validating program that checks whether date values—month, day, and year—fall within appropriate ranges.

DBMS   *See* database management system (DBMS).

debugging   The process of identifying and correcting syntactical or logical errors in a program.

decompose   To break down an overall job or program into smaller, more manageable elements or steps.

decomposition   *See* decompose.

defensive programming   The inclusion in a program of instructions that test for and react to unexpected or erroneous data conditions.

descriptive information   *See* indicative information.

desk checking   *See* walkthrough.

destructive writing   A writing function on a storage device that erases or obliterates previously recorded data.

detail line   A collection of information printed on a report from a detail record within an output file.

detail report   A listing of all records contained within a computer-maintained file. Also called a detail listing.

direct access   The ability to find and retrieve individual records at random in computer files.

disk cartridge   A removable magnetic disk medium that usually contains a single platter.

disk drive   A peripheral device that reads from and writes onto magnetic disks.

disk pack   A removable magnetic disk unit containing multiple platters.

division   One of four basic parts into which all COBOL program coding is organized. Each division is further subdivided into sections, paragraphs, and sentences.

dynamic table   A table that is defined as the program is written and compiled, but whose actual data contents are loaded from an external storage medium when the program executes.

E

editing   The screening of input data to check for accuracy and completeness of characters, fields, and records; also a processing control over the formatting of numeric printed outputs. *See also* validation.

effective date   In a report heading, the date to which the delivered information applies.

electronic journaling   A procedure for logging all transactions into a computer system. Inputs are generally recorded on magnetic media, in order, as transactions occur.

elementary item   A single data field containing no separable subfields.

end-of-file condition   The point at which processing of a file is discontinued, either because a predefined flag has been sensed or because no further data records are available for reading.

even parity   Recording pattern on magnetic tape that uses an even number of binary bits in each byte as a check for character validity.

exception   Any situation defined as unusual or abnormal; a record that meets or fails to meet some pre-established test or condition.

exception report   A report that contains only those records that fall outside predefined limits of acceptability or normalcy.

execute   To carry out a program by performing the specified processing.

exit the loop   To terminate repetition processing and move on to the next instruction in the program.

F

field   A basic, processing-oriented unit of data formed by a set of characters in a predetermined format; usually combined with other fields of data to form a record.

figurative constant   In COBOL, a constant represented by a reserved word to which the compiler assigns a specific value.

file   A collection of data records with related specified content.

file description (FD)   Statement in the FILE SECTION of the DATA DIVISION that provides identification and physical structure information about a file.

file dump   Operation that prints out an unformatted listing of the contents of a computer file.

file maintenance   Procedure for modifying, or updating, master files to reflect the addition, modification, or deletion of records.

file reel   Reel of tape from which data are read or to which data are written; later removed for storage.

fixed disk   A nonremovable magnetic disk, usually with a large storage capacity. A fixed disk usually has a separate read/write head over each recording track, permitting access to any record in a single rotation of the disc.

flag   A signal or control field containing fixed information that is used as the basis of a condition test. The sensing of a flag value affects the processing stream of a program, often causing the invoking of a different processing module. Also called a switch.

flexible disk   A small magnetic disk with a base made of flexible plastic sheeting coated with iron oxide, generally used with microcomputers or data entry devices. Also called a floppy disk.

floppy disk *See* flexible disk.

footing A running total printed at the bottom of each page of a report, invoked by a predetermined line count.

FORTRAN (FORmula TRANslator) An early compiler language, designed primarily to solve mathematical and scientific problems.

function A usable item of data in a table, identified by a matching argument.

G

group indicating The printing of only the first occurrence of each control field value so that these identification lines will stand out clearly in the printed report.

group item A data field made up of subfields that can be used separately.

H

hardware An inclusive term identifying all computer equipment. *See also* central processing unit (CPU), control unit, arithmetic logic unit (ALU), main memory, and secondary storage.

hierarchical design *See* hierarchy.

hierarchy A top-down, multilevel organizational scheme in which components of problems, systems, or programs are layered in a top-to-bottom, general-to-detailed fashion.

high-level language A programming language that interacts with a compiler to produce multiple machine-code instructions for each source-code statement. *See also* compiler.

history file A chronological record of the past condition of a master file to reflect updating transactions.

home address The beginning location, or starting point, on a magnetic disk track.

I

identification field A field interspersed between data records on a magnetic disk track that is used to identify the size of the next data record.

identifier The name of the program represented by a structure chart, found at the top level of the chart; the name applied to any unit of data, whether a single field, a group of fields, or a complete record, that is input for processing as a single unit; the name of a paragraph, module, or subroutine invoked by a program instruction.

imbedded sign An algebraic sign (+ or −) stored as a zone bit over the rightmost character in an input data field.

implied decimal point   Indication of the position of the decimal point in a numeric data field, represented in COBOL data definitions by the symbol V.

increment   To add a specified value to a counter for each processing operation performed.

index   A computer storage item whose value represents the location of a particular element in a table.

indicative information   Report entries that serve as identifiers for detail lines, generally placed to the left of the corresponding quantitative or variable information. Also called descriptive information.

information   Processed data, developed according to a plan to fill a need of users in performing jobs or making decisions.

information explosion   Term indicating the enormous volumes of data created as byproducts of science, technology and business.

initiation   The component of a program containing the modules that provide startup, or initialization, activities. *See also* main processing and termination.

input   The entry of data into a processor. Also, to enter data.

insertion character   In COBOL, one of several special characters that can be used to punctuate numeric data.

instruction   A programming language statement that causes a computer to carry out a specific function.

interface   Any point at which people and equipment interact; also, an interconnection between units of equipment or modules of a program.

interrecord gap   The blank space between records on magnetic media.

invoke   To cause a program module or series of modules to be executed.

iteration   *See* repetition.

J

job control language (JCL)   The language of an operating system used to identify programs, data files, and equipment support requirements for processing.

L

layout form   Standard worksheet used in systems development and in programming to represent the configuration of data to be input to or output from a system.

leg   The vertical dimension of a structure chart, showing the hierarchical relationship among levels for a single segment of the program.

level Degree of depth to which the design of a program is carried. Can be represented as a horizontal row of modules in a program structure chart. Also called hierarchical level.

limit test Validating process that determines if data values are above or below some predefined value.

literal A numeric or an alphanumeric constant whose value is defined by the characters of which it is composed. A literal is used in the exact place and context where it is described.

log file A serial file representing a continuous recording of activity within a computer system.

logical error Program error that involves improper processing.

logical operator In a COBOL decision statement, an AND clause or an OR clause connecting two separate conditions. An AND clause means that both conditions must be true; an OR clause means that either condition must be true.

loop The repeated processing of a set of instructions that continues, over and over, until a conditional test is met.

low-level language A programming language that is at or close to the level of machine language. Requires a separate instruction for each operating function to be executed by the computer. *See also* machine language and assembler language.

M

machine language The internal representation language of a computer processor.

machine reel Reel used within a tape drive to hold the tape that is unwound from the file reel. Also called the take-up reel.

magnetic disk A data storage medium in which records are recorded as patterns of magnetic bits along circular tracks. A magnetic disk can store records for direct access or for serial, sequential, or indexed sequential processing.

magnetic tape A data storage medium in which records are encoded consecutively as patterns of magnetic bits on a long ribbon of oxide-coated plastic.

main memory Device connected to the computer processor unit that supports the handling of data by the control or arithmetic logic units. Used for temporary storage of data and programs during program execution.

main processing The component of a program containing the modules that carry out the primary data manipulation function. *See also* initiation and termination.

maintenance Updating and/or enhancement of an existing computer information system.

major key The name of the highest order of precedence of two or more record keys used in sorting records into sequential files.

master file A related set of permanent or semipermanent data relevant to a specific application.

match In merging or collating sequential files, a condition in which the value of a record key in one of the source files is the same as that of the active key, causing that record to be written to the output merge file. Also called an equal condition.

merge *See* collating.

microfiche Sheet of film used for recording and storing microimages.

microfilm Roll of film used for storing microimages.

microform A reference encompassing the recording of microimages on both roll film and fiche.

minor key Any record key other than the key used in sorting records for sequential files.

mnemonic A unique name assigned by a programmer.

model An outline, or "skeleton," of the program to be developed. Can be represented in a structure chart or flowchart.

module A unit, or part, of a computer program that corresponds to a complete processing sequence; can be represented by a single box within a structure chart.

N

named constant In COBOL, a constant that has an identified function within a program.

nested IF test A series of condition tests involving two or more levels of IF (selection) statements.

number crunching Nickname applied to scientific, as opposed to business, computing. Signifies large volumes of computations.

numeric Data consisting only of the digits 0-9, indicated in COBOL data definitions by the symbol 9. *See also* alphabetic and alphanumeric.

O

object program The machine-language program generated by a compiler, translating a source program.

odd parity Recording pattern that uses an odd number of binary bits in each byte to represent valid characters.

operating system A program that controls the configuration and functioning of computer equipment.

order of arithmetic operations The predetermined order in which arithmetic functions are always executed under the COBOL COMPUTE command: operations within parentheses, exponentiation, multiplication and division, addition and subtraction.

output The results of computer processing, delivered in a form and format—and on a schedule—that makes the end products usable by people.

P

page eject   A function that causes the printer to space vertically to the top of a new page.

page number   Part of a report heading, incremented by a counter as each page is printed.

pagination   Subroutine that causes the printer to advance from the bottom of one page to the top of the next after a predetermined number of lines have been printed, invoking the heading routine and resetting the line counter to zero.

paragraph   One or more COBOL sentences that constitutes a logical processing unit.

parallel installation   An approach to implementation of a new system that permits both systems to operate at the same time, with the old system being gradually phased out as the new system proves itself.

parity bit   The channel or position in a data recording pattern used for automatic checking of the validity of a character. The parity bit is used to check that the appropriate number of bits, odd or even, is present in each byte. Also called the check bit.

partitioning   The process of breaking down problems and programs into a series of manageable parts that can be understood and handled individually. Also called decomposing.

physical record   *See* block.

platter   An individual magnetic disk.

present data check   Part of a validating program that checks whether data exist within specified fields of records being processed.

priming read   Preliminary reading of the first data record in a file before the main processing loop begins.

printer   Output device used to deliver computer-processed information to users in the form of printed reports.

print layout   A diagram showing the planned format and content of a printed report, including headings, detail lines, summary lines, pagination, and totals.

processing control   A routine that permits or prohibits processing of records on the basis of data content and format. *See also* authorization, validation, editing, and balancing.

program   A set of instructions that causes a computer to perform a series of steps without human intervention in processing data so as to solve a problem or meet a need by delivering specific results.

programming language   A set of terms and symbols used by people following specific rules of syntax to convey instructions to computers.

program module   *See* module.

pseudocoding The use of English-like statements that describe the required processing steps in a program.

punched card A data storage medium in which data are recorded by means of patterns of holes arranged in columns and rows.

Q

quantitative information In a report, the variable content or value of a detail line, usually placed to the right of the corresponding indicative information. Also called variable information.

R

random file A computer file whose records are not arranged in any logical order or sequence, but are accessed instead by a system in which record keys are used to determine storage location.

range check Part of a validating program that checks whether data values fall between some predefined minimum and maximum values.

reading The function of sensing and capturing data nondestructively from a recorded medium or source for processing or storage. Reading sources or methods can involve magnetic media, documents, or outputs from compatible devices.

reasonableness test Part of a validating program that checks whether data values are appropriate for the context of their use.

receiving field The area within computer memory to which an identified data item is to be moved.

record A collection of data fields relating to a single entity, such as a person or a business transaction. A number of records with related content make up a file. Also called a logical record.

recording density The closeness, or spacing, of bit positions on magnetic storage media. The three standard recording densities for tape are 800, 1,600, and 6,250 characters per inch. On disks, recording density varies from track to track.

record key A specific content item, such as name or employee number, on which the ordering of a sequential file is based.

record test Part of a validating program that tests whole records for completeness or accuracy.

recovery A set of procedures used to rebuild a computer information system through the use of backup files.

relational test In a COBOL decision statement, a condition test involving a logical comparison of two data items to determine whether the second item is equal to, greater than, less than, not equal to, not greater than, or not less than the first item.

removable disk Magnetic disk that can be mounted on or removed from a disk drive for access by a movable read/write head.

repetition   A routine or module that is processed from beginning to end, over and over, with newly presented data items, until some predefined condition is encountered. The term is synonymous with iteration.

replacement character   In COBOL, a character that substitutes for a leading, nonsignificant zero in a numeric data field.

report   A document produced by a computer from the contents of computer-maintained files.

report heading   Heading printed at the top of each page of a report, including the title of the report, the page number, the effective date, and possibly the run date.

reserved word   In COBOL, a word with a special, predefined meaning that can be used only for a specific purpose or to convey a specific meaning.

rigid disk   An inflexible magnetic disk with a metal base, or substrate, usually an aluminum alloy, coated with an oxide material.

rolling total   A feature of a control break program that provides for transferring an accumulated total to the next higher summary level called for in the program.

round   To eliminate rightmost, unnecessary decimal places by dropping the unwanted digit and, if it has a value of 5 or greater, incrementing the digit to its left.

run date   The day on which a report is actually prepared, not necessarily the same as its effective date.

S

search   The act of accessing data stored in tables. Also called table lookup.

secondary storage   Devices for retaining files outside of main memory for program-controlled access. Secondary storage is lower in cost and slower in performance than main memory.

section   A major unit within a division of a COBOL program. A section, in turn, is made up of paragraphs and sentences.

sector   One of a number of equal segments into which the tracks on a magnetic disk are sometimes divided.

selection   A program control construct that chooses processing statements for execution on the basis of condition tests.

sending field   A data item to be copied to another area within a computer memory.

sentence   One or more complete, syntactically correct COBOL statements terminated by a period.

sequence (processing)   The execution of program steps in the order in which they are written.

sequence check   A processing control applied to make sure that the next record accepted for processing is in proper sequential order.

sequential file   A computer file consisting of records stored and processed in a specified, logical order.

sequential search   A table search conducted in order, from beginning to end, covering all elements in a table.

serial file   A file consisting of records recorded chronologically, in the order in which they are received by a recording device.

sign condition   The presence within a numeric data field of algebraic signs indicating positive or negative data.

sign test   In a COBOL selection statement, a condition test that determines whether the algebraic sign of a numeric field is positive, negative, zero, not positive, not negative, or not zero.

software   Computer operating systems and application programs, together with the operating procedures for their use.

sort   Program routine for arranging records in a prescribed order.

source code   The coded statements prepared by programmers under the rules of a specific programming language.

source program   A set of processing instructions written by a programmer for translation to machine language.

statement   A program instruction, or command, that directs computer processing.

static table   A table whose data contents are defined when the program is written and are embedded within the program itself when it is compiled.

stepwise refinement   The top-down approach used in decomposing a problem to identify the program components, or modules, required to solve it.

structure chart   Programming tool used to break down a problem or program into manageable modules and to show the relationships among them.

structured flowchart   Programming tool that uses standardized symbols to describe the sequence of processing and the controls applied in implementing a program.

structured walkthrough   A peer review of the basic design or pseudocoding of a program to identify logical corrections.

subroutine   A sequence of instructions that causes a specific processing function or activity to be executed. A subroutine represents a change from, or branch in, the main sequential processing stream of a program. A subroutine can be invoked at any point in the program where it is needed.

subscript   A number or data name that identifies the occurrence number of an element within a table. Written in parentheses following the identifying argument.

substrate   The base material of a magnetic disk to which the oxide coating is applied.

summary report   A report in which information is consolidated so that each line represents more than one detail record from a computer-maintained file. Summary reports are often used to provide status information for managers. Also called a tabulation.

supplied word   In COBOL, a word invented by a programmer, following certain rules, that is used in writing program instructions.

switch   *See* flag.

syntactical error   Error in the use of a programming language, violating its structure or usage rules, that prevents compilation of a source command.

syntax   The structure and usage rules of a programming language.

system flowchart   A graphic presentation, using standard symbols, that documents the processing steps within a system.

system maintenance   *See* maintenance.

system printer   Device designated by the programmer or by a default instruction from the compiler for printing computer output.

systems analyst   A CIS professional who specializes in the the analysis, design, and development of computer information systems.

systems development life cycle   A project structure that guides development of a system by establishing a manageable structure consisting of phases, activities, and tasks.

T

table   An area defined in computer memory to hold repeated occurrences of a particular set of data items. Also called an array.

table lookup   Method of finding needed data items in a table by using the corresponding arguments. Also called table search.

tabulation   *See* summary report.

take-up reel   *See* machine reel.

tape drive   Machine that reads from and writes onto reels of magnetic tape. Also called a tape transport.

task   One of a series of steps or procedures followed in completing an overall job. Tasks are short, minimum work assignments.

termination   The basic component of any CIS program containing the steps that close out the processing. *See also* initiation and main processing.

test data   Data developed and used for testing purposes, designed to represent all types of data to be processed by the finished program, including all types of errors that might be contained in the actual data to be processed.

testing The process of analyzing output produced through use of a program and comparing it with expected results to identify any logical errors in the program.

throughput The volume of processing that a computer system can handle within a given time.

top-down design *See* hierarchy.

top-down testing The standard approach to testing program logic, beginning at the top level of the structure chart and working across each subsequent level from left to right, making sure that each module invokes the succeeding module correctly.

total The sum of an arithmetic processing sequence. Also, any numeric value in a report, printed under the column whose accumulated value it represents.

track (disk) Locus of data on magnetic disk. Tracks are concentric circles on the surface of the disk on which data are recorded in linear patterns.

track (tape) Locus of data on magnetic tape. Most tape drives record data in nine tracks, eight of which are used to represent data values and the ninth to check the accuracy of recording or reading operations. Also called a channel.

transaction file A file consisting of the records created as a byproduct of individual acts of doing business, such as sales slips, checks, or time cards. Transaction records are generally used to update master files, after which they become part of history files.

transient data Data that will be used within a specific program but will not be retained permanently.

truncate To drop excess characters when a data item is moved to a receiving field with insufficient room to hold it. In numeric moves, truncation occurs at the left of the field; in alphanumeric moves, truncation occurs on the right.

U

unit record Another name for punched card records.

update report A type of control report used in master file maintenance, permitting easy review of updating activities.

updating The process of modifying master files to reflect the addition, change, and deletion of records.

user Any person or organization served by an information system.

V

validation A processing control that, through a series of calculations, determines the accuracy and completeness of characters, fields, and records. *See also* editing.

variable   A named data item that may change with the execution of the program. A variable may change, for example, each time a new data record is presented.

variable information   *See* quantitative information.

verb   A command or instruction that invokes a processing action.

vertical spacing   Arrangement of lines on the page of a printed report.

W

walkthrough   The process of checking and validating the logic of a program using test data, either mentally, with pencil and paper, or with a calulator, to eliminate bugs before submitting the program to the computer for testing, and to verify correctness. Also called desk checking.

INDEX

A margin, 92, 103, 225
"A" PICTURE symbol, 94, 175
ACCEPT command, 63, 69
  for automatic printing of dates, 275
  [FROM] clause, *122*, 123, *123*, 136
  restrictions on use, 122
  SPECIAL-NAMES paragraph, *123*, 123–124
Access time
  defined, 346, 350
  for fixed versus removable disks, 350
Accumulators, 97, 193–195, 198
  applications, 194
  control break programs, 356–357, 378
  defined, 194
  multiple, 194–195
Accuracy of data, 169, 272, 283. *See also* Validation
Active key, 319, *321*
Activity directing item, 322
ADD command, 128, *129*, 136
  GIVING clause, 129, 136, 137
  TO restrictions, 136, 137
Addition functions, 128–129, 132, 133, 135
Algebraic signs, *95*, 95–96, 132, *133*, 281
Algorithm development, 7–15, 17, 24
  business application example, 10–13
  steps in, 8–10, *12*, 17
Algorithms
  characteristics, 7
  defined, 6, 17
  programs in relation to, 24
ALPHABETIC class test, 174–175, *176*, 197
Alphabetic data, symbol for, 94
Alphanumeric data
  moving, 126, 127, *127*
  symbol for, 94
  tests for, 171, 175, 197

Alphanumeric fields, truncation of, 127, *127*, *128*
Alphanumeric literals, 99, 100
  quotation marks for, 100
ALU. *See* Arithmetic logic unit
American National Standards Institute (ANSI) standards
  ASCII code format, 166, *167*
  COBOL, X3.23–1974, 60
  flowchart symbols, *38*, 38–39, *39*
Analysis and general design phase, systems development
  life cycle, 25–28, 47–48
AND logical operator, 185–188, *186*, 198
ANSI standards. *See* American National Standards Institute (ANSI) standards
Application programs, 2. *See also* Programs
  development, 23–49
  for file creation, 314
  organizing for coding, 43–44
Archival files, 309, 310–311, 324
Argument values
  in sequential search, 401, 402
  in tables, 392, *392*, *393*, 401, 409
Arithmetic logic unit, 3, 4, 17
Arithmetic operations, 4, 17, 128–137
  errors, 135–136
  order of, 132–133
  size of results fields, 134–135
  symbols, 95–96
Arrays, defined, 393. *See also* Table data; Tables
ASCII (American Standard Code for Information Interchange), coding sequence, 166, *167*
Assembly language, 59
ASSIGN TO clause, 223–224
Assignment statements, file names, 223–224
Asterisks (*)
  arithmetic symbol, 132
  as check-protection character, 102

for identification of report totals, 280, 377
AT END clause, 230–231, 232, 406–407, 410
Authorization of transactions, 28

''B'' insertion character, 101
B margin, 92, 103, 225, 228
Backup files, 309, 310, 324
Balancing, as processing control, 29, 272–273
Binary digits. *See* Bits
Binary notation, 58
Binary search, 403–405, 409
   flowchart, *404*
   SEARCH ALL statement, 405, 407
   sequential order needed, 405
Bits, 340, 348
Black box, computer as, 4–5
BLANK WHEN ZERO clause, 282
BLOCK CONTAINS clause, 342
Blocking factors, 342
Blocking of records, 341, *341*, 342, 345
Blocks, defined, 96
Brackets, 123, 124, 136
Bubbles, in data flow diagram, 28
Budgets, in systems development, 25, 27
Buffers
   defined, 338
   in main memory, 342
BY, in DIVIDE command, 130–131, *131*
Bytes, 340, 348
   defined, 91

Calculation commands, 128–137
Capstans (tape drives), 338
Carriage control, 238–240, 242, 280
   WRITE . . . ADVANCING statement and, 239
Case construct
   defined, 185
   flowchart, 44, *46*, 49
Cathode ray tube (CRT) terminals, 313
Central processing unit (CPU), 3–4, 17
Character set, COBOL, 64, *64*, 76, 91, 103
Character testing, 268
Characters
   collating sequences, 166, *167*, 171, 197
   in data names, 93, 104
   defined, 91
   insertion, 101–102
Chronological records, 307, 310, 323
Class tests, 170, 174–175, 197, 286
   ALPHABETIC, 175, *176*
   NUMERIC, 175, *175*
Clauses, in COBOL programs, 64
CLOSE statement, 229–230, 242
   format, 229

COBOL (COmmon Business Oriented Language), 2, 16
   background, 58–60
   character set, 64, *64*, 76, 91, 103
   coding (*see specific statement or clause, e.g.,* WRITE statement; VALUE clause)
   compilers (*see* Compilers; Compilation of COBOL programs)
   naming rules, 65
   program divisions and subdivisions, 60–64
   words, 65, 76–77
COBOL coding sheets
   special positions on, 66–67
COBOL programs. *See also* Programs
   compilation of, *71*, 71–73, *72*, *73*, *74*
   file definitions in relation to program divisions, 230–238, 242
CODASYL (Conference On DAta SYstems Language), 59–60
Coding
   defined, 13, 17
   in relation to structured flowcharts, 68–69
Coding sheets, COBOL, 66–67
Collating sequences, 166, *167*, 171, 197
Columnar headings, 273, 276
Columnar information, 276, 277, 280
   detail lines, 276
   totals, 277, *279*, 280
Commas (,), 136
   insertion character, 101
   in numeric fields, 281–282
Comments entries, 222
Comparisons. *See* Relational tests
Compilation of COBOL programs, *71*, 71–73, *72*, *73*, *74*
   error messages, 72, 73–74
   Job Control Language statements in, 71, 72, 77
   post-list, 72
   test data in, 73
Compilers
   COBOL, 60, 69, 71–72
   defined, 16, 60
   source programs submitted to, 69
Completeness of data, 272, 283
Compound conditional statements, parentheses in, 187–188
Compound conditional (AND/OR) tests, 170, 185–188, *186*, 198
COMPUTE command, 69, 132–133, *133*, 137
   arithmetic symbols, 132, *133*
   ON-SIZE ERROR option, 134–135
   ROUNDED option, 133–134, *134*
Computer decision making, 165–188, 197–198
Computer information systems (CIS), 6. *See also* Systems development life cycle
Computer-input microfilm (CIM), 313
Computer-output microfilm (COM), 313
Computer systems, defined, 4, 17

Computers
  defined, 1, 2, 4, 16–17
  hardware, 2
  as tools, 4, 17
Condition name tests, 170, 176–178, *178, 179*, 197, 198
Conditional statements
  AND/OR clauses, 185–188, 198
  compound independent conditions, 185–188, *186*, 198
  IF . . . THEN . . . ELSE statements, 167–188, 197–198
  multiple dependent conditions, 179–185, *182, 183, 184, 185*, 198
Conditions
  exception report tests of, 268–270
Conference On DAta SYstems Language (CODASYL), 59–60
CONFIGURATION SECTION, paragraphs in, 222–223, 242
Constants (COBOL)
  calculation, 97
  figurative, 99
  names, 99
Control break programs/reports, 355–378, *356*
  accumulators in, 356–357, 378
  characteristics, 355–357, 378
  coding (case study), 359, *369–372*
  control field, 355–356
  defensive programming, 375
  defined, 355, 378
  detail lines, 376
  group indicating, 377, 378
  preparation, 357
  printing options, 375–377
  program development, 358–359, 373
  program structure chart (case study), 359, *360*
  pseudocode (case study), 359, 361
  significance of totals in, 377
  two-level (case study), 357–358, *357–372*, 373–375
Control breaks, 355, 356, 373, 374, 378
Control data, 275
Control fields, 355–356
  defined, 355, 378
  multiple, 355–357
Control reports, 265, 272–273, 283
  defined, 272
  examples, *272*, 272–273
  techniques used, 272–273
Control unit, functions, 4, 17
Controls
  in data processing, 28–29
  flags and switches, 195–196, 198
  in program structures, 44–45
  purposes, 166, 197
  sequence check, 375
  in structured flowcharts, 37–38
  for validity of data terms, 169

Copy functions
  MOVE command, 126
  system utility packages, 314
Costs and benefits, 25
Counters, 97, 198
  defined, 193
  use, *194*
CPU. *See* Central processing unit
''CR'' insertion character, 101, 281
Creation of files, 315–318, *315, 316*, 317, *318*, 323
Credit (CR) designation, 101, 281
CRT (cathode ray tube) terminals, 313
Cylinders, defined, 345, *345*

DA designation, 224
Data, 89–104
  defined, 4, 17
  hierarchy of, 90–91, 103
  independent items, 92
  logical units, 347–348, *349*, 350
  physical record, 348, *349*, 350
  physical units, 348, *349*, 350
  processed, 4, 17
Data definitions, 91–100, 103–104
  alphabetic data, 94
  alphanumeric data, 94
  elementary items, 96
  examples, 96–100
  group items, 96
  numeric data, 94
  PICTURE clause, 94, 103
  VALUE clauses, 98
DATA DIVISION, 60, 63, 76
  FILE SECTION (*see* FILE SECTION)
  in payroll program, *62, 67*
  vertical spacing control established in, 239–240
  WORKING-STORAGE SECTION (*see* WORKING STORAGE SECTION)
Data fields
  initial values, defining, 97–98
  sizes, 127
Data flow diagrams, 6, *27*, 32, *32*, 36, 48
Data formats, 28. *See also* Formatting
Data movement
  alphanumeric, 127–128, 136
  commands, 125–128, 136
  field sizes, 127
  numeric, 126–128, 136
Data names, 68, 93–94, 104
  characters allowed, 93, 104
  for input data, 94
  numeric, 94, 128
  for output data, 94
  prefixes, 93–94
  rules for, 93–94, 104

Data processing. *See* Processing of data
Data records, types of, 98–100, 104
Database, defined, 306, 323
Date fields
  date checks, 270
  in headings, 273
"DB" insertion character, 101, 281
Debit (DB) designation, 101, 281
Debugging. *See* Testing and debugging
Decimal fields, 133–134, 135
Decimal points, 100, 282
  implied, 94
  "V" symbol, 94–95
Decision making, computer, 165–188, 197–198
  COBOL programming, 169–188
Decision tables, 42, 43, 48
Decision trees, 42–43, 48
Default input device, 123
Defense, U.S. Department of, 59
Defensive programming, 375, 378
Design
  detailed, in systems development life cycle, 28–29, 48
  of program processing, 37–47, 48, 49
  of program structure, 36, 48
Desk checking. *See* Walkthroughs
Destructive writing, 339
Detail lines, 276
  control break reports, 376, 378
  indicative (descriptive) information, 280
Detail reports, 265–266, 282
  defined, 265–266, 282
  examples, 266, *266*
Detailed design and implementation phase, systems development life cycle, 28–29, 48
Direct access, 308, 312, 324
  for on-line systems, 347
  storage devices, 311, 347
Direct files, 306, 308, 323
  record keys, 308, 324
Disk cartridges, 343
Disk drives, 311, 342–343, 350
  access times, 346, 350
  fixed, 343, 350
  read/write heads, 346
  removable, 343, 350
Disk packs, 343
  multiple, 348
Disks. *See* Magnetic disks
DISPLAY command, 63, 69, 76, *124*, 124–125, *125*, 136
  in debugging, 125
  [UPON] clause, 124, 136
DIVIDE command
  BY, 130–131, *131*
  GIVING option, 131–132
  INTO, 130–131, *131*
  REMAINDER clause, 131–132, *132*

Division functions, 130–132, 133, 135
Documentation
  of current system, 25–26
  design of program processing, 37–47, 48, 49
  of program development process, 31–46, 48, 49
Dollar signs ($)
  insertion character, 100, 101
  in printed reports, 281
DOUNTIL loops, 191, 198
DOWHILE loops, 191, 198
  PERFORM . . . UNTIL command, *191*, 191–193, 198
Dynamic tables, 399–401, 405, 409
  defined, 394, 409
  entry of data into memory, 394, 395, 399, *399*, 409
  program definition, 394, 399, *399*, 409

EBCDIC (Extended Binary Coded Decimal Interchange Code) character system, 166, *167*
Editing, 29
  of data, 268–270
  insertion characters, 101
  numeric fields, 100–103
  for printed output, 29, 100–103 (*see also* Printed reports)
  replacement characters, 102
Effective date, 275
"88" level entry, 93, 98, 177–179, *178*, *179*, 198
Electric journaling, 306–307
Elementary item, 96
ELSE clauses, 171, 173
End-of-file condition, 230–231
END OF PROCESSING, 69
ENVIRONMENT DIVISION, 60, 61, 76, 221, 222–224, 237–238, 242
  CONFIGURATION SECTION, 222–223, 242
  in payroll application, *61*, 67
  SPECIAL-NAMES paragraph, 123–124, 125
Equal condition, 322
EQUAL TO relation, 171
Equals sign, 132
Error checking, 268–273
Error messages
  in compilation process, 72, 73–74
  display of, 125
Errors
  calculation, 135–136
  due to truncation, 136
  improper parity bit, 340
  input/output, 340
  in sequence, 375
  syntactical, 69, 72, 73–74, 77, 359
  testing for, 72–76, 77
Exception reports, 265, 268–272, 283
  defined, 268, 283
  examples, 270–271, *271*
  types, 268–270
Exponentiation symbol, 132

FD (file description) statement, 225
  blocking factor in, 342
  format, 226–227
  PICTURE clause, 242
  in WORKING-STORAGE SECTION, 226–227
  and WRITE command, 236
Fiche, 313
Fields
  data definition and, 96, *97*
  defined, 90, *90*, 91, 103, 347–348, 350
  physical arrangement, 96
  size, 134–135, 171
FILE-CONTROL paragraph, 223
File creation, 313–318, *315, 316, 317, 318*
File definitions, 225–228
  in relation to COBOL program divisions, 230–238, 242
File dump, 314
File names
  assignment, 223–224
  READ command, 230, 237
File organization, 306–308, 323
  control break reports, 356–357
  direct, 306, 308, 323
  indexed sequential, 306, 308, 323
  sequential, 306, 307–308, 323
  serial, 306–307, 323
File reel (tape drive), 338, *339*
FILE SECTION, 96, 98, 178, 196, 221, 224–228, 242
  data tables, 393
  file descriptions, 237
  ''01'' record name area, 93, 103, 238, 342, 394
  PICTURE clauses, 242
  record definition in, 238
  and WRITE . . . FROM command, 237
File structure
  multiple-level control break processing, 356–357
  and recording density, 341–342, 350
Files, *90*, 90–91
  archival, 309, 310–311, 324
  backup, 309, 310, 324
  in COBOL programs, 221–242
  defined, 90, 91, 103, 306, 323
  history, 309, 310, 324
  LABEL RECORDS clauses, 225, 226
  log, 309–310, 324
  on magnetic disks, 347
  makeup, 305–306, 223
  master, 308, 322–323, 324
  merging, 318–323, 324
  organization, 306–308, 323, 356–357
  transaction, 309, 322–323, 324
  updating, 322–323, 324
FILLER, 94, 238
Flags, 195–196, 198
  end-of-file, 231, 242
Floppy disks. *See* Magnetic disks

Flowcharts. *See* Structured flowcharts
Footings, 277
Formatting, 273–282, 283
  printed outputs, 238–241
  of reports, 273–281, 283
  specifying in WORKING-STORAGE SECTION entries, 282
FORTRAN (FORmula TRANslator), 59
[FROM] clause, *122*, 123, *123*, 136
Functions, in tables, 392, *392, 393*, 409

Gaps, interrecord, 340–341, *341*, 344
Garbage, defined, 231
GIVING clause
  ADD command, 136, 137
  DIVIDE command, 131–132
  MULTIPLY command, 130
GIVING option, 129
GREATER THAN relation, 171
Group indicating control break reports, 377, 378
Group item, 96
Grouping of terms, symbol, 132, *133*

Hardware, defined, 2, 16
Heading designations, 240–241
Heading line, 97
Headings, 273–276, 277
  columnar, 273, 276
Hierarchical structure
  of data, 90–91, 92, 103
  of program requirements, 35–36
History files, 309, 310, 324
Home address (disk track), 344
Human-machine interfaces, 27
Hyphens, 61
  in data names, 93, 104
  in numeric fields, 281
  in supplied names, 77

IDENTIFICATION DIVISION, 60, 61, *61*, 67, 76
Identifiers
  in ACCEPT statement, 122
  defined, 122
  in PERFORM statement, 188
IF statements, 167
  AND/OR clauses, 185–188
  control break report, case study, 373
  nested, 179–185, *182, 183, 184, 185*, 198
  NOT clause, 172–173
  one-way, 167, *167*
  THEN and ELSE options, 63, 69, 167–188, *173*, 197–198
  two-way, 167, *168*, 169

Imbedded overpunched signs, 95, *95*
Implementation phase, systems development life cycle, 28–29, 48
Independent data, 97
INDEXED BY clause, 397, *397*
Indexed sequential files, 306, 308, 323
Indexes
 defined, 308, 397
 establishing or changing values, *398*, 399
 SEARCH statement used with, 397, 409
 sequential files, 308
 SET statement and, *398*, 399
 table data, 396, 397, *397*, 399, 407, 409
 two-level tables, 407
Indicative information, 280
Information
 defined, 4, 17
 indicative, 280
INITIALIZATION procedures, 231, 236
Initiation component, in structure chart, 34, 35
Input, 313–314
 data names, 94
 in data processing cycle, 5
 defined, 2
 defining, 7, 8, 11, 17
 flowchart symbol, 38, *38*
Input commands, 122–124, 136
 ACCEPT statement, 122–124, 136
INPUT designation, 228, 230
Input/output devices
 default, 123
 SYS numbers, *223*, 224
INPUT-OUTPUT SECTION
 file assignment statements, 223–224, 242
Insertion characters, *101*, 101–102, *102*
Installation phase, in systems development life cycle, 28–29, 48
Interactive systems, and direct access, 347
Interfaces, human-machine, 27
Interrecord gaps, 340–341, *341*, 344
INTO
 DIVIDE command, 130–131, *131*
Investigation phase, in systems development life cycle, 25, 47
IPO (Input/Processing/Output) charts, 33–34, *33*, 36, 48
Iteration, defined, 44. *See also* Processing loops; Repetition in programs

JCL. *See* Job Control Language (JCL)
Job Control Language (JCL), 71, 72, 77
Justification, 280

Keys. *See* Record keys

LABEL RECORDS clause, 225, 226
Layout, of printed outputs, 273, *274*
Layout forms, 32–33, *33*, 48
 control break report, case study, 359
 input, 33
 output, 32–33, *33*
Leg, vertical (structure chart), 35–36
LESS THAN relation, 171
Level numbers, 92–93, 103
 "01," 93, 103, 238, 342, 394
 "77," 92
 "88," 93, 98, 177–179, *178*, *179*, 198
Limit tests, 269
Literals, 99, 100
Log files, 306–307, 309–310, 324
Logic switches, 97
Logical errors, 29, 69–70, 77
 identification of, 74–75, 77
 post-compilation testing for, 69, 71
Logical functions, computer, 4, 17
Logical operators, 185–188, *186*, 198
Logical records, 347–348, *349*, 350
 defined, 96
Loops. *See* Processing loops

Machine language, 58
Machine reel (tape drive), 338
Magnetic disks, 312, 342–347, 350
 advantages, 347, 350
 copying, 314
 file assignment clause for, 347
 file storage, 347
 fixed, 343, 350
 flexible (floppy), 342, 343, 346, 350
 identification field, 344
 recording devices (*see* Disk drives)
 recording patterns, 343–346, *344*, 350
 removable, 343
 rigid, 346
 substrates, 343
 tracks, 343, 344, 345
Magnetic tape, 312, 338–342, 348, 350
 archival files on, 311
 copying, 314
 nine-channel, 339–340
 recording densities, 340–341, 350
 recording device assignment, 338
 recording devices (*see* Tape drives)
 recording patterns, 339–340, *340*, 348, 350
 tracks, 340, *340*
Main memory, 3, 17, 342
Maintenance
 of sequential files, 322–323, 324
 in systems development life cycle, 29

Major (record) key, 307, 324
Management
  approval, 28
  needs, 25
Margins A and B, 92, 103, 225
Master files, 308, 324
  updating, 308, 322–323, 324
Master records, 322
  in archival files, 311
Match condition, 322
Match/merge procedures, 322, 323
Memory, 3, 17. *See also* Memory, main; Secondary storage
    headings
Memory, main, 3, 17
  buffer, 342
Merging files, 318–323, *319*, 324
  active key, 319
  defined, 318
  match/merge procedures, 322, 323
  program, 319, 320
Microfiche, 313
Microfilm, 313
Microforms, 313
Minor (record) key, 307, 324
Minus (–) arithmetic symbol, 132
Minus (–) insertion character, 101, 102
Mnemonics, for hardware devices, 123
Model, structure chart as, 35
Modules (program), 190
  defined, 28, 190
  flowchart symbol, 38, *38*
  invoking of, 36
  reusable, 315
  testing, 75
MOVE statement, 63, 69, 76, 126–127, 136
  numeric, *126*, 126–127, *127*
Multilevel (nested ''IF'') tests, 170, 179–185, *182*, *183*, 184,
    184, *185*, 198
Multiple totals, 278, *279*, 280
Multiplication function, 130, 132, 133, 135
MULTIPLY command, 130, 136, 137
  GIVING option, 130

Names, hyphens in, 77
Naming rules, COBOL, 65
Nested IF tests, 170, 179–185, *182*, *183*, 184, *184*, *185*, 198
NEXT SENTENCE clause, 167, 170, 172
''9'' PICTURE symbol, 94, 126, 128, 136
NOT clause
  in IF statements, 172–173, *174*
  use of, 173
NOT EQUAL TO relation, 171, 173
NOT GREATER THAN relation, 171, 173

NOT LESS THAN relation, 171, 173
Number crunching, 59
NUMERIC class test, 174–175, *175*, 197
Numeric data
  calculations, 128–137
  insertion characters, 101
  justification, 280–281
  moving, *126*, 126–127, *127*
  relational tests, 171, 197
  replacement characters, 102–103
  symbol for, 94
  test for, 174–175, 197
Numeric fields, 276, 277, 279, 280, 281
  algebraic signs, *95*, 95–96, 132, *133*, 281
  commas in, 281–282
  data definition, 94–96
  decimal points, 94–95, 100, 282
  dollar signs, 100, 101, 281
  editing procedures, 100–103
  MOVE statement, *126*, 126–127, *127*
  negative, 281
  printed output, 100–103
  size, 95, 134–135, 136
  truncation, 127, *127*, *128*
Numeric literals, defined, 99

OBJECT-COMPUTER, 222–223, 242
Object program
  compiler displaced by, 72–73
  defined, 69
  generation of, 69, 72
  testing and debugging, 73–76, 77
OCCURS clause
  for table definition, 394, 395–396, 409
  use with VALUE clause, 395
Offpage connector, 39
''01'' level entry, 93, 103, 238, 342, 394
On-line systems, and direct access, 347
ON-SIZE ERROR option, 134–135, *135*
OPEN statement, 228–229, 236, 242
  execution, 229
  format, 228, 229
Operating systems
  defined, 2, 16
  input submitted to, *71*
  record blocking function, 342
  utilities programs, 307, 314, 315
Option terms, bracketed, 123, 124, 136
OR logical operator, 185, *186*, 187–188, 198
Output
  data names, 94
  in data processing cycle, 5
  defined, 3

editing for, 100–103
flowchart symbol, 38, *38*
predefinition of, 7–8, 17, 76
printed, 100–103, 238–241, 242, 273, *274* (*see also* Printed reports)
and WRITE command, 236–237
Output commands, 122, 124–125, 136
OUTPUT designation, 228, 230
Output devices, SYS numbers, *223*, 224
Overflow, 136

PAGE, 240–241
Page, top of, 240–241, 277
Page length, 277
Pagination, 274, 276–277, *278*
Paragraph (COBOL program), 64
Parallel installation, 29
Parentheses
in compound condition statements, 187–188
for grouping of terms, 132, *133*
Parity, 340
Parity bit, 340, 348
Payroll application programs
algorithm development, 10–12
CALCULATE module, 68
coding, 14–16, 67–69
DATA division, *62*, 63, 76
data fields, 96, *97*
data flow diagram, *32*
ENVIRONMENT DIVISION, 61, *61*, 76
IDENTIFICATION DIVISION, 61, *61*, 76
INITIALIZATION module, 69, 75
input record layout, *33*
IPO chart, 34, *34*
output record layout, 32–33, *33*
PROCEDURE DIVISION, 68–69
PROCESS-DATE module, testing, 75
repetition in, 44–45, 47
selection (program control), 44, *45*
structure chart, 34, *35*
structured flowcharts, 39–40, *40–42*, *68*, 68–69, *69*, 70
top-down testing of, 75
PERFORM statement, 63, 68, 188–190, *189*, 198
identifier, 188
transfer of control by, 190
UNTIL phrase, 190–193, *191*, *192*, 197, 198, 231, 409
VARYING phrase, 401, 409
Periods (.), 61, 64, 69
ending FD statements, 226
ending nested IF structure, 184
Physical records, 348, *349*, 350
blocks, 96, 342, 345
volumes, 348

PICTURE (PIC) clauses, 94–95, 103, 242
absence, 96
contents, 94
data table, 394
in editing, *101*, 101–103, *102*, *103*
receiving field, 126, 136
Platters. *See* Magnetic disks
Plus (+) arithmetic symbol, 132
Plus (+) insertion character, 101, 102
Priming read, defined, 231–232
Printed outputs, 100–103, 238–241, 242. *See also* Printed reports
carriage control, 238–240, 242
layout, 273, *274*
numeric fields, 100–103
Printed reports
control break options, 375–377
design, 280–281, 283
formatting, 100, 273–280, 283
types, 265–272, 282–283
vertical spacing, 238–240
Printers, 312–313
Problem analysis, in program development, 6, 8, 31–36, 48
Problem definition, in systems development life cycle, 23–28, 29, 30–31
PROCEDURE DIVISION, 14, 60, 63, 76, 221
instructions, 228–241, 242
literals in, 100
in payroll program, *62*, 67, 68–69
references to external files, 238
Processing controls. *See* Controls
Processing loops
basic characteristic, 193
defined, 190
DOUNTIL, 191, 198
DOWHILE, 191, *191*, 198
exiting, 191
within loops, *192*, 192–193
Processing of data, 5–6, 17, 121–137
cycle, 5, *5*, 12
defined, 3
requirements, defining, 8, 9, 12
as step in algorithm development, 8, 17
structure chart component, 34, 35
Processor, components, 2–4, *3*, 17
Program design
algorithm development, 7–15, 17
validation of logic of, 45–47, 49
Program development life cycle, 30–47, 48–49
coding program, 57–77
control break report, case study, 357–359, 373
design of program processing, 37, 48
design of program structure, 36, 48
importance of adequate planning, 57–58
problem analysis, 31–36, 48
steps in, 31–47, 48–49

in relation to systems development life cycle, 30, *30*
testing and debugging, 69
PROGRAM-ID, 61
Programming languages
business versus scientific applications, 59
COBOL (*see* COBOL headings)
defined, 60
FORTRAN, 59
high level, 59
low level, 58
Programs, 4, 17. *See also* Application programs; COBOL programs; Utilities programs
algorithm development, 7–15, 17, 24
completeness, 7
components, 34
decomposition/partitioning, 43
defined, 1–2, 16
execution, 7
repeatability and reliability, 6, 7, 17
testing (*see* Testing and debugging)
types of, 2
Proof machine, 272
Pseudocode/pseudocoding, *13*, 37, *38*, 43, 48
control break report, case study, 359, *361*, 373
defined, 13, 17, 37
for file merging program, 321
independent of programming language, 37, 58
structure chart in relation to, 37
structured walkthrough, case study, 373–375
Punched cards, 268, 312

Quality assurance, 45–47
Quantitative (variable) information, in printed reports, 280
Quotation marks, use of, 100

Random access. *See* Direct access
Range checks, 268, 270
READ command, 122, 230–236, 242
AT END phrase, 230–231
file names, 230, 237
INTO phrase, 236
in relation to PERFORM . . . UNTIL loop, 231
placement, 231, *232–235*, 235, 242
Read/write heads
disk drives, *343*, 345–346
for fixed versus removable disks, 343, 350
tape drive, 338
Receiving fields, 126, 136
ADD command and, 128–129
addition functions, 135

RECORD CONTAINS clause, 225, 226, 242
Record descriptions, 96, *97*
Record keys, 307, 319, 323–324
active, 319, *321*
control break reports, 355–356
direct fields, 308, 324
indexed sequential fields, 308, 324
sequential files, 307, 323–324
Record names, and WRITE command, 236–237
Record tests, 270. *See also* Validation
Recording densities, 340–341, 350
and file structure, 341–342, 350
magnetic disks, 345–346, *346*
magnetic tape, 341
Recording patterns
magnetic disks, 343–346, 350
magnetic tape, 339–340, *340*, 348
Records, 90, *90*, 91
attributes, 347–348
blocking/blocks, 96, 341,*341*, 342
chronological ordering, 306–307, 323
defined, 90, 91, 103, 306
logical versus physical, 96, 347–348, *349*, 350
movement of, 125–127, 136
physical, 96, 342, 345, 348, *349*, 350
Recovery, defined, 311
REDEFINES clause, 394, 395
Relational tests, 170, 171–174, *173*, *174*, 197
alphanumeric data, 171, 197
condition name, 177–178, 198
numeric data, 171, 197
symbols not recommended in, 173–174
Reliability, 6, 7, 17
of data, 272, 283
REMAINDER clause, DIVIDE command, 131–132, *132*
Repeatability, 6, 7, 17
Repetition in programs, 17, 44, 68, 185, 188–193, 197, 198.
See also Processing loops
Replacement characters, *102*, 102–103, *103*
Report numbers, 275
Reports
control, 265, 272–273, 283
control break, 355–380
design requirements, 280–281, 283
detail, 265–266, 282
exception, 265, 268–272, 283
formatting, 273–282, 283
headings, *267*, 273–275
printed, 265–283 (*see also* Printed reports)
structural requirements, 273–280, 283
summary, 265, 266–268, 283
titles, 274
Reserved words (COBOL), 65, 69, 76
Result fields, 134–135, 136
Review phase, in systems development life cycle, 29, 30, 48
Rolling total, 347

ROUNDED option, 133–134, *134*
RUN, 63
Run date, defined, 275

''S'' PICTURE symbol, 95
Schedules, in systems development, 25, 27
''Scratch pad'' memory, WORKING-STORAGE as, 97
SEARCH ALL statement, 405, 407
SEARCH statement, 397, 405, 406–407, *406*, 409
  WHEN clauses, 407
Search techniques. *See* Table lookup (search) techniques
Secondary storage, 3, 17. *See also* Magnetic disks; Magnetic
    tape
  logical versus physical data, 347–348, *349*, 350
Secondary storage devices, 311–312, 324, 337–347, 348, 350
  magnetic disk recording, 342–347, 350
  magnetic tape recording, 338–342, 348, 350
Sections (of COBOL programs), 64
Sectors, of tracks, 344
SELECT statement, 223, 224
  ASSIGN TO clause, 223–224, 242
  for disk files, 347
  tape device assignment, 338
Selection mechanisms in programs, 167–188
  one-way versus two-way, 44, 167, 169, 170, 197
Sending field, 126, 128, 129
Sentence (COBOL program), 64
Sequence check, 375, 378
Sequence of processing, in structured flowcharts, 37
Sequential files, 306, 307–308, 323
  control break reports, 356–357
  creating, 313–318, 324
  indexed, 306, 308, 323
  maintenance, 322–323, 324
  merging, 318–322, 324
  punched cards for, 312
  reporting, 264–283
  S designation, *223*, 224
  sorting and merging, 307, 318–322, 324, 405
Sequential processing, 166, 169, 190
Sequential search, 402–403, 409
  argument value in, 402
  SEARCH statement used for, 397, 405, 406–407, *406*, 409
Serial files, 306–307, 323
  creating, 313–317
  punched cards for, 312
  sorting, 318, 324
SET statement, *398*, 399
  use with SEARCH statement, 406
''77'' level entry, 92
Sign tests, 178–179, *179*, 197, 268
Signed data, 95–96, 281
Slash mark (/), insertion character, 101
Software, defined, 4, 17. *See also* Programs

SORT statement, 307
Sort utilities, 307
Sorting, 307, 318, 323–324
  defined, 307, 324
  record keys, 307
  table data, 407
SOURCE-COMPUTER, 222–223, 242
Source programs
  defined, 69
  read into memory, 72
  submitted to compiler, 69
SPACE/SPACES, 99
Spaces, not usable in data names, 93
Spacing, vertical, 238–240
SPECIAL-NAMES paragraph, 222–224, 242
  in ACCEPT statement, 123–124
  outout device, 125
Static tables, 405
  defined, 394, 409
  entry of data into memory, 394, 395, 409
  program definition, 394, 395, 409
Status information, 266–267
Stepwise refinement.*See* Top-down testing
STOP statement, 63
Storage, defined, 3. *See also* Memory, main; Secondary
    storage
Storage media, 311–312, 324
Structure charts, 28, *28*, 34–36, *35*, 48
  component, 34
  control break report, case study, 359
  file merging program, 319, *320*
  identifier, 34
  levels, 34
  pseudocode written from, 37
  top-down design, 35
  vertical leg, 35–36
Structured flowcharts, 26, *26*, 37–42, 43–44, 48
  basic characteristics, 40, 42
  coding in relation to, 68–69
  control break report, case study, 359, *363–368*
  controls in, 37–38
  payroll program, 68, 69, 70
  sequence of processing in, 37
  symbols, *38*, 38–39, *39*, 169
Structured walkthroughs, 45–47, 49, 75–76, 373
Subfields, 92, 103
Subroutines
  defined, 190, 198
  in structured flowcharts, 39–40
  transfer to, 190, 198
Subscripts
  table data, 396–397, 409
  two-level tables, 407
SUBTRACT commands, 128, 129–130, *129*, *130*, 136
  GIVING option, 129
Subtraction function, 129–130, 132, 133, 135

Summary reports, 265, 266–268, 283
  control break reports, 355–378
  defined, 266, 355
  examples, 266–267, *267*
Supervisor, in compilation process, 73
Supplied words (COBOL), 65, 76–77
Switches, 195–196, 198
Symbols, flowcharting, *38*, 38–39, *39*, 169
Syntax, 29
  defined, 60
Syntax errors
  compiler identification of, 69, 72, 73–74, 77, 359
  defined, 29
SYS entry, *223*, 224
System utilities programs, 314, 315
    sort, 307
    versus standard application programs, 315
Systems analysts, defined, 25
Systems development life cycle, *24*, 25–30, 47–48
  analysis and general design phase, 25–28, 47–48
  detailed design and implementation phase, 28–29, 48
  installation phase, 28–29, 48
  investigation phase, 25, 47
  maintenance requirements, 29
  program development in relation to, 30, *30*
  review phase, 29, 30, 48
Systems development projects, defined, 24
Systems flowcharts, 26, *26*
Systems software, 307, 314, 315

Table data
    accessing, 396–399, 409
    argument, 392, *392*, *393*, 401, 409
    file maintenance, 399
    functions, 392, *392*, *393*, 409
    sorting, 405
    volatile, 399
Table lookup (search) techniques, 401–407
    binary, 403–405, 409
    SEARCH command, 406–407, *406*, 409
    sequential, 402–403, 409
Tables, 391–410. *See also* Dynamic tables; Static tables
    defined, 391, 409
    definition through OCCURS clause, 394, 395–396, 409
    dynamic, 39
    functions in, 392, 409
    multiple level, 407, *408*
    position value, 401
    program definition, 393–394, *394*
    references to, 401
    sequential order, 405
    single-dimension, 392, *392*, *393*
    single-level, 392–396
    static, defined, 393
    use of, 391–392, 409

Tabulations. *See* Summary reports
Tape drives, 338–339, 348. *See also* Magnetic tape
    tape up reel, 338
Termination component, in structure chart, 34, 35
Termination point, flowchart symbol for, 38, *38*
Termination procedure, 7
Test data, 73, 75–76, 77
    construction, 75–76, 77
    control break report, case study, 359, *372*
    criteria, 75–76
    development, 29
Testing and debugging, 29, 72, 73–76, 77
    control break report, case study, 359, *372*, 373
    DISPLAY command in, 125
    top-down, 75, 77, 359
Tests
    computer decision-making, 170–188, 197–198
    of record contents, 268–270
THEN clauses, 63, 69, 167–188, 171, *173*, 197–198
Throughput, defined, 345
TO, 126
    in ADD commands, 136, 137
Top-down design, structure charts, 35
Top-down testing
    control break report, case study, 359
    of programs, 75–76, 77
Top-of-page, 240–241, 277
Totals
    columnar, 277, *279*, 280
    multiple levels, 277, *279*, 280
    rolling, 374
    running, 280
    significance, in control break reports, 377
    summary, 355–356
    symbols for, 280
Tracks (magnetic disk), 344
    cylinders, 345
    home address, 344
    sectors, 344
Tracks (magnetic tape), 340, *340*
Transaction fields, 309, 322, 324
Transaction records, 322
Transactions, defined, 309
Transient data, 97
Transfer of control, by flags and switches, 195–196, 198
Translation, in program compilation, 2, 16, 72
Truncation, 127, 136

Underscoring, 123
Unit records, 312
UNTIL phrase, in PERFORM statement, 190–193, *191*, *192*, 197, 198, 231, 409
Update reports, 273

Updating
    of files, 322–323, 324
    of systems, 29
[UPON] clause, in DISPLAY command, 124, 136
UR designation, 224
UT designation, 224
Utilities programs, 307, 314, 315

''V'' PICTURE symbol, 94–95, 135
Validation
    of data, 28–29, 169, 268–270, 269
    of program logic, 46–47, 49, 75–76, 77
VALUE clause, 98
    constants in, 99
    literals in, 99, 100
    placement, 98
    use with OCCURS clause, 395
    uses, 98
    in WORKING-STORAGE SECTION, 227–228
Variable information, 280
VARYING phrase, in PERFORM statement, 401, 409
Vertical spacing, 238–240
Volumes, of physical records, 348

Walkthroughs, 45–47, 49, 75–76, 373
WHEN clause, 407
Words (COBOL)
    reserved, 65, 76
    supplied, 65, 76–77

WORKING-STORAGE (WS) SECTION, 94, 96–97, 98, 104,
        178, 194–195, 196, 198
    active key, 319
    counters and accumulators, 193–195, 194, 198
    data tables, 393, 394
    file description in, 226–227
    and formatting of reports, 282
    level ''88'' entries, 178, 196
    reading data values from, 122
    use of, 97
    VALUE clause, 227–228
    and WRITE . . . FROM command, 237
WRITE statement, 236–241, 242
    AFTER ADVANCING phrase, 239, 277
    BEFORE ADVANCING phrase, 239–240
    format, 237
    FROM phrase, 233, 237–238
    function, 236
    integer for vertical spacing control, 239–240
    OPEN statement and, 236
Writing, destructive, 339

''X'' PICTURE symbol, 94, 127, 175

''Z'' PICTURE symbol, 102
Zero (0) insertion character, 101
ZERO/ZEROS/ZEROES, 99
    test for value of, 179